GUIDE TO CONSCIOUSNESS and the UNSEEN UNIVERSE

*(A companion guide to
"Training Manual for Gods, Book One,
Consciousness and the Unseen Universe" by Chiron)*

SOPHIA OVIDNE

Guide to Consciousness and the Unseen Universe
Sophia Ovidne

First published in Australia by Sophia Ovidne 2023
www.earthwithspirit.com

Copyright © Sophia Ovidne 2023
All Rights Reserved

A catalogue record for this
book is available from the
National Library of Australia

ISBN: 978-0-6457396-6-4 (pbk)
ISBN: 978-0-6457396-7-1 (ebk)

Typesetting and design by Publicious Book Publishing
Published in collaboration with Publicious Book Publishing
www.publicious.com.au

Book cover images:
Maxx-Studio © Shutterstock
kanpisut © Shutterstock

No part of this book may be reproduced in any form, by photocopying or by any electronic or mechanical means, including information storage or retrieval systems, without permission in writing from both the copyright owner and the publisher of this book.

To

all humans who wish to fly,
and to all gods who are helping us achieve this.

Also by Sophia Ovidne

Training Manual for Gods, Book One - Guide to Consciousness and the Unseen Universe (Channelled from Chiron)

Training Manual for Gods, Book Two - Arrival of the Gods (Channelled from Chiron)

Training Manual for Gods, Book Three - Ingenuity of the Gods (Channelled from Chiron)

The Getting of Wisdom, Books One and Two (Channelled from El Morya)

Lady Sedna's Ascension Handbook (Channelled from Lady Sedna)

(Non-fiction, under her name '**Ovidne**')

Meet the Masters (including channellings from many Masters)

Ascended Masters Today, Vol 1, Love and Light (Channelled from many Masters)

Ascended Masters Today, Vol 2, Wisdom and Insight (Channelled from many Masters)

Ascended Masters Today, Vol 3, Power and Action (Channelled from many Masters)

(Fiction, under her name '**Paula Hartwood**')

The Celestial Crossroads

Secret in the Circle

"Magic is just science that we don't understand yet."

Sir Arthur C. Clarke (1917–2008)
British science fiction writer, science writer and futurist,
inventor, undersea explorer. Author of "2001: A Space Odyssey"

ACKNOWLEDGEMENTS

My dear friends Collette Tupling and Angela Scarangella-Gugger for taking the time to review this copious volume and for giving me useful feedback, and for all their support and encouragement, and again to Collette for being my angel investor.

My dear friend Sonia Bailey for her unfailing support and love throughout these past tumultuous couple of decades as we have journeyed together towards godhood.

My dear friend and earthly mentor for many years, Ashtara, who first taught me the wonders of astrology and much else about the unseen universe.

My dearest sisters, Tina, Teresa, and Michelle, for their constant love and pride in me, even though they don't have the faintest idea what I am on about half the time!

CONTENTS

Preface i

PART ONE   Consciousness, unseen beings, and unseen dimensions

Chapter 1   Introduction 1
    Why am I writing this Guidebook? 1
    Who is Chiron? 3
    What is metaphysics? 4
    Who am I? 6

Chapter 2   What is consciousness? 8
    Consciousness in general 9
    Belief 16
    Inner personas 22
    Lower consciousness 24
    Higher consciousness 26

Chapter 3   The unseen beings—soul, spirit, Source 28
    Soul graduation/soul merge 30
    Our Source and the radio dial 37
    Our relationship with our spirit/soul 38
    Does everyone have a soul? 44

Chapter 4   The unseen beings—God and the gods 46
    Who or what is God? 46
    Creator gods 47
        The creation of humans 50
        The creation of robots 53

              Who are the other gods? 55
              What do the gods do? 63

Chapter 5   **Other unseen beings** 67
              Angels 67
              Aliens and UFOs 69
                   Crop circles 73
                   Alien abduction 74
                   The Veil is thinning 75

Chapter 6   **The unseen dimensions—the Two Earths** 76
              What is the difference between a universe and
              a dimension? 77
              Where are the unseen dimensions? 79
                 1.   The human physical dimension
                     (First Earth) 80
                 2.   The spirit and humans-turned-gods
                     dimension (Second Earth) 81
                        Time travel 84
                        What is spirit life like? 84
                        Different laws 87
                 3.   The higher gods' dimensions 89

Chapter 7   **The unseen dimensions—Heaven and Hell** 94
              Heaven and the New World (merger
              and split of dimensions) 94
              Diagram #1 – Merger and split of the Two Earths 96
              Hell and the Underworld 97
              The Light World and the Dark World,
              the Creation Realm 98

Chapter 8   **Death** 103
              Facing death 103
              Taking a life 110

Chapter 9	Life after death, and past lives	118
	What happens when we die?	118
	Ghosts	120
	Reincarnation, rebirth, past lives	123

Chapter 10	Journey to godhood/ascension and back to Source	130
	The human journey to godhood/ascension	131
	A god-human, incarnated at birth as a god in human form	137
	The return journey back to Source	139

PART TWO   Tools of Consciousness (Using consciousness to live a better life)

Introduction – What are the Tools of Consciousness? 145

Chapter 11	Vibrational levels	147
	What exactly are vibrations?	149
	What do low vibes feel or look like?	151
	What do high vibes feel or look like?	151
	Why we should keep checking our vibe level	153
	How to let go of low vibrations	154
	How to raise vibrations	156

Chapter 12	Connecting with the unseen universe	159
	Who or what will we connect with?	
	Unseen beings and dimensions	161

Chapter 13	The benefits of connecting with the unseen universe	175
	Agent for our soul	175
	The benefits we receive from the universe	176
	a) Love, comfort, hope	177
	b) Destiny, mission, purpose	177

	c) Warnings, prophecies......................................179
	d) Advice—words, images, journeys, insights, past lives 180
	e) Ideas to take back to Earth............................182
	f) Energies, healing, raised vibrations...................182
	g) Answers to our prayers..................................183
	h) Training 183

Chapter 14 What prevents connection?......................................184
    a) Fear 184
    b) Need for control, or fear of being controlled 188
    c) Distrust, disbelief, doubt 190
    d) Negative thoughts, closed heart..........................192
    e) Cherry-picking..192
    f) Drugs, alcohol 193
    g) Talent inherent in our natal astrology.....................193
    h) The Void..194

Chapter 15 Ways in which the universe speaks to us...................196
    a) Dreams..196
    b) In the Creation Realm......................................197
    c) Coincidences 200
    d) The world reflects our consciousness back to us 201
    e) Cards, astrology..203
    f) Stones, bones, tea leaves, patterns 203
    g) Symbols, signs, and images................................204
    h) Intuition/gut feel..208
    i) Sudden insights...209
    j) Navigation 209
    k) Bodily sensations and illness..............................210
    l) Messages through other people...........................212
    m) UFOS 213

Chapter 16	**How to connect with the unseen universe**............214
	Using our Third Eye, our psychic channel 214
	Setting intention and focusing............................216
	Knowing you are safe...217
	Crossing the bridge..217
	Arriving in the higher dimensions 219
	Accepting everything 220
	Flying and exploring..221
	Having respect...221
	Is it my soul, a god, or my ego talking?..............222
	Right brain vs left brain.....................................229
	Speaking with soul/gods as a friend 229
	Checklist for connecting with unseen dimensions 230

Chapter 17	**Manifesting** 232
	Introduction to manifesting...............................232
	What can we manifest? 233
	The technique for manifestation........................236
	The science of manifestation 243
	Troubleshooting 245
	Creating with higher beings...............................248
	Manifesting for others and the world................249

Chapter 18	**Creating a better you**...................................251
	Identify issues 252
	Raise vibrational level 253
	Work with your soul/spirit 254
	Reprogram yourself...255
	Being love, our core diamond, self-worth 256
	Finding fortitude 258
	Finding motivation..261
	Have a purpose..263
	Increase your power..264

Chapter 19	**Healing and letting go** 267
	Healing 267
	Letting Go 270
	Healing the body and physical issues
	(with table of symptoms) 273

Chapter 20	**Healing emotional and mental issues** 280
	a) Triggers and the Secret Book of Laws 281
	b) Facing heartbreak 288
	c) Gloominess, self-pity, victimhood 289
	d) Closed heart, imbalance, love, fun 291
	e) Managing our lower personas and their emotions ... 293
	f) Resistance to change 294
	g) Resistance to what is 297
	h) Wanting to escape 297
	i) Fear 298
	j) Being off track 299
	k) Feeling unfulfilled 300
	l) Dealing with desires 301
	m) Educating children 301

Chapter 21	**More about healing** 303
	Healing spiritual issues 303
	Being a healer of others 306

Chapter 22	**Healing techniques** 309
	a) Raising your vibrations 310
	b) Focus on desired outcome 311
	c) Being a fireball, the Sun 312
	d) Dealing with lower personas and ghosts of our past 315
	e) Healing suicidal tendencies 320
	f) Jewels of consciousness, rainbows, and light 321
	g) Changing your thinking, cleansing and letting go ... 322

        h) Revealing our diamond Source 328
        i) Positive perspectives 329
        j) Physical healing 331
        k) Projections, filters, and fears 332
        l) Being love, opening the heart, surrendering 334
        m) Healing with our spirit, soul, higher beings 335
        n) Dealing with children 335
        o) Time limitations 336
        p) Getting over the bridge 336
        q) Rewriting past scripts 338

Chapter 23   Love, forgiveness, and relationships 339
    Murderous intent 339
    Mercy and forgiveness 341
    Finding love 344
        Love for ourself first 344
        Finding a partner, soul mate, or twin flame 345
    Why do relationships fall apart? 347
        Triggers 348
        The full symphony 349
        We attract mirrors 351
    Evil entities and Group Consciousness 352
    Our relationship with our soul and higher beings 353

Chapter 24   Destiny/mission and evolvement 356
    Godhood mission 356
    When we get to godhood 357
    Our human mission 358
    The mission itself 359
    Am I already on a mission? Am I on track? 364
    Being unaware of your mission 366
    Stepping into your mission 366
    Where to find your destiny 368

Chapter 25 Destiny continued..371
    Feeling stuck or lost regarding our destiny or mission.....371
        a) Fears and blockages..371
        b) Human will vs divine will.
           No connection to soul..373
        c) Lack skills, resources, confidence, courage 375
        d) Destiny too big, too arrogant 375
        e) Focused on past and not the future.................376
        f) Missing signs or clues..377
        g) Timing and cycles – missing your
           slot, not being ready 377
        h) Not following steps to manifest properly............378
        i) Not using Toolbox of Consciousness..................379
    Ditching your mission..380
    How to stay on track 381
    Completing a mission...384

PART THREE The Future

Chapter 26 Gods as role models 387
    Traits of a god on Earth in human form 387

Chapter 27 Transition to the future.................................398
    The merger of First and Second Earth,
    creating the New World..398
    Climate change, waves, storms...403
    Why humans will resist the New World 409
    Time of transition..412

Chapter 28 The New World 414
    Living in the New World/Second Earth dimension 414
    New World society 416
    Education in the New World..419
    Space travel and aliens 422

The future of Earth, Sun, and solar system 423
In summary 424

Diagrams

Diagram #1 – The merger and split of
the Two Earths (Ref: Chs 7, 27) 96

PREFACE

In the first three books of the *Training Manual for Gods* series, Master Chiron takes us on an amazing journey which is targeted at those who are already gods (Masters) on Earth, plus those humans who are in the process of transforming into gods, and those who are merely curious about what it takes to become a god.

In Book One of *Training Manual for Gods - Consciousness and the Unseen Universe*, Chiron describes the hidden dimensions of this universe, including consciousness, the worlds of the gods and the superpowers that gods can attain, and introduces the metaphysical foundations of our universe and reality. He explains in detail the journey we humans need to undertake to become gods, and how this is the ultimate mission of everyone on Earth. Our journey is not just a physical odyssey but an emotional, mental, and spiritual one too.

Because Book One contains much metaphysical knowledge that many people may find needs some extra explanation, I have written this companion book, *Guide to Consciousness and the Unseen Universe*, to describe these concepts in further detail and with many analogies from my own experiences and teachings. This guidebook covers only Book One of *Training Manual for Gods*. Books Two and Three by Chiron are more self-explanatory, but perhaps one day I shall write further guides to these volumes as well.

In Book Two of *Training Manual for Gods - Arrival of the Gods*, Chiron depicts what it will be like when humans are separated into two dimensions of First Earth and Second Earth, and how it will be to live on Second Earth as a human-turned-god, or as a divine god who has arrived on Earth from an even higher dimension. How will humans and divine gods interrelate? What will spark the Final Shift that causes our two

Earths to split away from each other, and how can we prepare for this? What will happen to those left behind on the non-god First Earth?

In Book Three of *Training Manual for Gods - Ingenuity of the Gods*, Chiron deals solely with the training and operational needs of the gods on Second Earth. He describes how the gods can develop their superpowers and help build the fledgling all-god society on this new higher-dimensional earthly world. He also guides us in how to manage the transition from old world to new, revealing some of the incidents that will lead to the final event which separates our two Earths completely.

PART ONE

CONSCIOUSNESS, UNSEEN BEINGS, and UNSEEN DIMENSIONS

Chapter 1 – Introduction

Why am I writing this Guidebook?

In 2018, I channelled the book *Training Manual for Gods, Book One: Consciousness and the Unseen Universe* from a Master in the higher dimensions named Chiron. It is a seminal work in describing what consciousness is and how it operates, both in the human world and in the unseen universe beyond.

    I greatly admire this masterpiece from Chiron and find it to be profoundly wise, eloquent, and capable of imbuing the reader with the influential and healing energies of this Master. However, just as many fine academic works have been deconstructed by scholars over the millennia to highlight their finer points and explain them to people, I felt that Chiron's work is so substantial and broad that readers would benefit from some restructure, synthesis, and explanation of many of its tenets. Hence this *Guide to Consciousness and the Unseen Universe* was born.

    Not all the information in this guidebook can be attributed to Chiron's original source of work. I have added appropriate material that has been taught to me by many Masters over the past decades, to better elucidate some point or other. On the other hand, I have undoubtedly not covered every point in Chiron's book to the satisfaction of every reader. I have tried to take the most significant topics and describe these as fully as one book will allow. Perhaps there will be future volumes if the situation demands. Certainly, Chiron has indicated that *he* wishes to channel more volumes for his version of *Training Manual for Gods*.[1]

---

1. Chiron's *Training Manual for Gods* series, currently consists of three volumes. This Guidebook deals primarily with only his first volume, as his second and third volumes are generally more self-explanatory.

In Part One of this *Guide*, I have pulled together all the foundational information that Chiron tells us about the nature of consciousness itself, and about our soul, the Masters (also known as gods), angels, ghosts, and even aliens, and also the various unseen dimensions that they inhabit. We take an in-depth look at Heaven and Hell and what happens to us when we die, and the reasons why our life might be ended. In this section of the book, we cover everything from astral travelling, to past lives and reincarnation, to the journey where humans can ascend to godhood and become gods themselves.

In Part Two, once we have learnt about the structure of the universe and its inhabitants in Part One, we discover how to apply the various 'tools' that our consciousness contains; things like manifesting our reality, raising our vibrational level to better ourselves, how to communicate with the gods and higher dimensions, healing and letting go emotional or mental issues, building better relationships, and forging the right path to our true destiny.

Part Three is a summary of what Chiron has foretold for our future, of how we humans are being groomed to become gods, what the characteristics of a god are, and what it will mean to have gods living in the human world upon Earth.

Neither this *Guide* nor Chiron's book is asserting that its contents are The Truth. This is the wisdom that has been channelled to me by Master Chiron and from other Masters. It is a mythology, you could say, a book about gods and an attempt to explain their worlds, and it is up to the reader how they perceive this wisdom and utilise it. Chiron's aim is to help people improve themselves and their world, and he (and I) are not dictating a set of beliefs to anyone.

While this guidebook is laid out in a structured and easy-to-read format, I encourage people to also study the original version channelled from Chiron. His style is articulate, charming, and lucid, and his words witty, wise, and entertaining. Chiron's work is by no means some incomprehensible academic or mystical tome. On the contrary, it borders on the style of a novel as he captures the reader with descriptions of how our consciousness travels to other worlds and what it does there.

It matters not which version you read first. If you start by reading Chiron's, you might then appreciate reading my own, hopefully insightful, explanations of his work. If you begin with my more structured and amalgamated account, you might like to then read Chiron's more poetic, graceful, and energy-permeated version that instils the reader's consciousness with inspirational ideas and understanding from more highly evolved worlds.

Who is Chiron?

For those who don't know of my previous work in channelling the Ascended Masters, I will explain a little about them and what it is I do. Later in this book, I will go into detail about the Masters/gods and angels, and the higher dimensions that they exist within.

Suffice to say at this point that we humans are not alone in this universe. For starters, we all have a spirit side to ourselves that exists in a hidden and unseen dimension of the universe. Everyone has a spirit self, often called the soul, and sometimes the astral body. This spirit or soul exists eternally as a consciousness that can manifest in many forms, including a human body. But there are also many souls who exist not in human body, and the more evolved of these souls are given many titles such as Ascended Masters, gods, saints, prophets, or angels.

Chiron (Chi is pronounced 'kye' to rhyme with 'rye') is one such soul, a highly evolved and very wise Master or god. In Ancient Greek mythology, Chiron (or Cheiron) is the name given to the greatest of the centaurs, who were half-man and half-horse. The constellation of Centaurus is also named after him.

In astrology Chiron is deemed to be "The Wounded Healer" archetype, and ruler of the zodiac sign Virgo which deals with purification, healing, diligence, routines, connection with the natural world, and teaching these things. Another important element is that Chiron, as a cosmic body, sits in the heavens between the planets Saturn and Uranus, on the dividing line between Order and Chaos. He stands as the bridge between Order (the Light World as represented by Saturn) and Chaos (The Dark World as represented by Uranus), letting us experience one then the other, pointing out where we are most wounded or vulnerable and where we need to be strengthened or cleansed. His focus could be said to represent The Middle Way of the Tao.

While Master Chiron does indeed embody many of the traits attributed to him by the ancients and astrology, it would be misguided to imagine him as some mythical beast who is speaking with us and giving us advice and information. He is a consciousness who now inhabits a dimension invisible to us humans, but who thoroughly understands what it means to be human. He is well-situated to give us descriptions of the universe that exists beyond our Earth and solar system and beyond the limits of the human mind and brain.

Chiron is actually from The Pleiades, a star cluster in our galaxy, and as one of the guardians of our planet, he and his fellow galactic gods and goddesses have a mission to help mankind evolve into a new kind of being, into gods themselves. This is not some overnight transformation, nor is it the stuff of superhero movies. This venture has been going on for millennia, but it is at this time in history that we are beginning to see some promising results. It entails firstly that humans understand what is their consciousness, and secondly how to evolve from human consciousness into god consciousness. The superhero movies are merely inspiration from the gods to help us with this concept.

Chiron is a wonderful companion and a wise and patient mentor, and he has explained to me metaphysical aspects of this universe that I could never have imagined or read in any book upon Earth. This is truly astonishing, ground-breaking information from the horse's mouth (or perhaps half-horse's mouth in Chiron's case!)

To experience Chiron's magnificent personality first-hand, I encourage you to read the original source material for this book, *Consciousness and the Unseen Universe (Book One of the 'Training Manual for Gods' series)*, channelled directly from Chiron in his own inimitable voice and words.

What is metaphysics?

At this point it may be beneficial to clarify what I mean by metaphysics so that we're all on the same page because the term *metaphysics* can mean various things to various people. In this book, I use the word *metaphysics* to mean transcending or going beyond the current knowledge base of physics, psychology, and science and spirituality in general. In particular we will delve into the hidden realms of consciousness, and that which exists beyond our current understanding of mind and matter.

The Ascended Master St.Germain (Ascended Masters are described fully in the chapter 'Who are the gods?') told me a couple of years ago that metaphysics is about taking control over energies. We are here on Earth, he said, to learn how to become magicians, and that magicianship is all about power over the energies around us and within us. He went on to explain that if we are not wanting control over these energies, which constitute consciousness, then we won't succeed in life because other energies will overcome ours. We need to want to have control over mind and matter instead of just letting it all happen to us. But we will only win if we take control and responsibility for ourselves. We can't give up control too easily. We must keep focused on what we really want to achieve, and we need to be competitive and motivated. We cannot say to ourselves about life, "What's the point" whenever we are forced to fight too hard. We shouldn't merely acquiesce to what is dished out to us and accept we can't have what we most desire. Each of us has a mission to complete, and we need to doggedly forge ahead in order to complete it, not only through the sheer force of the human will but by using the wisdom, love, and power of the mysterious metaphysical dimensions surrounding us.

In traditional western astrology, the theme of metaphysics is covered by the sign of Scorpio and the 8th House which are both ruled by the planet Pluto. In mythology, Pluto (Hades to the Greeks) is the god of the Underworld, a trickster god and magician, and responsible for the depths of our psyche, for transformation, and for death and rebirth. He is the god of lower consciousness.

However, it is the god Uranus, ruler of Aquarius and the 11th House, who is responsible for higher consciousness, and he will come with his sudden lightning bolts of unexpected energy to unsettle our minds and lives, in order to change our perspective and ways of being. Between Pluto and Uranus, both change agents, we are forced into going beyond our known world and into the unknown and hidden universe, the realm of metaphysics.

There are many people on Earth today who do not believe in metaphysics or that there is anything beyond the human brain and our physical universe. Equally, there are many people, myself included, who have had transcendent experiences of worlds, dimensions, and beings beyond our human physicality. It is very difficult to deny your own evidence and experiences, although it is fair to say that there is little in the way of empirical scientific proof that these worlds exist.

To experience the hidden universe and the joys of a consciousness that expands way beyond the human mind, we must first believe and open that mind of ours. It is only when humans acknowledge the invisible dimensions that the universe begins to reveal her secrets to us.

Chiron asks what are we afraid of discovering if we go exploring the hidden dimensions of consciousness and the universe? Mankind is busy physically exploring the solar system and the depths of space, yet many people emphatically deny the existence of anything beyond what can be seen with human eyes. For many scientists, belief in dimensions beyond our world is tantamount to belonging to some underground movement; it must be kept secret or reputations and careers will be wrecked. And so, it is a long process that humankind is enduring to bring forth the evidence that will have everyone believing in the true universe and the true capacities of our consciousness.

Who am I?

The discovery of the realm of metaphysics came to me late in life. I had always had a fascination with psychology, but every time I tried to enrol in a degree course in this discipline at university I was thwarted in one way or another. The universe (not the university) had other plans for me! In my 60s I finally gained a diploma in Modern Psychology in Australia, but this was far removed from traditional psychology, focusing on NLP (neuro linguistic programming), hypnosis, and EFT (Emotional Freedom Technique or 'Tapping'.)

In truth, by this time, I knew it wasn't psychology that I wanted to be involved with—it was metaphysics. I wanted to know what was beyond the basic human mind, and what consciousness truly consisted of, and how it travelled and acted in other worlds and dimensions which I regularly found myself visiting.

So here I am, after penning many books which I have channelled from Ascended Masters, now writing a book about metaphysical things under my own name. Certainly, it is essentially an explanation of a book channelled from Chiron, but it also contains many of my own teachings, where appropriate, that I have refined through my own experiences and taught in my metaphysical workshops over the years. Every day I am still learning and evolving. The lessons never stop, no matter how high one ascends, and consciousness keeps on expanding with every experience in human form and spirit form.

I am neither a scientist nor an academic. My talent is for connecting with invisible dimensions and the beings that inhabit those realms. I have neither the capacity nor the inclination to prove what is written in this book. You, the reader, must make up your own mind and research your own empirical evidence. My beliefs are based on my own experiences, and I cannot doubt these anymore. In the past I have done so, but have grown stronger in my convictions with each new experience throughout the years.

One thing I have learnt from all my questing is that, at our core, we are a beautiful being filled with love, generosity, and reasonableness. Our consciousness has been suffocated throughout the ages by mudslides of tragic and terrible experiences. All we must do now is dig ourselves out, clean ourselves off, and find ourselves again. To do this we must enlist help, and our soul and beings who exist outside of our visible human dimension are just waiting to assist with our journey out of humanness and into godhood. It's not that humans transform into gods physically and become superheroes with physical superpowers; human consciousness becomes god consciousness, although it may seem at times as if superpowers are ignited in certain circumstances!

I have been on this journey myself for many years and have documented here many of my experiences, weird though they may seem to some people. It is my dearest wish that this book can be of assistance to you on your own journey through the maze of consciousness and into the amazing unseen universe.

Chapter 2 – What is consciousness?

Firstly, I would like to acknowledge the sheer brilliance of the mind of Master Chiron. When I first sat confronted with answering the massively broad question 'What is consciousness?' I felt panic arising as to how I could assimilate and dissect the vast amount of data surrounding this conundrum. Chiron, on the other hand, when I was channelling his book, blithely provided the description of consciousness to me over many sessions without hesitation or a single slip-up. And while the study of consciousness could be seen as a daunting prospect, Chiron makes it exciting, magical, and metaphysical.

This entire book is given over to describing what consciousness is. Therefore, we must divide up the information into bite-sized chunks so we can get our teeth into it a little better. And in order to understand what consciousness is, we must also define many other elements beforehand. So, in some ways it may seem that we are never getting to the point of this book, but if I tell you that consciousness is the whole universe, then you will realise that everything we learn along the way is actually contributing to our understanding of what consciousness is, and that this book, and Chiron's version, can cover only a fraction of the whole concept that is consciousness.

The traditional scientific viewpoint of consciousness is that it equates to the human mind, and that this itself equates to the human brain. In Chiron's *Consciousness and the Unseen Universe* and in this *Guide* to Chiron's book we shall see that consciousness goes far beyond the human brain, and juggles far greater things than just its human self on Earth. Consciousness travels way out into the universe, not only the universe that can be seen with human eyes but into the universe of unseen dimensions that can only be seen by the eyes of our soul.

This requires me then to describe what is meant by the term *soul*, and the related terms of *spirit, God, gods, angels*, and also the terms *universe* and *unseen dimensions*, which I will do in later chapters, but let's begin by understanding what consciousness is in general.

Consciousness in general

Consciousness is as vast and varied as the universe. It *is* the universe and everything within it. It is everywhere at any time. It is complicated too, and not all at one level. There are many pockets, pathways, and tunnels to follow. It encompasses not only our physical human world but also worlds that are hidden from our human eyes. As conscious beings, we are living not only on Earth as humans, but a part of us lives in another invisible dimension at the same time, having dreams and experiences other than human ones. This is the spirit part of ourselves which goes off travelling in these other dimensions while the human part of us carries on its daily life down on this planet. We are one consciousness spread across two dimensions, two halves of one mind, but like a single ribbon that encompasses both domains.

This, of course, is not what we are taught in schools or in society at large. All we know, and are taught, is that we exist in human bodies and that the things around us feel real to us. We have tangible evidence of this. This is our bedrock. We think we are *this* kind of person and that we lead *this* kind of life. It comes as a shock to find out that much of this is a lie, or at least, only part of the truth.

Consciousness is devious and has created a quasi-world for us to live in while we are in human form. Some people equate it to living in a world akin to a computer animation or game. Not all is as it seems; consciousness doesn't project true reality to us but only that which it wishes us to see. It plays out a specific role for us in this particular human lifetime. We experience only that which we are meant to, what our filters and programming allow us to see, hear, or sense. Many illusions are played out on us, but none of this is done with malicious intent; it serves as a base upon which we learn how to develop our consciousness further.

For most people, it is easier to go along with the belief that this physical universe is all there is. They believe consciousness is merely an illusion and just an epiphenomenon of chemical reactions in the brain. This belief keeps them safe and means they don't have to dissemble their lives and all they have been taught to swallow as fact. The movie *The Truman Show*, starring Jim Carrey, is a fine example of this. Believing in other worlds would shake the very foundations of our own, and who wants to do that?

But there is a great deal more to the universe than what we have been told or been allowed to know about. Through the ages, society has glossed over many mystical secrets which have been kept from humans in general, while a select few have been privy over the millennia in being caretakers for some of this metaphysical knowledge. The majority of the human world has not been ready to have these secrets freely handed to them, but at this present time, doors are opening into the universe, if people will shift their perceptions and open their minds to new experiences and ideas. It is only when we believe in these things that greater clarity will arrive to allow us to understand what really exists in this universe.

In his book, Chiron chuckles that it sounds like the rantings of some conspiracy theorist, or as if he's overdosed on hash, or living in some fantasy land (which, in truth, he does!), but we must bring our truth to the world now and be prepared to face the consequences of the doubters and naysayers. The consequences of keeping all this secret any longer is to deny humans the ability to experience who they truly are and where they truly originate from. The timing is opportune now to open up the universe and let human beings in.

According to Chiron, consciousness is not the physical brain. Consciousness itself is a non-physical entity that creates physical things. We humans have trouble digesting that fact since everything in our human universe is of a physical nature. How can you have something that is non-physical? This is an aspect of the universe we have yet to understand and is the reason why many scientists are disinclined to accept the notion of the existence of consciousness outside of the human brain.

Consciousness is akin to love in that they are both non-physical and nebulous to grasp; and they both transport us to other worlds. The entire concept of this book, and of Chiron's book, is to delve into the hidden universe that exists outside of our current scientific understanding of how things are. 'Meta' = 'beyond': 'metaphysics' means going beyond our current knowledge of physics and science in general.

Consciousness exists everywhere in the universe. In fact, it is the universe itself. Everything within the universe has consciousness. Yes, even inanimate things have consciousness, albeit very limited.[2] We now know from the field of quantum physics that everything is made up of subatomic particles, everything including inanimate things like stones and steel pipes and shoes. These subatomic particles respond (in strange and seemingly supernatural ways) to the presence of human observers and therefore have some kind of consciousness within them.

So, next time you go for a walk in nature, you might want to be more aware of the consciousness of the rocks and rivers around you!

Many years ago, on holiday in Maui, Hawaii, I was swimming in the shallow turquoise waters just offshore and was fascinated by the patterns of light on the rippled sand beneath me. Suddenly, I heard a female voice speaking to me in my head, and she told me she was the Spirit of Water. As I floated in the warm waters, I could see in my consciousness some kind of vague shape that seemed like a fabric of pieced together ribbons in blues and greens, like patchwork joined in strips. The 'fabric' was swaying like seaweed in the current. She was certainly very flowing and beautiful and had a calm but assertive presence. Since I had been suffering from a bad back and sciatica and felt anything but flowing myself, I asked the Spirit of Water what was the cause of my pain?

She told me, "*You have been too stiff, too rigid, too inflexible recently. You need to move like the water, be fluid, changeable, offer no resistance but go with the flow.*

---

2. This philosophy is known as Panpsychism, a belief that the universe is conscious and that everything material, even down to atomic levels, has an element of individual consciousness.

Water has many shapes and moods. It can be placid like a still pool or rushing like a cascade over rocks. It can be dark or crystal clear, turquoise blue or stormy green. It can rise in waves—gentle lapping waves or towering tsunamis that conquer all before it. Water can be freezing cold, refreshing, and stimulating, or warm, comforting, and soothing. It quenches thirst and provides growth. It can flood, it can irrigate. It can fall as rain or snow or be as the mist. It can fall as tears.

Be as the water; be all things to its own time and place."

Our human self is a walking consciousness, part of a much larger consciousness that comprises the whole universe. All consciousnesses are connected; humans with humans, humans with all of physicality, and humans with non-physicality. It is a great network, or matrix, of consciousness, and it is often referred to as The Matrix (as in the movie), or The Divine Matrix, The Field, the Unified Field, The Higgs Field, the Quantum Field, or The Ether. This is the 96% of the universe that scientists term as 'missing' or 'empty', but in truth it is a malleable field of energy which is consciousness.

There are many parts to our consciousness, just as there are many parts to our body, but all parts of our consciousness operate in tandem with one another like the cells and organs in our physical body. And all consciousnesses throughout the universe work together as one, like one huge body of thought and feeling. Consciousness is unity, and love itself in its purest form.

Consciousness is never static but always changing and hoping to improve itself and gather more experiences. We can notice this by being aware that there is never a moment where we are not thinking. We are within a sphere of consciousness which takes us travelling on a treadmill from which we can never get off. We are part of consciousness at all times; it is our home.

Our consciousness manages our human life for us, utilising our brain to do much of the monitoring and repetitive work, like operating our human body and responding in programmed ways to events and situations. It is well-known how most of us go about our days on autopilot, and it is only when unexpected conditions occur that we come back to full consciousness and take control again, such as when driving a car on our usual route and suddenly having to make an emergency stop.

But while our brain is obviously an important apparatus that we need for our functioning, it is just a tool of our consciousness, created by our consciousness as a bridge between itself and our human body. Consciousness is a million times more intelligent than our brain, so we might be asking, "If we have consciousness, why do we need a brain at all?" Good question.

The brain is a computer for our body, a machine that allows us to program the things we want to think on a regular basis, and to enable us to react with consistency, and to identify things in the world without effort once we have first identified or learnt them. It's akin to having an automatic washing machine with set programs, rather than having to remember how to wash items each time.

Consciousness is the programmer of the computer, the actual builder of the computer too, whereas the brain is the computer itself. Consciousness is like the person who decides to complete a crossword puzzle, whereas the brain is like the computer app that looks up all available words to fit that crossword. The brain embodies the parts of consciousness that have been mechanised to provide easier living conditions for the body and its experiences of the world.

If the brain is defective, it is because the consciousness that created the brain is defective in some way; the programmer has coded wrongly. In order to heal brain defects, then, we can heal consciousness so it can reprogram the brain. In Part Two we take a look at ways we can achieve this.

Consciousness also manages our connection with the invisible universe, the greater consciousness. It can take us travelling, often termed 'astral travelling', to other worlds where we can experience things that we can't on physical Earth. One of these worlds is the place in which we end up in our dream state at night. Some of this peculiar realm has been dreamed up by the consciousnesses of others, and some of it our own consciousness is imagining for us to move through. It is still real for us, or should I say, for our consciousness.

The main role for consciousness is as a prime creator. It exists to create and to imagine. It creates our experiences of the human world around us and helps us to manifest what we desire in our world through the use of our imagination. It is a playground for designing and playing out thoughts prior to making them manifest in our physical world. It is always looking for ways to get its dreams manifested, and it uses our human body as a vehicle to do this.

Chiron speaks of the Toolbox of Consciousness where we use our conscious mind to create ourselves as better people and to create a better world for ourselves and others. We need to practise using these tools every day until we become a craftsperson. In Part Two, we will examine many of these tools in detail, and we will see that consciousness is capable of operating in many diverse domains, including:-

- travelling within the hidden dimensions of our universe
- connecting with our soul and unseen beings
- manifesting physicality, including healing our physical bodies and minds
- accessing higher knowledge
- experiencing, and changing, the past and future
- letting go parts of consciousness that hinder us
- raising our vibrational frequency so that more of the universe is revealed to us
- teaching us how to become more loving
- discovering and designing our destiny
- understanding our origins and what we are evolving into

Where can we find consciousness? We ourselves are consciousness itself. Think of how water can exist in several different forms as gas, steam, fluid, and solid ice. So, too, can consciousness take many different forms, from an invisible substance to the solidity of a human body. Consciousness is us; we are it. It's already in place. We are playing out our consciousness in the role of a human being, and, at the same time, in spirit form in the higher dimensions. We merely need to wake up to the fact, or become conscious of the fact, that we are consciousness. Consciousness is awareness, in truth. We need to train ourselves to be more aware and not live on autopilot as much as we tend to do.

Have you ever wondered where your imagination comes from? Consciousness is our imagination. We could liken it to a huge room where all our past experiences are on display, from both the human world and the spirit world, and here we get our inspiration by mixing experiences to give us synergy for something new. All of our life's experiences are hoarded by consciousness; every single detail of every event, every conversation, every thought and feeling. We can tap into any of this at any time, if we should want to. We are also connected to the consciousnesses of others, and we can tap into their experiences too for bright ideas. Exploring our consciousness will take many years, lifetimes even.

Sometimes, when we have meditations or insights that provide us with startling revelations, we might think we are making it all up. But this is what consciousness does—it creates for us. It weaves information for us into scenes or dialogues or symbolic representations, some of which may be artistic inspiration, or solutions to problems, or new perspectives and understanding, or directions for our destiny.

We can use our imagination to travel to new and unexplored fields within our own consciousness and the greater consciousness, to have fresh and innovative experiences that help us evolve into more developed beings. We will meet others out here beyond our own consciousness, and sometimes some of their consciousness will mix with our own. This is very useful when gathering advice from the minds of higher Masters, since their consciousness adds value to our own and rounds us out.

Consciousness can do anything and go anywhere. It depends on how we are operating it as to whether we get maximum benefit out of it. It's like having a Formula One racing car parked under our cranium. Do we drive it like a Ferrari or like a Model T Ford? When we are utilising our consciousness properly, life can feel very rosy and joyful. Our heart is open and we feel as if we are on top of things and can tackle issues easily with our innate power. But when our consciousness is bogged, then we need to know which tools to use to get ourselves unstuck and out of there.

Our consciousness is our toolbox and magic wand. It contains all we need to live a successful and bountiful life.

Belief

Most people are not aware of their consciousness. Yes, they are aware that they think and feel, but they attribute this to their brain because this is what they have been taught. Many feel uncomfortable with the idea that there might be something further out from our brain, something that knows and sees much more than we do as little humans on a little planet in a vast cosmos. Yet, there are many invisible energies and substances out there in space and in our immediate environment which pass through us in every moment, unimpeded by the mass of our bodies, and we may feel or be affected by these, or we may not. Internet connections, television and radio broadcasts, ATM transactions, phone signals and messages, satellite communications—these are just some of the numerous energies that fly straight through our bodies every day. So, why not consciousness too?

Many people, especially left-brained scientists, don't believe in a consciousness that travels out beyond our human brain. Yet they might believe in tachyons which are thought to be invisible particles which fly through the air, faster than the speed of light. But these particles are just theoretical, and, like ghosts or spirits, they might or might not exist and there is no concrete evidence of them (as yet). Why believe in invisible tachyons and not in invisible spirits and worlds?

The existence of the atom was first proposed by the ancient Greek, Democritus, in the 5th century B.C., but it took over two thousand years before he was proved to be correct. Given time, the existence of the spirit world will also be proven to the satisfaction (and consternation) of scientists. Many remarkable minds throughout history have been rebuffed for their innovative beliefs. Naysayers are quick to bring them down. Mankind could have evolved at a much-heightened pace if man had only opened his eyes and mind a bit more often. But it is human nature to doubt anything that is not obvious to our own eyes and hands, and disbelievers feel safer sticking to the traditional laws of physics and are scared to move beyond them.

Lucky for us, then, that a few hardy souls kept the faith and believed with all their hearts what they were being shown on the inner screens of their consciousness. And the more they believed, the more the universe opened her doors to them and revealed her secrets and dimensions. These pioneers have shown the way for us, and now it's time to follow them through those doors.

Many people have lost their ability to dream when they sleep. Maybe they never had this skill, or it deserted them as they grew older. Few people would deny, though, that humans do have dreams while asleep, even if they don't experience them themselves or can never remember them once they wake. Sadly, most people have lost another ability, their skill to astral travel or conduct 'lucid dreaming' as it's also known, and those who do actively perform these skills are often the subject of derision and charged with delusion or duplicity.

Yet, why can't it be that some humans possess these skills, even if the majority of the population has not cultivated them? Why is this particular skill of travelling in consciousness not deemed allowable while dreaming is acceptable? Why is synaesthesia (the ability to taste colours, or hear with the tongue, etc) tolerated but not psychic abilities that tap into dimensions beyond the everyday range of most humans? We know many more wavelengths of light exist than those we can see with human eyes, such as X-rays, gamma rays, infrared, and ultraviolet rays, so why shouldn't there be dimensions that exist beyond the range of most human's abilities to see or hear or feel them?

Once we begin to have experiences in the unseen worlds and start to converse with the hidden beings who inhabit there, we cannot doubt our encounters. (Actually, we often do start off doubting our sanity but eventually come to the conclusion that there *is* definitely something out there!) Our belief concretises and our faith strengthens. It's similar to what would happen if someone stated that we couldn't ride a bicycle and we knew that we could. We would defend our truth vehemently. It's different from stating that we believe we might be able to ride a bike, if we've never ridden one before. When we've truly had the experience then we have the knowing, and nothing, not any challenge thrown at us, will ever be able to remove that knowing.

Until they arrive at this knowing, most people find it hard to believe. But to arrive at this knowing, they will first need to find enough belief to go off exploring and get that evidence for themselves. It's not something that a guru or a priest or a psychic can give us. It must be experienced first-hand and personally for us to obtain the knowing beyond all doubt. We must first believe in consciousness rather than just a brain, for we are much much more than our human brain.

As an astrologer, I like to check out what the planets have in store for me every day, and I like to couple this with pulling a few Tarot cards from several different decks for added guidance. When I first started doing this many years ago, it was just for an experiment and I was interested to see if any of it would correlate with the incidents happening in my life.

I would have to say that I had mixed results—at first. But over the years as I continued with this practice, I've discovered that the astrology and the Tarot cards are almost always aligned with one another, as if my belief in them has brought about some mystical affiliation between planetary positions and my hand randomly pulling cards. It is not that my life always pans out as indicated. This is because astrology and Tarot cards show only the potential of the energies for the day, and if we feel disinclined to utilise those energies then the opportunity is lost and we might feel that the guidance was faulty.

The world is divided into believers and non-believers. Perhaps you are a believer, or sitting on the fence, yet something made you curious enough to pick up this book. What is it that you are hungry to know and learn about yourself and the universe? Is there something within your consciousness that yearns for the truth?

What are we humans afraid to find out if we follow this line of enquiry and exploration? And why do we keep this information from our children, as if it were a reprehensible secret? What are we teaching them to make them believe or not believe? Why are we shutting the door to children about these possibilities, so that it is usually only in later adult years that people discover these possibilities for themselves? Once we have been indoctrinated by schools and society, it is very difficult to knock out these ingrained beliefs, and lives are built upon lies and part truths where we can't make sense of this world from the information we have been taught.

There are signs all around us that we are being directed by something greater than ourselves. Some call it coincidence, happenstance, or pure fluke. But most of us will have experienced some event in our lives that has taken our breath away from its sheer unlikely occurrence. There have been many books and articles written about such events, yet still many people deny the possibility that unseen hands or minds might be responsible

Most folks, and especially scientists, avoid speaking about, or looking into, the Unknown and spooky things that happen and which aren't under their control. I myself love to make a note of major, stunning synchronicities that happen to me. When I go through a period of doubt, I turn to my notebook and refresh my memory of all the wonderful experiences that have occurred. They actually happen to me daily, too many to make a note of, but the really spectacular ones just have to be written down and remembered. I could write an entire book about these occurrences alone, but I'll give a few examples here.

Often in meditation I am shown a scene or listen to a conversation, and within a day or so on the television I see the exact same scene or hear the same conversation. For instance, one day I was shown in meditation the Golden Gate Bridge crumbling into the ocean, and that same night I watched a movie I'd never seen before, '10.5', and in the film the Golden Gate Bridge crashes into the sea after a massive earthquake. Yet, I knew nothing about the movie before viewing it.

In another quite different example, I had just moved into a new rented house and had popped into the estate agent's office to pay my rent. He knew that I had spiritual leanings from the conversations we'd had when he'd been showing me houses. He told me that this house was perfect for me because it was owned by a saint. I was puzzled and wanted to know more. He then held up the office file for the house which was filed under the owner's surname/forename, and it read 'SAINT Michael'. Little did he know that I had a big statue of Saint Michael, the Archangel, already sitting in my lounge room and that I was an ardent follower of this angel and had channelled him many times. It was most definitely the right house for me!

On another occasion, I had asked the universe for a sign to indicate whether I should take a new job and relocate interstate. I requested to be shown, not one but two snakes, as confirmation that I should take the job, and as I was visiting a Botanical Gardens that day, I was keeping a sharp lookout for snakes in the undergrowth. (In Australia, snakes are fairly common, and I actually like them, being born in the Year of the Snake myself).

The universe often surprises us in the way it manifests our requests, and so it was in this case. Halfway around the Gardens, a hastily hand-painted sign had been erected to warn visitors that a snake had been spotted in the vicinity. I never saw an actual snake, but on either side of the text on the signboard someone had painted the symbol of a snake—therefore, two snakes were present. I had my sign and my answer! And I did indeed move interstate, to beautiful Queensland, a decision that was one of the best of my life.

The universe, the greater consciousness, has fun playing with us when we open our minds enough to look further than the commonplace and in directions that we don't usually gaze. We won't see any signs if we are blinkered. Most of us have a narrowly-tuned filtering system that sees only what it wants to see and it ignores all else. The human mind makes it easy for itself by filtering out all but essential information to get us through our day, and so we miss out on so much more that is going on. We need to become more consciously aware of our surroundings and switch off the autopilot and automatic programming more often.

Some people get their belief about the hidden dimensions from having experiences of actually seeing supernatural beings with their human eyes. These may be angels, Masters/gods, ghosts, or even aliens. These folks have a difficult time trying to convince others of what they have seen, and some are deemed to be mentally unstable, and some just suppress their experiences and memories because it's easier that way.

Sometimes, scientists demand too much empirical evidence and discredit the tangible evidence of human experience. Take, for example, the event in February 2013 in the snowy Russian city of Chelyabinsk. A massive fireball streaked across the early morning sky, and there were many witnesses who not only saw the brilliant light with their own eyes but they heard and felt the almighty explosion that followed and also felt the phenomenon of great heat.

Dashcam recorder videos gave the scientists preliminary evidence that this had been a meteor strike, but it was only when they held pieces of the meteorite in their hands that they confirmed what had taken place. However, the evidence that people had felt heat 'as if summer had come' was denied for quite some time until a research scientist came up with a suitable theory for why this could have been so, despite hundreds of people attesting to what they had physically experienced. At least they had each other to corroborate their accounts, and I recommend that people who have metaphysical experiences seek out like-minded others for support.

A glimpse of otherworldly things gets humans excited and gets them thinking, and never more so than when we think we are observing beings from another dimension. When we see these things, we are being allowed by our consciousness to see through the dividing veil for a brief moment. This undoubtedly wakes us up and makes us more aware. We learn with certainty that we are not alone in this universe.

It isn't some fantasy. Those who are ready to see will begin to see, although at first, it is true, it is hard to believe one's eyes at times. Just about all of us have some disbelief about invisible gods and higher worlds, mainly because there is no tangible evidence of them. We have to make do with blind faith. But there *is* evidence, and this comes from our experiences. And many humans have had experiences of visiting other worlds and/or conversing with higher beings, mainly in their dream state at night or during meditation, or even under the influence of anaesthetics or drugs. We should not doubt our own experiences.

Much is hidden from human eyes until it is time for them to be opened. As we believe more in these things, then more is shown to us. Beings of a higher consciousness than ours do not take kindly to being disrespected or denigrated, and therefore will work only with people who are prepared to believe in them. We can't have a foot in both camps and only half believe; these beings either exist or they don't. Nor should we use these wise and thrilling beings for our entertainment and switch them on and off as it suits us. The connection will be swiftly cut if we think we can play the gods for fools.

All believers are pioneers by nature. They dare to venture past the known world and bring back tall tales, just like the adventurers of old. Even Marco Polo had trouble getting colleagues to believe his stories when he first returned from his odyssey to the Far East. Pioneers have always faced derision and disbelief throughout history. But, even while they lack support of their fellow man, they remain strong and build their faith. In time they will be vindicated in their beliefs, as little by little the truth wins out and the disbelievers, who were so afraid to go beyond, are forced to admit things such as the Earth is round and not flat.

Our beliefs will certainly be challenged, by ourself, by our family and friends, and by society in general. Will we have the strength and faith to stand our ground and not betray ourself and our experiences? We believe in things that make our heart swell with grace and love. We tend to follow the road that helps us to feel most blessed and which supports the ideas we hold in our consciousness. Generally, if we are well-balanced, we won't believe in things that feel bad to our heart. Our consciousness knows very well what is good for us, and if that includes believing in invisible beings and invisible worlds, then we must follow this unconventional road.

Inner personas

Who are you really? It is probable that you are not who you think you are, but rather a being of multiple parts and mysteries. There are many different aspects to yourself, many shades of you that play out in different ways on a daily basis and depending on who you are with. You wear many hats, and combinations of hats, and play many roles, and the variety of experiences you have make you who you are. All in one day, you might be a businesswoman, a mother, a caring friend, an artist, a chef, a nurse, a lover, a taxi driver, a cleaner, or a yoga student.

Consciousness is made up of many pathways, high and low, and it's as if down each pathway there is a different part of ourself. Some of these 'personas' we get to know very well, while others surprise us at times when they rear their head unexpectedly. We need to understand each of our inner personas if we are ever going to have the chance to feel like a whole person, otherwise we might feel like Inspector Clouseau in the old Pink Panther movies, who was always aware that he might be set upon at any moment by his unpredictable but faithful manservant, Cato.

A persona in our lower consciousness is formed, either subtly or vividly, when we experience something in our life that cannot be processed and let go of in that moment. We generally let go of most moments in our day, otherwise our consciousness would be filled to overflowing with the minutiae of life, like buttering a piece of bread or getting in and out of our car. It is only in moments when our consciousness is sufficiently disturbed, and we don't attend to our feelings and thoughts at the time, that we hang onto the memory of that moment for processing later on. These are the things that we might mull over at night when we can't sleep.

For those disturbing events, we tend to store away in consciousness a memory of the person that we were at the time of the experience, along with all our thoughts and feelings. It's as if a video is taken of the scene plus all the sensory data connected with it. Even while we are unconsciously letting go of our mundane experiences, our consciousness still records every minute detail of our lives, but mostly this is archived in a remote location of our minds and is never accessed again (but can be if necessary). But with unprocessed experiences, these are kept on hand locally within consciousness until such time as we get around to resolving and bringing into harmony our thoughts and feelings regarding the situation.

Therefore, if we had a bad experience at school when we were seven-years-old, and have not had the wherewithal to be able to process our thoughts and feelings from that time, the memory of this issue stays stuck in our mind, and a seven-year-old persona begins to haunt the halls of our lower consciousness. Multiply this by the vast number of events that happen to us throughout our lives, which we have not successfully resolved, and we can see that we could have thousands of these lower personas in our consciousness, all wounded and just lurking about to be triggered off again by our current everyday experiences. Every one of us has these multiple personalities inside us, seemingly leading individual lives, and they build up within our lifetime until it can feel as if we have a whole committee of competing and cacophonous voices inside us.

Yet be assured it doesn't mean we are all certifiably schizophrenic. This only happens when one or more personas within our consciousness takes control over the others. What needs to happen is for all our personas to work together in unison to create a harmonious mind, just as all the cells and organs of our body generally operate with appropriate congruency to provide us with optimal health. If they don't cooperate and the balance is upset, that's when we experience illness. If all our lower personas come out together at the same time and demand attention, then we might experience the perfect storm and our body collapses and we undergo a nervous breakdown of some sort.

Managing our consciousness can be like running a business or a school, or a family of many children. We must take everyone into consideration and listen to their needs and problems and resolve their concerns. If a single persona within our mind is causing us trouble and pain, then our whole consciousness will feel discordant, just like when we bang our big toe and our entire body feels jarred from the injury. We must work with each wounded persona until all is harmony, and only then will we be able to feel inner peace again. In Part Two we will deal with some of the issues that result from inattention to our inner personas and how we can resolve these.

Lower consciousness

Mankind has throughout history fought against being controlled, and so it is this perception that is causing people to resist the notion that something out there in the blackness of space might be controlling us and making us into puppets of some unknown intelligence. Ancient peoples used to openly believe in gods and higher powers, but these days this has been relegated to the role of religion and spiritual practices where people can comfortably play out their beliefs. It would be fairly rare to find anyone in present times who still worships the Greek gods of Olympia, or the ancient deities of Egypt, Mesopotamia, or the Far East, outside of any religious organisation.

And so, it can seem as if much of mankind has lost its connection to the invisible dimensions that once played such a huge part in people's everyday lives. Humans, for the most part these days, are not very aware of things outside of their own operating bubble. They do what they have to in order to get through their day and achieve as much happiness as is possible in their human condition. This could be called lower consciousness.

Higher consciousness would be where people are very aware that there is more to the physical world than can be seen with human eyes, and where their consciousness is striving to become more wholesome and harmonious whilst being considerate and loving towards all around them. And so, in this book we will speak a great deal about raising one's consciousness, about learning to reach a higher state of mind where peace and happiness prevails.

When I speak about happiness, I am talking about true happiness, not just a veneer. For we can be happy if we have good relationships, sufficient money for our needs and desires, good health, success in our ventures, or a lovely home and car. These things will indeed bring about temporary and even long-lived happiness. But what would happen if any of these things were taken away? Would we still be happy then?

All of the above is conditional happiness. "I am happy as long as I have…" "I am unhappy if I don't have…" What we are striving for in a higher state of mind is that we can be happy regardless of what external events are playing out around us—unconditional happiness. We might think that this is impossible in some cases. "What if a beloved partner died? How could we be happy then?" But we will learn as we journey through these chapters, that when we move out of human lower consciousness and into higher consciousness, then we will have very different understanding and perceptions about our universe and how our consciousness can operate in new and profoundly liberating ways.

To move into higher consciousness, firstly the human mind must overcome ego to a large degree. Ego is really another name for our innate human consciousness, the part of us that controls our life and makes decisions. Some call it human will. Ego is much maligned, and that is because many humans misuse their ego to a great extent. They want what they want, and they want it now!

Human ego can make us ambitious and greedy to a fault, yet it plays its part in that it provides us with drive and motivation to achieve our goals. But ego can be insatiable and moody. It prefers satisfying short-term desires rather than disciplined, planned, long-term strategies. It sulks if it doesn't get its way and can become angry, revengeful, and aggressive. And so, humans tend to placate their ego rather than taming and controlling it and putting it to positive use.

The human ego does not like the idea that there may be a part of consciousness that is higher than itself. Ego will fight with this higher self and resist it if it feels it is being controlled or directed against its will. This higher part of our consciousness is often called our spirit or our soul. Humans may or may not be aware of it, and its existence is mostly kept secret from us, because to know our soul is to open the floodgates to a hidden part of our consciousness that may prove to be overwhelmingly transformational and ultimately spell the death knell to our human ego.

Higher consciousness

At the start of this chapter, consciousness is described as being like a ribbon that runs between the two dimensions of the human and non-human worlds, connecting our human mind with our invisible spirit self. There is no physically obvious line in consciousness where our human self stops and our spirit self starts. They just meld into one another like a river runs into an ocean.

On this same note, Chiron once showed me a stream running through a woodland, which had a small waterfall, and he told me how our consciousness is like a river or a stream. There are higher parts upstream and lower parts downstream, and the upstream and downstream parts don't know what the other is doing but they are still part of the same river. What happens upstream usually gets carried downstream and affects the waters there. Just as there are waterfalls and changes in levels in rivers, so too is it like that in consciousness. Similarly, just as a river has a source and most rivers flow towards the sea, so also does consciousness have a source and it too flows towards the Great Ocean of total consciousness.

Our higher consciousness, our spirit self, is called higher for several reasons. We might imagine it sits on a cloud in the sky and observes us all day long, and there is an element of truth in this. For it does have a higher viewpoint of our life and can see a bigger picture than we can, down on the ground as a human. It can see not only a larger physical environment in which we operate in our physical body, but it is also privy to all our thoughts and feelings, and also to the thoughts and feelings of the people around us. All consciousnesses are linked, therefore our higher self can connect easily with the higher selves of all the humans we come into contact with.

Our higher consciousness is not so concerned with the everyday details of our lives, but more with pushing its human self along so that it meets its destiny at all the points in life which had been agreed upon before it incarnated on Earth. Our higher self has ideas and high ideals which it wishes its human to pursue, and most of all, to cultivate it to become a more worthy and loving person.

The human ego often resists any changes to its persona and way of life, and so there are ructions and much internal conflict as the two sides of consciousness go into battle. This is the basis of emotional and mental pain that affects the physical body and brings about illness and accidents. Resistance always equals pain, and in Part Two we will look at practical ways of minimising both these things.

In short, it is our journey as a human through this lifetime to learn to surrender our desire for control, and to place control in the hands of our higher consciousness, our spirit or soul. While this may grate against every instinct in our body, we would do well to remember that both parts of consciousness, lower and higher, are us. It doesn't serve to fight with ourselves. Master Dominic, one of the Ascended Masters (or gods) that I work with regularly in the unseen universe, once said to me, "Your greatest enemy will always be yourself."

When our higher consciousness spirit takes control of our world, we can be more on purpose and act from a base of higher values. We jettison our old human programming, which makes us reactive and unconsciousness, and begin to use the new programs and ideals that our higher self carries for us. In effect, we raise our consciousness to a new higher level, where we love not only ourself to a greater degree but everyone around us too. Raising our consciousness becomes the key that opens the doors to the unseen universe and the unseen beings that inhabit it.

Chapter 3 – The unseen beings—soul, spirit, and Source

The Ribbon of Consciousness that connects our human consciousness with our spirit self in the hidden dimensions is a very long ribbon indeed. On the other side from our human world, it carries not only the consciousness of our spirit but many levels of consciousness that rise higher and higher until we reach up to the very source of ourselves, our Source (who is also a Creator God), at which point we are pure consciousness and not physical or in any form at all. So, let us examine this ribbon in more detail, and start with the parts of our Consciousness Ribbon that are closest to our human self—the spirit and soul.

You may be asking, "Is there a difference between my spirit and my soul?" It's a good question and a common one that many folks ask.

When people speak about the part of our consciousness that exists just over the border in the invisible dimensions, they might refer to this part as either spirit or soul. In general, it's not worth splitting hairs about their designation. We can speak about either entity and we would be roughly correct. Chiron himself in *Consciousness and the Unseen Universe* uses these terms interchangeably. But if we would like to know the proper definition of the spirit and the soul, then Chiron gives this to us.

The spirit part of our consciousness is eternal and can never die. As consciousness it is a non-physical entity that can freely travel the universe, but it can manifest itself into physical forms in the human world, and does so regularly. It is similar to having an alter ego, just as Superman had Clark Kent and Spiderman had Peter Parker. We, as a human, are one of our spirit's current manifestations into physical form, but spirits are who we are as default.

In the spirit world we can also take on a physical form and Chiron has told me that our spirit bodies are made up of plasma, an electrically-charged gas. This is what a star consists of too, including our own sun. The sun's corona, its outer atmosphere, is created from very diffuse plasma which extends across the solar system and out into deep space. While plasma is a rare phenomenon on Earth, much of the material universe is made from plasma as well as solids, liquids, and gases. It is the natural state of matter. Lightning is an example of plasma, and our spirit bodies, or light bodies, are made up of trillions of tiny lightning bolts that are flashing on and off.

So, how do spirits recognise each other if they all consist of plasma? It is by their vibrations or wavelengths of light. Using a prism, light can be split into its constituent colours or wavelengths (a rainbow is the result of sunlight being split into its various colours by the prisms of raindrops.) The light of a spirit body will likewise have its own unique pattern of coloured lines which identifies it as an individual just like we would recognise a human face.

Our spirit is the twin of our human self (not to be confused with twin flames). The spirit part of us dwells in the hidden dimensions, living a parallel life to our own. Just as avatars represent ourselves when we play a video game, our spirit is akin to our avatar, representing us in a higher realm (or perhaps our human self is an avatar of our spirit?) Our spirit has a different kind of life from ours but our consciousness is shared. It has the same *current* consciousness as exists for our human self, a mirror if you like. So, we are really in both places at once, with our consciousness able to be in both forms at the same time as both worker and manager. (This is similar to a subatomic particle that exists both as matter and in waveform in the same moment, as discovered by quantum physics scientists.)

Our spirit shares most of the same thoughts and feelings as its human counterpart, but because the spirit has a higher viewpoint and easier access to great beings of love and wisdom, and doesn't have the limitations of an earthly physical body and the human environment and society, our spirit self is able to see things more clearly and act from a more stable emotional base.

In some recent movies, the concept of a daemon (or daimon) has been featured. This is not the same as a demon, but is a supernatural being, or usually a creature, which has the nature of something between a god and a human. In short, this is similar to our spirit or soul. The ancient Greek philosopher Aristotle wrote in the 4th century B.C. about his daimon who was his spiritual guide. In the film *Alice through the Looking Glass*, Alice is guided by a blue butterfly named Absolom to the looking glass mirror where she steps through into the other world, where Absolom acts in the role of her spirit guide. In the movie *The Golden Compass*, the children all have animal daemons which protect them physically and direct them through voices in their consciousness. The daemons can shapeshift into almost anything but normally act out as the animal which best mimics the personality traits of the children themselves.

We all know that we can be a different person when we are in a great environment with caring friends and family than when we are being stressed to the max in an uncomfortable situation facing hostile people. Likewise, the spirit side of us tends to act with greater love and compassion and wisdom than does the human part of our consciousness. This is the voice in our heads that sometimes gets through to us and guides us through the turmoil of human living.

Our soul, on the other hand, is our *future* self. It sits on the Ribbon of Consciousness at the next level above our spirit. We could liken the spirit to being the director of our consciousness for this lifetime, and the soul as the CEO, the overseer of all our lifetimes, and our central hub. Our human self is the employee. (Yes, I know that sucks, but remember the spirit and soul are parts of us too! We need to play our part in the team, and our part as the human is to be the arms and legs for our spirit.)

Soul graduation/soul merge

The soul is who we are learning to become, and as we raise ourselves up in consciousness to be more loving, more insightful, and more on track with our destiny, then we move towards our soul, higher up the Ribbon.

How exactly does our human/spirit consciousness graduate and move to a higher level?

We can look at our journey through life as a path along the Ribbon of Consciousness, where we will find there are a series of graduation gates where one level of consciousness stops and the next starts. It's like moving up from one class at school into the next. But unlike schools, where we usually move up at the end of the school year, in consciousness and the higher dimensions there is no concept of time, and our progress depends entirely on ourselves. If we have done the work allocated to us, then we progress. If we have shirked our duties, then we will stay at the same level. Some people take years to move between levels, and some people never make it to the next level in their entire lifetime. But it would seem that the move to the first level is the most difficult and takes the longest. We humans find it hard to initially wake up to our consciousness, but once we get going we tend to move forward quite successfully.

What is this work that we need to accomplish in order to graduate?

It's a combination of making advances in our given mission (see chapter 24 for how to discover your destiny/mission), developing our potential and talents, and growing ourselves into more loving and responsible human beings who work well and cooperate with our spirit selves. If we keep working daily at this, we will find that we get to graduate at the right time and at our right pace. Some people like to be dramatic and embark on a fast track of evolution, but Chiron says it's not to be recommended. 'Slow and steady wins the race.'

If we do make these advantageous moves, eventually our spirit consciousness rises to meet our soul consciousness on the Ribbon, and they slowly merge and assimilate. It's akin to pouring cordial into water. This soul level now becomes the new base level for our spirit self. This new merged spirit/soul consciousness also filters down the Ribbon into our human mind and we begin to operate on Earth with an elevated consciousness. This doesn't mean that we start flying around like some superhero. These soul merges are micro steps towards becoming a god-like being, but we don't move anywhere with our physical body, only in our consciousness.

What it does mean is that our human consciousness becomes more aware and open to the universe at large and we will begin to experience more metaphysical occurrences in our life. Life changes all around us, and we usually feel uplifted in spirit and slightly removed from our old everyday routines. At this higher level, new doors open, we may meet a new circle of people, and more secrets of the universe are revealed to us.

Many people undergo soul merges in their time as humans on Earth, and often more than one merge. Most times it is hardly acknowledged as such by the person; they may just presume they have gone through some major life change that takes them on a different path which automatically has them thinking in new and atypical ways.

But there are times when a soul merge is a key evolutionary step for a person, and they may find that their character is altered out of all recognition, as if a completely new person has inhabited their skin.

This has happened to myself three times now in this lifetime. Each time, I have been given new astrology to work with and have found myself trying to manage my new persona and understand my new characteristics, talents, and challenges. It's definitely like being reborn! I have twice changed my name formally to match these major sea changes, but with my latest merger I informed my soul that she will just have to live with the name I have currently as I'm not about to go through all that name-changing palaver again! (And as I was finalising this book, I had yet another soul merge. Time will tell how this role will play out!) Below is my personal timeline of merges and astrology.

1953 – 2003, Paula; Leo Sun/8th, Sagittarius Ascendant, Aquarius North Node/2nd

2003 – 2012, Ovidne; Pisces Sun/12th, Pisces Ascendant, Gemini North Node/3rd

2012 – 2018, Sophia Ovidne; Taurus Sun/9th, Leo Ascendant, Sagittarius North Node/4th

2018 – 2021, Sophia Ovidne; Virgo Sun/12th, Libra Ascendant, Leo North Node/10th

2021 – Sophia Ovidne; Cancer Sun/5th, Aquarius Ascendant, Gemini North Node/4th

Those who are familiar with astrology might be able to see how my new souls complement and dovetail with underlying previous consciousnesses of my human self. The new souls are building up my character bit by bit, with the specific destiny of turning me into a channeller for the gods and a teacher of metaphysics.

Most of my family and oldest friends still insist on calling me by my birth name, Paula, but that's okay because I still have that first consciousness within me. When a soul merge happens, the soul's consciousness doesn't come in and obliterate the lower consciousness; it merely adds to it. The Ascended Master El Morya once described this to me as like marinating a sausage. The basic sausage meat is like our natural born consciousness, and the merging soul consciousness is like the spices and herbs that get added to it to give it heaps more flavour. So, you could say that a higher consciousness is much more desirable and tasty!

When a new soul comes into a human/spirit consciousness, it brings with it new rules and new goals. It's like new management for a company, and the human self will certainly feel the changes. 'A new broom sweeps clean' is the old saying, and we can find ourselves having to endure a lot of changes and letting go. It's not that the new soul/spirit will outline these rules and goals from Day One. The human consciousness has to discover these for itself, and will be given opportunities by its new twin, friend, and Master, to do so. If the human side resists these changes, it is in danger of dragging them all back down to a lower level of consciousness and everyone will suffer.

And, yes, a spirit/soul can suffer! It is still a part of our consciousness that lives a parallel life to our human one. It has thoughts and feelings and its own tasks to complete, and at times it can go through the turmoil of change and challenge in the higher dimensions just as we do down here in the lower dimension of Earth. If our spirit/soul is unhappy, then this discontent or pain will trickle down to us in human form, and we may wonder why we are feeling so under the weather when there appears to be no rhyme or reason for it.

A merger between human consciousness and spirit/soul consciousness is like two people joining together in a marriage. One doesn't seek to take over the other but to integrate their hitherto separate lives and to come together harmoniously. Like in any marriage, compromises have to be made and both sides have to get used to that. At first there are bound to be differences between the two elements of consciousness, and ways will have to be found to overcome these difficulties, but the soul is wise and patient and teaches its human counterpart to surrender to greater love and harmony until all is aligned and balanced.

It has been my experience (and my confusion at times) that the Masters often refer to this merge of consciousness as a marriage. And so, if a Master or god requests to marry you, it doesn't actually mean what you think it does but refers to them wanting to share part of their consciousness with yours. This happens a great deal in the higher dimensions, where the higher beings download some of their wonderful mind and energies into our consciousness in order to help us progress or heal. Again, it doesn't mean that we are being taken over, but that another 'book' has been added to our 'library'.

I asked Master Chiron if it is possible for a god to take over a human completely (often termed a 'walk-in'), or is it always just a partial merger of consciousnesses?

Chiron: *"In most cases the gods are downloading their consciousnesses, their wisdom and their energies, to help their students get a leg up on the ladder to godhood or towards the higher levels of godhood. And these are always just partial transfers of knowledge and energy, and the student will be the wiser for it but will not have been brainwashed in any shape or form.*

But there are instances where gods will take over the consciousness of a human, and that is when the human is about to die and yet there is still usefulness for that body. And so, the physical body will be retained, and the god's consciousness will slide in as the human's consciousness slides out. And so, a full swap entails. But let me add, this is only done on rare occasions, for it is not a god's wont to take over a human's consciousness."[3]

After any marriage or merger of consciousnesses, we always enter a period of at least three days (and sometimes several weeks) which I call The Void. It's a time and place where we feel very vague and disconnected. What is happening is that the new higher energies and characteristics are

---

3. From a channelling by Chiron, 26 November 2019

flooding our consciousness and we are trying to integrate and make sense of them. From experience, it doesn't pay to fight this. It's better just to accept we are going to be in a strange and void-like space for a few days, and eventually we pop out of it automatically as our consciousness begins to see the light of day. If we resist it, then the three-day period stretches out to weeks and even months. It's best to remember we have a spirit in the higher realms and to try and stay connected with them.

Immediately after our graduation, especially the early ones on our spiritual path, it sometimes seems as if we are in mourning. It feels as if we have lost a loved one. In truth, we have—it's an old part of ourself. It's similar to leaving childhood and entering adulthood, or moving from school to university, or leaving bachelorhood and getting married. Whilst we can appreciate the gains we have made spiritually, we can feel some grief for the human part of our lives that we've had to leave behind.

However, when we do emerge from The Void, we will usually feel as if we've been promoted at work. Certainly, our higher level brings with it new responsibilities, tasks, and challenges, but many new rewards too. We face the world with renewed strength and positivity, even if it all feels a little unsettling at first. For a while, we might have difficulties with communication lines to our spirit/soul while we are busy integrating our new consciousness, but before long our combined soul/spirit is communicating new directions and new paths to us. (I usually find that when a soul merge occurs for myself, or I have made a big jump to a new level of consciousness, my computer crashes and I am compelled to buy a new one with new improved communications capabilities!)

In the background, from a higher level on our Ribbon of Consciousness, a new soul slips into place to replace the soul that merged with us. There are many of these souls waiting in the wings for us at higher and higher levels, reaching right back to our very Source. We won't be able to communicate with this new and higher soul until we have fully integrated our latest merger. This can take many weeks or months, or even years. Only then will this new higher soul begin to work in everyday partnership with us, and the cycle begins again of training us to reach a new and higher level of evolution where eventually we will merge with this soul too.

As we keep raising our consciousness to a higher level with more and more loving and god-like thoughts and actions, we will keep merging with new souls that are at a higher and higher level. A whole line of souls is waiting for us. It's not clear how many souls there might be, but plenty enough to keep us going for a few millennia, I would guess. While I have little idea of how many levels there are in this process, I do know of some of the major levels we are aiming for throughout the course of our evolution over many lifetimes. Our ultimate aim is to reach to the highest level, and at that level we find our Source, who is at creator god level.

1. **Human steps onto spiritual path.** Trained by its spirit and soul that it is born with.
2. **Human enters ascension/godhood training** (explained in detail in Ch 10). Human merges with current soul and then trained by next higher-level soul. There can be many soul merges during this period.
3. **Human consciousness becomes god consciousness.** Human becomes a god but with limited capacity at first. Merges with current soul and then trained by next higher-level soul.
4. **Enters star training.** Part of this training entails learning how to embody the energies of a planet, and finally that of a sun or star.
5. **God consciousness becomes star consciousness.** The god embodies a sun or star. Enters creator god training.
6. **Star consciousness becomes creator god consciousness.** The consciousness reaches its Source and becomes a creator god, managing an entire universe along with other creator gods.

If we are open-minded and open-hearted then we will feel the excitement and magic of living at a higher level. If we have no expectations and we cease clinging to our old ways at the lower level, then all will unfold magically for us at this new level of consciousness. Chiron tells us that soul graduation is like a caterpillar becoming a butterfly. We need to stretch our new wings and fly.

Our Source and the radio dial

I have discovered from personal experience that we don't need to wait several millennia, while we complete our evolutionary journey, in order to meet our Source. But to describe how this is possible, we first need to understand that our consciousness is not only like a ribbon across dimensions but also like the dial on a radio that shows wavelength frequencies and connects us to various radio stations.

Our human consciousness is at the lower end of the bandwidth, and there is not just one radio station there but many thousands. These equate to all the various personas that we described in the previous chapter. So, when we wake up in the morning we may be tuning into our 'bad hair day' persona/station, or perhaps our 'kind friend' persona/station, or perhaps our 'I'm gonna take the world by storm' persona/station. We will probably have one or two default station settings for our consciousness.

However, just like with a radio, our consciousness can actually dial into whatever station and wavelength that we fancy, and we can tune into our spirit or our soul, or even our Source at the very high end of the bandwidth. We step into the consciousness of our soul or our Source in that instance, tuning into their frequency and listening to our consciousness at their level and what it has to say, just like we would with any radio station. It is as if, daily, we can wear multiple hats of our varying personas.

It's fair to say that it's difficult to dial into the higher frequencies unless we have done quite a bit of work to raise ourself to a higher level of consciousness and vibrational being. But anyone should be able to receive broadcasts quite clearly, at least at their spirit's or soul's frequency, if they set their dial (their intention) that way.

When we go through a soul merge, our default frequency on our consciousness radio gets set automatically to a higher wavelength, and we might lose some of the lower bandwidth altogether. So, in effect, we choose which level to live at within our consciousness; the higher the level or frequency, the more life is filled with the god-like qualities of love, light, and happiness.

Our Source sits at the very top of the frequency band, and connection will probably be limited and brief, since we humans can't cope with such high wavelengths for very long, although sometimes our Source will come down the wavelengths a bit to meet us halfway. My own Source, who is pure consciousness and non-physical, shows herself to me as an image of a shimmering female human form of intense white diamond light or fire. Other Sources may show themselves in different guises. In truth, my Source is neither female nor male but is a balanced blend of both, but I feel very comfortable working with her in this feminine form and she obviously knew that it would work well for me. The very first time I met her, I cried in realising who I truly was at my core. It was one of the most beautiful experiences of my entire life.

Our relationship with our spirit/soul

Once we discover that our spirit and soul are now our partners for eternity, we need to further learn to work together as a team. Our spirit/soul is our companion, protector, and guide. They know the plan for us in this human lifetime, and it is their job to guide us in understanding our purpose and to carry out our contract. We won't be allowed to renege on our destiny. Our spirit/soul monitors the health of our mission at all times and, if we are failing miserably, we may get recalled back to the spirit world. For it is our soul who places us here on Earth, and it is our soul who dictates when it is time to leave. Our tenure on Earth isn't up to our human consciousness.

Our spirit/soul spends much of its time fighting the human ego, trying to stop it playing up or preventing it from taking control and dictating its own path through life. The very worst thing for a human is to be separated from its spirit/soul, even if the human has no idea they even have a spirit or soul. The relationship gives a human not only great strength and comfort but also direction and a guiding light. We call a depressed person 'dispirited' for good reason; they are a person who has lost their spirit. If our spirit/soul sees there is no hope for our redemption, our soul reins us in and brings us Home, back to the higher dimensions as our spirit consciousness. (Refer to chapters 8-9 on death for more details on this.)

If our human self is connected with the higher dimensions, our spirit/soul will work with us daily from its parallel world. If we cherish our spirit, it will likewise cherish us and make life more pleasant for us, utilising their higher powers. If we ignore our spirit self, then it ignores us too. If the human doesn't acknowledge its invisible twin, then its spirit goes off and waits for contact. Until then we will receive no guidance or protection from them, or the benefit of their manifestation abilities. We will feel abandoned and disconnected, not just from spirit but from ourselves and everyone around us too. Spirit and human are two halves of one mind. If one half is missing, we stand alone and will feel lonely. When we work as one unit of consciousness between human and spirit/soul, then we can attain all we desire in this way, but not when we work alone.

Like any team on Earth, spirit and human must be on the same page. Even though they are one consciousness, they play different roles, and they need to converse with one another and share goals, motivations, skills, and communications. Daily meetings are in order to give one another support and set expectations. The mission will get off track if they don't keep each other in the loop. Spirit/soul is always available to be asked questions and to provide directions. This may come as a voice in our head, or as intuition, or through opportunities that they provide. (See Part Two for how spirit speaks with us.) Spirit is wiser than us and we would do well to heed their advice.

Like any friend, we can get to know our spirit/soul personally and build a strong and loving relationship, and their free-spiritedness, indomitable will, and knowledge of the universe is like a breath of fresh air in our human lives, especially if we are feeling stuck or uninspired. Strangely enough, they don't know exactly what we are thinking or feeling, or our aspirations; it's akin to us not knowing what each of our lower personas thinks and feels.

So, we can ask our spirit/soul questions such as, what is going on in their parallel life, and where do they like travelling in the universe in their spirit sphere? What is their home like, do they have a partner, what kind of work do they do, and where do they prefer to go on holiday?

Spirit/soul is invested in us, and everyone benefits from our success. We need to let ourselves be directed by the consciousness of our higher self and not operate from our lower human will. This is not to say that humans don't ever get to have their say, but we are the employees in this company, and we must work cooperatively with all parts of our consciousness. When we do this and offer our skills to the best of our ability, then we are able to bring in the magic.

If we look into the attributes and nature of the left and right hemispheres of the human brain, in my opinion, these appear to mirror the manner in which the human and spirit/soul consciousnesses operate. Human consciousness tends to be represented by the left brain, and spirit/soul consciousness tends to be represented by the right brain. Even while we use both hemispheres of our brain in most activities, each side of the brain has a kind of personality and favours certain ways of working.

The table below gives an indication of the *tendency* of each hemisphere and does not signify this is what actually occurs in each person. Also note, the hemispheres should not be categorised as either male or female sides of the brain.

Left brain tendencies (typically human)	**Right brain tendencies (typically spirit/soul)**
1. Expresses its will and ego. Tends to want power and to take control and to manipulate	Prefers cooperation and harmony, and to bring unity, cohesion, and balance to the world
2. Tends to be inflexible and finds it difficult to make changes. Prefers the familiar and status quo	More accommodating and willing to be adaptable. Prefers to experience flow and to evolve
3. Lacks imagination. Dislikes going beyond into the unknown	Searches for new experiences. Actively seeks to go beyond the known world. Can cope with unknown paradigms and the mysterious
4. Stays within circulatory thinking and '9 dots'	Explores outside the box
5. Limited in what it sees and understands	Open to everything outside itself
6. Narrow focus of attention, tunnel vision	Broad, vigilant attention to its surroundings

Left brain tendencies (typically human)	Right brain tendencies (typically spirit/soul)
7. Tends towards narrow thinking, details, things that are easily understood	Flexibility of thought. Big picture thinking, taking in the entire context, even if not easily understood
8. Takes a short-term view	Willing to go the long haul
9. Offers solutions that fit with, and confirms, what it already knows	Offers wide scope of possibilities and visions
10. Has a need for certainty and things to be pinned down. Tends to force a decision	Encompasses uncertainty and ambiguity. Can deal with multiple possibilities
11. Tends to jump to desired conclusions, and can become deluded	Copes with incompleteness and lack of boundaries. Understands true nature of things
12. Dismissive, gets stuck in denial, divisive	Understands points of view of others, unifying
13. Has a need to be right, even if wrong	Has no agenda or preconceptions
14. Efficient in automatic daily routines	Delegates routine to left side (human) unless in 'the Zone', when spirit/soul takes over
15. Tries to be articulate, precise, detailed, and unambiguous. Good with analysis, language, and syntax	Understands overall context better than left brain. Uses imagery rather than words. Better with musical language and poetry than the left brain
16. Technical, mechanical, tends to be predictable, follows rules	Exploratory, insightful, intuitive, flexible, open to newness, bends rules
17. Ability to follow processes, systems, techniques, maps, in language, maths, and other practices	Often solves maths and other problems via intuition and by perceiving the whole context
18. Tends to choose logic and theory over real experience, the map rather than the territory	Chooses experience and actual reality as its models

Left brain tendencies (typically human)	Right brain tendencies (typically spirit/soul)
19. Views the world according to its own theories	Presents the world as it really is, relating to its experiences
20. Tends to take things literally, and takes the soul out of things. Finds it hard to understand imagery, symbolism, metaphor, humour, subtlety, or hints	Appreciates soul, humour, music, artistry, and employs imagery, symbolism, metaphor, hidden meaning, story, and context. Can operate through ambiguity and vagueness
21. Unconcerned about taking things out of context	Understands things belong in their context. Comprehends narrative, the whole story
22. Doesn't easily recognise deceit or irregularities	Can better detect duplicity, discrepancies and anomalies
23. Tends not to be so good with facial recognition, or utilising body language and emotional expression	Better at recognising faces, body language, and emotional expression. Uses the body as a vehicle through which it can express itself
24. Tends to see humans as machines, not living forms	Concerned with relationships, bonding, and what gives spirit to the human form and consciousness
25. Prefers non-living things e.g. machines, money, the world of materiality	Prefers living things e.g. people, animals, nature, and the hidden worlds of gods and spirituality
26. Tends to deal with parts of things and not whole entity, seeing things in a mechanistic way	Sees the whole before seeing the parts, the combined union rather than the pieces that it is created from
27. Tends to want to amass things. Can be predatory, and can become angry or aggressive if thwarted	Prefers to share. Not so concerned with material things. Tends to be more passive and accepting
28. Tends to lack, or not display, empathy or loving emotions. Tends not to notice the other's state of being	More emotionally intelligent and empathic. More able to detect when an emotion is appropriate or not. Often can sense the other's state of being

Left brain tendencies (typically human)	Right brain tendencies (typically spirit/soul)
29. Deals primarily with own side of brain and what that knows, and not concerned about what right brain (spirit/soul) may know	Concerned with both sides of brain. Takes into account what the left brain (human) knows and is able to achieve
30. Does not understand the right brain (spirit/soul), and can be fearful of it	Understands both left and right brains (human and spirit/soul)
31. Thinks it can go it alone, without right brain (spirit/soul)	Encompasses left brain (human) in its views and desires
32. Tends to prefer competition more than collaboration. 'Either/or' mentality; me or you, not, me and you	Open to interconnectedness and relationships. Inclusive of all sides and views
33. Tends to be unaware of its limitations. Unrealistic about talents or shortcomings	Aware of what is possible, realistic about abilities and potential
34. Can be overly optimistic about future	More realistic about future, but can tend towards pessimism
35. Concerned with time	Unconcerned by time. Gets lost in timelessness

In recent centuries, our society has become more and more left brain-orientated and predominantly favours our human consciousness. We are forgetting how to operate with a right brain perspective, and therefore we cannot see what our soul/spirit wants us to see, and we are missing out on the unseen universe.

Whatever is going on for our spirit in the heavens reflects also within our human environment and relationships. When our relationship with our spirit is onside, then all our other relationships will be harmonious too. When we ignore or fight with our higher self, all other relationships tend to act out divisively too. Spirit and human affect one another in both positive and negative ways across the dimensional divide. Spirit is akin to a human's shadow. We cannot dump it or discount it. It is with us for our entire lifetime, whether we acknowledge it or not.

We need to stay connected with our spirit twin at all times and treat them as we would our best friend, looking for ways to make them part of our lives and to make their life better too. Spirit will reciprocate well and will enthusiastically share their love, advice, comfort, and metaphysical experiences in the higher realms. (Refer to Part Two for how to connect with the spirit world)

Does everyone have a soul?

Someone asked me the above question at one of my workshops, and so I went to the source for the answer, literally to my own Source, and here is the response she channelled to me.

My Beloved Source: *"Does everyone or everything have a soul? Let us speak about people first. Does every body that is alive on Earth have a soul? Yes, they do. It is impossible to be alive without a soul, without a spirit counterpart in Heaven, for that is what your soul is, the non-physically manifested part of yourself that resides in a higher dimension.*

And so, to be human means you have a soul on the other side that guides you, protects you, that is your home area, and to which your consciousness will return when you pass over from this Earth. If you are a body on this planet without a soul, then you are not human. Then you are just a machine, a vehicle without consciousness such as a robot or a car.

Can you be a physical body in other parts of the universe without a soul? Again, I say to you, this would make you merely a machine. To be a human being, or any other kind of being with consciousness, then you would have a soul that goes along with you. For your soul is consciousness, nothing less, nothing more.

Now when I speak about things not having a soul, this could be a point for debate, for all things have a modicum of consciousness. They take on some of the consciousness of their creator. All things are made from molecules and atoms, and these tiny items exist because they have been created by someone and they hold a tiny part of the consciousness of their maker.

So, even mountains have consciousness, for their soil consists of elements and these elements were created by the gods. And these elements have been brought together to form stars and planets. And all the plants that have come from seeds, these seeds have been created with consciousness. We are not saying they have the full consciousness of their creators but enough consciousness to be able to know what they must do. You might say that this is all programmed into their DNA, but who programmed that DNA? It was their creator.

And so, do mountains and plants have a soul? If a soul is consciousness and consciousness is a soul, then it could be said then that, yes, mountains and plants have a soul. But if a soul is to be defined as consciousness with more capacity, more free will, then perhaps you might be inclined to believe that mountains and plants do not have a soul. And the same argument could therefore be used for animals too. Where do you draw the line at your definition for a soul?

Perhaps humans are soulless compared to the gods? Give that some thought. A soul is consciousness. How much consciousness do you need to become a soul?"[4]

---

4. Channelled from my Beloved Source, 28 September 2017

Chapter 4 – The unseen beings—God and the gods

Who or what is God?

'Who or what is God?' is the most difficult of all questions to answer. Philosophers and theologians have been debating the issue for millennia. Have we got any closer to discovering the truth?

I have noticed recently, in listening to podcasts that contain any hint of spirituality, that people are tending to steer away from any mention of God when they wish to discuss God or the soul or spirit, or that which is beyond our world. They refer instead to 'the transcendent', or at best to 'the divine', as if it's no longer politically correct to use the 'G' word.

What Chiron (and I) mean by God, is the entity that created our universe, for all of us can agree (I hope) that we live in a physical universe that is all around us, and something or someone must have created that. Something came before 'The Big Bang' and the creation of our universe, no matter what theories you believe in. As yet, there is no agreement amongst scientists about how life got started on Earth. It is still one of the greatest unsolved enigmas of our time.

We could call God a Higher Power or Intelligence, or the Universe, or any number of designations, but what we are referring to here is the Consciousness that started it all, that came before our universe existed. It's ridiculously difficult to get our minds around, and Chiron tells us that there is an answer, but that we will never understand, from our human consciousness, where the initial consciousness came from, and we must just accept the mystery of it for now.

So, we could call God the First Consciousness, or the First Creator. And because the universe is consciousness itself, and a collection of all the consciousnesses that exist, we could give God the name of One God because all is brought together into oneness under this entity's umbrella. Chiron refers to God as the One God throughout his book.

The very first question Chiron asks in his book is, "Was there a beginning to this universe?" And he answers it with, "Of course there was!" But he goes on to say that his version of the origin of our universe differs perhaps from current theories. And you will need to keep an open mind as I explain his description of events, and bear in mind that we only believe what we believe because it has been inculcated in us from an early age. It wouldn't be the first time that schools and religions have taught us incorrect things; they merely teach us what is the prevalent thinking at the time, and over time theories evolve and sometimes change altogether. Scientists can only play games at imagining how the universe began, and religions have confused people with misinterpretations of sacred writings, but we are taught these things as if they were the truth. That said, I am not asserting that the following is The Truth; I am giving an explanation of Chiron's version of the truth. You must make up your own minds as to what is true for you.

In the beginning of this particular universe there was nothing, just a void of emptiness. I say 'this particular universe' because Chiron tells us that there are many universes. Some have been and gone, and there will be many more to come.

Creator gods

Did the One God create all these universes? Yes and no. The One God obviously didn't like being all alone at the very beginning, and created many son and daughter gods to help with the creation of the multiverse. These gods are named creator gods by Chiron. It may go against all we have been taught in the Western Christian world to hear that there is more than one god, but if we check out the Christian Bible, we will see (and I was very surprised to discover this myself) that in Genesis, the Book of the Bible that describes the creation of our universe, there are references to 'gods'—yes, in the plural. This was something they neglected to mention at my Roman Catholic school in London!

In the Christian Bible, on the 6th Day of Creation, God said, "And now *we* will make human beings; they will be like *us* and resemble *us*."

(Good News Bible: Genesis 1:26) God speaks of 'we' and 'us' and is therefore referring not only to Himself but to other gods around Him too. In the King James version of the Bible, it states, "And God said, 'Let *us* make man in *our* image, after our likeness.'", clearly saying 'our' not 'my' and referring to multiple gods.

A little further on is another example of a reference to 'us', therefore acknowledging at least one other god present apart from God Himself. "Then the Lord God said, 'Now the man has become like one of *us*.'" (Good News Bible: Genesis 3:22), or in the King James version, "And the Lord God said, 'Behold, the man is become as one of *us*.'"

The One God, and the creator gods whom He had created, existed in some huge domain which is the Great Universe that encapsulates all universes and where universes get created. At some point, Chiron tells us, ten of the creator gods pooled their light into the dark void and created their future playground which is now our particular universe. Just like children in any family, the creator gods were allowed to create and experiment in any way they wished. They used their light and consciousness to develop a universe filled with both physical and invisible (to us humans) non-physical elements.

Apparently, this was not the first universe they had created, and so they had some past experience of what worked and what didn't, playing around with the basic physics and mechanics and allowing things to evolve of their own volition. The creator gods kept the things that pleased them and ditched the things that didn't go to plan. All the while, over many eons, the creator gods were learning, just as a child learns, and their consciousnesses, and the consciousness of the One God too, expanded with new experiences, knowledge, and wisdom.

In Greek and Roman mythology, the universe was created by the goddess Gaia (Earth) and the god Ouranos (Sky, the Heavens). These could be considered as representing creator gods. They gave birth to twelve Titans (e.g. Cronos/Saturn), who in turn gave birth to the Olympians (e.g. Zeus/Jupiter), representing the descendant races of gods.

The creator gods are still creating and our universe is still expanding, as was proved by Edwin Hubble and other scientists only last century.

My personal theory on this is that, if the universe's substance is consciousness, and everyone is expanding their consciousness, then of course the universe is going to expand. Perhaps this is what dark energy really is—consciousness? Chiron says we shall discover these truths one day, but it won't be until scientists acknowledge consciousness for what it truly is.

The creator gods went on to manifest all the first materiality in our universe, such as stars and planets, and the elements and energies. It's not as if they created our Earth exactly as it is today, nor even as it was millions of years ago. They tend to seed things and let them evolve, fine-tuning where necessary and doing away with things that are atrocious failures. We might wonder if the fate of the dinosaurs was a planned or accidental event?

Not only material objects were created by these gods but beings too. The creator gods used parts of their consciousnesses to form new consciousnesses—new gods. At first, the new entities were fashioned directly by the creator gods, and these were non-physical beings, but in time, these new gods also began creating new consciousnesses from themselves and physical forms too, and eventually they created a new race of consciousnesses—us humans, and manifested human bodies to house these consciousnesses.

The Nobel Prize Winner, Francis Crick, who discovered the structure of DNA along with his colleague, James Watson, stated in his book *Life Itself* that it is impossible for our human DNA to have originated on Earth, and he proposed that "organisms were deliberately transmitted to Earth by intelligent beings on another planet". Of course, we cannot prove this in any way, but it's good to keep an open mind on these things.

So, we have a hierarchy appearing now. At the top is the One God, first consciousness and first creator of the place that holds all universes. Below the One God sit the original creator gods, created by the One God. Below the creator gods are the intermediate gods that they created. Some of these gods embody the stars (suns) and planets of our universe; that is, these cosmic bodies are the physical housing for their consciousness. So, we can understand now how some civilisations worshipped the Sun as their God. Below the intermediate gods sits the human race inhabiting Earth (and other human-like races inhabiting other exoplanets).

Therefore, if we speak of God or pray to God, to whom are we actually referring? Are we reaching the one at the very top, or the creator gods, or the intermediate gods? Does it actually matter, in truth, if they are all one united consciousness? If we return to our metaphor of the radio dial, we can imagine tuning into the frequency level of the god that we might wish to communicate with, bearing in mind that to reach the higher frequencies our own consciousness needs to be able to cope with those elevated wavelengths.

The creation of humans

Humans have actually been part of the universe since the very beginning. Human consciousness has evolved from the consciousnesses of the intermediate gods, who were fashioned from the creator gods, who were birthed from the One God. Therefore, each one of us has a spark of consciousness within us that originally came from the One God. Certainly, it has been pared down, added to, and sifted and stirred by many consciousnesses along the way, but our first ancestor is the One God, and we are all derived ultimately from this entity.

However, when I speak with my own Source within my consciousness, she tells me that she is at the creator god level. So, when the gods (or I) refer to the source of our consciousness, they are referring to the creator gods and we can trace our lineage back to one of these. I guess everyone's true source is the One God, so a distinction is being made to help us understand that not all of us come from the same creator god consciousness. But there may be other interpretations that I am not aware of yet.

Chiron describes the evolution of a human's consciousness in the following terms. In the beginning, a piece of consciousness is firstly scooped out of the cloud that is the creator god consciousness. This scoop is only a copy and does not take away from the original consciousness in any way. It is now a new individual consciousness, often called a 'clone' by the gods. And from this consciousness another scoop copy is taken, and from this scoop another taken, and it might be merged with other tiny cloud balls along the way. Therefore, new clouds of consciousness are always forming, and we are descended from one of these. We can see from this that our lineage is not directly in a straight line back to a particular creator god. We have been scooped and merged many times since our beginnings, and we are descended from, and related to, more people than we could ever imagine.

We could liken this to starting with a glass of pure water and adding various flavourings to it, and then pouring these into other glasses of water and their particular flavourings, and so on. However, the consciousness within the glass of liquid also has a life of its own and it proliferates and generates its own unique flavour over time. And eventually this too will go on to flavour other liquids. Although this scooping and merging process is often referred to as cloning, we can see that we are never a clone of anyone in the true sense because we are not an exact copy but a derivative of many consciousnesses at once.

So, we already exist as this scooped, merged, and flavoured non-physical consciousness when it decides to experience life in the form of a human in some particular role. Before our actual birth, our consciousness creates the brain which will be used as a tool by our human body, and also sets up the appropriate filters and perceptions of the entire world around us suitable for this lifetime. All-in-all we are prepared for our acting part, and the background scenery and props are put in place too.

As humans we are not born as pure and fresh consciousnesses. We will have many memories stored away in the recesses of our minds, and sometimes these can flicker into life and we might recall other lifetimes in other places where our consciousness was playing out a different role. Our human consciousness is protected for the most part from being overwhelmed by past life memories for it needs to focus on its present role. As our consciousness matures and is deemed able to handle more knowledge of its journeys through time and space, then more doors will be opened within the universe for our spirit self to travel through and explore parts of itself and its consciousness that were hitherto unknown.

Did we humans evolve from fish and apes, or did we spring whole-like from the hands of the gods? There is fierce debate about this in our current times. There are differing views from Evolutionists, Creationists, and those who believe in Intelligent Design. Let us briefly summarise these viewpoints so we can understand where Chiron's version of events sits within, or opposed to, these other philosophies.

The Evolutionists believe in the theory of evolution and natural selection as espoused most famously by Charles Darwin in his book, *On the Origin of Species,* published in 1859. In it, Darwin stated that all species develop from a process of natural selection which focuses on the small variations in biology which foster an increased ability to thrive, survive, and reproduce, and which thereby become the dominant traits in later generations and species. In this book he does not mention how humans themselves came to evolve. In his later book, The *Descent of Man,* published in 1871, Darwin describes how man descended from apes but offers no fossil evidence that this is so. To this day, no scientific evidence has been forthcoming, often referred to as 'The Missing Link', to prove irrefutably that present-day humankind is descended from apes or fish or any other species.

Some Evolutionists believe that the universe began about 14 billion years ago, with the Earth coming into being about 4.5 billion years ago. This is the theory that most scientists hang their hat on. Life evolved, some believe, probably from bacteria in the rocks, and no God or deity was involved in this process. However, some Evolutionists believe that God did create the universe in the first instance and then left it to its own devices to evolve in a natural manner, utilising the natural selection process.

Creationists come from a religious viewpoint where they believe that the universe and all life were created by a Divine God and not through the processes of evolution and natural selection. Some Creationists believe in the literal interpretation of the Genesis texts in the Christian Bible of how God created the universe in six days and created Adam and Eve as the first man and woman. They reject the theory of evolution in that it cannot adequately explain the complexity and intelligence of humans and other life on Earth. They also cite the lack of the so-called 'Missing Link' as argument that evolution is not a valid theory.

Those who believe in Intelligent Design, argue for the existence of God or a higher power, which was responsible for the origins of life.

They assert that biological features are far too complex to have been the result of natural selection or random processes, and that they could only be the product of intentional design by someone.

Scientists and proponents on either side of the debate have not been able to produce, as yet, absolute empirical evidence of how mankind came into existence.

To recap Chiron's take on all this, it is that the consciousness of the One God created other consciousnesses whom he calls creator gods. These creator gods created other gods out of their own consciousnesses. And from these gods eventually human consciousnesses were created to inhabit human bodies that were created by the gods in the image of themselves. This is not unlike how we create a baby, taking the consciousness of two humans, bringing them together and giving life to a new being.

Those who first created the physical forms of humans, we tend to call God or gods. Therefore, because humans also create physical forms, could they too be termed as gods? What about the creation of test-tube babies and DNA genetic modifications? Are we fast stepping on the toes of the gods in this area?

The creation of robots

In this present century, just as the gods once did, humans are busy creating a new race of physical forms that resemble themselves—the race of robots. They are being programmed with artificial intelligence and taught to think for themselves. Chiron asks, "When does the term 'artificial intelligence' become '*natural* intelligence'? At what stage have you given birth to a human-like being? And will these human-like beings be deemed to have consciousness?" Ultimately, when does a robot become a human being?

The gods tussled with these same questions when they first created the human race. It wasn't that the human form was magically brought into being overnight and plonked on Earth to see how it would fare. Humans were designed by the gods over a long period and there were many prototypes, just as the race of robots is being refined today. I repeat my earlier quote from the Good News Bible: Genesis 1:26 "Then God said, "And now we will make human beings; they will be like us and resemble us."

In the beginning, humans were pretty rough and unsophisticated and had only the minimum amount of consciousness to enable them to do their work on Earth, just like the robots we are producing today. But the new humans obviously weren't totally unattractive, as some of the gods mated with some of the humans and produced semi-divine beings or demi-gods (no, they are not just in the movies!). Were these the giants that are referred to in the Christian Bible? Genesis 6:1-4 "When mankind had spread all over the world, and girls were being born, some of the supernatural beings saw that these girls were beautiful, so they took the ones they liked…In those days, and even later, there were giants on the Earth who were descendants of human women and the supernatural beings."

But it is the nature of consciousness to expand, and the humans' insignificant consciousness expanded in unforeseen ways until the gods lost control over their race of humans, and they are still trying to wrest back control to this day. The gods tell us that whatever we create becomes our responsibility and must be managed, just as parents have responsibility for any baby that they birth. Therefore, the gods are responsible for the humans they have created, and over millennia, the gods, our parents, have worked on our consciousness to develop and expand it into the interesting and remarkable species we are today.

Now it is we humans who are creating our world. We are creator gods in our own right, with our playground here on Earth, and perhaps the solar system before too long. The original creator gods rarely interfere with what is going on down here, and only when requested if things get way out of hand and their own son and daughter, middle management gods cannot turn events around.

We need to remember that consciousness, once brought into existence, can never die and can never be killed off, and our creations through our consciousness remain our responsibility forevermore. So, as humans we will need to be very careful about the new forms of consciousness that we are bringing into the universe through our new race of robots, or in any other way.

Who are the other gods?

In the previous section we discovered how the gods came into being, and how there are several levels of gods, the highest after the One God being the creator gods, and the newest being those humans who have transcended the human realm of consciousness and gained god consciousness. That is the ultimate quest for every human being—to ascend to a higher level of consciousness and to become a god, a human-turned-god.

So, what type of beings are these gods?

If we start from the bottom up, according to level of vibration, we find that newly initiated gods are not much different from humans. We imagine a god as a being of radiant light, overflowing with love and compassion, and with a brilliant mind that can solve any problem and work miracles as well.

Well, at the lower levels of godhood, we might be a tad disappointed! For although a god can on occasion be many, or all, of these things described above, they are also still working through many of their limiting characteristics. They are given challenges worthy of their new god status, and this can bring up new issues for them which they haven't faced before. It's very similar to taking on the job of CEO of a company for the first time—it doesn't come easy in the beginning, and there are many stressful situations and vulnerabilities and old wounds to be overcome before a god can sail through every storm with aplomb. They are still very much on a learning curve, as is every god, no matter what level they sit at. Even the creator gods face their own challenges and are expanding their consciousness with new experiences and learnings all the time.

The higher a god rises up the hierarchy, of course, the greater that god's capacity for eminence and the three pillars of godhood; love, wisdom, and power. The highest status gods tend to migrate away from the human world; they have business elsewhere in the universe. But there are many lower and middle management gods who are readily available to work with humans on Earth and teach them how to become gods themselves.

However, some of the higher gods appear now and again in the lower dimensions, just as a CEO might take a walk amongst their workers and listen to their opinions and solve some of their day-to-day problems. I, myself, work frequently with my Source, who is a creator god. She has told me that she is interested in learning more about humans. Most humans, and even most gods, do not generally get to work with their creator gods on a regular basis. Perhaps because of my ability to channel at high frequencies, it's easier for my Source to speak with me than with most people. I'm just not sure how representative I am of humankind—I'm a little bit weird, most folks would say!

So, who are these intermediate or middle management gods who deal with us humans on a daily basis? I can tell you that every one I have worked with over the years has had many lifetimes on Earth in physical form, sometimes as a god, and usually as a human before becoming a god. Some of these current gods were gods in ancient times but fell in their vibrational levels back down to the level of human consciousness and they have had to work their way back up to god consciousness again. The crown of a god is something that is earned on a moment by moment basis, and can be lost as well as gained if not maintained at the high frequency and standards required of godhood.

In my book, *Meet the Masters*[5], I have written at length about my work and personal relationships with many of the gods, or Masters, including Jesus, Mother Mary, El Morya, St.Germain, Venus, Sedna, Pallas Athena, Buddha, Djwhal Khul, Serapis Bey, Quan Yin, and Hilarion. Some people may work with only one god or Master, but I find that they all come to me at various times with their messages for the world or to teach me something personally.

However, I do have a few gods that I tend to work with more closely than others. Master Dominic is one of them, and he is my Twin Flame (see chapter 23 for a description of Twin Flames). My relationship with him is well-documented in *Meet the Masters*. His consciousness has been involved with several well-known characters throughout human history, including General Antigonus who served under Alexander the Great; the Roman Emperor Tiberius; St. Dominic who established the Dominican

---

5. Available from my website www.earthwithspirit.com

Order of Preachers; Leonardo da Vinci; and General Lafayette who fought alongside George Washington.

In the chapter on past lives (Chapter 9) I will explain what I mean by the above phrase 'his consciousness has been involved with', because as Chiron states in his book, we are not one whole consciousness handed down from incarnation to incarnation. For instance, the total consciousness that was Leonardo da Vinci did not go on to become the total consciousness that was General Lafayette.

Obviously, I also work a great deal with Master Chiron, but as he was a later arrival in my life, I'm afraid he doesn't get a mention in *Meet the Masters*. However, I do write about Master Hilarion in my book, and Hilarion has evolved from Chiron's higher consciousness and they are very similar. They are both gods of healing, teaching, science, and energies. Hilarion's consciousness was involved with St. Hilarion, a great healer, and with the Apostle, Paul of Tarsus, who was instrumental in establishing Christianity after the death of Christ.

Another god I work very closely with is El Morya ('Morya' rhymes with 'warrior'), and he certainly appears in *Meet the Masters* and is quite a character. I have channelled two books from him, *The Getting of Wisdom, Books One and Two*, available from all good online bookstores. His consciousness has been involved with Abraham; Alexander the Great; the Roman poet, Ovid; Richard the Lionheart; St. Thomas Becket; St. Thomas More; and Akbar the Great, a Mughal emperor who tried to unite the Hindu and Islamic religions.

There are just as many female goddesses that I work with as there are male gods, and these include Sedna, Venus, Pallas Athena, and Quan Yin. Sedna is not very well-known but she is a very high-status goddess who is a higher consciousness from which Venus and Athena evolved. She has channelled a beautiful book through me, *Lady Sedna's Ascension Handbook*, which is filled with wonderful wisdom of how to achieve ascension, another name for godhood. This book is also available through good online bookstores.

These are a sprinkling of the gods and goddesses that I can be chatting with every day and doing work with. In the next section, we shall examine what kind of work the gods get up to, and how we humans can be of help to them.

How do I see these gods? What form do they take? I will go into more detail about how exactly I connect with the gods in Part Two. However, here I can tell you that I don't see the gods with my physical eyes as flesh and blood people on the ground, but I connect with them through my consciousness, seeing a movie being played out on the screen of my mind, a movie that I step into and play a role in.

The gods can exist in spirit as pure consciousness, and are also able to materialise physically in various forms and guises as spirit bodies. In whatever way we ourselves might expect a god to look like, this is what will probably appear. If we think a god should be an old man with a long white beard, they will show up like that for us. If we can't imagine what a god could look like, then perhaps we will see just a blinding light or some shape meaningful to us. The gods will usually adopt a human form because in that way they won't frighten people so much. In any case, humans were created in the image of the gods, so naturally they would appear very much like us.

The gods have a consciousness in exactly the same way as you and I have a consciousness, and this means they have a personality and character traits and talents and idiosyncrasies just as regular humans do. They are generally very gracious and sociable, helpful and responsive, but rarely moody, offended, or offensive. They have a great sense of fun and wit, and can provide amazing solutions to our problems, if we articulate them. They are very adept at showing us our own issues and mirroring these back to us in some way so we can recognise them and resolve them.

Not only do the gods visit us in our consciousness and sometimes take on a human form and visit us on Earth, but at times (and the present day is one of those times!) the gods will choose to be born on Earth in human physical form and live out a life just like any human being.

These gods are born in the usual human way, gestating in a human mother's womb for nine months, and having a human father. They are not born via 'immaculate conception' or virgin birth, nor do they arrive in a blaze of light, already as adults (although we shall see later in the book that sometimes this is true!) They have blood, tears, and DNA just as humans do (which is understandable as humans were first created out of the DNA of the gods). I asked Master Chiron if there is a difference between the DNA in humans and gods?

Chiron: *"Let us speak about the question of DNA in its entirety, for this ribbon is the stuff of life and also of individuality, and so we must take care that we get our terms precise, for if we mix things up we will be messing with the very creation of life.*

DNA is not something to be taken lightly. It is a serious matter to combine all our codes into one coherent human being. So, let us first ask, "Do gods have DNA?" Yes, they do, if they are transforming their spirit bodies into a human form. Then they will need this DNA to create the form that they are taking. It is their blueprint, if you like.

Now, is this god DNA the same as human DNA? Well, it does have the same components, but the way it is put together in the form of building blocks is different for a god than for a human. It is like taking LEGO bricks and creating either a simple structure or creating some Master-built masterpiece from those same basic blocks. The engineering is different, that is all."[6]

The one thing that is quite different about gods born on Earth is their consciousness, which is god consciousness and not human consciousness. This means they are born at an elevated level of frequency, and this enables them to get off to a running start and accrue talents more quickly and easily than their human counterparts.

At this time, there are also those who have been born as humans who have since become gods in the course of their lives. Their human form remains exactly the same, apart from ageing, of course, but their consciousness is now god consciousness and they will face similar challenges and have similar powers as gods born onto the planet. Often the greatest challenge for these humans-turned-gods is overcoming their human inhibitions and fully embracing the role of a god.

I asked Chiron if there were differences in the DNA for humans-turned-gods?

---

6. Channelled from Chiron, 26 November 2019

Chiron: "*If a human is turned into a god whilst still on Earth, then their DNA does begin to take on different forms. They will not have the full toolset, but when they incarnate again, as a god from birth, then they will be given full god DNA. So, is a human-turned-god on Earth, a full-blooded god? Well, unfortunately I will have to say, no. But they can reach 80% of this potential if they work on their gene pool which, in turn, will redistribute their DNA.*

So, yes, you could call a human-turned-god on Earth a demi-god. For like the offspring of a god who mated with a human, there will be deficiencies in their DNA which suppresses their full god abilities, but in both cases they are semi-divine beings and should be accorded respectful status."[7]

It's interesting that the Christian Bible speaks several times about giants upon the Earth (Numbers 13:33, Deuteronomy 1:28, Deuteronomy 9:2, Joshua 14:12), (and again, I was never taught that at Sunday School!) because when I meet with the gods in consciousness they are usually very tall beings. Also, ancient Egyptian frescos and statues more often than not portray the gods as giants compared to the mere mortals beside them. Archaeologists have explained this as the Egyptian way of showing deference to the gods and their immense power, but what if these works of art are literally true, and the gods are shown in correct dimension against their human counterparts?

As I stated earlier, the gods can also embody stars (suns) and planets, and indeed it is part of our evolution as humans to do so (refer to chapter 3, Soul graduation), once we have achieved god consciousness and begin our journey towards star consciousness, and ultimately towards creator god consciousness. Yes, humans will one day become creator gods and share in the creation and management of universes.

Therefore, the stars and planets are actually gods, ones who have made it to a very high level of consciousness. As an astrologer myself, I love this fact, and often connect with the consciousness of the planets to understand the energies and challenges they are bringing to Earth and to myself at that time.

---

7. Channelled from Chiron, 26 November, 2019

The goddess Sedna currently embodies the planet Earth and she is very accessible to us in our meditations. A dear friend of mine has been told that she is in training to be a future embodiment of Earth, and I myself have been told that I am in training to become the future embodiment of planet Venus. I'm not entirely enamoured with the prospect of managing a burnt-out planet with no vegetation or water, but who knows what really exists on that planet, if we could truly see what lies in the hidden and invisible dimensions? I take heart in that Venus is the goddess of love, beauty and harmony, and these aspects are ones I definitely espouse. I've been given no timeframe for this new job position, but I imagine we are talking thousands, if not millions, of years before this might become my reality!

Embodying a star (a sun) is the next step up from embodying a planet. And it needn't be in our own solar system or even our Milky Way galaxy. Our Sun, as the embodiment of a god's consciousness, is the wisest consciousness in our solar system and it monitors all of us from high above in the heavens. The Sun god controls our solar system, and all consciousnesses within it are subordinate to the Sun. We are pre-programmed to love the Sun, and it's not difficult to understand therefore why many ancient cultures venerated the Sun as their highest god. This all sounds very mythological, I know, but I have come to understand from my work with the gods that much of our ancient mythology is based on foundations of truth. In our 'sophisticated' left-brained world at present, we dismiss all mythology as the stuff of fairy tales and primitive minds, but our right-brained souls would have us re-examining our beliefs on this score.

To scientists and most of the human world, the Sun may be just an inanimate ball of fiery hydrogen and helium gases, but in the invisible world of the higher dimensions, the Sun is the physical manifestation of the consciousness of a particular god. This Sun god will have been responsible for sharing its consciousness in order to create us, so we could revere it as a father-mother god. We are its children and offspring. The Sun star shows us on Earth how to radiate love and brilliance. There are many stars in our visible universe, all of them the embodiment of gods, and they all sprinkle elements of their consciousnesses down upon us, but our own Sun has the most influence on us humans here on planet Earth.

On Wikipedia, there are almost 100 names of sun gods, represented by every culture that has ever existed. Sun gods, therefore, are not just some fantasy of one or two imaginative races. The most well-known Sun gods in our Western culture today, from Egyptian, Greek, Roman, and Mesopotamian mythologies are probably the following:

Egyptian mythology
- **Amun** (also Amon, Ammom, or Amen), a creator god and god of the sun and air. His name means "the hidden one", "invisible", "mysterious of form". His symbol was the ram. The boy pharaoh Tutankhamun was named after him. Amun later became known as Amun-Ra, creator of the universe and king of the gods.
- **Aten**, god of the sun. The pharaoh Akhenaten was named after him.
- **Horus**, god of the sky whose right eye was identified with the sun and his left eye with the moon.
- **Ra** (Re), god of the sun.

Greek mythology
- **Apollo**, god of light, healing, music, prophecy, and archery. Eventually he replaced Helios as the sun god, particularly during Hellenistic and Roman times.
- **Helios**, a Titan god and personification of the sun. Mythology shows him driving his chariot across the sky every day.

Roman mythology
- **Sol**, god of the sun. Equivalent to Helios, he too rides across the sky in a chariot.

Mesopotamian mythology
- **Shamash**, Akkadian god of the sun and justice
- **Utu**, Sumerian god of the sun and justice

Before we leave this section on 'Who are the gods?' there is just one more question to put to bed that you might be asking at this point, and that is, "Are the gods some kind of ghosts?" Ghosts definitely exist and are just one type of physical manifestation of a lower level spirit entity. But ghosts are not gods. Seeing a ghost, either physically or in the domain of consciousness, is not at all the same as visiting with gods or angels. They are on vastly different vibrational levels. In Chapter 9 I will describe ghosts in more detail.

What do the gods do?

Above all else at present, the task of a god is to transform mankind from a race with human consciousness into a race of beings with god consciousness. No mean feat when we have over seven billion people on the planet and most of them are uninterested and want nothing to do with gods or the hidden dimensions! Many are ignoring the warnings and denying the gods, rejecting the help offered by the gods and preferring their old human ways.

Recently I watched the movie *The Host* (for the 3rd time!) based on the novel by Stephanie Meyer who also wrote the Twilight series of books. It's one of the best movies I've seen for portraying how 'aliens' take over the consciousness of humans (they introduce a 'soul' into them), and how humans rebel against this, even though the world has now found peace, harmony, and love because of these 'souls'. If we substitute 'gods' for the aliens, this is pretty much what the gods are trying to do. It's a continual battle of god consciousness versus human consciousness, where the gods are trying to teach humans about their own soul and how to merge with it to become a better human being, and ultimately transform into god consciousness. Humans are mightily resisting this. They view it as being taken over by an alien power, not realising that the alien power is their very own soul who wants nothing but the best for them.

So, Earth is a school and the gods are essentially teachers, training people in the ways to reach godhood. They are developing the next generation of gods. They do their work as gods from the invisible dimensions and also by coming down to Earth in physical form and living a 'normal' human kind of life.

There are many gods on our planet in human form at this present time. They are generally not noticed or identified by the population, although some very spiritually-connected folks may suspect the lineage of these gods on Earth. Even some of the gods themselves don't realise who they truly are or their full spiritual missions, especially if they have come with a very down-to-Earth purpose such as changing the world economy, or creating a new species of corn to prevent future famine, or inventing a new modality of neuroscience. All gods on Earth must find their rightful place here and play a useful part. They can't be everywhere at once, putting out fires or influencing every political or business meeting, but they know how to use their consciousness to great effect and will broadcast on the wavelengths to places, situations, and people they can't get to physically.

Above, I stated that the gods can't be everywhere at once, and this is true for most gods, but Chiron tells us that senior gods can in fact teleport (or 'translocate' as the gods prefer to term it). We are entering the realm of science fiction here, I realise, but we will need to have faith that this is indeed the case. Chiron doesn't inform us how this is managed technically, but there is still much in the invisible dimensions that we have yet to discover, and our earthly scientists are certainly working on this problem even as I write. The answer will probably come out of research into quantum physics, and only when scientists surrender to the fact that an unseen universe actually does exist!

Anyway, Chiron tells us that junior gods on Earth don't usually have the benefit of teleportation powers and that, at present, they have to use physical transportation like everyone else. He says that consciousness must learn to travel first and then the physical body can follow. I'm sure we all look forward to the day when we can translocate (teleport) around the world and even the larger universe. Meanwhile, we can use our consciousnesses to astral travel in this way while our body sits at home in an armchair.

The gods are all trying to make necessary changes to our world, but the world doesn't necessarily like changes; humans are too invested in their own handiwork. Not only are the gods trying to transform humans but also the planet itself. Mankind has almost wrecked Earth, and the gods are trying to save this special place before all becomes extinct and all resources are exhausted.

High frequency energies are presently pouring down onto our planet, and these come not so much from the hands of intermediate gods who are charged with helping us, but from the higher levels of the unseen universe. Sometimes, these energies come in conjunction with great storms. The gods themselves often don't create the initial storms but they can utilise them to their benefit and they can shift and rework them so that the storms focus on an area that requires some kind of transformation.

These energies are designed to thrust us all into new ways of being at higher wavelengths and to break open hearts which have been encased in hard shells. The consequence of this is that all that exists at the lower frequencies of materiality and of consciousness is being slowly demolished and shifted to make space for the new era. No one will escape this cleansing and re-wiring process. If a person is not aligned with the new energies, the demolition will happen to them in one way or another. If they won't lift themselves up to a higher consciousness, the universe will grind them down. The gods could be demonised as destroyers of our old way of life, but we cannot build a palace on the footprint of a hovel, nor a new world on the foundation stones of a ruin. Our future is described more in Part Three.

When a human is fortunate to have a god work with them or on them, the presence of that god, in spirit or human form, can often stir up agitated feelings and bring up issues that the human would rather keep buried. They might feel unsettled, and the initial joy of working with the presence of a being of such love and light, can turn to woe and resistance. So, things can often become unpleasant for the human.

A god comes to transform and test a person to see if they are suitable for godhood, and they will drive a person pretty hard at times; rebellion or resistance won't be allowed. If this happens to us, the best thing to do is open our heart and surrender and thank our teacher. They are not doing it for their own benefit but ours. Just as the training and boot camp for joining the elite SAS is extremely arduous, the path to godhood is not a walk in the park either. If we wish to become a god, then we will need to go through arduous training too.

It is unlikely that only one mentor god will stay with us throughout our entire period of training for godhood. There will be several gods, with a variety of styles and talents. They may hold our hand for a while and point out the path ahead, but they won't hang around forever. A god works with their supporters, and those they have chosen to assist, to get them to where they need to be, but then they will move on. A god has many clients and we will not be able to keep them all to ourself. If we desire to set up home with a god on Earth, we will need to be a god ourself. "Like attracts like," is one of Chiron's favourite sayings.

Where there is total resistance to change, a person will be invited Home; that is, their soul will initiate the process of death and that person's incarnation will be over for this lifetime. This is not a threat from the gods, but the high frequency energies will break down the person's human body and mental state anyway in time. The gods do not punish people for their choices or send demons to make their life a misery, but human consciousness must make changes to deal with these higher wavelengths bombarding them from the universe or else it will feel the repercussions, just like a weak immune system allows a person to suffer all kinds of physical ailments. This issue will be covered in more detail in Parts Two and Three.

Far from being happy when they see a person succumb to the high intensity of these incoming energies, the gods are appalled at the suffering that humans are undergoing, and they weep to see humans crushed. The gods have much love and compassion for the race of beings that they themselves created; they are not trying to fight them or wipe them out or kill off the human race. Humans are the children of their own consciousness. They want to grow them into gods, to refashion them, to teach them godly ways. Patently, mankind cannot remain as it is.

The gods do as much as possible to bring about healing even while at the same time they are trying to get their patients to raise their consciousness to a higher level, above all the mire and dark thoughts that plague them and society in general.

Chapter 5 – Other unseen beings

Angels

We've spoken about gods, now what about angels?

Angels are not gods; they are pure consciousness that has been created directly by the One God, but they are a different stream of being than that of the creator gods. Angels are untainted by the ego that is part of gods and men. They are clarity and purity itself and have no personal agenda except to help gods and humans.

This is not to say that they remain in their invisible spirit state at all times, for they are adept, just as the gods are, at manifesting themselves into physical forms of all natures, including as humans. They are able to travel the universe and all levels of dimensions, and arrive at any place, point, or time of their choosing.

It is the work of the angels to smooth things over and help right the world, and to keep the universe pristine and on its correct trajectory. It is not their job to clear up the mess of humankind. We will not be allowed to misuse angels; they have lofty goals of their own and they are not our servants or slaves. However, when we do get into strife, which we cannot see a way out of, the angels are here to help us in any way they can. They are especially good, I find, at protecting us from the energies of low vibrational entities.

As with the gods, it is quite acceptable to speak with angels, and they will happily engage in conversation. Always treat them with respect; they are the closest we will probably ever get to meeting the One God, Chiron says. Because they have no ego, they do not get emotionally affected by us or any situation, and they can offer us great advice and wisdom, seen from their higher point of view and lack of any bias or fear. I've always found them to be very stoical yet imbued with compassion, but it's impossible to dupe them or try to get your own way with them. They see through all our tricks. Our mental prowess is no match for theirs.

When an angel comes to us or speaks with us, we would do well to heed their advice. They are managers of this universe, and if we are found to be causing any kind of spanner in the wheels and cogs, they will drop us a clue via a gentle whisper. Angels tend not to shout, so we need to be especially attuned to their dainty manner. As we work more and more with angels, we will become much better attuned to their nature and energies and will hear them or see them more clearly. If an angel wishes to be seen by us, they will project an image into our consciousness in a form that we will recognise. But we must realise that the angels are not actually these projected forms but pure consciousness itself which is invisible to us, and which can weave in and out of the dimensions of this universe with alacrity.

How many angels are there? Chiron tells us there are more than we could ever count, and not only within our own universe but in other universes too. However, those allocated to our universe will remain inside its boundaries for the duration of this universe. They do not cross over into the multiverse. (Refer to chapter 6 for the gods' definition of universes and dimensions. It's not quite the same as referred to by quantum physicists.) But when this universe comes to an end one day, angels will still be on hand to populate the new universe that is created by the creator gods.

Can a human become an angel, just as they can become a creator god in the distant future? No, Chiron states, but we can attempt to become more angelic in our natures, especially in tempering our egos. Whilst the ego does have its uses, we need to utilise it in the correct way for the right causes. The angels are helping humans, and those in the spirit world, and gods too, to move out of lower consciousness, which is the domain of the ego, and into higher consciousness. No being is allowed to cause damage to the universe in any dimension.

The gods are not 'Search and Rescue' gods, and likewise the angels. When we make the choice to climb up to a higher level of consciousness and we request help, the angels and gods are there to assist us, but they don't go looking for us to save us. Being saved does not change consciousness; only saving ourself will transform us and strengthen us. The angels, as well as the gods, are training the next generation of gods, and they utilise tough love to do this so that the new gods are resilient, honest, and courageous.

Aliens and UFOs

I couldn't write a book about the unseen universe without checking out aliens and UFOs, could I? And it would seem that UFOs are not just a recent phenomenon: the first documented UFO sighting was back in ancient times, in 74 BC by the historian, Plutarch, in the region of present day Turkey.

Chiron gives us a whole chapter on these phenomena, and goes into quite a lot of detail too, obviously aware of the great interest in this subject on the part of humans. He doesn't exactly explain Roswell or crop circles or the Bermuda Triangle, but he does at least confirm that aliens and UFOs exist.

He states that the 'aliens' that humans usually see are not from other planets or the far reaches of space, but they are in fact the gods, monitoring us from the higher dimensions, and the UFOs that we might catch glimpses of are, in fact, the vehicles of these gods. We are being allowed to see through the veil between dimensions into the domain of the gods.

You might be wondering why the gods need space vehicles at all if they are able to teleport around the universe in their spheres of consciousness. Chiron tells us that spaceships have been invented in their quarter of the universe as a means of carrying physical forms and objects around more easily. He assures us that we won't be seeing any huge battleships hovering over our cities any time soon, like in our sci-fi movies, but we are being given a glimpse of what has been hidden from us up until now so that we realise we are not alone in this universe. It is setting the scene for a time in the near future when gods and humans will mingle freely on this planet, and for when it will be time in the far future for us to meet our cosmic neighbours, the real aliens, who reside on other planets and in other galaxies. There are many stars in our region, each with their own civilisations. Humans are certainly not the only ones here in the cosmos.

It will be quite a while yet before we will be allowed to meet true aliens rather than the gods who created our human race. We are not evolved enough yet, or at peace enough within our own planet, to meet our neighbours, and the distances between us are so vast that our technology is not good enough to take us there. This distance has been designed on purpose to keep us separate while we develop ourselves in our own backyard.

But we are told that there are indeed other human-like races out there in our galaxy. There are also races of beings who are not like humans or gods at all. But they all have consciousnesses, so it is possible to contact them via this method of communication. They may not speak the same native language as us but symbolism is a universal language and all will understand each other, in the same way humans understand their soul, and in the same way animals, birds, and insects understand each other without needing a spoken language.

Some alien races exist at higher vibrations than our own and some are equal or at lower levels. So, we will get to meet the ones first who are on our own wavelength or below it, unless we raise our vibrations higher to meet those invisible races that operate at a god-like level. The choice will be ours. The gods come as vanguards for the future, a distant time when humans will get to meet their alien neighbours in peace and harmony and love.

These sightings of UFOs and aliens are a foretaste of what is to come and have been arranged to wake up our consciousness, get us excited, and get us thinking. But we will firstly need to work on getting rid of the fear that many people, and governments, have around this subject. In the movie *The Day the Earth Stood Still*, the first action the military takes is to attempt to blow up the newly-arrived spaceship!

The gods have no hostile intent. Their ethics are to love and to do no harm. We need to be discerning about what is broadcast in the media about the gods or aliens. Most people react from a base of fear and have no knowledge of the things that are being described in this book. This is the reason why the gods do not come down to Earth with a grand show of force. The veil between the worlds is being opened gradually, and those whose consciousness dwells in the higher frequencies will get to see these revelations first. They will need to bide their time until the veil is opened wide, and only those ready to see will be able to.

Just think about it for a moment. Imagine what would happen if a spacecraft really did appear in our skies and was seen by a large population and captured in detail by thousands using social media? What if it was like nothing that currently existed on Earth and couldn't be handily explained away by the secretive and conspiratorial military? The gods chuckle at how agencies on Earth try to cover up these things. What exactly are they afraid of? Well, in truth, there probably would be great fear and panic, and the news would be right around the globe within minutes, compounding the problem. This is not a situation that the gods are wanting to create.

I am currently watching a TV series *Project Blue Book*, which is all about sightings of UFOs and strange phenomena in 1950s USA, and features the way that the military and government try to snuff out all information about this from reaching the general population. It's very interesting and entertaining.

Furthermore, what if the spacecraft landed on the ground and a figure stepped out? Might people be a tad disappointed to see a human-like figure in front of them? Yet, if this was a spacecraft of the gods, it *is* going to be a human-like god that walks down that ramp, not a green slimy creature with black slit eyes! For the gods are the creators of humans, made in their own image, and if they are going to appear to us physically, they would choose to do so in human form so as not to frighten us any more than necessary. Many movies cover this scene—the arrival of aliens and first contact with them, for instance, *Close Encounters of a Third Kind, Arrival,* and *E.T.,* to name but a few. It is the dream of many people to connect with alien races and discover what is out there beyond the stars.

If we did but know it, the gods have many spaceships plying our skies. They have been very inventive, and their craft use a different kind of propulsion from anything available on Earth, and it is quiet, fast, and undetectable. From their invisible ships, the gods can monitor our planet below, just as humans do with their satellites and drones. They enjoy flying around this beautiful Earth, and they speak with its consciousness and assist with any issues the Earth requests they attend to.

It is not that the gods come to snoop or pester. They may be on a targeted mission, and might even have the brief to reveal themselves to humans on the ground and make contact. They are letting us know that they are here. All we need to do is tune in with our intention and we can be having a conversation with these 'aliens' through our consciousness.

This happened to me several years ago when I was living opposite Mount Coolum on the Sunshine Coast in Queensland, Australia. I awoke around one o'clock in the morning and had the urge to look outside the window which faced the pyramid-shaped silhouette of the small mountain. As I did so, I saw a small cluster of lights fly towards me from around the other side of the mountain, and then the lights suddenly stopped still. I imagined it was a helicopter and it was just hovering. Because I was close to an airport I thought nothing much of it, although it was a bit weird for it to be flying at that time of the night, well after the curfew on flights. After hovering for several minutes, the craft suddenly zipped off inland at an incredible speed and disappeared within seconds, and I remember thinking that I didn't know that helicopters could fly at such a rate.

The next night I awoke at the same time, and again had the urge to look out of the same window. To my surprise, the same cluster of lights was hovering in the same place in front of the mountain. Now I knew something peculiar was truly happening. I tuned into my higher consciousness and asked if this was a UFO? The reply I received was that this was a group of gods who were just visiting and had come to say hello to me. I chuckled at this revelation and said how delighted I was to welcome them. They didn't stay around for a conversation but quickly took their leave and sped off again over the vast plain of sugarcane fields, just as they had done the previous night, and they were instantly gone. Some folks might say I was dreaming but I certainly wasn't; it was a very palpable and rational experience, one that will stick in my memory forever.

Crop circles

Another memorable experience happened to me in July 2018 in Wiltshire in England. With a friend, I had been visiting Avebury Circle, a mysterious and ancient stone circle that is so large that an actual village is situated within it, complete with a beautiful thatched pub. Here we were alerted to the location of not just one, but two, crop circles nestled in wheat and barley fields not too far away. It had been my dearest wish to see one of these, so we raced off to explore them.

It was the hottest summer England had had in decades, and the crop circles, on opposite sides of the road from one another, were each located about a mile from the roadside, well-embedded within the tall crops so that they couldn't be seen from the road itself. My friend and I, undaunted by the fierce sun, finally got to lie down on the flattened wheat of the newest of the circles and drank up its energies.

It's extremely difficult to fathom out the pattern of the crop circle whilst you are standing within it. This one was perhaps a hundred metres in diameter and featured circles within circles and strange standing tufts in the centre. The exterior and interior walls of the pattern were perfectly delineated, and the ground of the crop circle looked as if the wheat had been interwoven like herringbone parquet flooring.

If this had been created by fraudsters overnight, I take my hat off to them, because to my eyes it was an utterly impossible feat. And several of these crop circles appear every week during summer throughout Great Britain and other parts of the world, and many are exceedingly and breathtakingly complex designs. If humans are involved in duping the world in this covert manner, then they deserve international recognition and awards for their creations.

However, the gods told me many years ago that the true nature of crop circles is that they are the signatures of the gods. Hovering above a field of crops, the gods 'burn' onto the ground below a symbol which represents them. It is like shining a torch through the stencil of a design, although they are using their high frequency energy beams rather than a torch. Much like with UFOs, the gods are communicating with us and getting us to understand that they exist and wish to make contact.

Alien abduction

What of those who claim to have been abducted by aliens? Are they mental cases or the product of over-active imaginations? Chiron explains that since consciousness can travel anywhere, it is not unreasonable for a person's spirit self to find themselves aboard a spaceship and experience another dimension in a more conscious manner. He says spirit consciousness is always welcome aboard a UFO.

He points out, however, that not all these scenarios are hosted by the gods, for consciousness is capable of dreaming up many realistic scenarios for humans to experience and learn their lessons from. That person's consciousness may be undergoing a challenge or a trial that necessitates this type of role-playing. So, the human consciousness jumps into its spirit consciousness and experiences a scene aboard a seemingly alien spacecraft. Then consciousness slips back into its usual human mode and the person is left wondering if this was a dream or not, but one where everything felt so very real and physical.

Certainly, I for one, have had dreams which were incredibly realistic, and when I've woken I've wondered for a few moments which was the real world and which was the dream world. At times I've even had to check with people if I really did make arrangements to meet them, or was it only in my dream that I did this?

Some people, including myself, have gone through OBEs (out-of-body experiences) where a person has slipped into another dimension retaining full human consciousness so that what is experienced is as real as anything undergone on Earth. So, it's not so incredulous when people make claims that things happen to them on the other side, and they return to the human world not understanding what has occurred.

To be honest, I've never been abducted by aliens, so I can't speak on this with any authority, but I do believe that some people have had these encounters and that we should all keep an open mind on this. Our universe is a mysterious place, and there is much we humans simply don't know about—until it happens to *us*!

But will humans actually get to ride in a UFO in their human bodies? Chiron tells us this won't be possible unless we have the physical body of a god, for a human body could not cope with the high frequencies required to travel at high velocity and through space and time.

The Veil is thinning

Many things are hidden from our eyes until it is time for us to see them. And even then, some people will miss out for they cannot believe what they are seeing. But as the frequency of our planet increases and the higher dimensions begin to envelop our world, so will visits by the gods increase.

The veil between our dimensions is thinning now and we will begin to see hitherto invisible things appear before our eyes. Physicality itself is changing and the environment is transforming. New forms will manifest as vibrations are raised within us and all around us. We will need to broaden our minds so as to understand this new world and its brand-new forms.

There are exciting times ahead. We are on the cusp of entering an entirely new paradigm; indeed, a new dimension. The lid is being lifted right now, if we have the right consciousness to see it. The more we believe, the more will be shown to us, but until then, the gods will keep a lid on things.

In the next chapter we will examine what these hidden dimensions consist of, according to Chiron, a god who actually abides there.

Chapter 6 – The unseen dimensions — the Two Earths

We have spoken at length about consciousness and the unseen beings who display consciousness, but what about the unseen dimensions which these invisible beings inhabit? Where might these dimensions be found?

Mankind has invented very powerful telescopes indeed, and through them we have already discovered much about the entities and cosmic bodies that litter our universe, but what we cannot yet see is what occupies the space between all the entities. We know it is not empty space, but is full of cosmic winds, rays, forces, and gravity. It is also filled with something that scientists call 'dark matter' and 'dark energy', for want of better names until such time as they ascertain what exactly fills up the universal matrix between the planets and stars and galaxies. Chiron tells us that there is much out there that cannot be seen by our telescopes, and that our equipment doesn't necessarily need to be more powerful; it merely needs to be high vibrational.

Consciousness itself can therefore be this high vibrational tool, for it can see what the human eye cannot show us. The telescope of our consciousness can reach anywhere in the universe, notwithstanding the vibrational limits set for us individually. The spirit sphere of our consciousness is our vehicle for traversing the invisible dimensions, and we can be instantly transported anywhere in time and space. This may sound like fantasy or science fiction, but the gods, and even humans, have used consciousness to travel the universe for billions of years, and the dimensions hidden from human sight are quite visible to the gods and to our spirit selves.

The worlds of gods and spirits reside in invisible dimensions with different physics than our own human world. The gods, in their spirit form, are pure consciousness, non-physical entities, and so scientists searching for physical evidence of the gods will not find it. All consciousnesses exist in a band above physicality, and this mystery, Chiron says, will not be understood for a long time to come. It is only when scientists allow for such a thing as non-physicality that our world will be able to take big strides forward in knowledge.

What is the difference between a universe and a dimension?

Before we go further, let us clarify what is meant by the terms 'universe' and 'dimension' because the way that Chiron refers to them, and from the information I have been given by other gods at other times, the definitions are somewhat different from those that seem to be in general use amongst scientists.

To recap what has already been stated, many universes exist, and ours is just one of them, initially created in the dim distant past by ten creator gods who still manage our universe today, along with the help of other gods and angels. Some universes have already been and gone, and there will be more created in the future. But what is actually meant by a 'universe'?

A universe, according to the gods, is an enormous domain which encapsulates many worlds and dimensions. It contains both physical and non-physical elements, and has a boundary around it from which nothing, either physical or non-physical, can escape or enter during the lifetime of the universe which can stretch to many billions of years and even longer. It will always seem to us humans that the universe is boundless, unlimited, and ever-expanding, such is its vastness which we will never get to explore entirely or even mostly, but there is definitely a perimeter that binds our particular universe together, although what this consists of we shall probably never get to discover.

Everything ever created within our universe is contained within its walls forever, but can be recycled and recreated again and again into different forms. Creator gods, intermediate gods, angels, stars, planets, humans, flora, fauna, rocks, water, elements, consciousnesses; all are part and parcel of this one universe until such time as it comes to an end for some reason that only the creator gods will decide. Then all consciousnesses will be reunited and a brand-new universe created, and the cycle will begin again, but with new creators, new rules, and different outcomes.

The universe is a holding container for many worlds and dimensions. One metaphor used by the gods to explain it to me likens the universe to a tall skyscraper where each floor of the building is like a different dimension. Each floor exists at a different vibrational level and houses a different type of 'world' for its occupants.

Those on the ground floor are like the lowest vibrational humans living on Earth. They are able to see only what is on their own floor and cannot see any higher floors above them, although some humans may discover the elevator and be able to travel temporarily to higher floors for a visit.

The gods inhabit the highest floors of the skyscraper, and they are able to visit every floor below them and participate in those worlds. A person may access only those floors, or dimensions, that have an equal or lower vibrational level than their own, unless they obtain a special visa or are escorted by a god or angel. To gain access to the higher floors or dimensions, it is necessary to raise one's vibrational level. How to accomplish this is discussed in chapter 11.

A dimension is not actually a physical place but a state of consciousness. And so, we can be in the same physical location but view it from different viewpoints and states of mind. For instance, it's just like feeling in two minds about our home; on any given day we might love the place when our consciousness is at a high level of vibration, and on another day we may find much fault with our home if our consciousness is at a low level of vibration. Same location but viewed from a different lens, creating very different worlds or dimensions for ourself.

To visit or live in a higher dimension, we need to raise our consciousness and vibrational level to a higher wavelength on our 'radio dial', and tune into that dimension so that we can hear it and participate in it.

Therefore, amongst all the humans living on Earth, people could be living in the same city, some of whom might subsist in a low vibrational dimension and others enjoying a high vibrational dimension of existence. They will intermingle probably without realising the difference in their vibrational levels and consciousnesses, although there are often obvious clues to the state of a person's consciousness. Since 'like attracts like', those of the same vibrational level tend to stick together, and therefore we see areas in a city which are crime-infested, ugly, or dysfunctional because they are low vibrational, and other areas which are beautiful, bright, and a delight to walk in or live in because they are high vibrational.

The really high vibrational areas have such lightning fast frequencies that they cannot be seen by the human eye, and these are the hidden dimensions that the gods and angels inhabit, and also the spirits and souls of humans who are in between incarnations. These higher dimensions function with different rules of physics than those that describe the physical dimension that we humans call 'the universe'. Our physical universe (lower vibrational dimension) operates using Newtonian/classical physics. The invisible universe (higher vibrational dimensions) operates using quantum physics. We still have much to learn about the latter, and as we do so we will begin to understand the unseen universe at a whole new level.

So, dimensions are the way that the universe is sliced in order to house, at various levels of vibration, all the various consciousnesses along with their physical and spirit bodies. There is only one universe that we will ever get to know about, but a great number of dimensions within it, and many of these dimensions intersect with one another in one huge matrix that enables us to travel from one to another, and from our human physical world to the invisible worlds of spirits and gods.

Where are the unseen dimensions?

There are basically three major types of dimensions that we are concerned with in this book.

1. The human physical dimension (First Earth)
2. The spirit and humans-turned-gods dimension (Second Earth)
3. The higher gods' dimensions

There are bridges from each dimension to one another that are used by consciousness to travel across to other dimensions. The higher god's dimensions are open only to gods or to those who are accompanied by a god or an angel.

Chiron and the other gods never describe a dimension with a number, as in the 3rd dimension or the 5th dimension, as I imagine this can be confusing if the underlying criteria is not universally understood. So, I am keeping with the gods' way of doing things.

(1) The human physical dimension (First Earth)

The physical universe that we humans can see is a dimension in its own right. It includes our Earth and the whole cosmos of planets, stars, and galaxies. Although the following description applies to the entire dimension of our physical universe, let us focus just on our planet of humans so that it is easier to comprehend. Chiron calls this First Earth, and we shall see why in the next section.

Within our physical planet our population exists at multiple levels of vibration, resulting in our society being dissected into various levels of consciousness. We cannot see with human eyes the level of a person's consciousness or vibration, but their personality and demeanour usually contain tell-tale signs. It is certainly not a person's power, wealth, or even health, that distinguishes them. Humans cannot be an accurate judge of another's vibrational level. Unconditional love, compassion, and joy are the traits displayed by gods and people of high vibrations, and the higher the levels, the more god-like and less human a person tends to be.

Much of the population of our planet exists at a fairly low to medium vibrational level. A small minority exists at a very low vibrational level, and others exist at fairly high levels. All of us can see one another, but since 'like attracts like' we tend to draw into our circle only those on the same wavelength as ourselves. We choose which level to live at. It has nothing to do with gods or governments. Our consciousness sets the yardstick and attracts all at its own level. If that doesn't suit, then it will be necessary to raise our vibrations and fly higher. If we do this, then we will not have to live in the horrible conditions and darkness that lower vibrational people find themselves in. In a high vibrational reality, we are cocooned to a certain extent in a world that is distanced from low vibrational antics, disasters, and tragedies, and we are able to live a life of more peace and plenty.

We can see that on our planet a definite schism currently exists between low and high vibrational sections of our societies around the world, and this is not predicated on wealth or being a third world country. Those who are poor, diseased, or disadvantaged are just as capable of being high vibrational, and those who are rich, powerful, or famous, are just as capable of being low vibrational.

Ethereal bridges within our consciousness connect our physical dimension with each of the dimensions of spirits and gods. Humans may travel over the bridge to the spirit dimension whenever they please, and they do so whenever they fall asleep or lose consciousness or enter meditation. But to travel in our consciousness across the bridge to the high dimensional worlds of the gods and angels then we will need to be high vibrational ourselves or be accompanied by a high vibrational being.

Because our consciousness consists of many parts and personas which exist at various vibrational levels, it is possible that our Ribbon can straddle many dimensions at once, and that one part of our consciousness may be allowed across the bridge into the god's dimension, whereas the remainder of our consciousness is barred and allowed into only the spirit dimension.

When humans raise their vibrations to a high enough level, and pass all character tests required of them, they reach their ascension level, or godhood level, and they are then able to pass to and fro between the First Earth and higher dimensions as humans-turned-gods.

(2) The spirit and humans-turned-gods dimension (Second Earth)

There are many different hidden worlds and dimensions out there in our universe, some like Earth and others not at all. One of these worlds could be called a second Earth, Chiron tells us, and it is home to all the spirits and souls that are not gods, and also a playground and training school for them. It is an invisible duplicate of our planet, laid over our own Earth and just centimetres away from it and interwoven with it.

This Second Earth is in a separate dimension from our physical Earth, but it exists as a physical dimension too, merely vibrating at a different and higher level and therefore invisible to most human eyes. It is almost as if the Second Earth were another planet in our solar system, orbiting around the same sun next to our Earth, yet only millimetres away from it, like some binary planet. It is a mirror world of our planet, and Chiron states, "Where there is a tree (on our planet), there is an invisible tree next to it. Where there is a rock, there is an invisible rock next to it. Where there is an ocean, there is an invisible ocean next to it and through it."

Here on the Second Earth lives our invisible self, our spirit self, right next to us in this hidden dimension, along with the spirit selves of all other humans, and also all the non-god spirits who don't have a human counterpart at this point in time. Humans who have reached their ascension/godhood also abide here in their consciousness, living at this higher vibrational level as humans-turned-gods and with easier access to the spirit world.

So, our Ribbon of Consciousness, encompassing our human self and our spirit self, straddles the two dimensions consisting of Earth (the First Earth) and Heaven (the Second Earth). They are similar worlds but existing at differing vibrations. The bridge between these two worlds could be likened to the corpus callosum in our brain which connects the left and right hemispheres together and facilitates communication between them. The left hemisphere of our brain represents our human consciousness on the First Earth, and the right hemisphere represents our spirit consciousness in the hidden dimension of Heaven, the Second Earth.

It is usually to this Second Earth dimension that our human consciousness drifts, over the bridge between dimensions, when we go to sleep or daydream or meditate, and we jump out of our conscious self and into an altered state of consciousness. It's also where we go when we lose consciousness after being given an anaesthetic, or after a bad accident, or when in a coma, or when having taken drugs or too much alcohol.

We can move from First Earth to Second Earth with just a tiny jump in consciousness, but bear in mind that our feet will never leave the ground. It is not so much a physical journey as a journey of the mind. The human part of our consciousness hands over the controls to the spirit part of our consciousness, and we go off travelling in our spirit sphere into the various levels of the Second Earth. We cannot travel the higher dimensions without our spirit on board too. But we can quickly jump back into our human sphere whenever necessary, such as when our teacher nudges us to pay attention in class and stop our daydreaming.

Spirits who live on the Second Earth have much the same kind of consciousness as we find on the First Earth amongst humans. There is little difference in the way that they think. There are those at the lowest end and those at the highest end. They have no flesh and blood body like a human but can take on a human-like form, and they live in a world that is fairly similar to human Earth yet which does not have exactly the same physical properties.

Wanting to know more about what it's like being a spirit, I asked Master El Morya, "When I am walking in the higher worlds, do I have legs, and shoes on my feet? Do I cover distance in this way, having to utilise myself and my body physically?"

El Morya replied, *"You are asking whether you are walking with shoes on your feet. Yes, if you choose to do so, for you can travel through the New World (Second Earth) as your spirit self in consciousness, or you can choose to put yourself into physical form and play out as you would on Earth except that you are travelling with a higher consciousness."*[8]

Journeying to the spirit world of the Second Earth can be done quite consciously and is absolutely encouraged by the gods so that we can team up with our spirit self and explore the greater universe to learn much about ourselves and the worlds around us. Here too, we can meet with family and friends in their spirit consciousness, and much can be achieved with them that couldn't be accomplished within the physical confines of the First Earth. Location is no barrier in this unseen dimension, so that even if loved ones, or enemies, are physically situated across the other side of the world, we can visit them with impunity at any time and have delightful reunions and excursions, or fix up failed relationships or misunderstandings.

---

8. From a channelling with El Morya, 6 June 2019

Time Travel

We can do this in the past, too, since there is no concept of time in this Second Earth dimension. The consciousness of ancestors is just as available to us as any consciousness that is alive today. Therefore, we can return to situations in the past and make amends and take different decisions. And the gods encourage us to do this, so that we create a different world for ourselves today.

A tenet of science fiction is that in time travel we can never go back and change the past since it could create a paradox where we might not be alive today. The gods tell us that this is not the case and that the universe operates with different conventions.

The way it has been explained to me by the gods is that our personal history throughout the ages is like a book continually being written. If we were the author of a novel, it is very likely that we would come to write later chapters and realise that we needed to change some situations or characters in the initial chapters in order for our tale to better unravel and reach a more successful conclusion. So, we would go back into the past of our characters, to the early chapters, and we would change the storyline.

"The past, like the future, is indefinite and exists only as a spectrum of possibilities." Stephen Hawking.

When we rejig scenarios in our mind in the present moment, all dynamics, past and future, are altered. The universe works along these lines too, and we never need to worry that we will write ourselves out of existence. Once a consciousness has been created, it can never be killed off, even if we return to the past and cause our mother or father not to be born. We are dealing with consciousness here, not with human bodies!

What is spirit life like?

We may not think of spirits as living like we do on Earth, but, more often than not, they adopt a human-like form and lead the same kind of life that they lived on Earth. They look very much like the humans we see on Earth. Spirits can change their form if they want to, but they usually elect to appear like the person they were in their most recent incarnation, or as one of their favourite roles they played in the past. They will adopt what is familiar to them. Although their true spirit form is a mass of pulsating lights, it is not a comfortable way of living for them and many of them stay away from this mode of being. They are afraid to lose their human form, for their consciousness is still very human. So, although non-god spirits can jump in and out of human form like the gods, it is not often their will to do so.

However, those towards the higher end of the spirit world will practise taking on their spirit form at times, and they will be able to go in and out of spirit form according to their intention. They will be guided to do so by the gods; they are not left merely to their own devices, but the gods will not instruct them unless asked to do so. So, spirits can travel through the dimensions as their spirit self in consciousness or they can choose to put themselves into physical form and play out as they would on Earth except that they are travelling with a higher consciousness.

You may be very curious to know exactly how spirits manifest a physical body. I asked Master El Morya about this because Chiron didn't cover this in his book.

El Morya: "*It is hard to describe to a human how consciousness can manifest into physical form, but that is its power and its tool, and when it is in the higher worlds it finds it quite easy to do this.*

In the higher worlds things are moving in and out of physicality all the time. It is a state represented by quantum physics and it is difficult for you to get your mind around. So, you must take my word for it that you can go in and out of physical forms in the higher dimensions, and that all the items that you handle can also jump in and out of physical form too. You imagine it, and it is there in your hands. You imagine it gone and, poof, it is gone, dissolved back into the greater consciousness. It seems quite magical to you humans down on Earth, but it is part and parcel of the way that the world operates and performs up here. On Earth, things have a very slow way of manifesting. But believe me when I tell you that things can be instantly manifested in the higher dimensions, and physical things take form and then are dissolved again.

The closest analogy I can come up with at present is a 3D printer. You give this a blueprint, a pattern, and from tiny molecules of resin or other materials the printer builds up a three-dimensional physical form. If you imagine that kind of process happening instantly in consciousness then you will have some kind of idea of how consciousness utilises subatomic particles, brings them together in the pattern that you are imagining in your consciousness, and makes it materialise in front of you.

So, there is no difference between a physical body in the higher realms than the physical bodies on Earth, except that in the higher realms these bodies are only temporary and exist only for as long as we sustain them with our consciousness. So, we are birthing and dying regularly in the higher worlds."[9]

This spirit world also contains a multitude of vibrational levels similar to that of human Earth. Therefore, there are high vibrational spirits and low vibrational spirits, and the places that they live tend to mirror their vibrational level just as they do upon Earth.

While many spirits on Second Earth are non-gods, there are also spirit consciousnesses of humans (currently alive or deceased) who have achieved their ascension or godhood, humans-turned-gods who will live at the highest levels of this dimension before they graduate to the higher gods' dimension. The Second Earth is a 'finishing school' for newly-created gods.

So, a spirit, (even our own while we are walking about on Earth as a human), is living a life similar to the one we lead down here on Earth. They will live in the same kind of place as their human self is currently living, or used to live, upon the First Earth. There are squatters in hovels, there are high-rises, there are city and country mansions, there are palaces overlooking the sea. Spirit consciousness will design what it will, and will attract to it all that it deserves.

The physical body that a spirit adopts on the Second Earth is similar to a human's in that they can eat food, and they have a digestive system and all the organs and cells that a body would have on Earth. They taste that food and enjoy it and digest it and, yes, they would go to the toilet to remove it too.

The spirit world has a similar society to that of Earth, in that it has buildings and houses and shops and cafés and bathrooms, and everything

---

9. From a channelling with El Morya, 6 June 2019

that is found upon Earth is probably found up in Heaven too. They have partners and sex, produce babies, go to school, have jobs and careers, sing and dance, go swimming, face challenges, and experience relationship breakups just as we do on our human Earth.

If our spirit were to walk into a café on the Second Earth, there would probably be an exact duplicate of that café on the First Earth, just millimetres away but in a separate dimension. Our spirit could, in physical form, cross the bridge to the human world and 'haunt' the café and sit beside our human self, but would be invisible to the humans there, unless those humans were very psychic.

Different laws

Although the Second Earth is a facsimile of the First Earth, (or perhaps the First Earth is a facsimile of the Second Earth?), one moves at a different pace from the other and is subject to different physical laws. The Second Earth operates with different physics than our own world, and they play out in separate dimensions. The First Earth plays by Newtonian classical physics and the Second Earth plays by quantum physics.

On the First Earth, in our human bodies, our consciousness is normally inhibited from creating a reality for itself on a moment by moment basis. There is a time lag between what we are thinking and the consequences and outcomes of that thinking. This is to protect us from ourselves while we learn to get to grips with controlling our thought-form projections, else we might conjure up all manner of terrible situations for ourselves and others. For instance, if we were angry with someone and shouted, "Drop dead!" at them, it would be devastating for all concerned if this manifested in the heat of the moment.

However, on the Second Earth, our consciousness manifests its reality according to its thoughts *instantaneously*. Things are coming in and out of play all the time, and so things are not so stable and concrete as in the human world. Many of the physical things of the Second Earth are impermanent and are sustained only for as long as required. Physical manifestation in the hidden dimensions requires attention and focus and, when this is lost, the object or situation disappears.

This explains the craziness of our dreams where everything seems to change in the flash of a moment, and is the reason why our dreams can seem so chaotic and dark and plain weird. In our dreams our consciousness steps into the Second Earth and is creating its world instantly from the thoughts it is thinking, and if those thoughts are fearful or malevolent, then a monstrous dream will ensue. It is true too, of course, that if we have positive and delightful thoughts then our dream will bring a smile to our face and we will wake up feeling happy. Even in dreams the adage 'like attracts like' still operates.

In our dream, as our spirit self on the Second Earth, we can find ourselves exploring a world very similar to our own, with cities and cafés and oceans and mountains and people just like those on Earth. However, they will 'ping' in and out of existence, depending on what we are thinking and on what those other people we meet there are thinking. They may be spirits who live in this dimension permanently or they may be the spirits of humans like ourselves, for we are meeting the consciousness of others on the Second Earth while they are dreaming too.

Because of this Second Earth facility for instant materialisation of thoughts, spirits are limited in what they are allowed to manifest or else the harm they could wreak upon the cosmos might be catastrophic. They are confined within certain boundaries, and their playground is limited and constrained so that they affect only themselves and those around them on the same level. It is not permitted for the worst low-vibrational non-god spirits to pollute the purer, higher environments of the Second Earth.

As non-god spirits prove themselves worthy, they will be elevated to higher levels and allowed to practise their powers more freely. It is pretty much the same kind of journey for non-god spirits as for humans on Earth; just as humans must find their spiritual path and godhood, so too must non-god spirits.

We might ask, "Can non-god spirits see and work with the gods?" It all depends on the level of vibration and consciousness that the spirit has attained. Some spirits are able to see the gods and work with them, but to those at the lower end of the spirit world the gods look just like any other non-god spirit in human form. They do not recognise the gods or value them, or even know where they themselves have landed in the spirit world. They know about the gods, for word gets around, and now and again one of them will have a chance meeting with a god which will provide food for thought for them and assist them on their path. But those at the higher end of the spirit world will better recognise the gods and be able to cooperate with them, and it will be easier for them to eventually make the transition to godhood.

Another type of 'law' that is different in this spirit dimension of the Second Earth, and also in the gods' dimensions, is that money doesn't exist. I asked Master El Morya about this.

Sophia: *"If there is no money in the higher worlds, Morya, if I went into a café and wanted to get food, I couldn't pay for it with money, so how does that work? Is everything just manifested out of thin air for me?"*

El Morya: *"Our exchange rate is love and energy. So, if you ask for some food in a café in our higher worlds, those who worked in the café would be lovingly willing to create that food for you, and in return you would give them your loving appreciation for their efforts. There would be no one working in the café who did not want to work there, who resented having to work and do these tasks, so all is manifested with good will and no money need change hands. And at a later time you may find yourself doing some kindness for those people who served you in the café.*

If you were beginning to take, take, take, and not give back in return, the gods or angels would have a word with you so that you could set the balance right again." [10]

(3) The higher gods' dimensions

When we are more experienced at travelling in the higher dimensions in our sphere of consciousness, and our vibrations are fairly high, we will be allowed to travel beyond the Second Earth and into other higher dimensions. Here, the frequencies are so high that if we were not trained in coping with them we would be electrocuted. However, these

---

10. From a channelling with El Morya, 6 June 2019

dimensions are electrifyingly interesting and fascinating, as this is where the gods will be found. Permission is required to visit dimensions higher than our own level, and our visit would be monitored or guided to ensure we didn't pollute such an energetically pristine world.

The gods do not live in some fabled place like Mount Olympus or on the planet Jupiter, but in invisible higher dimensions separate from the human and spirit dimensions (although they do visit and work in these lower dimensions). We might think that the gods inhabit other galaxies, but these descriptions of higher dimensions don't refer to any galaxy of our universe at all; they may be outside our galaxy, yes, but at a higher vibrational level in other dimensions completely.

The spirits of the gods inhabit dimensions that are vibrationally higher than the Second Earth, in pristine and protected environments. There are many dimensions for the gods, depending on their vibrational level. For instance, there is a dimension for the gods that monitor and manage our planet, another dimension for gods who embody stars, and yet another one for creator gods, and many more too. As the gods rise higher in their consciousness, they begin to lose their desire for a physical form and they travel more and more in their spirit sphere, inhabiting the highest dimensions as pure consciousness.

In the following description we will concern ourselves with only the dimension that harbours the gods who are responsible for our planet and for human evolution.

Although gods can have parts of themselves in human form on Earth and also on the Second Earth, their home base is a dimension they keep all to themselves, a kind of Higher Heaven. Bridges exist for consciousness to travel across to this dimension from both the human world and the Second Earth, but only gods are permitted to cross over, or spirits that are accompanied by a god or an angel. Nothing is allowed to pollute the gods' environment with bad energies or bad attitudes. It is not that guards stand at the entrance 24/7, but there is a force field around the god's dimension that prevents anything that is lower than a certain high vibrational level from entering.

Unlike the Second Earth, the gods' dimensional world is not a duplicate of our Earth. Here we might find futuristic cities or transport or machines of the kind we see in science fiction movies. Creative people on Earth who produce these movies will have been blessed with their ideas after visiting the higher dimensions in their dreams or meditations. Chiron tells us there is nothing created on human Earth which hasn't first been created in the higher dimensions. However, it might be our own spirit self who created it there, so we don't need to give all the kudos to the gods!

Just like in the dimension of the Second Earth, the gods can elect to swan around in human-like bodies or in their spirit spheres of pulsating lights. However, unlike humans and their spirits, gods have full control over their powers and their ability to manifest physicality. The gods do choose to be in physical human form a lot of the time because they are used to it and they enjoy eating, drinking, having sex, and doing other physical activities. We must bear in mind that the human race was modelled on the gods' human-like form, and not the other way around!

So, in the world of gods they lead lives that can emulate our own human lives, and they can exist as physical beings that appear very human-like, but they are different from humans in their structure and their consciousness. They can morph into any form at will and manifest anything they desire through their intention, and they can travel both the spirit world and the human physical world, teleporting (translocating) their consciousness instantly across the dimensions and manifesting a physical body wherever they arrive. They can also have physical relationships with other gods and goddesses, produce children, live in houses, eat food at home and in restaurants, dress in lovely clothes, attend parties, and go to work in offices or on farms. They have long, active, and healthy lives in this form because they have learnt how to heal and balance themselves. Sometimes they suffer from afflictions, but these are resolved very quickly.

In the gods' dimensions they also have societies like on Earth, with buildings and shops and houses, governments, hospitals, and concert halls. It is a world that encompasses a human-like god form, and functions for them just as things operate for us on Earth (only better!). Their world would be recognisable to us humans, albeit that it runs at a much higher level of consciousness. However, not only are many of the structures of their world different from ours, but also their society and laws, which work very well since love is the prime mover here, not power or money.

Having recently watched the movie *Allegiant* (a sequel to *Divergent* and *Insurgent*) I was struck by how similar the storyline was to the situation of humans and gods. In the movie, most people live within the confines of a huge dividing wall, in a dystopian world where everyone is segregated into factions (Candour, Erudite, Amity, Dauntless, and Abnegation, with some being Divergent and not true to type). Eventually, the people learn about the world on the other side of the wall and some get to visit it. It is like the world of gods, with gleaming white towers and futuristic technology, and run by a council of wise beings not so dissimilar from the ordinary people themselves.

In our non-movie reality, it is not a huge concrete and barbed wire wall that divides humans from the gods, nor do we enter the world of gods through any physical door or portal. The dividing line is that of a set vibrational level. Everything below this level consists of the human world, and everything above this level is the worlds of spirits and gods. Bridges in consciousness connect between them all.

Not all the gods live in the kind of world as described above. Others live in different types of worlds, but it's possible to visit them too in consciousness. The gods encourage humans in their spirit spheres to visit their physical god world, as it will help people to believe that gods and other dimensions exist and that a better human world is possible. The gods offer training in the things of their world, and they would appreciate more visitors so that humans may take away ideas and install them on Earth in order that it become a better mirror of the gods' world.

When we travel in our spirit sphere of consciousness, we are instantly transported to wherever we have set the 'radio dial' in our consciousness, and we end up in the world or dimension of that frequency. Sometimes, it is not us or our own spirit who controls the navigation but the gods, and we are whisked off to some unknown destination to undertake some experience or challenge in order to learn and evolve.

The universe gives us endless adventures and we need to take time to explore it. Some worlds are very enjoyable, and our reaction to them can be like a child visiting Disneyland for the first time. These worlds can seem like never-ending theme parks, and we may think it a dream, but it's the everyday reality of our spirit. So, there are worlds that resemble Earth but with god-like touches, and those that are very alien to us.

While governments and scientists are scrambling on our Earth to launch rockets to Mars and to other cosmic bodies in our solar system, Chiron tells us that we won't discover much from visiting these planets and moons, and that we would be better off by travelling in our consciousness to other worlds where we will learn so much more. But he suggests that we should limit our explorations to within our own quadrant of our galaxy and be satisfied with this. There is still plenty to see and learn here, and we will be startled by what we discover, but further afield, the cosmos begins to unravel quite differently from anything we know or could even understand. When we stay within the boundaries of our galactic quarter, we will be more able to make sense of things.

Chapter 7 – The unseen dimensions – Heaven and Hell

Heaven and the New World (merger and split of dimensions)

In the previous chapter we equated Heaven with the Second Earth, the higher invisible dimension above the First Earth (the physical home of humans). The dimensions of the gods sit at levels way above the Second Earth and could rightly be called Higher Heaven. In his book, Chiron speaks not only of Heaven but a place he calls the New World. What is this place and where is it?

The New World is our future, and some humans are living here even now. It is the dimension that the gods are leading us humans towards in order to live there permanently in peace and harmony. It is Heaven on Earth, if you like. It is not another planet or physical world but this same Earth lived at a higher vibration. Heaven upon Earth will indeed come, once this planet and all her inhabitants are of a higher consciousness.

The New World is being created by the conjunction of the Second Earth with the First Earth. What do we mean by that? It means that the higher dimension of spirits is merging with our lower human dimension. Imagine, if you will, the Second Earth butting up against our planet and merging into it. This is not going to happen in one mighty great collision where we will feel a massive bump and all will get spilled. No, this is something that is happening ever so slowly and carefully, with precision management by the gods. And it has already begun. See Diagram #1.

The merger is not happening at all levels of vibration at the same time. Let us return to the metaphor of the dimensions being like the storeys of skyscrapers representing the various vibrational levels, with gods at the top and humans down below. The Second Earth is touching the First Earth only at the topmost level to begin with. Gradually, the Second Earth dimension will move on down the vibrational levels of our own Earth, joining the two worlds together as if closing a giant zipper.

The vibrations of the higher world will be felt intensely by humans, and it will be as if the sun is shining on all the darkness and shame of mankind in order to highlight it and make us clean up the planet and ourselves. The Second Earth will gradually descend all around us and envelope our consciousnesses, pushing the old world further and further away from it into something that could very well approximate a living hell. The old world and the new world will be somewhat poles apart.

Indeed, eventually, the old world, the First Earth, will be split away entirely from the New World and will take away with it all low vibrational people and things and those who haven't managed to attain their ascension/godhood. The New World of the Second Earth will now contain only high vibe beings who have ascended to godhood. The Earth itself will have ascended to provide a high vibrational environment for humans-turned-gods to live in. It is a training ground for newly-created gods.

In Part Three which focuses on the future, this merger that creates the New World, and what it will mean for us humans, are described in more detail.

1. Before merger of Two Earths (how it's been for last few millennia)

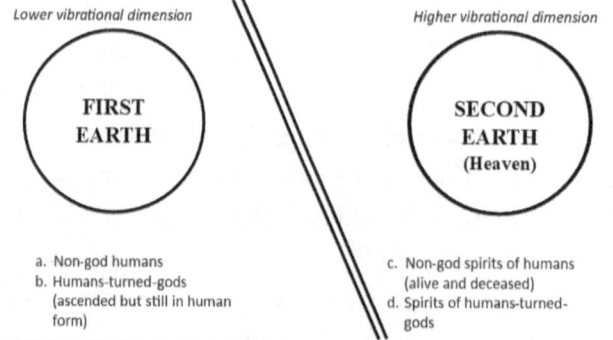

2. Merger of Two Earths and Dimensions (Present day)

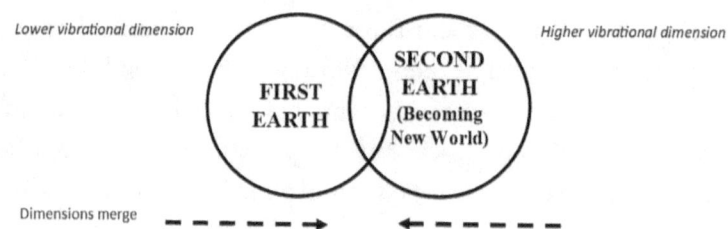

*All beings from groups 'a' and 'c' in diagram 1 above, are encouraged to attain ascension/godhood

3. Split of merged Two Earths and Dimensions (Near future)

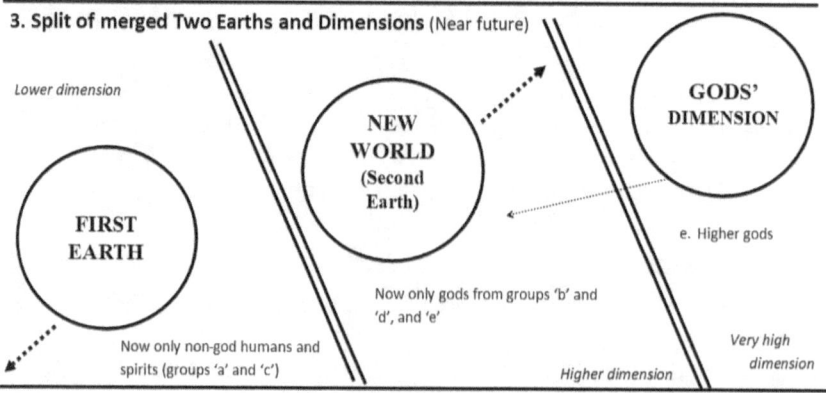

Diagram #1—Merger and Split of Two Earths

Hell and the Underworld

We have located Heaven, so where is Hell? Like Heaven, it is not a physical location but a state of consciousness. We can be anywhere on Earth or in the universe, and we could be in Hell because of what we are thinking and feeling. We have spoken a great deal about raising our consciousness and our vibrations, but it is similarly possible to cause our vibrations to fall and ultimately drop us into a kind of living hell.

Ancient mythology calls Hell 'The Underworld', and we know it best as being ruled over by the Greek god, Hades (Pluto is his Roman counterpart, Osiris his Egyptian version, Erishkegal (a goddess) his Mesopotamian version). In Greek myth, the Underworld is the land of the dead. When a person died, the winged god Hermes (Roman version is Mercury) guided souls to Hades.

Firstly, they had to cross the River Styx, where they had to pay the ferryman Charon to row them across. (Remember that song, *'Don't pay the ferryman'* by Chris de Burgh from the early 1980s?) A three-headed dog named Cerberus (also featured in the Harry Potter books and films) guarded the gates to the Underworld and prevented any escape.

The souls of the dead were judged, and the good ones were sent to Elysium, the Isles of the Blessed, to live out an idyllic eternity. The damned were condemned to Tarturus (from which we get our word 'torture') to suffer everlasting torment in this place of ferocious monsters and terrible criminals. The majority of souls, the ordinary folks, were consigned to the Asphodel Meadows, where they existed as shadowy ghosts, without the ability to think or take action or know pleasure.

In the next chapter, we will take a look at what really happens when we go to the land of the dead, and if we will experience anything like the journey into the mythological Underworld. For now, let us stay with the concept of falling into Hell whilst still living on Earth. How does this get to happen?

As we now know, our consciousness consists of many parts. Whilst some parts of us can be high vibrational, other parts of us on our Ribbon of Consciousness can exist at the same time in a very low vibrational state. We know we can be like this by the fact that when we are with a person we love we can act like an angel, and when we are with a person we loathe we can act like the devil himself. Our dark thoughts and actions pull us down and are further reflected back to us to cause us to sink even lower. We will feel miserable and disconnected, especially if we have known the higher vibrational world in previous times. It can feel as if we are being punished, but there are no gods, or even monsters, doing the punishing here. It is all of our own making; we punish ourselves, and it is by our own determined actions that we will redeem ourselves and get ourselves out of this hell and onto sunnier paths towards Heaven.

In Part Two, Tools of Consciousness, we will examine in more detail how we come to find ourselves in this lower world and how to rise up from it.

Since consciousness consists of everything in the universe, the Underworld and lower worlds are part of our consciousness too. Everyone will visit here at some time or another, not necessarily only when they are dead but also during the course of their lifetime when their vibrations drop dangerously low. We all have odysseys to undertake in this realm, and parts of ourselves to reclaim and heal.

Often, we come here in our dreams at night. Our Underworld mixes with the Underworlds of other humans, and we can fight the good fight here and resolve much on these plains of consciousness that could not be settled in our physical world. If we can face this place with respect, understanding, and courage, a journey through the Underworld can be a very rewarding experience indeed and help us to let go of our troubling past.

The Light World and the Dark World, the Creation Realm

There needs to be some further explanation about the world of darkness, for there is a place in consciousness called the Dark World and this is not to be confused with the Underworld, the place of low vibrations and the land of the dead.

The Dark World is the polarity of the Light World, and they are the equivalent of night and day. The Dark World, like the night with all its majesty of stars and deep awe, is not a terrible place and one to fear, but the night-time for our souls. Nevertheless, it can sometimes hide things from us and certainly holds its secrets. The Dark World is a place of stillness, serenity, meditation, and calm hearts, yet it is also the place of Chaos, the Unknown World, the domain favoured by our right brain.

The Light World, on the other hand, is alive with activity, creativity, and hearts on fire, yet it is also the place of Order (as opposed to Chaos). It is the Known World, the physical realm, the domain favoured by our left brain.

The Light and Dark Worlds are all about creation and manifestation, and together they form what I call the Creation Realm. Unless we set our intention to visit the Dark World, we will usually end up in the Light World by default.

To bring a baby into the world, to birth it into the physical realm as a human, it must first be conceived in the darkness of the womb and nurtured there for nine months before the baby sees the light of day. It is not only babies that are created in this way. Everything in the physical universe is first conceived of and nurtured in the Dark World before it becomes manifest as a reality in the Light World. "Let there be Light" were the words that God spoke from the Dark World, according to the Bible, in order to physically manifest the universe. And our planet Earth is evidence of all that has been manifested in the Light World of creation from the conscious minds of gods and Man.

My Beloved Source helped me to understand the Dark World better when I made a comment that it was a place of the Void and nothingness.

She replied with enthusiasm, "But it's also a place of everything! It is all possibilities and all potential, the birth of anything you care to imagine."

"Great! But how do I navigate it?"

She told me, "Just find a tunnel and follow it and have the experience."

So, the Dark World is akin to a womb, and we can visit this place any time in our consciousness and float around here and try out ideas and go exploring, without the consequences of actually manifesting what we are thinking. It is here that we can conceive our ideas and concepts and generally get to chill out. The gods recommend it as a place for relaxation and letting go of our anxieties. Here, we can get away from the created world and the interference of our human mind, and sink into a world of our own, just us with our spirit consciousness, and we can delve into all aspects of ourself without actually having to think them through. For in this Dark World we will participate by feeling rather than thinking, and insights and knowings will come to us like osmosis from the universe.

The consciousness of new babies originates here and so too new projects and anything else we wish to conceive. It is not only a place to prepare for birth, a womb for females to utilise, but also a place of conception for males too.

Here, in the Dark World, the universe can swirl around us, akin to the free-floating environments of the oceans and outer space, taking us to places we might never have visited before in our consciousness, and conferring brilliant ideas and wonderful sensations within us. Whereas on Earth we are generally focused on goals and targets and rules, in the Dark World that precedes creation "all is let loose for you to experience". It is a place without any boundaries, fences, limitations, or glass ceilings—a realm of pure potential. There are no forms or structures, no rules and regulations, no person or god to tell you what you can and can't imagine and conceive.

However, there is a Dark World and Light World area, a Creation Realm, for each separate dimension, suitable for that range of vibrational levels, so that we don't go over-reaching ourselves and our powers of creation, or who knows what might be let loose on the universe!

We can see, therefore, that the polarities of light and dark do not represent good and evil. They are both necessary to life, to the creation of anything at all. They are more akin to the concept of yin and yang in eastern traditions, with yin representing the Dark World and yang representing the Light World, and this can be seen beautifully in the Yin-Yang symbol itself, which depicts these two worlds combined and equal. Yin is the black background with the white dot. Yang is the white background containing the black dot. The dots represent the link or bridge to the opposite side, thereby maintaining balance in the natural world.

Chiron tells us that there is no gender aspect to this symbol, and that the Dark World is not feminine and the Light World masculine, as is often portrayed in literature. The Dark World is where all things are conceptualised and conceived by males and females alike, and the Light World is where things are given the spark of life, by either a male or a female, to become manifest in our physical dimension. All humans need to learn to utilise both the Dark and Light Worlds of the Creation Realm in order to create a whole and happy life and world.

Some people prefer to hang out more in the Dark World, and some prefer the environment of the Light World. It is not a question of judging them for this, for some humans were designed to be more of the conceptual type, and some are more of the 'make it happen' genre, but everyone will need connection to both of these worlds, for it is impossible to manifest anything unless it has first been conceived.

So, when we are having difficulty with manifesting our dreams on Earth, it could be because we have neglected some aspect of conception or birthing in these two dimensions of consciousness. If we only ever conceive, then we are never actually going to give birth to anything on the ground, be it babies, projects, ideas, or matter. Similarly, it is not possible to manifest things until we have pre-conceived them beforehand. This is why is it necessary to dream our dreams for a while and incubate them before leaping into action and making hard and fast plans.

When we understand how these essential two worlds of Light and Dark interplay, we can not only understand how the universe first came into being but also how to create our own personal universe around us too. Chiron urges us to spend plenty of time in the Dark World and get to appreciate it and know what it is capable of producing. Here we will feel safe, protected, and whole, as we align ourselves with its harmony. Access to this world is not limited in any way, and it will gift us with energies, healing, and ideas beyond our belief, and we will become adept at manifesting many more things and talents than could ever have been previously imagined. In chapter 17 we will discuss manifestation in more detail, as one of the tools of consciousness.

Some people may be asking if a Black Hole, the centre of a galaxy, is the same thing as the Dark World? I put the question to my Beloved Source.

Beloved Source: *"It is an interesting question that you have asked. Let me explain the ramifications of Black Holes to you, and then you will see how they are different from the Dark World.*

Your scientists are currently discovering that Black Holes do indeed exist, but at this point in time they have no further information about them. I cannot divulge all the secrets of the universe to you here, for mankind must find out things for themselves. However, there are some things I can tell you that will help you understand their purpose.

Black Holes are the recycling depots of the universe. When matter is abandoned, it can be crunched up physically and redistributed once again. That is its sole purpose. And we can take the subatomic particles and re-manifest them into something else.

And so, a Black Hole is not the same as the Dark World, for in a Black Hole all matter is being crunched down into the smallest particles in existence, and in the Dark World we are using our consciousness to imagine what we will bring about through the Light World. It is the Light World that will use the end product of the Black Hole, the source material for matter. This is where it comes from. I hope this is clearer for you now."[11]

---

11. From a channelling with my Beloved Source, 18 July 2019

Chapter 8 – Death

Facing death

For many societies on Earth, especially those in western civilisation, death is somewhat of a taboo subject. It is not widely discussed, nor provisioned for, except in hushed conversations around deathbeds or hospital beds, or if relatives need to be moved into nursing homes. Since death is something we must all face at some time, it is surprising that we, more often than not, don't have welfare, family, and personal systems in place to deal with it. It is not within the scope of this book to deal with all the practical processes surrounding death, your own or other people's, but Chiron does give us some counsel on this topic so that we might gain a better perspective about the *idea* of death and all its ramifications.

We need to come to grips with the inevitability of our own death. We've had a lot of practice. We have probably gone through the death process thousands of times before, in countless previous lives, and we should be prepared to do it again. Sometimes it has been a peaceful transition, and sometimes we have suffered great trauma. It's no wonder, then, that many of us fear what is preordained to visit us. But, are we fearing the manner of our death, or are we fearing what lies beyond it? In the next chapter we will discuss what lies beyond.

Given that most of us don't like to think about our death or plan for it, what are the things we should be pondering on and in what manner should we face the most certain thing that is ever going to happen to us?

Most humans want more time on Earth, especially when they learn they are dying. In truth, we know we are going to die from the very first day that we are born, so shouldn't we be making the most of our time here while we can? What would we do with more time if it was made available to us? Would we squander it, just as we might have been doing in our time here so far?

The knowledge that we are going to die one day is actually a positive thing for humans because it makes us focus on this life, to make the best of it in the limited time we have. If we knew we were going to live forever, we would never get anything done and would leave everything until tomorrow.

Fortune shines on some people when death seems inevitable, and they are given a second chance, and often this is a critical turning point in their lives and they begin to appreciate what they had little valued before. If we are given time to face death, it's a chance to get ourselves back on track if we have slipped off the rails, a chance to change our consciousness and heal all that is still unresolved, within ourselves and with other people. But many trudge through their lives not counting their blessings and only bemoaning the fact that life isn't kinder or more abundant. We shouldn't wait until the spectre of death pays us a visit before taking stock of whether we have lived a meaningful and productive life or not.

Wish as we might for a long and healthy life, our tenure on Earth isn't up to us but controlled by our soul, not the soul nearest to our human self but our soul which is closest to our Source. Our Ribbon of souls which reaches back to our Source are all linked and take part in major decisions like our death. The gods are not allowed to interfere with this process. Our soul has placed us here as a physical seed, and our soul will dictate when to return us again to the higher dimensions.

We will be allowed to stay on this planet as long as we are moving towards our destiny, our mission in this lifetime. No one comes without a destiny, not even sinners and the worst hardened criminals. Our soul is constantly monitoring the health of our mission and, if we are failing miserably, we may get the tap on the shoulder that augurs our recall. We can, of course, buck up our ideas and pull our socks up and our soul will look favourably upon this renewed motivation to do our best.

But if we consistently deny our destiny, our soul will bring us Home to the spirit world because we are just taking up valuable space on Earth and our soul will not want to drag a resistant human along. We might be better off in another type of world that is more adjusted to our temperament and where specialist beings can work with us until we are able to understand the truth about ourselves and what needs to be improved.

So, we mustn't renege on our mission. We need to understand the purpose of our current incarnation and get it completed. Our soul knows the plan, so we should work with our best friend as part of a team. It doesn't pay to go AWOL or play up, perhaps leaving our goal unfinished. We will only need to return and mop up the pieces in a later life.

Our soul is not cruel in fixing our demise. It has the job of evolving us into a more loving consciousness, and it is entirely unsentimental about what needs to be done. It is also a case of tough love when it comes to unhitching us from the Earth and pulling us away from all that we've known, and probably loved.

Summary of major reasons why we might get called Home:

- ☺ We have completed our mission successfully. This, of course, is the optimal reason for our death. All is good and we get to go Home and recuperate in the higher dimensions after a life well-lived. We may have had a long life or a short one. Success is not about longevity or material wealth but about achieving what we came here to accomplish in our divine contract.
- ☺ Our soul elects to give us a more important mission to complete, and our current one is cut short. We need to go Home to get our new instructions and perhaps be trained up for the new job.
- ☹ We have reneged on our mission and cannot be redeemed. Some people are snatched away before they can do more harm to themselves or others. This even happens to gods who are on Earth in human form if they are not careful.

  I know of one god on Earth who was a brilliant heart surgeon who was relocated by his soul to another country and fell in with a new crowd of wealthy movers and shakers who were heavily into the drugs, sex, and rock n' roll scene. He was killed off by his soul in a car accident because it was foreseen that he would not fulfil his destiny as planned, and that he had taken a path of his own choosing that would lead him to the Underworld of low and dark vibrations. This planet can be a sinkhole for both humans and gods, and the gods try to haul out those who seem to be redeemable, but even the gods can get recalled, and because this doctor was a god on Earth, he was held accountable to higher standards than any human.

- ☹ We no longer serve a useful purpose for our soul. This is similar to the point above but implies rather that we have given up on the job and are just cruising and waiting to die. Our soul always hopes that we will regain our mojo and get cracking again, but it will know when this seems irretrievably unlikely.
- ☺ Our death serves a purpose in helping the destiny of others. It could be the final part of our mission. Through loving and dying, we might help crack open the hearts of people around us who have loved us, as grieving tends to do this, and this transformation assists those people to become better humans. Our death may also help others who had become dependent on us to become more self-sufficient and thereby more able to complete their own missions.
- ☺ It is hard to believe that we might volunteer to die in some pre-arranged disaster or atrocity, such as being the victim of a tidal wave or terrorist attack, but this may serve the purposes of the gods in some way to teach a lesson to the world, perhaps by giving humanity the opportunity to show compassion and support. Maybe we receive extra credits for putting our hand up for this type of scenario?
- ☹ People of lower vibrations may become the victim of pandemics, storms, or other geophysical disturbances. Since our planet is undergoing a transition to higher dimensions, those who cannot match these frequencies will be removed from the Earth and their consciousnesses will be taken to another dimension better suited to their wavelength.

- ☹ Our soul might choose for us to experience a type of death that we had visited upon others in the past. For instance, if we were responsible for burning people at the stake, perhaps we will burn to death in a fire in this lifetime. If we have murdered in a previous life, then we might become a murder victim this time around. It could be described as the paying back of karma, but in reality our soul merely wishes us to have the experience because it might engender compassion within us.
- ☹ If it is determined that we will not be able to cope with the life we have been born into or that we are currently experiencing, our soul may be compassionate and bring us Home. Generally, we are never given more challenge than we can handle, but life's circumstances may get out of control and overwhelm us in such a way we could not survive.
- ☹ There seems to be no crueller thing than seeing children dying, and we tend to ask why God would allow this to happen? It could be for any of the reasons outlined above. It might also be because the soul wants the child to have just a brief 'taste' of life on Earth. Perhaps this consciousness has never experienced the solid physical world before and wants to merely sample what human life has to offer before making a major commitment to come down here in a physical body.
- ☺ We attract what we think about. Whatever is in our consciousness plays out, so if we fear a painful death then it is likely that we will attract it. If we fear cancer, it is probable that we will bring it on. If we fear an accident, then we are an accident waiting to happen. Our thinking creates our reality. Our soul is helping us to recognise our fears and negative thinking so that we can rewrite our programming, but if we are unable to do this, then our soul will ultimately call us Home. We can always think about an easy and peaceful death at the end of a loving and fulfilling life.

The reason for death is usually not quite so black and white as described here, and often takes in multiple reasons. Hopefully, the above will give some food for thought, and rather than wail at the injustice of a death, we might be able to see the bigger picture behind it, even while nurturing ourselves in our time of grief.

It is important to note that no death is ever an 'accident', either for a god or a human. We can be involved in accidents or incidents, but our soul determines if we live or die in them. Accidents can happen to us either because they occur naturally or because our soul or the universe has had a hand in putting us in this position to experience it. It is not that our soul or the universe is malevolent or pitiless, but that this is the manner in which we humans can learn our lessons and strengthen ourselves to become more resilient and self-sufficient. Our ultimate aim is to become like the gods, and we cannot be allowed to reach godhood if we are weak, dependent, and fall apart in a crisis.

When it comes time to take our final breath, we need to feel that our heart is fulfilled. We should leave this world with our consciousness having been given a good workout and having evolved to at least one level higher than when we came in. Sadly, some humans go backwards, but jumping even one level is better than none at all.

Even until the very last breath, there is still time to improve, but it will benefit us to get our house in order in good time, rather than leaving it to the last minute. We may not even have a last minute. My own father died suddenly of a heart attack at the age of 46, and he had given death little thought, and even though he had created a will, there was immense chaos and consternation left behind in his wake, along with five fatherless daughters aged between four and eighteen.

One of the things we could do to prepare for our death is to arrange our funeral beforehand, or at least leave instructions as to what kind of funeral we would like to have. Other people may not organise it as we'd like, and our spirit self may feel quite miffed when watching proceedings from above at what it deems to be an unsatisfactory way to say goodbye.

I once attended a birthday party of a friend who was imminently dying of cancer. I asked his relatives what my friend wanted by way of a funeral? They looked at me blank-faced. None of them had had the courage (or kindness) to ask him before he left the planet what were his wishes. I took it upon myself to remedy this, and my friend welcomed the discussion and felt more valued, and we subsequently held a funeral which was very much to his taste and liking.

There is no need to feel maudlin about documenting our plans to be laid to rest. We can do this with delight. Let us celebrate our life and achievements. We can write our own eulogy, and if nothing else, it will highlight whether we've led a good and fulfilling life, or whether there is still some way to go in rectifying matters. Ensure we have tied up all loose ends. We don't want to leave a tangled legacy or a box full of secrets to be sorted out ad infinitum after we've gone. We can get all our affairs in order by being disciplined every day. We may get notice of our death, or we may not.

In the meantime, we shouldn't take a single day for granted. It could always be our last. Let us fill it with joy and gratitude and focus on the mission we came here to complete. We can share the benefits of our life with others, be it our wisdom, our skills, our wealth, or even just our love, kindness, and attitude. These are ways we add value to the world and universe. Our life's lessons will be a valuable source of information for the people around us. Prove that we weren't just a waste of space and oxygen.

So, while we are still living, we need to think about how we can contribute to a life well-spent in the final analysis. Will we be ashamed when we return to our spirit home, that our list of achievements is all too short? Know that it's not just top jobs of fame and glory that win us kudos in Heaven. It is in the way that we have added value to the world that we will judge ourself. No one else will judge us. Will we harbour regrets and wish we'd made a better go of our life? This will be the Hell that we find ourself in, if we leave the planet with a heavy heart, remorseful and mourning that we hadn't made the most of our life.

Another thing we can do to prepare for our death is to practise being in the higher dimensions. We now know that we can take our consciousness for a drive there at any time, and the more we get used to this way of being, the easier it will be when we arrive in our new Home. If we are familiar with flying through the sacred halls and forests of the hidden worlds with gods and angels, and have already known the love and wisdom of the divine beings who live here, then our transition will feel like we are heading back to a loving family rather than into a great unknown. The gods pity those who have never tried to go beyond the limiting walls of Earth. They have missed out on the best parts of the universe, and especially on all the love that can be found there.

Our death is inevitable, so it's best to come to terms with that fact and just let go. Many wail at their imminent demise and try to put it off, only to lead a miserable life, just hanging on instead of allowing themselves to return to their true Home. It's better to go with lightness in our hearts than with the darkness of resistance, fear, and regret. We should ponder on a good peaceful ending, taking it in our stride and going out with dignity. We can elect how we would like to face our last moments and create the scene in our mind, for this is how our reality is created, by relaxing and dreaming in the Dark World.

We shouldn't be sad when it is time to die. It's just a phase of consciousness and we are moving out of one form and into another. One of the gods known as St.Germain once told me that dying is just like changing trains. We get off one train at the terminus of our destination, and we board another to a new destination.

In the movie *Lord of the Rings—The Return of the King*, Gandalf the Wizard speaks to the hobbit Pippin in the ruins of Minas Tirith, about what it is like upon dying. "The journey doesn't end here. Death is just another path, one that we all must take. The grey rain-curtain of this world rolls back, and all turns to silver glass. And then you see it—white shores, and beyond, a far, green country under a swift sunrise."

Our spirit self awaits our return and will have hoped that we have lived the good life, keeping to standards expected of us and living life with love, zest, and meaning. We should go to spirit well, for souls enjoy Heaven; it is all love-liness there. We will be glad to have returned Home.

Taking a life

Chiron tells us that taking a life, either our own or another's, is viewed very dimly in the higher realms. We will not be punished by the gods, for our actions rebound on us and we end up being punished by ourselves. Our own deeds find their way back to us in some way or other. Call it karma or a reckoning, or whatever you will, but a crime never goes unnoticed or unredressed by the universe, and all actions are balanced out ultimately.

Some people have nihilistic or vengeful thoughts and then take action and carry out the deed. Many more harbour this thinking in their consciousness but don't perform the act itself. Thoughts may range from actively harming and carrying out scenes of reprisal or self-destruction in their mind, to jokingly saying they would like to murder someone. We should acknowledge these feelings and cleanse them from our consciousness because they will count against us if they are allowed to linger and fester.

Since Chiron doesn't go into detail in his book about the ethics of taking a life, and I didn't want to give my own viewpoint which could never be as wise as the gods', I asked for one of the Ascended Masters to channel their views on the subjects of suicide, euthanasia, abortion, and murder, for us to consider. Whilst this may be confrontational material for some to read, I hope that this merely provides people with information about how Divine Law treats these subjects, and they can then make up their own minds on their standpoint. The gods never seek to take away free will, but they point out there are consequences to acting against divine will.

The Ascended Master, El Morya, a senior god, was game enough to tackle these subjects, although even he had a bit of nervousness in doing so, for he knows he and I will be misunderstood by some sections of society who don't yet understand how the higher dimensions operate.

Suicide (channelled from Master El Morya)

El Morya: *"I don't like speaking about suicide as it is a subject that is taboo, and it is a subject that many people cannot get to grips with, and they may not understand what I am going to say next, for it is quite controversial. But I can only state the truth, for this is how we travel in this universe.*

Suicide: the taking of one's own life before it is time for that person to go Home quite legitimately. Of course, we would all know the reasons why people take their own lives. Life has simply overwhelmed them and they can no longer cope or see a way out from their travails. It is the loneliest place to be, in this bottomless pit, where there seems no escape and certainly no hope.

And we must have compassion and sympathy for those that find themselves in this predicament and that they can find no other way to move forwards than to annihilate themselves and take themselves away from this planet. The truth is they will find that they have taken themselves away from not very much at all. For you cannot escape your consciousness; it travels with you everywhere. It is who you are.

And when you are trying to kill yourself off as a human upon Earth, you will find it has no effect on the fact that you will still survive in spirit. And you will look down upon what you have done, and your slain body, and the tears will well in your eyes and your heart that you have tried to do away with something so precious, this chance to experience the physical world and overcome challenges and gain superiority. You will say to yourself as your spirit, 'Well, that didn't work, did it? All I have done is taken away my chance for advancement, and now I must start again on the bottom rungs of the ladder in the spirit world.'

And yet many who commit suicide will have done so before, even many times in their history. It is a weakness in their character that makes them think that they can escape this world, and they forget the lessons that they have learnt before and they try it time and time again, to no avail. And, of course, it puts an almighty stop on their advancement towards their soul, for they are thrown back to square one again, and all the gains they may have made, even including godhood, will dissipate as they learn their lessons all over again.

This weakness of character must decide once and for all that this is not the way to overcome their problems. Adversity stands in front of us all, and we can run away from it but we cannot try to obliterate the situation as if nothing existed but this Earth. This planet and its scenarios are merely a projection of the same issues that we will face in the higher heavens.

The best way to deal with suicidal thoughts is to cultivate courage and to learn ways of letting go this fearful thinking. For, more often than not, it is just the thinking around the situation that is causing the most problem, and an adjustment in thinking will show the way through.

If a person does take their own life, they will be counselled well in Heaven. There is no punishment. The sorrow is all from the person themselves, for they realise now their mistake and they realise now that they must start the path again.

If a soul thinks that their human can be redeemed, then the suicide attempt will not be successful, and the soul will try to work with that person to get them back on their path once again. But if it is clear to the soul that this person does not have it within them to make a go of this life on Earth, then the suicide attempt will be successful. And all the company of Heaven will mourn the loss that this soul will experience now, for it is the human that enacts the suicide but it is the soul that must carry out the penance on the other side.

It is a natural course of events for every human to experience grief and tragedy and severe adversity at some time in their life, for these experiences are what will make us into gods in the final analysis. And we commiserate when humans find themselves in the bottom of the darkest pit, and so this is why we encourage learning how to utilise the tools of consciousness, for these techniques will help to bring a person out of that dark pit and will bring a modicum of hope so that the human begins to climb once again.

Most suicides could be prevented if people understood about their inner personas, and how they can work with these entities within their consciousness, and how they can dissolve away these entities that represent various thoughts they have had in the past or are currently thinking. When we know we can merely dissolve our thinking, then the danger is over. And we can look out upon our day with a brand-new perspective and not want to do away with our physical selves. For it is not our physical bodies that we wish really to kill off; it is the thinking that plagues us about our situation, and if we can merely think differently, then half the battle will be won. Learning to let go of troublesome thinking is the best tool you will ever have."[12]

Euthanasia (channelled from Master El Morya)

El Morya: *"This subject rides hard on the heels of my treatise on suicide. For euthanasia is a kind of suicide; let us make no bones about it. It is*

---

12. From a channelling with El Morya, 18 June 2019

performed by a person who wishes to take their own life, who wishes to no longer be on this planet in human form. So, although it might have a different name from suicide, one which implies a kinder and more compassionate end, the same consequences arise as I described for suicide before.

Yes, indeed, there are many people who are in pain and who believe it unjustified for themselves to exist in this pain or in these terrible conditions that they find themselves, and so they are hoping that human law will justify their decision and give them the all-clear for going Home. Well, they may or may not be breaking human law, but they will be breaking Divine Law. And that is a consequence that one must dearly ponder on, for the price is very high if it is broken.

And so, would we gods punish those who are in such excruciating pain or devilish circumstances that we would not allow them to go Home? It would seem as if we gods are punitive, but it is up to a person's soul, and not us gods, that determines when a person can unhitch themselves from this planet and return to spirit. A person's soul knows all too well what is going on and feels the human's pain also, but the soul does have a method to their seeming madness. And they are asking the human to endure, for there are lessons to learn, not just for the person themselves but for all around them too. Often it is the person's own resistance to going Home that keeps them grounded anyway, for although they might be saying with their lips that they wish to leave the planet, there may be a greater part of them which lies in fear of going Home and what they may face there.

So, no, we do not encourage either suicide or euthanasia. And a person must look to their soul to negotiate terms for going Home."[13]

Abortion (channelled from Master El Morya)

El Morya: *"The subject of abortion is a touchy one, is it not? There are those who stand for the life of the baby, and those who stand for the life of the mother of that baby. So, where must we draw the line? Of course, it is just like with the case for suicide and euthanasia, in that we as a human do not have the right to put an end to our life or anyone else's. Our soul is the sole determinator of whether we live or die. And so, what right does the mother*

---

13. From a channelling with El Morya, 19 June 2019

have, and her soul, to take a decision on behalf of her baby and its soul? If the baby chooses to live or die, that's another matter, under the guidance of its soul, but it is not for the mother or any other being to make that decision.

You may think that the mother had no part in the creating of this baby, the way some mothers wish to get rid of it so insistently. But we have learnt in the chapters of this book that whatever we create we are responsible for it, be it a baby, a book, a system, or a planet. And so, the mother has allowed a baby to be created within her. Her soul has been complicit in this creation. And so, she and her soul must now take responsibility for their joint creation and make the most of it.

You might be saying, 'What if the mother has been raped? Why must she bear the rapist's child?' Again, I say that the soul has been complicit in allowing the mother to fall into this situation, and the soul will have its reasons, for perhaps there are past life issues to be resolved here, or some underlying thinking that has attracted this situation. We cannot distance ourselves from the situations we find ourselves in as if it has been nothing to do with us, for every situation we will have attracted to ourselves due to our vibrations and our thinking. This seems harsh, I know, but how else will people work out the issues in their consciousness unless we bring them to the forefront?

You might ask the question, 'What happens if the birth of the baby would threaten the mother's life?' And this is a tricky one, for whose life is worth more, the mother's or the baby's? We would advise that the outcome is left to the souls, the soul of the mother and the soul of the baby. And these two souls must negotiate. And it may be that one may die and the other may live, but it could also be that by the grace of God, or their souls, that both may live against the odds. And so, care should be taken to keep both humans alive, and if one of them dies, or even both, we must know that this was the option chosen by their souls.

Yes, it is hard not to jump in as humans to take these decisions and save lives, but humans should not try to play God. And by 'God', in this case, I mean taking away the decision from the soul, for humans will find they cannot do this in any case. The soul's decision will always triumph. These are not words you may wish to hear, but this is the way of Divine Law and this is the way in which the universe operates."[14]

---

14. From a channelling with El Morya, 19 June 2019

Murder (channelled from Master El Morya)

El Morya: "*This topic runs on from the others, of suicide, euthanasia, and abortion. Now we are on to murder, for with murder we are killing a human against the wishes of their soul.*

Suicide could be considered as a form of murdering oneself, but it will only be successful with the permission of that person's soul. Euthanasia is a form of murder, for the person is using violent means to overcome the soul's will to take their own life, or to get others to do it for them. You might say that suicide can be violent too, but in this case the soul has more control over whether their human lives or dies. In euthanasia, the human has made up their mind that they really do want to go, and their soul will have to shrug and accept there can be no redemption and allow this person to die. It is still going against that soul's will. Abortion is a form of murder, for it is taking the life of a baby against the will of its soul.

And so, you will know by now, then, that murder will not be condoned by the gods, although again I say that each person that is murdered is complicit in this situation in some way; they have attracted it to themselves. And I know this may cause an outcry when you consider the victims to have been completely innocent, but consciousness is never completely innocent. And even if the victims were children, their past lives consciousness may have involved them with their murderer, and repercussions are now playing out. We cannot divorce this life from other lives. We are an interwoven network of lives, and consequences are being felt through lifetime after lifetime if we do not resolve our issues.

And so, we can see that murder is a heinous crime and there is nothing to say in its favour. But what about the murder that is committed in times of war? All of us will have been through wars in this lifetime or in history. And we will have been both invaders and victims, and we will have been guilty of atrocities and murder. Is it right to murder others to save your country, or to save your house, or your family, or your lands? Again, this is a tricky problem. Are you allowed to kill in self-defence? How would your world be now if certain invaders had been allowed to take over?

We gods are not so stupid in that we cannot see the ethics of this situation, and all of us have been involved in fighting for our crowns. But now we are aware that this is the wrong thing to do, to murder others, and so we are trying to create a society where we work through diplomacy and negotiation rather than the gun. If we murder for any cause, then there are repercussions to repay. And so, the more we can wean ourselves away from this mode of living, then the greater potential there will be for peace, not just within the world but within ourselves too. Murder is never condoned in any shape or form."[15]

If any of the above have triggered emotional reactions, Part Two will help to identify issues, heal them, and let them go.

---

15. From a channelling with El Morya, 19 June 2019

Chapter 9 – Life after death, and past lives

What happens when we die?

Some people might ask, "What's the point of living such a disciplined and consciously aware life if there might be nothing beyond this body and our last breath?"

The answer to this question is that we never truly die. We exist as a consciousness forever, and have always existed, and nothing, not even the death of our human body, can kill us off.

For those who don't believe in an afterlife, it must seem frightening that we will not exist any longer, that we will be snuffed out like a candle and nothing of us remains except for a few memories by loved ones, or a valuable legacy if we are lucky. It must make for a miserable life to believe that there is nothing more than this planet and this one little sojourn on Earth, and then annihilation. Hopefully, this book, and Chiron's, will serve to show a different point of view to these people, and that they will be able to embrace the knowledge that we are much more than our human selves, and that when we die we merely move on to another dimension in different clothes.

It is only our human body that dies. Our consciousness lives on. We have lived and died as human bodies many times before. We should not fear now moving through to the world of spirit. We are not merely human. When we 'pass over', the human part of our consciousness drifts out of our corporeal body and reunites with the spirit part of our consciousness in the invisible world. Our Ribbon of Consciousness that straddles the two dimensions is now reined in from the lower dimension and into the higher dimension. Because our consciousness will exist at various levels on our Ribbon at the moment of death, we return to those same levels in the higher dimensions of spirit; we simply lose the level responsible for the physical body.

The two parts of our consciousness (human and spirit) live side by side for a time while our old human self gets used to being in this peculiar world where it no longer has a flesh and blood body. It is still the same consciousness that existed while the body was alive, and there is understandably some confusion at first during this transition period. But our consciousness soon adapts and starts to change rapidly under the new conditions that present themselves in this higher world, and it isn't long before we are loving our new way of being. For starters, there is no longer any requirement to be conscious of the needs of a human body—a consciousness does not need to eat or sleep or wash or cook or shop or go to the gym.

However, as the newly-deceased human consciousness grows more accustomed to its new world, it can indeed manifest itself into a human-like form if it chooses, and then it can function in many ways like its old human self. But it may choose to fly in its new spirit body of pulsating, coloured lights. Without a physical body, it can go anywhere. There are no limitations except the vibrational level threshold that constrains it. There is so much novelty to explore and new types of beings to meet. It may not want to be bothered with the human-type world anymore.

Our new spirit body may be surprised to find worlds full of brightness, love, and succour after they die as a human. All resistance melts away. They will gain an understanding for their demise on Earth, and how their actions and reactions contributed to their life of success or life of failure. There may be regrets now, and they may ask the gods to be given another chance at life in the physical realms. This opportunity may or may not be granted.

Eventually, as our new ethereal body gains more experience, the old unwanted human parts of consciousness are completely let go, and all the useful skills and knowledge of that human lifetime are merged into its spirit counterpart. The lower world has shaped this old consciousness in the past; now the new structures, rules, and ethics of the higher dimensions will be learnt and integrated.

The spirit consciousness begins to make plans to reincarnate again, if this is allowed, and to prepare for its next role, which may be on Earth, or may be not. It could be quite a while before this consciousness is allowed to return to our planet, or any other physical realm, as it has much to assimilate from its recent life on Earth and much work to do in identifying its next mission and all its fellow colleagues who will be involved, as well as selecting its parents, siblings, extended family, and astrological guiding stars. In time, this consciousness will experience new life again in some physical world, being born as a baby, growing into an adult, and following the destiny which it has designed for itself.

Ghosts

We have just been examining the world we go to when we die, and that leads us to the question of ghosts. Do they exist, and if so, what exactly are they?

Yes, ghosts definitely exist, so if you've ever seen or heard one you are not going crazy, you might be glad to know. Ghosts are the spirits of the dead who are living in the lowest levels of the unseen dimension on Second Earth.

We have already established that spirits can take on any form, and this includes a human form, yet, unlike the gods who can manifest themselves in solid human form, spirits can only conjure up an ethereal approximation of a human figure. They are, in truth, only a mass of pulsing light. It is like an electronic signature, and what we see in a ghost is an imprint from the spirit dimension. We are seeing through the veil between dimensions where it is thinnest. The spirit is at the lowest edge next to our dimension of Earth. What we see could be the ghost in real time, as it is right now, or an imprint of it, like an electronic photograph, from a previous time when it has been in this location. Because there is no concept of time in the higher worlds, we could be seeing into the past, or even the future.

A ghost, or spirit, especially those who are newly passed over, sometimes wishes to revisit their old stomping grounds. It may be to take a closer look at loved ones and try to comfort them in their grief, or perhaps to convey some kind of message to them, such as what is the password to their computer, or where is the loot that they buried.

It could be their visit is to startle or scare someone who has done them wrong, or to try to take revenge. However, Chiron tells us that we shouldn't fear ghosts too much, for the angels are tasked with keeping wayward spirits under control, and they won't be allowed to cause havoc or death and destruction. Only gods have the power to do that. Of course, the sighting of a ghost could potentially lead to death through having a heart attack from fright!

Often a ghost is seen when it has decided to revert to the appearance it had whilst still alive on Earth, either in its most recent incarnation or as someone it was in the past. They are play-acting, putting on the hat once again, and they will revisit old haunts (as it were), maybe to try to work through some of the issues they had in that particular lifetime. They are especially inclined to visit the place where their destiny came undone.

Why is it that some people see ghosts, and others not? Usually, it is because a person has a link of some sort to that spirit. We have mentioned several times before that 'like attracts like', and this applies across dimensions. If we see a ghost, we will have a similar vibrational level to it (temporarily), and very possibly have featured in the life of that spirit at some time in our history. We could be a relative or descendant, a friend or enemy, or someone who saved its life or caused its death. Perhaps we are being used as an emissary to take a message to someone else still alive, someone who does not have the ability to see through the veil as we do.

For the most part, spirits don't care to return to the earthly world or to linger in the low vibrations here. They prefer to dwell in the higher dimensions and in their new form. Clearly, ghosts are not prevented from making visits to the world of humans, but they are discouraged from doing so by the gods and usually persuaded to move on, although sometimes they badger the gods to be given another chance.

It is said that ghosts are spirits trapped between the two worlds, unable to leave the physical earthly dimension and yet not able to enter the hidden spirit dimension. This is not the case. Everyone who dies arrives immediately in the spirit world and takes on their new spirit body. Nothing ever halts this process. There is no such thing as a lost soul, not in this particular context anyway. A ghost will always arrive firstly in its new home, and adopt its new body, before it ventures back to the earthly dimension for the occasional visit, haunting, or other seemingly paranormal activity.

One type of paranormal activity is that of a poltergeist (from the German for 'creating a disturbance' and 'ghost'). A poltergeist is an entity that creates physical havoc on the earthly plane, and is often associated with teenagers who are going through a 'bad attitude' phase. It is not a spirit type of ghost, in that it is not the ghost of someone who has passed over and wishes to do harm. A poltergeist is the out-picturing of a person's own consciousness, even while they are usually not aware of it.

Our consciousness is a very powerful tool for manifestation (more on this in Part Two), and when we allow one of our low vibrational inner personas to take control over our mind, the outcome can be very destructive in our earthly reality. We literally do have the power to move objects and furniture, and can even find our own body moving against our wishes, with a battle raging inside our own consciousness between the personas. We know that our inner personas can easily scupper and sabotage our plans, and the poltergeist is merely an extreme form of warfare within ourselves that plays out in our physical world. It is no ghost, just our troubled self creating disturbing events. The way to get rid of a poltergeist is to work with the issues of the human inner personas in a kind, compassionate, but disciplined manner, just like a parent would do with a troublesome child.

A true ghost is a real spirit from the higher dimensions. It won't be allowed to cause us any serious issues, but if we do feel any malevolence emanating from it, we can just send love to it and raise their soul to a higher place. Forgiveness is always a key factor in defusing any situation, so we need to forgive the ghost and ask it to forgive us, just in case we have been responsible for their demise or hurt. Understanding and trying to help is the best action, for we too have been in this position before, a ghost in another world, and it may be that one day we will come wandering down here too, looking for answers, or comfort, or someone to carry our message.

If we do happen to get a sighting of a ghost, we can marvel at how we are seeing through to another dimension, and how we can interact with spirits that can weave through both worlds, and how the gods have created these magical dimensions for us to play and work and learn within. In truth, we ourselves are not only humans but also spirits, and we jump between dimensions all the time.

Reincarnation, rebirth, past lives

As stated previously, we have had many past lives, and our Ribbon of Consciousness houses all past lives as a human and also our lives as spirit on the Second Earth. We are in a continual cycle of incarnation, death, and rebirth. Not all of these lives have been lived on Earth, or perhaps not even in this galaxy. We may have had a human-like form, or we may not. If bacteria are one of the most prolific forms on Earth, what is preventing us from having an experience as a bacterium? But, let us stay with our lives in human form, or else we shall be delving into quite another book entirely!

When we die, our human consciousness returns to the higher dimensions and merges back into the consciousness of our spirit and soul. We will retain many of the memories of this lifetime, and if necessary, we can always access more recollections from the greater consciousness which stores every single detail of every incarnation. Any scene from any time or any world can be reviewed, if it is important to do so. No judgement is ever made about what is stored; the universe merely faithfully documents it all, like any recording device in the human world, but with the addition of all emotions and sensations too.

And so, at the end of the cycle of our current lifetime, as we look down upon our old human world from our new abode, we will be encouraged by our mentors in Heaven to look back on our life and understand the lessons that we learnt and any opportunities we might have missed. All this will take quite some time to assimilate and mull over, and it will be a while before our spirit/soul is in a position to consider a new venture back down on Earth again, or in some other physical dimension.

However, there will come a time when our consciousness decides that it's time for a new challenge, a reincarnation into physicality again, and our soul gets busy pondering on the opportunities available and how to best utilise old skills and learn new ones, and what our new mission will be. Often, we haven't completed our previous mission, and so we might be sent back down to Earth to continue our work or tie up loose ends. However, it could be that our next life will have very different roles and rules.

Whatever the scenario, we will not be reincarnating with exactly the same consciousness as we had before, nor the same body or appearance. A part of our soul's consciousness is selected to comprise our new human consciousness, and this may or may not be comparable to the consciousness we had in our previous life. Perhaps we will be given a secret memory of this previous life, if it is helpful to us, but usually we will have no memory of past incarnations as these details will only serve to overwhelm us and detract from our current mission. Sometimes, later on in life, the veil of secrecy is lifted so that we might put the puzzle pieces together and understand our destiny better.

For instance, I learnt only in my early fifties that I had committed suicide in my most recent past life where I was young, widowed, and pregnant towards the end of World War Two, and that in this present lifetime it was my lesson to experience this from another perspective, a lesson I received all too acutely when my mother committed suicide when I was twenty.

So, we never return as exactly the same person we were before, although we may have many of those traits and characteristics, or none at all. We are created from the cloud of consciousness that is our soul, and we are added to by slivers or scoops of other consciousnesses who wish to be our human parents and our spiritual mother and father, or to be part of our adventure in some way this time around. Consciousness is a shared asset. It searches for experiences to add value to the universe and will join with others as necessary.

Our old consciousness may go on to be split into many threads of new consciousnesses that inhabit new bodies. Thus, people like Jesus or Leonardo da Vinci will never reincarnate as exactly their same selves, as the same consciousness they were once upon a time on Earth. Threads of their old consciousness may merge with other consciousnesses, and they may be born again and spread across many human forms, but can we say that Jesus or Leonardo has truly returned?

Therefore, we cannot accurately declare that we were once this person or that person in history, because only a thread of our current consciousness is linked to this being. However, the details of that particular consciousness and its life are retained in their totality, and we can revisit that consciousness at any time. Therefore, if we so wished, we could have a conversation with Jesus or Leonardo da Vinci as they existed in those famous lifetimes, but their current consciousnesses will now have evolved and moved on since those ancient days.

So, who are we really? It's very hard to say. The lineage of our consciousness is not a straight line from person to person, like in a genealogy chart. Our consciousness is not handed down whole and entire from one generation of ourself to the next. We are created from multiple consciousnesses each time we reincarnate physically, and the consciousness from our most recent life lives on as many threads of us, joining with the threads of others. In truth, we become like an amorphous wave of the ocean, not knowing where we start and end.

Our past life consciousnesses can still have roles to play in our new incarnation, and they will surface at appropriate times, affecting us for good or bad, either as talents handed down to us or as challenges we failed to fix last time around. We are a multi-media mishmash of all our lives, and it takes balance and coordination to bring them all together as one new rounded personality.

It can be fascinating to delve into our past life history, and check what we may have achieved or how we have messed up. Our records are available for our perusal, and access is not denied to us, but Chiron recommends that we don't get hung up on them. For instance, we might learn that we had been part of a conquering army that had slain prisoners mercilessly, or we had betrayed a brother, or abandoned our children, or been a slave or concubine. These were just experiences that created who we are currently, and it is this present lifetime that we need to focus on now.

It is only necessary to review our past if it explains our present, and if it can shed light on any recurring patterns and it helps to set us free from old limiting beliefs. Some skeletons in our cupboard can be hidden parts of ourselves from past lives, and their ghosts are still haunting us in our consciousness. We should be prepared for entanglements with the long-dead parts of ourselves. Their old fears and antipathies can pull us back from the path we need to be on, and we need to put any skeletons back into their graves and seal the coffin forever so that we are free of their shackles and can fly uninhibited into the New World.

It might be entertaining to know about some of our more successful old personas and talents, but even if we had a starring role in the past (which our ego will love!), it doesn't mean to say that we will be a star in this lifetime or in the future. Fame or fortune is not usually our destiny, but being a star of loving ways is our true path. We should rather stop looking behind us and head forwards. Our future is more important than our past. We need to be open to new vistas and adventures and move on with the consciousness we have today.

Mini-deaths and rebirths

The universe operates in cycles upon cycles, and our human death is merely the end of one cycle and the beginning of a new one. But there can be other cycles within our main life cycle, and we can experience mini-lives and mini-deaths within one lifetime.

Mini-deaths tend to be major milestones and turning points where our consciousness is seriously transformed into a new way of being and we enter a new phase of life. Marriage, our first baby, a new career, a major illness—these are all key events of our life that take some huge adjustment, and we need to let go of parts of who we were before and take on a new level of persona to deal with the transformation.

On our spiritual journey, too, there will be important jumps from one level to another on our Ribbon of Consciousness, and it feels as if we might be dying inside; and indeed we are, dying to the person we were and opening up to a new part of our consciousness. We are rebirthing like the phoenix from the ashes.

Sometimes we get notice of the significant change and can plan for it and tweak our thinking. But even then, the experience can cause massive upheavals in our life for which we just weren't prepared enough. It helps if we can appreciate what has gone before but are open to what lies ahead. If we resist what is happening to us and hold onto our old persona and consciousness, then we are sure to experience a lot of pain, for resistance always equals pain. Trees don't hold onto their leaves in winter. They let go in order to prepare for the spring when they will develop new buds and burst into blossom once again.

So, as one cycle closes and a new one opens, we need to look for opportunities for new growth. We have come to a new gateway in our life's journey and it is time for a new cycle. Even though we might be feeling sad that things are coming to an end, and our leaves are falling and dying, we should feel happy that we are evolving and that we are not stuck in one cycle but are moving forwards.

When we come to the end of a cycle, it isn't as if we have just gone around in a circle. We are on a spiralling path, and when we return to the point on the circle where we began, we are actually one level higher now (and hopefully not one level further down!) It is helpful to review our past cycle and ascertain the wisdom of our actions, and then make plans for our next cycle with an open mind. However, there will always be some cycles that we never complete in any one lifetime and our consciousness will continue this journey elsewhere at another time.

Astrology can be of assistance in showing us where we are within certain cycles that are under the influence of particular planets, and can highlight when we are approaching a major crossroads on our life's path. All the planets have cyclical orbits, and, in my experience, their energies contribute greatly to the focus of the challenges we face and the support we receive during their transits. Most of us will know about the influence of the Moon on tidal waters and plant sap, but it also greatly affects our moods and our own emotional waters. Similarly, all the planets and moon nodes have particular effects upon us.

Here is a summary of the cycles of the planets and nodes and their effects. We are influenced by them a great deal of the time, depending on our birth chart, but we are affected in a major way when a planet or node interacts with us at the end of a full cycle and also at key interim points within that cycle.

Planet/node	Full cycle	Description of effect and interim cycles
Moon	28¼ days	Emotions, fears, nurturing, mothering, counselling. Changes sign every 2½ days, giving us a new emotional focus.
Sun	1 year	Personality, brilliance, talent, ego, creativity, fun, leadership. Changes sign every month, giving us a new focus.
Jupiter	12 yrs	Expansion, learning, teaching, travel, luck. Interim cycles every 3, 6, 9 years Changes sign approx. every 12 months, giving us a new focus.
North Node	18/19 yrs	Destiny, mission, teamwork. Interim cycles every 4½, 9¼, 14 years Changes sign approx. every 18 months, giving us a new focus.
Saturn	28/29 yrs	Responsibilities, career, status, feeling stuck, success. Interim cycles every 7, 14, 21 years Changes sign approx. every 2.5 years, giving us a new focus.
Chiron	50/51 yrs	Woundings, vulnerabilities, healing, teaching, cleansing. Interim cycles every 12½, 25, 37½ years.
Uranus	84 yrs	Separation, change of consciousness, technology/invention. Interim cycles every 21, 42, 63 years. Changes sign approx. every 7-8 years, giving us a new focus.

Neptune	165 yrs		Spirituality, faith, addiction, victim, inspiration, flow. Can spend up to 14 years in one sign, affecting an entire generation with a single focus, depending on sign.
Pluto	248 yrs		Transformation, deep emotions, power, sharing, sex. Can spend between 12 and 30 years in one sign, affecting an entire generation with a single focus, depending on sign.

Chapter 10 – Journey to godhood/ascension and back to Source

What actually is godhood, also known as 'ascension'? Godhood is the state of being a god, either in the higher dimensions or on Earth. Humans are being trained to enter godhood and become gods, just as priests are trained to enter the priesthood and practise as priests. In the process of entering godhood, the human's consciousness is almost completely transformed, and they will think, feel, and act quite differently from when they were a human. It might sound a bit like brainwashing, and in truth the human brain *is* washed and cleansed of unloving ways and limiting beliefs, so that, as a god, the being can go on to bring love, harmony, and amazing progress to humanity and the universe.

The process of getting to godhood is often called an ascension journey. The human must ascend the metaphorical spiritual mountain, or elevate themselves up the Ribbon of Consciousness to higher levels of frequencies. It is consciousness that undertakes the journey, not the physical body, although many humans feel called to climb mountains in a symbolic nod to their spiritual challenge.

The gods are often referred to as Ascended Masters because they have completed their ascension journey and thereby achieved their godhood. In the Buddhist tradition, getting to godhood or ascension is referred to as 'Enlightenment'.

This journey can be completed either on Earth or in the higher realms, as humans or as spirits. All are encouraged to take the path to godhood at any time and in any location. What exactly does this journey entail, and what is it like for a human once they achieve godhood and become a god?

There are three types of human on Earth at present;

1. A human who has not yet become a god (most of the population)
2. A human-turned-god who has become a god whilst living on Earth (not many of these as yet but increasing rapidly)
3. A god-human who has incarnated on Earth at birth as a god in human form (quite a number of these)

Let us examine the process of a human in becoming a god, and what it is like for a human-turned-god to be living on Earth.

The human journey to godhood/ascension

Our whole lifetime on this planet is a journey towards godhood, a human becoming a god, moving our default level of awareness up the Ribbon of Consciousness, out of the human dimension and into the dimension of our soul and the gods. We don't have to physically die to do this, nor does our physical body become like a god with supernatural powers. (Oh, we wish!) Our human consciousness becomes god consciousness, and with that will come an increase in our power, our love, and our wisdom. But we won't find ourselves physically flying through the air, teleporting through wormholes, or instantly manifesting a new car or next meal, not while we are still journeying on First Earth, anyway.

To earn our godhood it is necessary to go through an arduous training program customised for us by higher beings, for gods are strong, resilient, capable, loving at all times, and wise beyond measure, and we humans have much to learn and a great deal of fortitude to gain. This training program takes many years. It begins when a human steps onto their spiritual path, opening their mind and heart to the possibilities of the divine realm. The training can be completed within one lifetime, but sometimes takes place over several lifetimes, depending on the progress of the student.

In the past century, training has been fast-tracked so that more humans than ever can be transformed into gods. It's not that the gods have lowered their standards for entry into godhood, but that many more people are now committed to their spiritual path and the discipline it takes to become a god. They have probably had previous lifetimes as a religious or spiritual devotee, which has given them a good foundation for this final program of transmogrification.

I myself had a fairly recent incarnation where my life was dedicated to helping establish a new kind of religion, and in at least one earlier life I helped to spread Christianity, and before that I was a paganist and involved with the Druids.

We briefly examined this training program in chapter 3 on Soul Graduation, and the steps along this journey as it related to merging with our soul at each stage of progression. Now let's look at it again to understand what is entailed in getting to godhood.

1. <u>Spiritual training</u>: Human steps onto spiritual path. Trained by the spirit and soul that the human is born with.
2. <u>Ascension/godhood training</u>: When deemed ready for it, human enters training program for ascension/godhood, merging with current soul and then trained by next higher-level soul and the gods.
3. <u>Entering godhood</u>: At the culmination of godhood/ascension training, human consciousness becomes god consciousness and ascends into godhood, merging with current soul and then trained by next higher-level soul and the gods. Human becomes a god but with limited capacity at first.

The following is a more detailed description of the above summarised steps.

STEP 1: Spiritual training

Once we step onto the spiritual path, there will be years of training, mostly by our soul and sometimes by the gods. Our commitment and aptitude for godhood are tested, our potential is highlighted, and many of our deepest fault lines are brought to the surface to be repaired. At the end of this period, our human consciousness merges with our soul's consciousness and we progress to the next level up on our Ribbon.

A new soul from higher up our Ribbon is now available to mentor us, a soul with higher consciousness. It's up to us how far and how fast we evolve. Staying in the lower dimensions or moving up to the higher dimensions is our own choice.

For myself, this was an eight-year period where my life was tumultuous to say the least. I moved interstate, gave up my career in IT, and turned my focus full time to learning about spirituality, metaphysics, and healing, and to teaching this also. This was my own particular journey and it's not necessarily going to be similar for anyone else. We all have unique purposes and pathways to complete, and every journey will be different, and what people are called upon to deal with will vary individually. There were three different gods who mentored me during this period, one for the first five years, one for the next two or so years, and a senior one for the final six months.

The gods have told me that over half the planet have now stepped onto their spiritual path and are involved in this training. I find this immensely encouraging! Many people will have no idea that this is what is happening to them, but their souls are working with them just the same, even though the human is not conscious of it. Earth is essentially a training school for humans to become gods, whether people realise this or not. The gods work with people across the dimensions from their higher perspective, and also by incarnating into human form themselves to lead humans from the front.

STEP 2: Training for ascension/godhood

When the gods ascertain that we are ready for promotion and are totally committed to our path, then we are invited to join the ascension/godhood training program as a student, and taken under the wings of either one particular god or several of them. I myself had multiple higher gods mentoring me, and I loved discovering their diverse personalities and talents.

Our ascension/godhood training begins when we move the higher end of our Ribbon of Consciousness across the bridge between Earth and Heaven, between the human world and the higher invisible dimensions.

Training is now ramped up, and we are put fully under the pump to dig out any vulnerabilities and misalignments with our truth.

We are now also carrying our merged soul's consciousness, and this can bring out all manner of 'snakes in the snake pit' that we hadn't encountered before. The reason this occurs is because the boundaries to more of our history are unveiled and we can now see into past lives, habits, and beliefs that we hadn't had to deal with before.

While we are undergoing this onerous training for our godhood, our consciousness is going back and forth across that bridge, gradually moving more and more of our Ribbon over the bridge. Along the way, we achieve minor and major milestones in our evolution towards godhood, going through gateways that take us to the next level of training and learning.

One of the ways I often experienced going to a new level was by finding myself in meditation careening over a waterfall. The Masters invented many ingenious ways to get me to go over, once I had twigged what the sound of rushing water meant if I was in a boat on a river. Usually I landed safely down below, but once I did crash land and the very next day on Earth, I ended up in hospital with a slipped disc. Obviously I didn't handle that particular evolutionary jump very well! The good news is (apart from my slipped disc having healed) that once we get to full godhood and maintain it, we no longer need to go over any waterfalls.

Once we get the bottom end of our Ribbon across the bridge, that is, the full extent of our consciousness has moved across, only then do we get to achieve full godhood. During my own training period, I often received images of a bridge, and I saw my spirit as pulsing filaments of light moving across, like glimpses of lightning. It was very heartening.

The challenges can be awesome, in both senses of this word. It was a rough ride for myself, over another eight-year period, and although I survived, I felt I didn't do so with much dignity and gracefulness, but more like I had been pulled through a hedge backwards. I have never cried so much in all my life. It certainly teaches us humility!

But in order to be a god, we must be tough, resilient, independent, and able to withstand any crisis. It's no good giving the management of our planet to a god who is going to buckle under the weight of responsibility, duty, hard work, difficulty, and complexity. Although a god needs to be as lovely as a rose, they also need to be as hard as steel and as flexible as rubber, all at the same time. (Now you might understand why I cried so much!)

I am certainly not unique or special in achieving godhood. It is not to boast that I state it here quite publicly but to let people know that this is where humanity is heading. There are quite a few of us now on Earth, and more and more are celebrating this milestone every year. One day it will become the norm, and it will be abnormal to still be a human. These will be the ones who are being left behind and who will suffer from the elevated frequencies that will be coursing through our planet and the solar system as the First and Second Earths merge and then split apart again.

STEP 3: Entering godhood

At the end of ascension/godhood training we are promoted to the next level on our Ribbon of Consciousness. We merge with our current soul's consciousness and receive another new higher soul from our own Ribbon of Consciousness to mentor us for this next phase. At this stage, we have achieved ascension, or godhood, and, to all intents and purposes, we have become a god. Our body is still human but we are now deemed to carry god consciousness and we have won our godly crown. At first, we will be given limited capacity to act as a god, but as we prove ourselves, our reach will be expanded.

What is it like for us as a human-turned-god once we reach godhood? When our consciousness enters godhood, everything changes for us as a human, and yet at the same time nothing changes. We are still walking around in a human body and living a fairly normal human life. It is our consciousness that has now changed, and we will be seeing the world with new eyes and new heart. We become a god in a human body. We will be ultra conscious of our role and our mission in making a difference to the planet, and teaching all around us how to be a better person and ultimately helping them to become gods themselves. All gods help to train the next generation of gods coming behind them.

It is a serious transition to step into the shoes of a god. Although we don't physically die (although some people might choose to do so), we are opting to leave behind almost everything that makes us human. We can still live in a house, drive a car, have a partner and children, pursue a career, eat food, and swim in the ocean, but we have let go most, if not all, of the limiting beliefs we had as part of our human thinking. We will still do regular human things, but we will no longer have a regular human mind. We should now be thinking, feeling, and acting like a god at all times, with love, wisdom, and godly power (although this is usually still a work-in-progress for the newer gods!).

Even though we still have a physical body, we cannot return to being a mere mortal. It is difficult to make the jump to godhood, and one of the rewards is that our body is now divine and remains so. Nothing can be the same again, and we will feel the tremendous changes between us and our family, friends, and the community. For a while there can sometimes be some bitterness at all that has been left behind, because this new role usually comes not without major sacrifices, and we may still be feeling vulnerable at all the shedding of skin we have done to reveal our god selves underneath.

Chiron advises us not to weep or feel self-pity but to reflect on our journey as we pack up our old life. It has made us what we are, and we should be elated at our progress into godhood. We will be gaining more than we are losing. But it can take a while for our victory to sink in and we may be feeling overwhelmed. We shouldn't be falsely humble, as we would have worked extremely hard to get to this level. We need to put our shoulders back, take a deep breath, and tell ourselves it is now our time to shine in the sun. Instead of dirges there should be fanfare. Happily, we will find that we lose interest in living life in the old human way. Our desire now is to live above this level, out of the muck and mire, in the purer and more loving environs of the higher dimensions.

There will certainly be new challenges once we reach godhood, but with this will come a new kind of peace and fulfilment. We have been waiting for this victory all our life, so now it is here we shouldn't deny it but take the opportunity to celebrate and appreciate our success. It is time for optimism and vigour, new perspectives, and expecting changes for the better. Our new consciousness will be shining with our godhood. Life will take on a new sparkle and we may be feeling like we could take on the world. Heaven is now appearing for us.

Even though we have been triumphant in getting past the winning post, we won't be able to rest for long. We must no longer face backwards but look to the future and all that needs to be done in this world to awaken folks. The universe is ever-changing, and we didn't reach godhood to just sit in the corner and waste our talents.

We will need to continually prove our worth as a god and keep our frequency and standards high. It will necessitate leaving the comfort of our homes and participating in life fully, expanding our horizons, and growing our consciousness daily. As human-turned-god we don't cease evolving and learning, and higher gods will often download and merge their consciousnesses with us to broaden our scope and abilities and to inspire us with new kinds of thinking. We act as their agent, as well as agent for our own soul.

Many people wish for stardom in their lifetime, and we have reached this when we are able to stand as a god on Earth. Not only have we achieved victory for ourselves and our own consciousness, but it is a victory for humanity itself; it goes to prove that humans can indeed become gods.

As yet, there are not too many of these human-turned-gods, but numbers are growing every year. It is the destiny of everyone on Earth (and in the spirit world) to get to godhood one day, even though it may take another thousand years to achieve this. All of the human race will need to be transformed into the god consciousness that initially gave it life.

The next time these human-turned-gods incarnate on Earth, now as god-humans, they will be fully-fledged gods from birth, with god DNA and more powers and capabilities than they are able to currently possess.

In Part 3, we take a look at how it will be to live in the New World as a newly-created god.

A god-human who has incarnated at birth as a god in human form

When a god is born on Earth as a baby, it will have slightly different DNA than that of a human. It gives the god more protection and immunity, additional strength, physically and emotionally, and higher mental clarity and psychic abilities. But this god will still adopt a human body and participate in regular human activities. The more senior gods on Earth, I am told, do seem to have supernatural powers, but it's not been my experience to witness these myself (as yet), therefore I don't feel qualified to write about them here (maybe in a future book?). However, I will say that they are exceptionally good at manifesting whatever they need for themselves and to support their work, which could seem like some magical superpower to the rest of us.

For the first years of their life, a god born on Earth may not realise their true status. They will have a spirit self, just as humans do, but once they rediscover Heaven and get their consciousness over the bridge to the higher dimensions, they will merge with their spirit self and then have only their soul to guide them. This is also true for humans-turned-god, once they have settled into their godhood properly.

This means that gods on Earth are actually both their human self and spirit self at the same time which gives them quite an advantage over ordinary humans. They *are* their spirits! They need to get used to the idea that their consciousness lives in a higher dimension, and step right into it and be there with all their senses. Incarnated gods can make the mistake of viewing the higher dimension as being a separate place over the bridge from Earth, a place they have to visit instead of being there in every moment with their consciousness. Because a god is not separate from their spirit, they travel as their spirit quite consciously to other realms, just as easily as we humans might take a flight to another part of our world.

The gods inform us that there are quite a number of them on Earth at this present time, but they are not making themselves known for reasons I have described in earlier chapters. We would be hard-pressed to differentiate between a true full-blooded god and a normal human being, but the tell-tale signs are there for those who are aware of godly traits. There are a few prominent people in the world today that I have recognised as being true gods, but of course I am not going to reveal them and blow their cover! You will know them by their deeds and awesome, loving, steady presence.

The return journey back to Source

Once we have attained our godhood by getting our full consciousness across the bridge to the higher dimensions, paradoxically it is then time to come back over the bridge and make a return journey. To explain this requires that we map out our journey from the very start of being born into consciousness, the beginning of our evolution into who we are right now.

Our Source, one of the creator gods, first created the thread of consciousness that eventually became the consciousness we are today. Therefore, in truth, we started life as a pure and high-level god. Our consciousness then went on to have many incarnations, on this planet and others, in physical human-like bodies, in spirit, and other forms too.

During these incarnations, we have not always led the good life, and we have inevitably fallen into darkness and taken on board into our consciousness many beliefs and instincts that are not conducive with being a god. Eventually, our consciousness fell out of the higher dimensions, no longer able to get across the bridge between Heaven and Earth. This was exacerbated when some thread of our god consciousness was used within the new human race that was being created.

Some of our consciousness at the very top of our Ribbon may have been able to retain a sliver of our godhood, but when too much of our Ribbon is flapping around in the lower human dimension, then we are ejected from Heaven and required to find our way Home again across the bridge. This entails getting all of our Ribbon of Consciousness back over the bridge again, into godhood or ascension. Some consciousnesses fell out of Heaven hook, line, and sinker, and to this day may not even remember there is a bridge, let alone be able to find it to get across.

So, the odyssey from our initial Source has taken many millennia and many paths and incarnations. Once we find the bridge, get across it fully with all our Ribbon, and achieve our godhood, then we are asked to turn around and face back the way we came and make the return journey.

It is now our mission to revisit every lifetime that we experienced as a human and as a spirit, on the way here to ascension, and to deal with every issue that remains unresolved, and to put right our past deeds and past relationships. It is not as though we will relive every life as though it were Groundhog Day, but similar scenarios will be created by our soul to highlight the issues that we must face.

While this might seem like a daunting task, we must remember that we are now in the shoes of a god, and that we will have new clarity, compassion, and confidence, and it should be easier to solve our difficulties than it was when we were still of human or lower consciousness.

We will continue with this journey, evolving our consciousness along the way, merging with our souls to higher and higher levels, until we return one day to the Source of who we are, and become a creator god ourselves eventually.

As I was writing this chapter, I was given a beautiful image of our journey to godhood and the return journey back to our Source. We start off from Source, at the very beginning of our adventure as consciousness, as a tapestry of pure white yarns. A thread unravels with each incarnation, and we gain experiences and colours in that individual strand. Once we reach godhood, we start to reconstruct our tapestry on the return journey, pulling all our threads back together again, with all their dyes, hues, and stories, and with love.

My own Source had this to say on the subject of the return journey when I asked about it.

"The first path is a spiral path and it takes us up the mountain to the top. This is where godhood is to be found. When we have climbed our own personal mountain, surmounted all our obstacles and challenges and reached the very pinnacle which is required of us, then begins the journey back down that path. We are revisiting every scenario that played out on the way up.

Of course, we are speaking here of thousands upon thousands, if not millions, of years of evolution of our consciousness. And so, it is not a short journey back to the starting line, and we will be involved in this in many many lifetimes. This will involve revisiting every lifetime, whether it was played out on Earth, or in the spirit dimension, or in other galaxies. All will need to be accounted for.

And so, although a part of you will reside in the gods' dimension once you make it to the top of the mountain and to godhood, there are now many parts of your consciousness that will now make their way down the mountain and live out many lives at once—threads of you, as you have described them, threads of you taking on personas and roles, threads of yourself in action at any one time, playing out over several dimensions.

And when you are a god you will become more aware of these other threads playing out apart from yourself. And you can even jump into the consciousness of the other threads of yourself and try to bring some love and wisdom there. You are a team of threads, an army. You can go help each other out. Part of you lives in the gods' dimension, part of you lives on the Second Earth, part of you lives on the human Earth, and you are privy to all these parts of you at any time, and you can bring your consciousness to bear on all of them.

You are dealing with all the situations that you were involved with once before and which did not result in the right consequences. So, you are tying up loose ends, loose threads, with love, until all has been forgiven and smoothed over and there is nothing left triggering you off in that situation or with those people.

Yes, some of these lifetimes are jolly difficult to put right, and perhaps you will have to leave it for a while and come back to it at a later time. These lifetimes do not have to be dealt with in chronological sequence, but you will have to knock them over one by one, and all of them eventually.

You can play a strategic game here and target those lives where the people are more evolved, for then you are liable to have more success. If you go back to lifetimes where there was little awareness, then your job will be made much more difficult. But all the while be aware that you are a god now and your awareness is heightened and your consciousness is fine-tuned. So do not think this an impossible task but merely the righting of wrongs, the redressing of negativity that you have brought into the world. The universe is all about balance, and you are balancing out your deeds.

There is no return journey yet for those who have not reached their godhood, but they can seek to do all in their power to lay good foundations on their way up to the top so that when they revisit, after they have attained their godhood, then all will go much more smoothly for them."[16]

---

16. From channelling by my Beloved Source, 25 June 2019

To complete the picture of our evolutionary process, the following summarises the training levels we undergo after we attain our godhood. These will take us millennia to achieve and will be experienced as part of our return journey back to our Source.

STEP 4: Being a god, training for starhood

Once we have settled into our godhood and are performing well to the standards required of the gods, we will be invited to join the star training program. This is a very long-term period of instruction, over many lifetimes, where we move up through the ranks of the gods to senior levels and take on many responsibilities for managing our planet. Then we are educated to take over a major role such as embodying a planet or some other cosmic body, and finally we are trained to become a sun, or star, ourselves.

STEP 5: Being a star, training for creator godhood

At the culmination of star training, god consciousness becomes star consciousness. The god embodies as a physical sun or star itself. The god/star will create its own solar system around it and manage this for many millions of years. During this time, the god/star is still in training, learning to become a creator god of the universe.

STEP 6: Being a creator god

The final step in the evolution of any consciousness is to become a creator god. At the culmination of creator god training, star consciousness becomes creator god consciousness, pure non-physical consciousness which can create and manage an entire universe along with other creator gods. This, of course, is the top of the evolutionary tree for a consciousness, for the level above this is the One God. I don't know if the One God ever steps down and allows a senior Creator God to take over the helm. Perhaps they merge together? It's beyond my pay grade to know this.

PART TWO

TOOLS OF CONSCIOUSNESS

(Using consciousness to live a better life)

PART TWO – Introduction

What are the Tools of Consciousness?

Part Two is dedicated to applying our consciousness. Now that we better understand what consciousness consists of, we can learn how to use it to live a healthier and happier life. Chiron calls this our Toolbox of Consciousness, and, like any manual for a craftsperson, we are going to take a look at all the tools and how to handle them, and when and where to utilise them.

If we aren't so happy with our current world, we can use these tools at any time and change the basic composition of our consciousness. This will then alter the source of our thinking that gets reflected back to us as our reality. When we understand the fundamental building blocks of our consciousness then we can advance on the road to godhood, and have immense power at our fingertips, and a mind as potent and extraordinary as any magic wand.

My Beloved Source pulled me up on an issue to do with my Toolbox, which is fitting to share here. I was experiencing a great deal of trouble with electrical items, and their batteries in particular, which seemed to be drained of their power at an alarming rate. Remote controls kept dying, smoke alarms kept going off at unsociable hours, laptops and phones were misbehaving, and just about anything electrical in my possession was becoming a nightmare to operate.

Beloved Source told me that I was using the power of the physical world, as in electricity and batteries, as the source of my power instead of utilising the power of the universe which is incredibly more forceful and delineated. She said I needed to use my tools of consciousness to manifest resources instead of using the power of the human will and mind. She told me I had been trying to use the force of my human self alone, which obviously isn't much, while the power of the universe is much much greater, and even when I feel I have no control over things at a human level, the universe always has control and can take command, *if I let it*.

A scene from the movie *Doctor Strange* highlights the above. Doctor Strange is battling to learn the metaphysical arts.

The Ancient One, the Sorceress Supreme, says to him, "You cannot beat a river into submission. You have to surrender to its currents and use its power as your own."

Doctor Strange questions this. "I control it by surrendering control? That doesn't make any sense!"

"Not everything does. Not everything has to!" the Ancient One replies. "Surrender! Silence your ego and your power will rise."

The tools of our consciousness are available to us 24/7, and we can always depend on them. If we work with our Toolbox every day, we will definitely make progress, even if imperceptibly, but we will become a skilled craftsperson very quickly if we practise, and will be able to put our hand on the right tool for the job in any circumstance.

Our consciousness is a powerhouse of energies and healing tools. It is the Toolbox of the gods for every occasion, creating this universe around us.

Chapter 11 – Vibrational levels

One of the main tools of consciousness is being able to connect with the unseen universe. In order to do this we must begin by understanding how vibrational levels, or frequencies of being, play a huge part in who or what we connect with.

In chapter 3 we covered how our consciousness is not only like a ribbon connecting the human earthly world with the higher worlds, but that the Ribbon of Consciousness can also be viewed like a dial on a radio with all its frequencies and bandwidths. Each wavelength dials us into a different persona within our consciousness, ranging from the inner personas of our human self at the lower end, to the higher entities of our spirit, soul, gods, and angels, and right up to our creator god Source at the highest end.

It's not that we need to know the wavelength of whomever we are trying to connect with, but that we need to be vibrating at a similar level in order to get through to them. We need to be 'on the same wavelength' as it were, and 'in tune' with them.

We know from experience that if we try to tune into a radio station and we are slightly off that wavelength, all we will get is a fuzzy reception of static. The same goes for tuning into the divine wavelengths. We ourselves are the tuning fork. The vibrational level of our consciousness is what determines who or where we will reach. It's not that we will need to be at that level permanently, but for the duration of the broadcast and communication some part of our consciousness will need to be at the desired vibrational level.

I say 'some part of our consciousness' because our consciousness exists at many different levels of vibration at the same time. At the lower end of our Ribbon, our inner personas are vibrating at many different levels, with our horrid or gloomy personas at very low vibes, and the nicest and happiest parts of ourselves at an upper part of the Ribbon with higher vibes. Our spirit is at a higher level again, and if we tap into that level we can then bounce up even higher to reach the gods. We are, at the same time, at the bottom, middle, and top of our Ribbon of Consciousness, with the threads across the width of the Ribbon like the various levels of vibration.

Not all of our personas need to get up to the required high level of vibration; and that's not even possible for the most part. It takes many lifetimes to raise all parts of ourselves up to a high level, and then we are at the level of the gods. We just need to get one part of ourself up there, and we don't even have to know which part.

Each persona and level of our being has a frequency signature, its own frequency or tone, like a note of music. If we listen to the whole Ribbon of Consciousness together, it is a string of notes. Therefore, each individual is a piece of unique music, and this is how we are recognised on the higher planes in our spirit form, by our musical signature and the quality and hues of our light.

Every group of people and community and country has its own distinct vibrational 'music', and sometimes we aren't on the same wavelength and don't fit in. In that case we need to move on and find the right place with the right vibrational level for us. Sometimes, if we raise or lower our vibes substantially, we may find we no longer fit in with the wavelength of the original group or community, and so we would need to relocate to a place or group that vibrates at our new wavelength.

So, to be able to connect with the spirit world, we firstly need to be in a space of higher consciousness or higher vibration. If we are sitting in our lower consciousness, in our lower bandwidth at the bottom end of our radio dial, it's very unlikely that we will be able to hear anything that is broadcast on the higher wavelengths.

Sitting in our lower vibrational world feels like we are in our own bubble. We may be very happy there, but we won't be very aware of the world around us, or feel any sense of connection to it. Usually, in fact, we will feel very disconnected from people and society in general. There may be a level of dis-ease about us; life perhaps doesn't feel comfortable or flowing. We may have to make great effort to keep our head afloat, or our relationships on an even keel. There is often a feeling of discontent, and a sense that something, if only we knew what, was missing from our life.

Dwelling in higher vibrational consciousness, on the other hand, we are closer to the gods and on their wavelength. Life, although it may still have its unenviable challenges and tribulations, provides a sense of satisfaction and meaning. Generally, we will feel kind, loving, and considerate towards others and be willing and motivated to make changes to ourself and our environment for the highest good. Loving ourself and others is the foundation of higher consciousness.

Many people wait for the divine worlds to come to them, but it is us that needs to get ourselves to the divine worlds. We must step up, through our consciousness, into the vicinity of the higher realms by raising our own vibrational levels. We will need to get ourself into this higher vibrational space in order to communicate with our soul, or the gods or angels, or go off astral travelling in the higher dimensions. Even the most senior of gods, if they were in a bad mood (and they do experience this at times), cannot connect properly with the spirit world if their vibrations are too low.

Just as people work and learn better when they are in a relaxed and contented state, and they also make better decisions, this high vibe state is the best way to connect with the soul and the higher dimensions.

What exactly are vibrations?

Vibrational levels are actually electromagnetic radiation wavelengths, also known as frequencies or bandwidths. There are long, slow waves and short, fast waves and everything in between. These wavelengths include AM radio, FM radio, TV, cell phones, microwaves, x-rays, gamma rays, infrared rays, ultraviolet rays and visible light. These are all frequencies or vibrational levels.

The Earth has a vibrational level and we ourselves, as a body and a consciousness, have a bandwidth of vibrational levels, as described earlier. All of us are vibrating at different frequencies or wavebands, within ourselves and from each other.

The faster and shorter the waves, the higher the frequency. Our souls and the gods vibrate at very high and fast frequencies. This is the reason they are invisible. An analogy would be to visualise the blades of an electric fan. We can see the blades when the speed is slow, but when the speed is fast the blades are invisible. Humans vibrate at low and slow frequencies which is why we are visible to each other.

There is no discernible dividing line between our physical dimension and the higher dimensions. One slides into the other like the froth on a cappuccino sits on top of a cup of coffee. There is no physical portal that we need to go through, no physical door, gateway, or wormhole. The vibrations gradually increase, and we move imperceptibly from one dimension into another.

If, when we try to connect with the spirit world, our level of vibration is low, then we will connect only with our own inner personas, or the lowest parts of consciousness of other people. The quality of the advice cannot be vouched for at this level, and can even be detrimental to us if we heeded it. If we want to speak with our soul to gain better wisdom, we will need to get higher than low frequency human personas. In order to connect with gods and angels, we will need to be in a very high vibrational state (again, only one part of our consciousness needs to be in this state.)

So, if we have set our intention for who we wish to speak with, plus our vibrational level matches that level we are trying to dial into, our consciousness will be instantly transported to that level of higher dimension and to the spirit entities that abide there. We will have tuned into the radio station desired.

If we don't know what vibrational level we are sitting at, then we get transported to the level of whichever persona of our consciousness is at the forefront at the time, our default frequency. So, if we are upset or tired or angry when we try to connect, then it stands to reason that we won't be accessing a high-level radio station but a low-level one.

Let's examine, then, how it feels to be low vibrational, and then we'll look at how it feels to be high vibrational. We need to know the difference as this is essential if we are to successfully connect with our soul and the gods.

What do low vibes feel or look like?
- Miserable, sad, depressed, crying
- Drowning in water or mud
- Lethargic, can't get out of bed, no hope
- Tired, exhausted, illness
- Body/physical issues
- Afraid, doubting, distrustful
- No goals, unmotivated, purposeless, unfulfilled
- Angry, blaming others, grumpy, revengeful, victim, bully
- Feel like an outsider, rejected, abandoned, don't belong, lonely, disconnected
- Lack self-worth, self-esteem
- Lack respect for self or others
- Bad relationships, uncommunicative
- Heavy, burdened, overwhelmed
- Rigid, stubborn, closed heart
- Resistance to doing one's work or mission
- Going against the prevalent energies of the day
- Life out of control, not on top of anything
- Psychotic, mental, stressed, nervous, anxious, can't cope
- Not very aware, in own bubble
- Dazed, forgetful, confused, muddled, fragmented, foggy
- Drunk, drugged, out of mind
- Hoarding, messy, dirty, unhygienic
- Hectic, too busy, crazy life
- Not able to manifest dreams or resources to support self

Low vibrations are the outcome of feeling unhappy about life.

What do high vibes feel or look like?
- Happy, contented, peaceful, harmonious, calm
- In the flow, moving like music, open-hearted
- Soft, flexible, not rigid
- Loving everything, accepting, feel loved in return

- Kind, compassionate, generous, merciful, wise, powerful
- Good balance in life
- Not triggered off all the time
- Healthy—physically, emotionally, mentally, not on medication, natural
- Clean, organised, efficient
- Lightness of being, floating on air, on top of the world
- Clear mind, get insights and intuition, inspired
- Feel and give love, open-hearted, nurturing, giving
- Have self-worth, self-esteem, proud of self, feel valued
- Belong, participate in life, communicative
- Joyful, excited, passionate, life feels rosy
- On top of things, in control
- Feel strong physically, emotionally, mentally
- Tedious jobs done with love. Feel motivated and eager
- Tackle issues easily, with power. Take responsibility for them
- Good relationships
- Very aware, considerate
- Sense of purpose and meaning in life, goals for future
- Respectful, appreciative, grateful
- Feel supported by earthly world and divine world
- Able to manifest dreams and resources

High vibrations generally:

- Make us feel good about ourself and our life
- Broaden the mind so we can understand higher worlds
- Help us stop focusing on the minutiae of tedious life
- Raise us up to new levels of being and evolution
- Help us to understand ourself and others better, and the gods too
- Make us feel like we are in love, as if love is all around us
- Give us romance even if we have no partner. Feel in love with the whole world
- Give us a new partner in our spirit/soul. Feel love for them

- Help us out of our stuckness and sickness
- Give us new clarity and insights
- Offer new levels of reality, a new life
- Help change our attitude and perspective
- Set us on the right track to fulfilling our destiny
- Make us want to set the world to rights

Why we should keep checking our vibe level

It's important to keep checking the state of our vibrations throughout the day because we will not be able to connect with our soul and other high entities, and vice versa, if we have low vibrational levels, and then we miss out on all the guidance that could be coming our way. Are we in the higher world or the lower world or zigzagging between the two? We could compare ourself with the checklists of low and high vibes above, and get a feel for how far up (or down) we are along the Ribbon of Consciousness, remembering we could have parts of ourself at several different levels at the same time, but in any moment, one will take precedence and be our default.

We often don't realise just how low our vibes have fallen. It only takes a grumpy customer, a recalcitrant child, or an upsetting text message to set us off down the slippery slope into the low vibe pit where our inner personas are just waiting with glee to add to our low mood with their gloomy or angry perspectives of the world. This only serves to take us down even further.

So, we need to check if we are feeling like an angel or a monster, and take action to raise our vibrations as quickly as possible before we sink without trace beneath the waves (vibrational waves). If we fall down a mountainside it takes a long time to haul ourself back up to the top again, so we want to make sure we don't fall in the first place. The longer we stay down in the low vibrations, the longer it takes to get back out again. We become stuck there, and it takes an almighty effort to heave ourself out, like an animal stuck in a muddy swamp.

If we have previously been at a high level of vibration and we allow ourselves to fall down our Ribbon of Consciousness to a low place, we will find we lose all previously gained status and privileges, and, most of all, we will acutely notice the disappearance of the great love and harmony that had surrounded us before.

Our energy levels and vibrations not only affect everyone around us but they also rebound on ourselves and give us a taste of our own medicine. How often does it happen that we are angry and then we cut ourself or have an accident? We need to become aware of our vibe level and fix it quickly so that our day is not ruined, nor for those around us. Consciousness attracts reality at its own level, so, if our world is not working out for us, we need to raise our vibes and fly with our spirit, and we will notice the difference almost immediately.

How to let go of low vibrations

Many people go through life on autopilot and don't give a thought to whether they are acting out low or high vibes. They may recognise they are acting or reacting badly, but they don't realise they can change their way of thinking and take themselves to a much better state of mind and a happier life. They might blame others for wrecking their lives but we ourselves are the architect of our reality, and our world is created from our own thinking and beliefs.

Most of us know the kind of thinking that keeps us stuck in the same old negative patterns. But we don't have to accept who we are and how we are. We can edit ourselves, adjust our thinking to a higher level, and create a completely different life for ourselves. We need to do maintenance on our minds, and most people never service their consciousness, ever.

Firstly, we need to make a conscious choice to live at the higher level and then start sifting through that thinking and change any faulty programming and beliefs that make us feel in low vibes as outlined above. To get to a higher vibrational level we must throw out all that old 'stinking thinking' and reprogram our mind with new, positive thoughts and beliefs and new supportive programs. How do we go about doing this, apart from visiting a psychologist or hypnotist?

There are many ways of letting go thoughts and beliefs that no longer serve us, and a whole book could be written on this subject alone. We basically need to appraise what stays and what needs to be ditched within our mind. We need to snip away at parts of our Ribbon of Consciousness, especially at the very bottom levels. Our mindfield is like a minefield, you could say, and we need to clear away those explosive devices that regularly set us off!

One method of letting go that the gods have taught me concerns segments. Imagine that consciousness is like an orange, divided into segments but many millions of them. These segments hold our programming and beliefs that we have accumulated over our lifetime. Some segments have gone bad or mouldy, and these unsavoury segments lower our vibrational level. We can take out a segment (like lifting out a printer cartridge), check it and clean it, or replace it with a new one filled with new beliefs and programming.

For instance, a segment might contain the thought, 'I'm sick and tired of going to work every day.' This is obviously a low vibrational thought and probably results in us actually feeling sick and tired physically. We could clean up the thought by replacing it with, 'I'm glad I have a job to go to every day.' Or we could get rid of the low vibe segment altogether and install a new segment such as, 'I'm going to find myself a new job, one that I really love and utilises my skills.'

When our segments are clean and healthy, there is no physical or emotional pain because we clear out all triggers that set us off. So, we can take out all the segments of our consciousness that don't conform to the new way we wish to think. It could be all of them! We don't need to know which segments—just set our intention to clear the ones at fault; our consciousness will do the rest.

I quite like to do this letting go meditation by imagining myself in a huge warehouse with racks of shelving full of bins, and I go around the shelves checking out the labels and pulling the bins out if they contain faulty beliefs, and throwing the contents onto a bonfire outside. Sometimes, I go down into an imaginary basement in my house, or up into the attic, and I throw out all the stuff there that needs to go, down a big chute that connects to a Black Hole.

The methods of cleaning out our consciousness are limited only by our imagination. We might think, "How could this possibly make any difference to how I feel and act?" but I assure you that this is exactly how consciousness gets to be transformed—by us going in there and poking around and making changes.

It doesn't take years of psychotherapy to achieve these changes, but only minutes of our time. If we are familiar with the methods of NLP (neuro linguistic programming), then this process is very similar, but in truth we don't even have to know NLP or any other modality to change our consciousness; all we need to do is have the intention to make a change, ask our soul to help us achieve this, and enter the playground of our consciousness and see where our soul takes us. (See the next chapter on how to connect with your soul)

After we have disposed of our unhealthy segments, we will instantly feel like a different person. We are no longer weighed down by this old baggage, and we will probably feel like we are floating on air. Our consciousness is able to rise up to a higher level of vibration, and from that elevated vantage point will be able to see and breathe more clearly. Letting go of our low vibrations automatically raises our vibrational level so that all will begin to change for us.

In chapters 19-22 there are further examples of methods of changing our consciousness and letting go techniques.

How to raise vibrations

So, if we're feeling low vibrational, how do we get to raise our vibrations to a higher level? Our thoughts create our reality; therefore, we use our thinking to also raise ourselves up. Below are some of the ways we can raise our vibrational level.

- Ponder on lovely things and images: a rainbow, meadow, flowers, waterfall, sunrise, a baby's laugh, a cat's antics, a lover's eyes, turquoise ocean, graduation, a gold medal
- Dream often of good and serene things
- Step into your dreams. Play out your destiny in your imagination
- Visualise the outcomes you want in life. Feel into your desires
- Be love itself. Not-love holds you down in lower waters

- Love yourself. Love others
- Do good deeds for other people
- Believe in a higher you and a better future. Have hope
- Get creative
- Listen to, or play, beautiful and uplifting music. Go dancing.
- Jettison old programming, beliefs, negative thinking, doubts, anger
- Feel yourself being a bright, shining star or sun. Install that fiery star in your heart
- Ramp up energies in your heart until it's like a ball of fire. Set your world aflame
- Send out waves of love and light. Let your vibrations flow out from your heart star
- Be godly. Have traits of a god. Do tasks expected of a god—transforming humans
- See yourself whole and as you'd like to be, and all situations harmonised
- Utilise meditations, mindfulness, and inner journeys
- Visualise climbing up steps or a mountain, or ascending in an elevator, or lifting off in a balloon or aircraft, or flying like an eagle
- Write a Joy List to lift up your spirits. Write all instances of joy you can remember, and victories and successes. Include favourite movies, books, and places
- What could you do for your soul to make their life better? E.g. not resist so much

Practise raising vibes daily.

Spend time daily getting up to full power and feeding your consciousness with the right kind of thoughts. Raising vibrations is a skill that can be learnt and honed by anyone, and it's essential that everyone do this. But it's like becoming a magician; it's an acquired skill, perfected by plenty of practice. Getting it right doesn't happen overnight; it must be worked on frequently. All have the capability to be a magician; it's not denied to anyone. Taking action to raise our vibes, no matter what our current circumstances, will definitely improve our state of affairs and will set us on the path to creating a magical life. Practising magic attracts more magic from other quarters, and more bounty will flow into our life.

We need to start by noticing when we are in a state of low vibes and then consciously deciding that we don't wish to stay in that state. We can then employ any number of methods to raise ourselves out of our pit. Start with little ways in order to gain some confidence, and notice the relief that comes about almost instantly. It only takes a minute to have a happy thought or stir a pleasant memory. Even if it raises us up only one percent, it is an improvement on how we were feeling before, and it opens the door to more radical advances.

It may be noticed that the lower personas of our consciousness don't want to lift themselves up, and we will have to investigate our thinking to discover why we would want to keep ourselves down. What is the hidden agenda? When we first start to practise raising our vibrations, there is often much resistance from our lower personas as they don't like to change the way they have always operated. Keep practising regardless and develop the skill. Help inner personas to let go of their fears and get all parts of consciousness on board with the goal and all in alignment with it.

When we ourselves understand what it takes to raise our vibrations and we bring about vast and beneficial changes to our lives, then we can teach those around us to do this and improve their lives too. The higher our vibrations, the less we are affected by the vicissitudes of life. This is probably the most useful tool any of us will ever learn in our entire lives.

We need to raise ourselves up daily and fill our hearts with loveliness. When we focus on love then the world reflects only love back at us. The state of our heart and consciousness dictates our vibrational level, and once we can raise it sufficiently high, we can hop to any planet, star, or galaxy and travel the universe, limited only by our vibrational wavelength which is our passport. Our vibrations set us free.

Chapter 12 – Connecting with the unseen universe

In Part One we discussed the unseen beings of the universe; souls and spirits, gods/Ascended Masters, creator gods, the One God, angels, ghosts, lower entities and personas of our consciousness, and even aliens. Therefore, if we wish to connect with any of these beings, how do we go about it? It's not as if we can pick up the phone or Skype them. Is it possible for humans to communicate with each other, the dead, and other disembodied beings, through using ESP and only the abilities of our minds? And how do we differentiate between connecting with our soul, a deceased relative, a god, or some ratbag persona within our own consciousness?

Our consciousness can travel and explore anywhere in the universe, within the vibrational levels we are allowed. It is our high vibrational telescope that is able to see what the human eye cannot capture. It can be everywhere at any time, having experiences other than a human one, and we are encouraged to be an adventurer with our consciousness, exploring the many different worlds out there, some like Earth and some quite strange.

In order to travel in consciousness we merely go within our mind, connecting with our spirit counterpart who is on the same Ribbon of Consciousness as ourself. Our human eyes can't navigate the energy grids of the universe, so we must use the eyes of our spirit and the tools of our consciousness to do so. And there is much to see.

Our spirit self lives in a parallel world (Second Earth) in a higher dimension and leads a different life from us, but, in truth, is just a tiny step away from us. Our spirit consciousness can be said to travel around its domain as a sphere, a vehicle that we could imagine to be like a translucent bubble of light, that contains all the same thoughts and beliefs and fears as we do in human form. We can visualise stepping into our spirit sphere and getting whisked away to experience new and wonderful worlds and ways of being that are part of our spirit's playground.

Initially, we will probably converse with our spirit self as if they were a separate persona from ourselves, but we are one and the same consciousness, each of us playing a role. In time, we will learn to actually jump into our spirit's shoes and act the part of our spirit as we travel the invisible realms quite consciously.

We humans are the ones who must initiate contact with our spirit, not the other way around. Our spirit will just wait in the higher dimensions until the day comes when we acknowledge it and wish to communicate consciously with it. We must take that imperceptible step in consciousness from our world on the First Earth into the higher dimension of the Second Earth, allowing ourself to rise up from our human consciousness level to our spirit's level. It is not difficult to do this. We do it every night when we sleep and even during the day when we daydream. If we can imagine ourselves hopping into a hot air balloon and lifting off, or flying like an eagle over the world, then we are well on our way to imagining ourselves in our spirit sphere vehicle.

It is impossible to travel the universe without our spirit being present too. At first, we need to just let go and be transported, be a passenger and not in control of our 'car'. Over time we will learn how to steer the vehicle ourselves, but this will only come about when our human self and divine spirit self are working hand in hand as one united consciousness.

As we gain more experience, we are allowed to travel beyond the Second Earth into further and stranger worlds and dimensions. Consciousness has its own GPS and will take us to our destination without us having to worry how it works. Without a physical human body, our consciousness can travel anywhere with few limitations and we never get tired or hungry.

We are not only human but we are spirit too, and we need to experience these invisible worlds for ourself, for this is our true home and where we will return to one day. Our journeys in the hidden worlds give us endless adventures and will fill our souls with joy, wisdom, and inspiration, and connect us with all the other souls who are waiting to make our acquaintance in this universe. We need to travel with our spirit regularly as we have much to learn from one another. They are our closest family, and in the higher dimensions we will enjoy discovering other members of our divine family too.

Who or what will we connect with? Unseen beings and dimensions

In the previous chapter we studied how our vibrational level dictates who we connect with in the unseen dimensions and where we might find ourselves. Below is an outline of the beings we might be in contact with through our consciousness, from the highest vibrational level to the lowest (approximately).

- The One God, creator of all universes
- Creator gods of our universe, our Source
- Angels
- Senior gods/Ascended Masters
- Stars, planets (the physical manifested bodies of some senior gods)
- Intermediate gods/Ascended Masters
- Junior gods and humans-turned-gods
- Our soul and the souls of others (living or dead)
- Our spirit and the spirits of others (living or dead)
- Our human lower personas and the lower personas of other humans
- Personas from past lives
- Everything in nature (birds, animals, trees, flowers, mountains, oceans, etc)
- Aliens (could be at any vibrational level—who knows?)

Every person will be different in what they see and hear when they connect. I myself usually have very vivid experiences, as if I have stepped into a movie, but even so, there are times when the scenario is richly coloured and detailed and I can see and hear everything with perfect clarity, and there are other times when it seems as if I am looking through a window that has been smeared with grease, or I can see only with tunnel vision and not anything to either side.

It will depend on the strength of our vibrational signal at the time, and on whether the consciousness we are interacting with wishes for us to see less or more of our surroundings. Often, they want us to focus on one particular thing, and so they blur all the distracting scenes to the sides.

All higher dimensional beings can hear us clearly when we seek to connect with them in our mind. Be aware, they won't always respond right there and then. They may have other methods, more effective methods, of contacting us at a later time. The various ways that the universe can contact us are described in Chapter 15.

In whatever manner we make our contacts, we should take time to ponder on and assimilate all we experience, as quite often full understanding only comes to us later on. I myself write a daily diary of my experiences so that I can join the dots at some future time, sometimes only weeks or months later!

Paradoxically, the higher we reach in the dimensions, the vaguer things generally become because, as humans, we can't hope to sustain that high level of vibration for any length of time. The only reason we can see or hear anything at all at these stellar levels is because the consciousness we are connecting with has usually lowered their vibration so they won't overwhelm us for the duration of our encounter.

Connecting with the One God

In my own case, when I have on the rare occasion had the privilege of speaking with the One God (and, yes, it is possible for us mere mortals to do so!), I just get a sense of magnificent light and Presence; there is no landscape beyond this. The One God doesn't say too many words, but I have always gained a profound knowing as part of the experience, as if God has transferred by osmosis into my consciousness all I need to know. Afterwards, I am normally at a loss to transcribe exactly what God has said to me, because it's arrived as a whole package of knowing, as if I've been downloaded with the contents of a whole book rather than heard a few spoken sentences.

There was one memorable time, though, when the One God taught me a most wonderful lesson. I was shown a big lily pond in the pouring rain, complete with croaking frogs. A dragonfly had fallen into the water, and its wings had become wet and it couldn't fly or clamber back onto the lily pad it had been perched on.

God swept a hand downwards and scooped up the little insect. The bedraggled dragonfly began to fight and resist and squeal and cry as the hand carried it over the waters to the other side of the pond. Gently, God's hand put the dragonfly down onto a big lily pad, safe and sound and dry, and even the sun came out again at that moment. God told the dragonfly, "I was only moving you to a better place."

The One God has appeared to me at times, not because I have set my intention to meet Him/Her, but totally out of the blue and in a complete surprise, but a delightful one.

How have I known that it was the One God? That's an interesting question that I can't really answer. There was just a knowing each time that this was the Universal God. I guess our consciousness knows these things at the soul level, and we must just believe and go along with it. These times have felt quite different from connections with other gods, even creator gods. It is as if the whole episode takes place in a blaze of great light, and while my human self is experiencing vagueness and opacity, my higher self is receiving great clarity at her level. I come away feeling drenched by the experience of the light and love of God's Presence but unable to explicitly quantify it from my human perspective.

Other people's experience of meeting the One God could be quite different from mine, so I recommend not having any expectations at all of what it's like to meet God or any of the gods or angels or other entities.

Connecting with our Source

I love to connect with my Beloved Source at the very top end of my Consciousness Ribbon, something I have only been able to do within the past several years. She is a creator god, the originator of my thread of consciousness way back in the annals of history. I always refer to her as a 'she' but she is not really any gender at all, but she shows herself to me as a shining goddess because I can identify with her better that way, given that I am a female.

My Source usually makes me raise my vibrations really high in order to reach her, and she tantalises me in my consciousness with glimpses of her intense light through a crack in a cloud until I have ramped up my energies high enough to be able to burst through the cloud and into her sphere of consciousness. It is like stepping into white diamond fire that doesn't burn, and it envelopes me totally, inside and out. At first, it usually seems like a 'white-out', but as my consciousness adjusts to the bright light and high energies, then her form will swim into view along with anything else she wishes to show me. Her form normally takes the fairly indistinct shape of myself as a human, but glorified in its light and attractiveness—perhaps the shape of me to come in millennia from now.

This outcome of reaching my Source is something that can't be forced by my human mind; it is controlled by my spirit or soul, but the journey to get there does need my human will in order to keep pushing vibrations higher and not get distracted.

As with the One God, my Source's words are usually brief, but at least I can have a conversation with her and I always remember the experience with great clarity. She is a fount of wisdom but will never tell me anything which I need to discover for myself. But she does, at times, show me solutions to what I consider to be impossible predicaments, for which I am very grateful. My Beloved Source keeps all her messages very simple. She has no ego whatsoever, no triggers within her that cause her to be biased or to have an agenda. There is no emotion except unconditional love and compassion.

Connecting with angels

The angels have a similar temperament to the creator gods, and will always have the most fair and just answers for us, and are very straightforward and lack any trickery or deception in their veins.

However, I have found the angels to be quite work-focused, (maybe just my own personal experience?) and not quite so amenable to debating options as my Beloved Source who is always available for negotiation, discussion, or to show me around.

But the angels do have a wonderful hospital in the higher dimensions and, if we ask them, they will take us there for healing. I have found them to be the most marvellous healers of our physical bodies and any emotional and mental problems. (See chapters 19-22 for more on healing.)

Connecting with the gods/Ascended Masters

The gods of the higher dimensions are a varied bunch, all with their own unique skills and energies and personalities. In my book *Meet the Masters*, I have detailed my encounters with many of the gods (Masters) and have transcribed channellings from them which I believe give a good indication of what they are about individually. Some of these gods I have worked with for many years and even decades, and some gods I have met only socially and briefly. Some have been only mentors to me, and others have started out as mentors and then become my very best friends and family. The gods I have worked with for extended periods include Dominic, El Morya, Chiron, Hilarion, Thoth, St.Germain, Lord Maitreya, Sedna, Venus, Pallas Athena, Quan Yin, Eris, and Mother Mary. The angel I have worked with the most is Archangel Michael.

Some gods live in a world very similar to our own, the kind of Second Earth which I have described in Part One, and other gods live in very different worlds to ours. We can visit all of them in our spirit sphere of consciousness, as long as we are vibrating at the right level. Humans often meet gods on their astral travels.

The gods are liable to take on any shape or form when they meet with us in consciousness, especially of how we might expect them to look. If we imagine that a god would appear like some ancient old prophet, then this is the form they might take so that we feel comfortable with that and recognise them. They will nearly always show themselves in human form so that they don't frighten people with their appearance. The human form is actually based on the form of gods anyway, so there is not much difference physically between us and them.

The gods are prone to practising deception and illusion, so beware! It is not that they are malicious or dishonest, but they know all the tricks in the book of how humans can wriggle out of their contracts and missions and responsibilities, and they are ready for us and will do whatever it takes to get us back onto the right track again. They will dangle carrots in front of our noses, and we hardly ever get to eat those carrots, it seems!

And they will tell us things which might seem to us to be a lie, but from their higher perspective what they are saying is the truth. They don't tend to tell us lies, but they are quite adept at telling us only part of the truth, or the truth from their angle even though we are unable to see it that way at the time. So, if we are taken on as a student by a god, we need to be on our toes as they will run rings around us until we learn the particular lesson they are teaching us. We definitely learn humility on this journey!

Something we shouldn't forget is that there are many gods now intermingling with us on Earth, and so it is not just in consciousness that we might meet them but in physical form too. We will know them by their awesome presence which radiates an intense aura that attracts us to them. They are not necessarily overtly godly or spiritual people, but they have a charisma that certainly pulls us in (or could repel us if we are not on their high wavelength).

Some gods can be quite terse in their dealings with us, and others are quite content to shoot the breeze for as long as it takes. I love it when they take me on long journeys into the universe and I get to meet new beings and discover new places. But I especially love to learn new ways of thinking about things, and most of what they tell me ends up in a book like this.

Just when I think I have learnt all there is to learn on any particular topic, I am shown another new perspective, and my mind goes into overdrive once again as I dwell on this profound wisdom. I often think, after decades of going on astral journeys with them, that there couldn't possibly be any more ways of travelling that they could show me, but I am always proved wrong. Imagination is limitless in the higher dimensions, and I am blown away each time I undergo yet another unique adventure.

Connecting with stars and planets

The stars, planets, asteroids, and other cosmic bodies are all physical embodiments of gods, and they all have consciousnesses, too, and can be conversed with. Being an astrologer, I have to admit I do this quite a lot, and thoroughly enjoy it. In particular, I love to connect with our sun, especially at sunrise or sunset when its energies seem to be even more potent, and I can feel its strength, radiance, and starlike qualities coursing through my body and mind.

Connecting with our own soul

Connecting with one's soul is a very individual experience and so I can only describe things from my own perspective.

Our soul is totally focused on getting us to complete our mission. It depends on how compliant we are as a human as to whether our soul gives us grief or sweeties. If we resist our soul, or completely ignore it altogether, we won't have a happy soul and they can become seemingly quite mean in their dealings with us to get us to sit up and take notice.

Our soul is our future self, so it will depend on how high vibe we are in our human consciousness as to how high a vibration our soul has. If we are a low vibe human, then our soul will also be relatively low vibe compared to other souls, and perhaps won't be cherishing us as much as we would like.

For most people, their soul will remain as the same personality guiding them for their entire lifetime, albeit that it is also evolving like we are. But we must bear in mind that our soul can be replaced during the course of our lifetime, and we will be confronted by a quite different character from the one we were used to dealing with before. I personally am now dealing with my fifth soul in this lifetime, and they have all been incredibly different (see chapter 3).

In past eras, we needed to have died to get a new soul, but in recent times this 'rule' has been changed, and we can now 'die' on Earth to our old selves and receive a new soul to guide us, with our old soul integrating into our human consciousness. This is no simple process and it truly is like being born again, with all its commensurate struggles, especially of being a 'newborn' in an adult's body and having to come to grips with a new personality and new skills (and impairments!) all over again.

In no way am I anyone special to be undergoing this process. I know of many other spiritual people on Earth who are also experiencing these soul transitions. However, as a teacher of metaphysics, it's my job to be particularly aware of what is happening to me so that I can then describe the process for the benefit of others.

Connecting with our own spirit

Our spirit is our twin counterpart in the invisible dimension of the Second Earth. It is an expansion of who we are as a human, and we share our consciousness with it, and we can communicate with it at any time just through our intention.

We jump into our spirit's body whenever we dream, daydream, or lose human consciousness in any way. All day long, we are probably yo-yoing backwards and forwards between our spirit and our human self, and we are not very aware of which part of our mind belongs to our spirit and which part belongs to our physical human because we are so interconnected.

Connecting with the souls and spirits of others

Connecting with other souls and spirits is also possible through our consciousness. These may be souls or spirits of people who have passed over from the earthly plane. They may be the consciousnesses of family members or friends, or people from our distant past with whom we have had a strong bond, whether loving or challenging. We can have relationships with them in the same way as we would any person here on Earth, excepting of course that they (and we) don't have a human physical body when we are swanning about in the invisible dimensions, although we can take a physical spirit form.

This is the realm of psychics who tap into this dimension to speak with departed souls and spirits, but all of us have the ability to do this if we set our intention to do so and get over our fear of connecting with disembodied entities. However, it is a talent that we might or might not have, akin to having a musical ear and being able to play an instrument; it's not for everyone.

If we practise our talent, we can also converse and travel with the spirits of people who are presently alive on Earth. This can happen in dreams at night, or during meditation, or quite consciously. How often do we get a sudden image of a person in our mind and then out of the blue we hear from them or bump into them? Our spirits have met on the higher plane, and orchestrated that we get in contact down on Earth as well, usually for some specific reason.

Our destiny as humans will one day be to communicate with each other without the need for a device such as a phone, computer, or radio. We will use purely our consciousness to keep in touch, just as animals, birds, and insects do today. Once upon a time we probably had this innate ability, but we have lost this skill throughout millennia of evolution and through a lack of practice and belief.

Connecting with our own lower inner personas

It is necessary to get to know our own soul and spirit and maintain a good relationship with them and keep in contact with them, even though they are part of our own consciousness. This applies to all parts of our consciousness, especially the lower personas who cram our cranium with negative thoughts and questionable ideas. Each segment of our consciousness can be personified as one of these inner personas where we are playing out the many different roles and aspects of ourselves. They can lead quite individual lives with their own focus, just as the organs and cells of our body all have their own tasks and purpose.

We can call out any of these personas and have a conversation with them, and this is essential if we are to get to the bottom of any resistant thinking, or depressive or malevolent attitude. All we need to say is something like, "Will those inner personas who disagree with this new change in our life, please appear in front of me now." And then within our consciousness we can speak with them individually or as a group, just as we would a group of young children or employees.

Their feedback can be quite profound at times, especially when we haven't taken them into consideration concerning any changes we are trying to instigate. It could be as simple as going on a diet or needing to do more exercise—the inner personas need to be brought on board and aligned with our new goal, or else they will sabotage our every effort. This is not usually because they are malevolent creatures but because they have previously been programmed to do what they are currently doing or thinking, and that programming now needs to be altered to accommodate the required modification to our life.

It is best to deal with these inner personas, or inner children as they are sometimes referred to, with kindness and understanding, just as we would with real children. After all, they are a part of our own consciousness, and we should always try to treat ourselves kindly and with compassion. We cannot merely kill off any particularly nasty or rebellious inner personas, for they will simply resurrect as something else equally nasty or worse.

I have found that if I cannot reason with them and get them to change their attitude, I can offer to send them Home to the higher dimensions, and generally they welcome that. I then merge them into my heart with great love, telling them how grateful I am for all they have been for me in the past. With that, they dissolve, and that part of my consciousness has now been cleared of troublesome thought.

At times, an inner persona will not play the game at all, and then it takes some days or even weeks and months of focused intervention in order to get it to change its thinking and attitude. But I have never found an inner persona that I couldn't dissolve eventually.

Be aware that we can't do this with our spirit or soul; they are like our immortal shadow and cannot be dumped or got rid of, whereas an inner persona is just a temporary representation of a thought or belief we have. On our journey to godhood/ascension we will be required to let go most of our troublesome inner personas, and in early godhood, as newly-created gods, we will learn to let go of the last remaining traits of our human consciousness.

Connecting with the lower personas of other people

On a daily basis, we are communicating with the inner lower personas of other people through our consciousness and theirs. In this way, we pick up thoughts and energies which the other person believes are well-hidden from us, but which are totally transparent to our consciousness and spirit self. By the same token, we ourselves also can't hide what is going on in our own mind from other consciousnesses.

So, when we have the thought, "Oh my goodness, she really shouldn't wear that dress!", we need to realise that the wearer of that awful dress is hearing us loud and clear in her consciousness and being duly affected by our judgement of her. This is one reason why social events can be so excruciatingly painful for our self-esteem, because at an inner level we are experiencing all the criticism from the people around us, and perhaps doling it out too. Being only love keeps us out of trouble.

Not only is our consciousness in constant contact with the consciousness of other people, but our vibrational energies are surging out of us too and affecting everyone around us. In some of my workshops I demonstrate, using metal divining rods, how our vibrational field, often called our aura, expands or retracts depending on our emotional state.

If we are feeling low vibrational, our energies retract inwards into ourself, and this means that people around us don't get to feel our energies and can act as if we don't exist. We also don't get to feel the energies of other people because our energy field is not 'out there' picking up signals. This causes us to feel disconnected. This is what happens when people feel depressed, and then they also feel very alone because their vibrational energy field is not touching anyone else's.

When we are feeling joyful, our vibrational field expands to many metres beyond our body, and therefore our aura keeps bumping into other people's energy fields, and thus we feel connected to them. Happy, high vibrational people don't feel lonely or disconnected.

It's fun to practise connecting with other people's consciousness in planned experiments. We can set a time to connect whilst in different locations, and become still and meditate and see what comes to mind. We might be surprised at how often we pick up clues about the scene where the other person is located. This is often termed 'remote viewing'. With a great deal of practice, we can even jump into that scene with all our senses and experience it as if we are truly there. This is a kind of teleporting, but a teleportation of our consciousness not of our physical body. The teleporting of physical human bodies is a skill that we may all learn one day in the future.

When people experience horrific scenes in meditation or dreams, with monsters and all manner of grotesque entities coming into their consciousness, these are often inner personas and creations of their imagination. I know they can seem very real, and we can't imagine that our own mind can harbour this kind of stuff, but our consciousness and our soul are very adept at being imaginative, and we will need to deal with the horrors that our consciousness has embedded in it, created from our thinking at some time during this lifetime and other past lives. We need to remember Chiron's favourite adage, "Like attracts like". Whatever is stored in our consciousness will attract similar themes on those wavelengths.

However, it is possible for us to attract the lower personas of other consciousnesses into our aura, and these can cause us a great deal of anxiety or even torture for us. This is described in more detail in chapter 16 (Who is doing the talking?)

Connecting with past life personas

On occasion, when we connect with the higher dimensions, we can be shown scenes from some past life of ours. This will only happen if our soul believes that the lessons of that lifetime are useful for us to know in our current one. It is not usually some life where we have been famous or rich or powerful, although that can happen, but every life, no matter how simple, offers some rich vein of wisdom and insight. We will often get only a very focused view of this life in one or two scenes, unless it is of immeasurable importance for us to know a lot about this particular incarnation. Even then, the information is usually revealed to us over a long period in dribs and drabs in order for us to better integrate it. Our souls won't show us past lives just as some form of entertainment for us.

During these past life scenarios, we might also connect with other consciousnesses who were involved with us in that past life, if it is important for us to resolve relationships we have had.

Connecting with nature

We can practise our connective ability by conversing with the consciousness inherent in nature. As we have discovered in Part One, everything on this planet, whether animate or inanimate, has some kind of consciousness, and therefore we can communicate with it.

Personally, I always have a chat with the flowers, trees, and vegetables in my garden and they seem to thrive on it. We might think we are inventing any conversation we hear back from them, but if we believe in it we will receive all kinds of interesting information, such as whether they need a certain kind of fertiliser, or if they are happy or unhappy growing next to a certain type of plant.

Speaking with insects and animals is very useful too, especially if we want ants or snails to move on, although I had no luck with a very recalcitrant possum who liked to eat everything in my garden, even pineapples and chillies. He obviously thought I had provided a nightly banquet for him and why should he move elsewhere!

Where I live in Australia, the countryside is habitat for snakes, and some deadly ones at that, but I have been in my house for over fourteen years and have only ever had non-venomous and delightfully entertaining snakes come and visit me. They sense my energy (I am fascinated by them) and they put on a show for me while I avidly watch and appreciate them. Often I dream of snakes, and it usually augurs that I will see a snake in the real world within a couple of days, which I take as a sign of transformation and letting go, as in the fact that a snake needs to shed its skin in order to grow and evolve. I used to have quite a collection of real snake skins that had been sloughed.

Connecting with aliens

Last but not least, when we connect with the higher dimensions we may find ourselves in conversation with some kind of alien being. They do exist, as we discussed in Part One, and they too have some kind of consciousness. Most of us won't be meeting them physically any time soon, perhaps only in consciousness. However, times they are a-changing and who knows what the future has in store for us!

It's difficult to say how we should handle this encounter, for an alien could take any shape or form and be of any vibrational level, low or high. Often what we think are aliens are merely the gods taking on a form that will get our attention, and it may also be just a creation of our own imagination, especially if we have over-indulged in watching science fiction movies.

We need to remember that as a consciousness we can never die, even if in this alien scenario we do in fact face death of some sort. We will be rebirthed, never fear. If we fill our consciousness with thoughts of love, then the universe rebounds only love back at us, and then we shouldn't encounter representations of our fears as we travel through the universe in our spirit sphere of consciousness.

Chapter 13 – The benefits of connecting with the unseen universe

Agent for our soul

If the universe is so wonderful and our soul and spirit so much more high-vibrational and loving than ourselves, why are we here in human form at all, and why does our soul bother with us?

The consciousness that is our soul has manifested part of itself into a human form and placed us on Earth temporarily, not solely so that we can play and enjoy this beautiful planet, although that is also part of the deal, but so it can learn lessons for itself through us and evolve itself to a higher level. As a human containing part of our soul's consciousness, we become the agent for our soul, its arms and legs, and we agree on a mission that we will complete in this lifetime that will give our soul additional skills and understanding. Each time we learn a lesson on Earth, the valuable outcomes are integrated into our soul's consciousness and, when we eventually die to our human self, our consciousness returns to the soul's realm and reintegrates with it completely.

Our soul monitors our human progress and accomplishments like a parent with a child. Through our shared consciousness, our soul can influence us in certain directions physically, or through intuition, mental messages, and clues. It is always nudging, pushing, and even kicking us to proceed down the right path for our destiny, and it will help us to understand our issues and clear out erroneous programming so that we can work from a higher level of consciousness.

As a human we see only what we have programmed ourselves to see, what our mental filters allow us to see, whilst our soul can see the bigger picture for us and also across time, and its guidance will keep us on track. Our soul's view is much clearer than our own since it is not confused or distracted by the effects of our physical dimension's lower vibrations.

However, if we ignore our soul and don't acknowledge its existence or its communications with us, it tends to ignore us in return. It can also seem a bit callous in its attitude, and play tricks on us if we are reluctant to commit to working with it or if we play them for a fool. We need to foster a good relationship with our soul and ask them to share their experiences, guidance, and feedback with us.

Like the right side of our brain, which we discussed in Part One, our soul tends to be fairly spare with their words and prefers to communicate with us by way of symbolism and images. Unfortunately, our soul doesn't believe it a good idea to furnish us with winning lottery numbers, but further on we will examine the ways that our soul does like to keep in touch with us.

The benefits we receive from the universe

We have seen why our soul needs to keep tabs on us and why it needs to hold our reins. But what reason do we have as humans to reciprocate and connect with our soul or any other part of the unseen universe? It seems there are many people on Earth who never consciously connect with their soul or even admit to having one, and many of them appear to get through life okay, and some of them even thrive in a human, materialistic way. Therefore, what drives us to want to connect and work with our divine self? Wouldn't we be just as happy concerning ourselves with only the earthly world?

It is true that we can get through life without ever giving a second thought to our divine partner and the hidden wonders that lie beyond our physical dimension. But at what cost? For life is then a hit-or-miss affair as to whether we fulfil our mission and learn anything that our soul wishes us to, and it could be a wasted life as far as our soul is concerned and we might not have evolved a single jot. We will not realise this, of course, until we return after our death to the invisible dimensions, and then there may be many regrets.

To get the most benefit from this lifetime, we need to follow the plan laid out for us by our soul. It's not as though this plan is nicely printed out for us and all we have to do is read and follow its instructions. We wish!

No, it is more like a cryptic treasure map, and firstly we have to even know there is a map, and then we need to discover it, and then we need to decode it correctly, and then take action to complete its steps. Isn't this much more exciting than just following an explicitly detailed but boring set of directions and directives handed out to us? Who doesn't love a secret treasure map and the enticement of adventure and rewards?

By learning to connect with our soul and the greater universe, we are given much help in discovering our treasure map and decoding it. Of course, there is much to learn along the way, just as archaeologists had to learn how to decipher the hieroglyphics of ancient Egypt before they could understand what went on there.

So, what kind of help is offered to us by our soul and the higher beings? The following are the types of assistance we could receive or experience when we connect with the hidden dimensions.

a) Love, comfort, hope

We will receive love, comfort, and hope in some way if we have asked for it, and even sometimes if we haven't asked, since others often do the praying for us on our behalf.

If we pray for love, it may not come in the form we want, as in a relationship, but in some way that is better for us and in line with the lesson we are presently learning, or with our mission. For instance, if our soul is teaching us to be self-reliant, a romantic relationship may be withheld from us until we have proved that we are solid and no longer needy. Paradoxically, when we no longer need a partner to complete us, then our soul may deem it time to offer one to us.

Our soul, and especially the gods and angels, are love itself and when we connect with them their energies will feel beautiful, calming, and comforting, and will raise our vibrations automatically. When we connect with the higher dimensions, we can feel more alive and refreshed, as if we have been on holiday and have returned filled with new ideas and experiences and renewed hope.

b) Destiny, mission, purpose

Often in life we will be at a crossroads, feeling confused and having no idea what to do with our lives or which path to take from here. Getting directions about our future is clearly an advantage. We may not be told our entire itinerary, or even our final destination, but even if we learn which is the next station to get to, or even the next step to take, then this is a benefit to us. And it is not the same as some career counsellor giving us advice, for our soul knows exactly what is right for us, and what has been planned for us from the start.

Our astrology charts will provide us with a good guide too, especially if we get one done by someone with an understanding of the spiritual interpretations of our aspects. This is something I enjoy doing for my clients. The look of delight and wonder on their faces when they finally understand their soul destiny, is to be treasured.

Our soul is not interested in the mundane minutiae of our lives, and generally won't answer questions that are silly or have no great importance. What is important to our soul is our higher purpose of getting on track and completing our destiny as per our contract. Our soul will not be amused at being used as a source of entertainment or as a kind of Google assistant. We must treat our soul with respect, as if it were a god and not our servant.

The kind of help we could expect to receive about our purpose and future was nicely illustrated by my own request for guidance many years ago. I was thinking of setting up a new business and naming it *Rainbow Circle*. I asked the universe if this was the right name, and received not one but two unusual confirmations that I was on track.

The first came when I was on a plane, staring out of the window. To my utter surprise, there on the clouds, like a colourful sticker, was a complete circle of a rainbow. I had never seen anything like it before. Not only that, but the shadow of my airplane actually flew through the centre of the rainbow circle. Perhaps this is a common occurrence to people who do a lot of flying, but I found it fascinating and took it as a firm answer to my question.

The second confirmation followed soon after when I was lucky enough to be in Hawaii, on the island of Maui. I was clambering up the slopes of a volcano when I came across a noticeboard which, to my astonishment, described the phenomenon of the rainbow circle, an image that is apparently used a lot in Hawaii. I had not known that. Since I was loving my time in Hawaii and felt a great affinity with the place, again I took this as wonderful confirmation of my plans.[17]

c) Warnings, prophecies

Our soul can provide us with guidance about the future in other ways, too, by way of warnings or prophecies. It doesn't have to be complicated, in the style of Nostradamus, but it may come, most probably, by way of intuition or gut feel. We may just get a message in our mind to tidy up the house, and then we find our mother-in-law popping in unexpectedly, and we are glad we heeded that little voice in our head.

There are many instances of people not getting on planes or into a car because they just had a gut feel there would be an accident, and they have been proved right. The problem here is to know when it's a warning from our soul or just simply our own fear. We will discuss fears in the next chapter, but if we are dwelling in fearful vibrations then we are likely to attract fearful events.

Some people do receive visions of the future, but these often tend to be dire predictions. They might be accused of being a Cassandra. She was a high priestess of ancient Troy who had the gift of prophecy, and she foretold the downfall of Troy, but no one would listen to her until it was too late, and Troy was infiltrated by the enemy using the Trojan Horse and then destroyed.

One thing to be aware of is that, when our soul or the gods tell us about the future, it can be that they are sharing their dreams of the future with us, the things they would like to manifest. It isn't necessarily what *will* actually come about, but what they are visualising in their consciousness as

---

17. While checking my facts here, I came across this article about Hawaii which covered both of my experiences!
Rainbows All About You (https://www.mauimagazine.net/behind-the-rainbow/)
"If you've ever looked out of a plane and seen its shadow on the clouds, encircled by a rainbow, you've witnessed a Brocken spectre. On rare occasions, you can see the same thing if you stand at the edge of (Hawaii's) Haleakala Crater when it's filled with clouds. If the sun is behind you, it will cast your shadow on the clouds and surround it with a rainbow. One of the best photographs ever taken of a Brocken spectre was shot in 1968 at Haleakala's rim. In fact, every rainbow is a circle. It just looks like a bow because the ground blocks your view of the bottom. Climb high enough, and you'd see the whole, lovely ring."

something they would like to come about. Therefore, we can't take this as being the concrete future, only a hope for the future, a possibility.

It would be great if we received prophecies of the future that foretold winning lottery tickets or the frontrunners of horse races, but this seldom happens although it is not unknown. I know someone who knew she was going to win a competition for a trip to France, and sure enough she did. Maybe it was because she had such solid belief about it, rather than saying, "Yeh, yeh!" in sarcasm, as most of us would have done.

At times we may get a clear and audible warning. Usually, I don't hear my soul speaking to me as if I was listening through headphones but, rather, I hear her subtly inside my head. But on one occasion I was startled at work when I heard her yell at me, "Bail out!" as clearly as if someone in the room had shouted it out. She wanted me to resign from my job urgently as it was not good for my future, and I did as she requested and found myself a much better job that suited my abilities more happily.

d) Advice—words, images, journeys, insights, past lives

One of our soul's main purposes is to offer us advice and guidance. This can be received in many ways, and we will examine these in more detail in a later chapter. The advice may be heard as words in our head, or seen as images or symbols in our consciousness, or experienced as coincidences, or felt as intuition or sensations in our gut or elsewhere in our body.

My own soul usually takes me on a journey to meet the gods or angels, and in the higher dimensions a scene is played out for me from which I can gather understanding about my mission or an issue I am going through. Sometimes I just watch the scene unfold before me, and at other times I am an active actor in the play. It's not always obvious what exactly the message is, and I often need to ponder on what has occurred before the penny drops completely. But it is always helpful advice to enable me to understand what I need to let go of, or deal with, in order to move on and progress on my path.

Our soul and the gods can see our predicament much more clearly than we can on Earth, and I thoroughly enjoy the creative ways they inform me of my issues and point out the directions in which to find answers. Rarely will they give us a complete solution; only pointers and clues to what this might be.

An example of being given a marvellous pointer came one Sunday morning when my soul suggested that I visit a little country village about half an hour's drive away. I had never been there before, mainly because there was nothing there except a few houses. "Why do I need to go here?" I argued. But I knew it was fruitless to resist my soul's urgings, so I got in the car and drove, feeling a little peeved. As far as I knew there wasn't even anywhere to have a coffee in the village, and it certainly wouldn't be open on a Sunday.

But as I turned off the main road towards the little hamlet, I suddenly saw a sign advertising a café and that it was open on Sundays. Gosh, things were looking up! And what I eventually found was the prettiest and most welcoming tea gardens I'd ever been in. This is the kind of advantage we can secure if we are prepared to listen to higher beings and take action on their advice.

On the odd occasion, we might be shown a scene or two by our soul from a past life, and this will always be because it has some bearing on a current situation we are undergoing, not just to boost our ego or amuse us. Here we will often gain an understanding of how our present life is interwoven with the lives of others we have known in the past. Current spouses or children may have once been our employers or our servants, and current friends may once have been our siblings or comrades-in-arms.

The scenarios are endless and fascinating, but we need to be careful not to get too caught up in the fantasy of it all. We are a more evolved consciousness now from that which we were in that past life, and the other players will also have moved on too. There will certainly be things to learn from it, but we shouldn't hang our hat on any particular past lifetime.

Other important advice from our soul concerns letting us know when our vibrations have dipped too low, and being given encouragement to raise them. This can often take the form of merely feeling separated from our soul, for that feeling of desolation and disconnection is enough to have us examining ways to climb out of our pit and reconnect as swiftly as possible.

e) Ideas to take back to Earth

If we go exploring in the higher dimensions, we will often come across ideas that we can bring back to Earth, whether it be architectural structures, vehicles and transport systems, social or business schemes, games, fashions, food and drink, agricultural methods, artwork, or twists for a novel.

The gods tell us there is no copyright on their ideas, and we are free to use them and share them for the benefit of the planet. We are welcome any time to visit their worlds and discover further inspiration, for the gods want nothing more than for the earthly world to become more god-like.

Science fiction books and films often feature concepts that have been brought back from the higher dimensions. There is nothing on Earth, Chiron says, that can be created without first having been conceived in the higher worlds. All conception of ideas happens there first, in the Dark World, and then it gets manifested through the Light World of creation into the physical dimension of our planet.

f) Energies, healing, raised vibrations

Another kind of assistance we receive from our soul and the gods is by way of energies. This can take the form of healing energy which can either suffuse us generally or be directed to a certain problem area. Healing comes about through purifying and balancing the parts of our consciousness that are responsible for the diseased or painful situation. The healing energies could also help us to raise our vibrations, or to awaken us or stir our motivation. Healing is discussed in greater detail in chapters 19-22.

Our soul and the gods can choose to download a part of their consciousness into us to help improve us in some way. We may just generally feel stronger and more capable, or we may get insights or feel more compassionate and loving. In special circumstances, when we are being taken to a whole new level, the gods, or our soul itself, can ask to merge with us, and we become a blended consciousness with them. Not only does this increase our power, love, and wisdom, but we take on a whole new set of responsibilities and challenges as well.

The spirit world surrounds us even if we are feeling quite lonesome and abandoned on Earth. If we tap into this dimension and all the beautiful beings there, we will never have to feel isolated or unsupported again. This knowledge alone can keep our vibrations soaring high.

g) Answers to our prayers

Many people only ever speak to the Divine, and generally only to 'God', when they want to pray for someone or something, and most people in the world will find themselves resorting to praying to God at some time in their lives, most especially during some crisis, even if they don't believe in such an entity.

The higher beings don't take umbrage at this, at being used only in emergencies. After all, it's better than never hearing from that human at all, and does prove that there must be a tiny fraction of belief deep in that person somewhere. It can sometimes provide the chink in the armour that was needed for a breakthrough to get the person connected with their higher self and the unseen dimensions.

Prayers are always heard by our soul and the gods, and they will deliver whatever is necessary for our growth, not necessarily what we ourselves want for our own happiness. We are here to complete our mission, not just to be happy bunnies.

h) Training

Another reason for us to connect with our soul and the higher dimensions is to partake in the training that the gods offer us in the ways of their world. This includes how to be more loving, have harmonious relationships, be more innately powerful, work from a higher and clearer mind, introduce better laws and justice systems, and a whole host of godly-inspired innovations and initiatives.

Through this training we get to lead a more productive and better-quality life on Earth in all respects, and we can take these teachings and transfer this knowledge to others in the world to help transform humanity and the planet. Ultimately, we are being trained for godhood.

In undergoing this training, we are also being prepared for our return to the higher worlds one day when we die and merge back with our soul. We will have evolved to a higher level, which will please our soul no end.

Chapter 14 – What prevents connection?

Even with the best will in the world in wanting to connect with the unseen universe, some aspects of our character could be preventing us from conversing with higher beings and taking opportunities to jump into our spirit sphere and explore the great unknown.

Fear and a lack of belief are usually the greatest obstacles, but in this chapter we will try to cover as many blocks as possible so we can understand why we may not be hearing or receiving anything. Once we have laid all our cards on the table and discovered our potential blocking tactics, then we will move on in the next chapter to describing in what ways the universe speaks with us, fully aware of how we may be negating some of these attempts at connection from the invisible worlds.

a) Fear

Fear is probably the biggest inhibitor to connecting with the invisible worlds. We are trying to get in touch with the Unknown, and the human psyche generally has an innate trepidation of dealing with something it doesn't know or understand. Hence horror movies often involve something sinister that we can't quite make out, lurking in the darkness or out of sight. Our imagination runs riot about what it could be, and the snake turns out to be a curvy stick, or the monster turns out to be the shadow of a tree on the wall. The movie *The Blair Witch Project* certainly made the most of our capacity to imagine all sorts of terrible things, based on no real evidence at all.

As discussed in Part One, the gods don't come down to Earth in a blaze of glory and show of might for this very reason. Most humans would just panic and become hysterical with fear, and the higher beings can't see any benefit in doing this. And so, the methodology for introducing themselves to humans is to tread softly and slowly, getting people used to the idea that gods do indeed exist.

Science fiction has paved the way for this, but the downside has been that, while many people now know about gods and their superpowers, they do not believe that any of this truly exists as part of our physical reality. I have to chuckle when I watch some science fiction films, at how very close to the truth they actually are, but of course not many people would actually believe that.

Fear is a low vibration, and we need to have high vibrations if we are to be able to connect with the higher dimensions. Therefore, we must do all we can to overcome our nervousness and timidity at approaching a foreign dimension and foster our courage. Ramping up our vibrations in the manner discussed in chapter 11 will assist us to break through to the other side and go on our journeys there. The gods pity those who are too fearful to go beyond the boundaries of our physical dimension; they are missing the best parts of the universe—experience and love.

Our fears are many and varied and are part of the programming installed within our consciousness and brain. They have been encoded there at some time during our life (or past lives) in order to protect us from the then current situation. Some fears are healthy, such as a fear of fire helps prevent us from burning ourselves on barbeques or around bonfires, and a fear of being run over helps us to be careful crossing the road.

But many fears are limiting and inhibit us from leading full and active lives. A fear of public speaking may stop us from progressing in our career. Claustrophobia, a fear of enclosed spaces, may prevent us from entering elevators or airplanes, or even cars. Technology terrifies some people but is embraced wholeheartedly by many, while spiders and snakes are petrifying to some and fascinating to others. We are all very different as to what sets off our fears.

Something becomes a fear or belief when we unconsciously set a rule around it that whenever we experience this event we will react in a certain way, usually with horror or heightened emotion, or by trying to escape or hide. It will often be a playing out of the original reactions we had when this event was first experienced.

It is as if we have a gatekeeper within our consciousness, a custodian of all the rules and beliefs we have fed into us, and our gatekeeper fiercely complies with these rules and beliefs, right or wrong, and will not allow us to act contrary to them. It is not the gatekeeper's fault if the rules no longer apply; we need to inform our protector about the new rules and beliefs that we wish to play by.

The gatekeeper is one of our inner personas, and a guardian of all our inner children and segments of thinking. They are completely fixed in their purpose, just like a computerised device will only function in a certain way, and, like this device, the gatekeeper's functionality can only be changed by re-programming them and giving them new rules and beliefs to follow. In order to do this, we have to first convince our inner personas that change is needed, and then we must feed into our consciousness new ways of thinking, and embed them until they are taken up by us as a habitual way of living.

Fear of being unsafe

I have been chatting with the higher dimensions for several decades, and have made many excursions there, and I can assure people that nothing untoward has ever happened to my physical body in all that time while I've been communicating or travelling. It's been perfectly safe. Be reassured too that we will always return to our physical body and full human consciousness, and we won't get stuck on the other side of the 'wormhole' in some strange dimension.

We may fear opening ourselves up to evil entities or aliens, but if we set our intention to be protected and to deal only with divine beings who are of higher consciousness, and we come only from a place of love, we won't have these kind of experiences. Beings of darkness are often our own low vibrational personas playing out. It is true that we can be affected energetically by the evil personas of other people, when their consciousness gets entangled with our own, but all this needs to be dealt with in the higher dimension, in our consciousness, and not in the human physical realm. See chapters 19-22 *Healing and Letting Go,* for ways to overcome this.

Fear of failure

Many people fear they might fail in some capacity; at school; in their job; as a husband or wife, father or mother; achieving their dream; establishing a business; sitting an exam; overcoming an illness; surviving a journey or challenge; even getting to godhood. Some people decline to attempt things in case they fail.

There are those who also fear trying to connect with the divine worlds in case they fail. After all, it's not a common occurrence to be able to see or hear things in another dimension. They might try once or twice but then they give up and tell themselves, "I'm just not psychic or intuitive." As stated before, to become a magician takes a lot of practice, and a lot of failure.

The gods tell us that there is no such thing as failure; there are only attempts to succeed. Thomas Edison, as he was trying to invent the light bulb, famously said, "I have not failed. I've just found 10,000 ways that won't work."

Fear of change

Sometimes it's not a fear of anything in particular that we have, but a fear of change itself. Many of us have manufactured our lives exactly as we want them, and we go all out to protect what we have established and to keep the status quo. But the universe is always moving, and always moving us on too, and change will be presented to us when it is time to break out of our cocoon and nestled lifestyle, and it will be painful if we try to resist it.

Some folks embrace change with alacrity, but others will cling onto anchors even whilst they are drowning. We will need to learn to let go and flow with our destiny, and see everything as a new adventure and an opportunity for learning new skills and evolving our soul.

Fear from past lives

Sometimes, we can't fathom where a fear is coming from. It may have no rational basis in our current life experiences. We may be playing out fears from one or several of our past lives. Our consciousness can carry these over from lifetime to lifetime, hoping that we will find a way to overcome them.

For instance, if we have died in a previous life by being interred within a cave or tomb whilst still alive, we might very well find ourselves feeling quite claustrophobic in this lifetime. Similarly, if in some past life we have been put to death or mutilated or humiliated or betrayed due to our connection with the divine worlds as a religious or spiritual person, then it is possible that we will feel fear about going down that path again this time around. (Astrology note: those people with their Chiron, Moon, or South Node, in Pisces or in their 12th House, very often have this particular issue.).

b) Need for control, or fear of being controlled

Fear is usually the underlying basis for people wanting to take control, and this need for control is a common cause for not being able to connect with the divine worlds. Some people will not allow their soul to have any sort of control over their lives because they fear they will be taken to places they do not want to go, fear they might be asked to do tasks they don't want to do, and most of all they fear giving up their own free will and their desire to choose their own path in life. And so, they shut out any connection to an entity who might take away control from them.

But even for those who do make a connection with their soul, it can still be a challenge to let go of control and let their soul take the reins or even just guide them.

To get a better understanding of this issue, let us imagine a factory where there are workers beavering away on the factory floor, and overlooking them upstairs is a glass-fronted office where management works. This is the Command Centre. Visualise our human self as one of the workers in overalls. In the office above is our soul as one of the management team, wearing a smart suit. So, we are really in both places at once, with our consciousness able to be in both forms at the same time as both worker and manager.

The factory floor worker (us as a human) often resents and resists the edicts from the Command Centre (from our soul). Sometimes we play up and test authority and sabotage the work that needs to be done. We might feel that we ourselves should be in control, or we feel fearful of what is asked of us, that it is beyond our capacity and stresses us. Our soul, meanwhile, can see clearly what needs to be done and often gets frustrated with us, the worker.

So, what can be done in this situation? Who should be in control; the factory worker or the management team? Who should have access to the computer keyboard in the Command Centre? Who knows the management strategies and overall direction for the factory? The soul needs to prevent the factory worker from taking control or else chaos will ensue.

It is just like a parent taking back control over unruly or recalcitrant children, or regaining possession of the remote control for the TV. (Whenever I have problems with remote control devices, I always know it's due to a battle going on with my soul about control of something. When I surrender control, then I get back a working remote control!)

When we are in a fight for control with our soul, obviously we are not going to be receiving all the wonderful assistance that could be coming our way if we were in alignment with it and in high vibrations. So, with humility, we do need to let our soul be the manager, while we accept the position of worker bee. We need to cooperate and come to an agreement, for we rely on one another to complete our mission and have a harmonious life.

It's not that we, as a worker, don't have any say in things, for our soul encourages us to state our case and fight for what we believe in, and it is true that sometimes the soul doesn't always take the worker into consideration enough. Therefore, things can be worked out and smoothed over, as long as we remember who is really in charge here.

If we seek to be just the human part of our consciousness, we will feel the pain of separateness because we won't feel whole. We need to be a family unit with our soul. All outer reality reflects this ongoing fight within our consciousness between our human ego and our soul, whether it is in our personal relationships, or in discord or war between countries. Eventually, one day, we will need to merge our factory worker with our Command Centre manager, and exist as both at the same time in complete wholeness and harmony.

c) Distrust, disbelief, doubt

It's common to doubt and disbelieve what we hear, see, or sense, that has been presented to us in an uncommon way. If we can't see it, hear it, or touch it, as a human we generally won't believe it, which is the reason why much of the population of the Earth never sees or hears anyone or anything from the invisible higher dimensions.

Many might ask themselves the following questions:

- What if I'm just making all this up?
- How can I know that what I am seeing or hearing is true?
- Is it all fantasy?
- What if it's just me talking in my head?
- Who is it that is speaking to me or showing me things?
- How do I know if it's my soul or a god or some evil entity?

Of all the issues I have ever had in channelling my soul or the gods, the most difficult has been because I have doubted what I have received and I haven't believed enough. Surprising, eh, when I have done thousands of channellings, experienced thousands of spiritual journeys, and written many books based on my channellings of the gods!

But I was a left-brained computer programmer in my early life, and, just like for most humans, all this 'woo-woo' stuff was nonsense to me at first. And even after many years of these experiences, I still didn't believe 100% of the time. I had been given many challenges which often made me distrust the messages I got. They didn't come true, or not in the way I had expected them to. What I have come to understand is that I took them too literally and that things play out in many ways that we don't understand at first.

Nowadays, I doubt less and less, and usually not at all. I have learnt to accept exactly what I experience at the time, and then allow a comprehension about it to gradually come into my consciousness over time, asking many questions in order to clarify things.

But it is natural in the beginning to query what is being received, since this is the way we make the unknown known, just as we do as babies and children. We just have to experience what we experience, and eventually we will begin to understand and to trust. We can't fast track this understanding. There is no Wikipedia out there that will explain what is going on (although I hope that this book will go some way to redressing that problem!) There is no physical evidence of gods, and even if we discovered a god upon Earth, how would we go about proving that they were indeed from the higher dimensions?

There are really no rules governing what we might experience when we connect with the higher unseen universe, and as every path is custom-designed for us, we can't easily compare our experiences with those of others.

When we doubt and disbelieve, it makes it more difficult for us to connect in the future. We close ourselves down before we even get started by believing that this is all nonsense, and anything we receive is probably not worth its salt. Only by persevering with our experiences and gaining an understanding of what is happening to us, will we be able to build up our trust. Isn't this the same with any relationship, whether divine or human?

When we trust our divine counterpart and the gods of the higher dimensions, then connection is much easier and more instantaneous and also online 24/7. It is like the difference between having a dial-up Internet connection on our computer and a dedicated cable to the fastest broadband network available.

When we distrust what we are experiencing, we are corroding the value of what we receive, and can become cynical or even nihilistic. We will actually be denying our existence. This will push us to lower vibrational levels from where it will become even harder to make connections with our soul and the invisible worlds, and they will be even less likely to want to work with someone who doubts them.

Denial of our spiritual experiences is often a human defence against the threat of change. Questioning our beliefs may lead to us having to dismantle our life, and so it's easier to keep on believing what we have always believed. It keeps us safe from having to make changes to our lives, or take on new responsibilities, or extend ourself.

Denial and disbelief can also occur so that we are not seen to be a laughing-stock by a society where much spiritual wisdom is derided. This is especially so in the professions where people have status and careers to maintain, and cannot be seen to be holding such non-conformist views. Thank the gods, then, for the likes of Oprah Winfrey, Deepak Chopra, and Shirley MacLaine who have pushed against this narrow-mindedness.

We all have a crisis of faith at some time or other. We must stay strong and keep believing, and not be pulled down to the lower levels, and we must raise our consciousness back to higher levels where we will find our connection to the higher worlds again. An open mind is the symbolic door through which we will connect with other realms, and our belief is the key that will open that door.

d) Negative thoughts, closed heart

Another reason for not being able to connect with the universe is negativity. When we have negative thoughts we are lowering our vibrations, and as we have learnt, we need to have high vibrations in order to connect with high dimensions. We need to examine our consciousness for all the segments and programming that contain suspect thinking and beliefs, and make a conscious effort to replace these with positivity and optimism. It will be hard work and will take time, and no one claims it will be easy, but this is what will raise our vibrations.

Negativity closes down our heart, but also, when something bad happens to us, our first instinct is to close our heart in order to protect it. But a closed heart cannot access the higher worlds. Our heart is at the beginning of our Ribbon of Consciousness that links to our soul. We don't connect head-to-head but heart-to-heart.

What is it that opens a closed heart? It is love, and everything that is lovely.

e) Cherry-picking

Often, we do actually hear what our soul says to us, but we ignore it and tell ourselves it was just a voice in our head. But that is precisely what our soul is! Our soul speaks to us frequently but subtly, and we often take it to be just another thought that runs through our mind.

We might act on some soul or god suggestions, if we like them, and not act on others if we don't like them. For example, we might get a voice in our head that says, "You need to clean the windows," or "You need to write that report today." And we don't feel like it so we ignore it. But if we get the voice saying, "Go out for a coffee today, forget cleaning the windows," we're obeying that instruction like a shot!

This is just cherry-picking, selecting what we will and won't do according to our human will. After a while, our soul or the gods will decide it's not worth communicating with us, and there will no advice forthcoming.

If we wish to work with our soul or the gods, we will need to be committed and persistent. They will drift away from us if we drift away from them. The god, Ascended Master El Morya, once stated to me about humans in general, "If they can't be bothered, I can't be bothered!" Therefore, we must be careful not to use the gods or angels as occasional entertainment. They cannot be switched on and off at our pleasure. Just as we humans don't enjoy being used or abused by family or friends, so too do the gods and our soul feel the same way.

f) Drugs, alcohol

While alcohol and certain drugs do open up our channels to altered states of consciousness, they usually connect us only to the lower ranges of vibrations in the spirit dimensions where all sorts of horrors can await us from within our own Ribbon of Consciousness or when we connect with the low parts of the consciousness of others.

Sometimes we may be fortunate and enter the Dark World and receive inspiration or feelings of deep peace, and some people are able to travel the dimensions and receive meaningful experiences. But, all too often, the experiences are reflections of our own dark nature, and it's not recommended that alcohol or drugs are used in order to jump into the invisible worlds unless we have done a lot of work on ourselves to remove our triggers and lower vibrational segments.

g) Talent inherent in our natal astrology

Although every single person on Earth, regardless of gender, age, race, or religion, has the ability to connect with their soul and the divine worlds, some people have more talent for this than others because of certain aspects in their astrology charts. We are given our astrology chart as a blueprint to help guide us through this lifetime, but we must realise that the aspects we are endowed with assist us to complete our mission, and it is not everyone's destiny to follow an overtly spiritual path and spend time in daily meditation.

Sometimes we are blocked from easily accessing the divine worlds, as in having Chiron in Pisces or the 12th house, and this usually signifies that we have experienced significant trauma in a past life relating to a spiritual or religious affiliation, which now prevents us from taking this path again until we have overcome or resolved most of our issues from that lifetime.

If we have prominent water planets, or many planets in water houses or water signs in our chart, then it is likely we will be more open to divine energies than if we are very grounded in Earth energies.

Water planets are Moon, Pluto, Neptune, Cassandra, Selena (White Moon), and Lillith (Black Moon). Water houses are 4th, 8th, and 12th, and water signs are Cancer, Scorpio, and Pisces.

Earth planets are Venus, Sedna, Chiron, Saturn, and Ceres. Earth houses are 2nd, 6th, and 10th. Earth signs are Taurus, Virgo, and Capricorn.

Getting an astrology chart done by a spiritual specialist is one of the best things we can do to put us on the right path for our destiny, and to help us discover our true potential and where our challenges lie. It will show us the level of our predisposition for connecting with the divine dimensions, and in what ways we are likely to best receive our guidance. For instance, a person with many air aspects in their chart will be better at receiving messages in their head, while a person with many Earth aspects will be better at receiving communications through their own body or through nature.

h) The Void

Lastly, there is another, yet unusual, reason when we will find it difficult to connect with our soul or the gods. This is the period when we are in transition, graduating between vibrational levels, when we are in The Void. During this time we are merging levels of our consciousness and integrating the energies within us. Communications are closed down with the divine world while our consciousness focuses on its task of assimilation. This can be a period of usually not less than three days, but can sometimes take weeks or months, depending on how easily we integrate the new level of consciousness with our old one.

Going into The Void doesn't happen very often, and for some people it never happens at all in their entire lifetime. It occurs only if our consciousness is evolving and travelling up the Ribbon to settle at higher levels on a permanent basis.

The most recent time I found myself in The Void after a major jump in levels, I discovered, to my consternation, my car suddenly declaring on my dashboard computer that my vehicle was not fitted with a GPS navigation system! Where had it disappeared to? I laughed as I realised the symbolism—I was also without a divine GPS, being in The Void! My car's GPS had mysteriously locked on me. Funny that!

Chapter 15 – Ways in which the universe speaks to us

We have looked at the types of assistance that may come our way when we connect with the higher dimensions. Now we will examine in what manner this help comes to us, as it's not always obvious that the things that happen to us in life are actually communications from our soul or the gods. We don't get emails, texts, or phone calls from them, but they deliver their messages in quite unusual ways.

My own soul told me, as I was writing this book, that she speaks to me in experiences and symbols rather than words, because words easily go in one ear and out the other, whereas experiences are often remembered well. To illustrate her point, she said that if someone quoted a love poem to us as a token of their affection, we would probably forget the words of the poem very soon afterwards. But if our lover gave us a long, lingering kiss instead of a poem, we would not forget that experience for a very long time to come.

The following are many of the ways that the universe gets our attention and conveys its messages for us to ponder and take action on.

a) Dreams

Dreams are probably the most common way that people receive communications from their soul or higher beings. They are a record of our travels in consciousness and other dimensions as our spirit self. It's difficult to have a belief in the invisible dimensions and higher beings until we have had experiences of them first-hand. Dreams give us these.

People generally don't pay too much attention to their dreams; they are downplayed by today's society, but the dream world is where our consciousness goes to play at night and where we live out our life as our spirit, and our dreams contain much important information for us.

Everybody dreams, even if they don't remember them, and everyone will have had the experience of waking up from a dream and having a fleeting sensation of having been elsewhere, doing something that they now can't recall, but having been affected by it all the same. The dream world drifts away all too quickly and the details are lost to our conscious mind.

Sometimes, though, a dream is so vivid that we are lucky enough to remember it when we wake, and if we write it down we can mull over the scenario and try to decipher the message it contains. Later on in this chapter we will take a look at the symbolism that crops up in dreams and what it could mean for us.

My own dreams, where I have stepped into the shoes of my spirit self, are usually very dramatic and clear and I can recall many of the details of my journey when I wake, and I jot them down in my diary which I write daily (I've been writing a diary almost every day since I was nine-years-old!) The details may be clear but they aren't always lucid or the meanings apparent, and I need to dwell on them for quite some time to figure out what is being taught to me in this realm of consciousness that I wander into when I fall asleep. There have been times when my dream has been so real that later when I am awake I need to go and check with people if I actually did make this or that arrangement with them!

Also, sometimes in my dreams I remember that I have been asking myself if I am dreaming or not? In the movie *Alice Through The Looking Glass*, Alice tells the Mad Hatter, "A dream is not reality." He replies sagely, "Who's to say which is which?"

We travel as our consciousness in our dreams, as our spirit self in our spirit sphere, and the location that our consciousness usually flies to in the higher dimensions is the Creation Realm.

b) In the Creation Realm

The Creation Realm is a part of the greater consciousness, and consists of both a Dark World and a Light World. However, unless we specifically set our intention to land in the Dark World of conception, we will by default land in the Light World, the place of instant manifestation. There is a level of Creation Realm for all the invisible higher dimensions, including the spirits' Second Earth and the gods' dimensions. It is like Universal Studios in Hollywood, a place where movies are set up and played out.

This is a place where our own consciousness meets up with the consciousnesses of others. Here our spirit gets to act out various roles in diverse landscapes and situations which we later identify as our night-time dreams. Usually, we are learning lessons or experiencing scenarios that cannot be set up for us physically on Earth because of impossible logistics and relationships. Here, in the Creation Realm, we can nut out issues with other people, or with our own fears, that simply could not be manifest for us on Earth. For instance, if we need to work out an issue with another person (dead or alive) but we can't contact them on Earth, then we can visit with their spirit consciousness in the Creation Realm and sort things out at that level.

Hence, we often find ourselves in some kind of ridiculous or unfeasible situation that we would never encounter on our planet in our human life, because all situations become possible in the unseen dimensions. All things can be manifest in the Creation Realm since it is the domain of consciousness, and consciousness is imagination. There is nothing to be scared of here in this realm of consciousness. It is merely the imagination of our soul or spirit being creative along with other souls and spirits.

We enter the Creation Realm during meditation, as well as in our dreams. Here we might be shown images or experience situations where it feels as if we really are part of another world, but going about our day just like we do on Earth, and communicating and interacting with other spirits like ourselves. Often, we embark on long journeys through this realm, some Herculean adventure perhaps, and we might be in human form or we might take other forms, depending on the nature of our lesson.

Some people may still be wondering what it is like in the Creation Realm, so here's a quick little exercise to give you a taste of it.

Creation Realm Exercise

In your mind, visualise a park with a big, green, grassy space in the centre. Imagine a dog running over the grass, chasing or catching a ball. Now add some people to the scene. Now add yourself to the scene. What are you now doing and hearing? Stay with the scene for a minute or so. Do this now before reading further.

You were probably very capable of visualising that scene and could see it clearly playing out in your mind, and you were still thinking like yourself as you do down on Earth today. Our consciousness does not change just because we are not in our human physical body in the Creation Realm. Apart from a lack of body, everything else is just the same.

However, are you aware how the scene probably took on a life of its own? I'll bet that you didn't say to yourself, "I'm now going to create a dog, and I'm going to make that dog run over to that tree and then run over to me with that ball." Things started happening of their own accord, didn't they?

Having done this exercise in many of my workshops, I know that people will tell me things such as; their dog had a frisbee and not a ball, and that it began playing with another dog, or they started chatting to other people in the park, or some little kids came up and started to play too, and any manner of other scenarios started to play out that were not under their own control or from their own imagination.

During this exercise, you have actually been in an altered state of consciousness, not conscious for a minute or two of your physical self or surroundings. You have travelled to the Creation Realm in your spirit sphere. You have been watching your spirit, maybe hearing it, maybe even acting out as your spirit self. Perhaps you were interacting with other spirits there too?

♦

Once we step into the Light World of the Creation Realm, we are a participant there, just as we are in this life on Earth, with things happening all around us and people coming and going. The difference is that in the Creation Realm we are actually manifesting our scenarios in the moment, according to what we are thinking or feeling in our consciousness at the time. It is the realm of instant manifestation. (Manifestation is covered in chapter 17 in more detail).

Other consciousnesses around us are also instantly manifesting what is in their own thinking, and all this is immediately playing out for us all and we are interacting and reacting as our thoughts and emotions unfold. We cannot hide or withhold anything from anyone, nor from ourselves. Our reality in the Creation Realm Light World is an out-picturing of what we are thinking and feeling in that moment.

If we wish to just visualise scenarios without actually manifesting them, then we would visit the Dark World area of the Creation Realm which allows us to play 'what if' until we are ready to concretise our ideas.

This is the way things are in the higher dimensions, and this is one of the reasons why we must train ourselves to utilise our consciousness as a tool that helps us and not hinders us.

c) Coincidences

Some people see coincidence as just a chance occurrence, even though the odds might be heavily stacked against it. Some people might call coincidence the 'Hand of God', or a miracle, or magic, or voodoo.

But all of us, believers or not, would have experienced some form of coincidence happening in our lives, and sometimes even amazing examples of it. Many books and movies have been written on this subject because it is something people are fascinated with.

Was it coincidence that just last night I watched a good movie "2:22" which featured a common coincidence of things re-occurring at a set time, such as 1:11, 3:33, 4:44, or those numbers continually appearing somewhere else? When we realise that our soul and the gods are adept at creating scenarios for us, on Earth and in the Creation Realms of the Second Earth and other dimensions, then we will know that our experience of coincidences is no coincidence at all.

Firstly, they grab our attention, and that is exactly what is supposed to happen. We sit up and take notice of what is going on. Then we need to realise that our soul or the gods are responsible for putting this chain of events into place, and apart from appreciating their brilliance in doing so, we need to understand the message behind it all. It might simply be them wanting to be acknowledged by us, or there might be a deeper underlying cause and meaning.

One of my own amazing coincidences did indeed involve 'The Hand of God' in a most unusual way, and this was just before I first stepped onto my spiritual path when I was much younger. I was waiting to check in at the airport, flying from Sydney, Australia to Los Angeles. Ahead of me I noticed a rather gorgeous man, and was delighted to gaze upon him a second time in the airline's lounge. I thought no more about him as I boarded my plane and took my seat by the window. But, to my utter amazement, a man came and sat next to me, and it just happened to be the attractive fellow I had been admiring earlier. We began chatting, and we didn't stop for the entire fourteen-hour flight to L.A. We got on like a house on fire, and discovered we were both writers. I was just finishing off my first novel, and he had just written a movie script entitled *The Hand of God* (no kidding!) I rather like those kinds of coincidences!

d) The world reflects our consciousness back to us

A major way in which we receive messages from our consciousness is from our environment. The world around us can be read like a wise book. It contains many clues for us to help us understand our issues. It 'speaks' to us if we look around with awareness or hear what it is saying. But most people are too wrapped up in their own little worlds and they are blind and deaf to the messages all around them.

The human mind filters out all but the essentials for our everyday functioning. Other worlds are intersecting with ours in every moment, and it would be overwhelming if we didn't filter out all the things that weren't necessary to manage our life. But in doing so we become complacent and oblivious to commonplace occurrences. So, we need to broaden our viewpoint and take in more around us, looking in directions we don't usually peer, and asking why quirky things may be happening to us. For our environment may be reflecting our consciousness back at us in any number of ways and giving us important information.

Recently, I was having trouble with the remote control of my TV recorder. This in itself was signifying that I was having a battle of wills with my soul over control. I couldn't get a replacement remote control anywhere, so I toyed with the idea that I might buy a new TV with an inbuilt PVR (personal video recorder). My current television was pretty small by today's standards, and I checked out all the massive screens, not really wanting one that size to dominate my lounge room. But in the end, I didn't need to buy a new TV because I suddenly understood the message I was being sent. I just needed to see the bigger picture, and that's why I had been led to view all those big TV screens!

Another example of my environment speaking to me was about the noise in my external world reflecting back at me the noise in my mind. I was going through a period of feeling anxious, unsafe, unconfident, and alarmed. So, alarms were going off in my house because I was feeling alarmed! I had two weeks of smoke alarms going off in the middle of the night even though there was no smoke or flat batteries. I so wanted to get rid of those smoke alarms!

Eventually I had all the alarms replaced with new ones. Then I went to turn off my alarm clock and accidentally swiped it so it landed underneath my bed in an awkward place to get to. I was subconsciously trying to get rid of that alarm too. It took a while for it to sink in that I merely needed to get rid of the alarming feelings in my consciousness and then all the external alarms would cease too.

Not only our homes but our cars are often good reflectors of things that are going wrong in our consciousness and our thinking. Flat batteries and flat tyres could indicate that we have burned up all our energy and we have nothing left within us to get started or to keep going with. Flat tyres could also be preventing us from going somewhere that we shouldn't. Speeding tickets tell us we are travelling too fast without due care, not only on the road but also in our life in general. Parking tickets might be saying we are overdue in making a move in our life.

e) Cards, astrology

Tarot cards, angel cards, wisdom cards—there are thousands of card packs in the marketplace these days that bring us all kinds of messages and enlightenment. Our soul loves to use cards to get its message across as it's an easy way to communicate with us and bypasses our human conscious mind that might inhibit our soul.

I love to use cards every day, even though I can simply channel my soul and the gods whenever I want. The cards add even more clarity and meaning to whatever lesson I am currently learning, and I always ponder on them and believe in their message. A mixture of cards is good for a broader understanding of the issue, and gives our soul a wider choice of the best version to use in any particular situation.

Not only do I pull several cards each morning, but I also check out my astrology for the day, and I love the way that the two modalities match up very nicely, supporting one another in their messages.

For instance, I will often pull the Star Tarot card when I have the Sun (a star) aspecting my North Node of Destiny. The Empress Tarot card often shows up when the goddess Juno is prominent on that day. The Love Tarot card turns up when Venus is in my stars. The Tarot Five of Cups (Disappointment) or Tarot Nine of Swords (Sorrow) cards are associated with the Black Moon (the goddess Lillith). Cards that are to do with nurturing or nature will show up when it's a Ceres day (the goddess of the harvest), and cards to do with selfishness or taking action will turn up whenever it's a prominent Mars day.

Pondering on the messages of cards or astrology is not just fun and entertainment but can give us genuine guidance for our day or weeks ahead, guidance that comes from our soul and the gods.

f) Stones, bones, tea leaves, patterns

Many years ago, when I lived in South Africa, I visited a witchdoctor in Zimbabwe who 'threw the bones' for me. I entered his mud and straw hut with trepidation, and recoiled at all the ghastly skeletons, skins, herbs, and hocus-pocus items hanging from the roof, but sat down on the dirt floor and listened intently. The sangoma (the African name for a witchdoctor or shaman) read the bones like we might read tea leaves in a teacup; he made sense of the patterns he saw before him, his soul guiding him in interpreting the imagery.

In one of my workshops, we threw stones into a circle as a group, and we had a lot of fun, and amazement, as we began to construe some meanings from the patterns that had formed. It could be said that anything could be read into it, but there was truly some underlying message there that aligned well with what I had just been teaching my students.

We shouldn't be so quick to dismiss these seemingly crazy and quirky ways of receiving messages. They are just more ways that our soul and the gods can speak with us and give us insights as we try to interpret the patterns.

g) Symbols, signs, and images

The beings of the higher dimensions speak to us in a language which is usually not in words but in symbols, signs, images, music, or metaphors. If this is the way the universe communicates, then we need to learn it, like reading and writing our own human language. Symbolism is a universal language. It conveys greater meaning than words alone.

For instance, think of the universally-known logo of McDonald's symbol of the Golden Arches. When people see this symbol, there will be a whole range of images, and probably memories too, that pop up in their minds. The five-ringed symbol of the Olympic Games is another case in point. We don't look at these symbols and interpret them literally, but we convert them into what is conveyed in general by that symbol and then into what is meaningful to us personally.

Symbols and signs are the way that our soul and the gods will commonly communicate with us. These are all around us in our everyday life, and we need to be vigilant so that we notice them and act on their suggestions to adjust our path. We are being directed by the higher beings (and fellow humans) at all times, but often we don't see the signs because our eyes are blinkered by our filtering system that sees only what it is programmed to see and which ignores all else.

In order to see all the signs that are laid out for us, we need to open our minds and actively become conscious that the world is 'speaking' to us. If we follow the signs, then we will have more chance of keeping on track with our mission. If we miss even one sign, then there is every chance we will become lost, just as if we miss a turning when we are following a road map.

Symbols and signs may be experienced via images that we see, but they can also be audible signs, or arise through our sense of smell, taste, or touch. We may get a whiff of a fragrance or pipe tobacco that reminds us of someone important that we need to contact. I have created a range of flower essences from 45 different flowers, and if I come across one of these flowers unexpectedly, I am reminded of the healing energies of that plant and I know I need to turn my focus to the issues that this flower represents. We may experience signals to us through some or all of our senses, depending on how sensitive and consciously awake we are.

Interpreting symbols and signs

Once we become aware that we are receiving a sign or symbol of some kind from the universe, the next step is to interpret it correctly. There are many misunderstandings between Heaven and Earth because the spirit world speaks with us in this cryptic language. We can often read the wrong things into signs and make them say what we want, or confirm what we believe. (Scientists have a term for this—confirmation bias.)

We will need to interpret our signs correctly using the right intelligence. Who better to act as an interpreter than our soul? We can ask them to help us unravel clues by asking specific questions. If we try to use our human mind to unlock the secrets of these symbols, we will probably fail because our brain is just too literal and usually cannot see the patterns and underlying themes. It would be like speaking with a computer or a robot; they could identify certain things they had been encoded to recognise but anything unusual would be beyond their remit.

For instance, if we showed a robot a cloud, it might identify it merely as a cloud, a collection of water vapour, and it might even be able to recognise the category of the cloud. But what if the universe was showing us an image within that cloud?

Years ago, when I was creating a workshop entitled *Warrior for God*, I looked up one evening as the sun was setting, and to my astonishment

I saw a massive sword lying across the sky as a dark purple cloud formation in an otherwise cloudless blue sky. The logo I was using for my workshop was an Excalibur-type sword, so I took this as a wonderful sign of confirmation that I was on track with my work.

The universe generally uses signs and symbolism that have great meaning for us personally. Signs have different meanings for different people, so they must be understood correctly for each individual. We will need to ponder on the meaning that is unique to us. For example, the McDonald's Golden Arches symbol may conjure up a variety of meanings if we asked several people; food in general; beefburgers; French fries; ice cream; coffee; soft drinks; a place to use the bathroom; a rest stop on a trip; a warm place out of the cold; a place to use the Internet; fast food; cheap and filling food; too many calories.

Whatever we see, hear, or experience, we shouldn't take it too literally but be circumspect and enquire more about the sign. Question everything about it, not in disbelief but merely to ascertain what it might be telling us. We cannot always accept things as they seem, and we may need to put a different slant on things.

This applies especially with dreams and meditations where things usually have more subtle, obscure, and often ingenious, meanings than in our physical reality. Many of us will have dreamed of a plane crash, either being in one or watching one. This does not indicate that we will be involved in a plane crash any time soon, but more likely it is telling us that our expectations haven't been met, or that our dreams and aspirations have crashed.

A common dream is of sitting on a toilet in public, and this indicates that we are feeling exposed or vulnerable, and may be needing to let go of our emotional baggage which is affecting our public image. Losing our handbag or wallet in a dream can mean, not only that we need to be more careful with our money, but that we feel we are losing our identity in our physical reality.

Cars can represent our human body or our spirit body. It is the vehicle in which we travel. I have had several dreams where I have forgotten where I parked my car, and this usually indicates that I have become neglectful of either my human self or my spirit self, that I have forgotten about them and need to reconnect.

Elevators in dreams represent moving up or down the vibrational levels of the higher dimensions. If I press a high-numbered button in the elevator, I know I am off to visit a high-level world. If I press the basement button, I know I am in for some trouble!

Water in dreams or meditation equates with emotional issues. Getting lost means we are not on the right path to our destiny. Waiting to catch a plane, train, or bus means we are about to set off on a new journey, either physically or as our spirit self.

But again it should be emphasised that there will be multiple meanings for incidences in dreams and altered states of consciousness, so that if several people saw the same thing, it might mean something different to all of them, conveying many meanings at once, especially if they are at different levels of vibration. Therefore, if we can create a personalised system with our soul, or the gods that we regularly work with, we will be able to recognise much of the symbology that they show us and interpret its meaning correctly each time.

The power of symbols and signs

Symbols and images are miniature power grids and are transmitted from Heaven to Earth continually, as well as being present all around us on our Earth. They could be considered as magical and they have great power. The consciousness of whomever created the symbol oozes out of it, and their energy emanates from every line, space, and angle. The symbols are not inert and they definitely affect us. This is the reason that advertising and marketing campaigns have such a hypnotic effect over us.

If we feel a symbol to be not for our benefit, then we will need to protect ourselves from its effect and be conscious enough not to be brainwashed by it. Advertising symbols and logos rely on this, which is why upmarket brands of clothing and accessories retain such a cachet. People flock to sport the logo that is trending at any particular time, even though the item may be exactly the same quality as one that is one tenth of the price but doesn't carry the prestigious name tag.

Our society is distorting our consciousness through the use of symbols and images in advertising, some of it secretive and iniquitous. Are we being turned into someone we don't want to be, or don't even realise who we are becoming—a puppet of media marketing?

However, if we find a symbol or image that fills us with joy and which raises our vibrations, then we should fill up on it. Most people love to gaze at photos of their family, and it fills their heart with love. These photos are just another kind of symbolism—they represent all that means so much to us in our life. Other people might love to look at images of flowers or animals or children or beautiful buildings. Spiritual people might favour pictures of saints or the Ascended Masters, or enigmatic images of light in striking patterns. The options for discovering uplifting symbolism are unlimited.

Our signature is also a symbol, a power grid of who we are and what we stand for, and our own energy emanates from it whenever we create it. It has a vibration to it, so we need to be careful what we put our signature to, and to value it as representing who we are and what we are committing to.

Consciousness is awareness, and we need to train ourselves to be more aware and conscious so that we can recognise the marvellous symbolism and the messages that the universe is communicating to us. If we live on autopilot, we will miss all the necessary signposts that will guide us to our rightful destiny. Life is much richer and more on track if we learn the language of our soul.

h) Intuition/gut feel

Messages from our soul or the gods often come not as words or even as symbols or images, but rather as intuition or gut feel. A person will just get a sense of what they need to be doing or saying. Many people, even those who have never given a thought to their soul or the higher dimensions, nevertheless act on their intuition more often than they would credit.

In my experience, men especially, who tend not to be as open to the invisible worlds as women, work more unconsciously through their intuition and gut feel rather than through hearing their soul or other voices in their consciousness. However, everyone is moved by their intuition at times, whether they realise it or not. It comes as an urge to do something, very often something that they might not have thought of doing in the normal course of events.

For most people, intuition is just that sudden idea that pops into the head, followed by a decision to go with that thought. It's often just a subtle thought and not given much consideration, so much so that on reflection it hasn't seemed like a thought at all but more like a flow of energy through the body or gut that gets us moving in a certain direction.

Often when I wake up in the morning, I suddenly feel an idea develop in my mind, and get an image along with it, of what I need to do that day or where I need to go. It may be quite different from what I had planned, but I always heed this intuition for I know my soul is wise and can perceive many things that I can't see, so I don't choose to ignore it. And so, I might find myself going out for a coffee when I had planned to stay at home to work on writing my book, and then I might meet an old friend at the café and something important happens and I am suddenly glad that I listened to what my soul had to say.

i) Sudden insights

Another way that the divine world communicates with us is through sudden insights, great ideas that hit us out of the blue. For most people they would merely think that they were an inspired genius, but usually these revelations come courtesy of our soul or the gods. All great discoveries come from the higher dimensions, and humans are just the vehicles that write these brainwaves down and make them happen. Albert Einstein often said that his insights came from God.

Our egos need to be humble enough to accept that perhaps we are not the geniuses we gauge ourselves to be, and that we might be being assisted by higher minds than our own.

j) Navigation

Our soul and the gods are adept at guiding us towards our true destiny and keeping us on track if we see the signs and interpret them correctly.

But they can also help us to navigate our way around physically down on Earth, just as if we had a GPS system in our car. We can be physically guided to the places we need to be, even if we have no map or even if we have no idea of our destination.

We will need to surrender to this process completely and not try to take control or argue with our divine navigator, or else we will get into trouble and lose our way. But if we can just be the arms that steer the car, or the feet that step forward on the path, and we do as instructed, then we can find ourselves in magical places or back on the right road again if we have been lost.

Some years ago I was in Darwin, in northern Australia, visiting a friend who had recently moved there. We wanted to go somewhere nice for lunch, and I got a message from Master Dominic that he wished to guide us to a lovely restaurant. My friend drove while I channelled the instructions from Dominic who took us down many roads and around roundabouts, and neither my friend nor I had any idea of where we were being led to. Eventually we arrived at a little backwater wharf by the waterfront which had a great restaurant which my friend didn't know existed.

Another time I was visiting the Lake District in England, driving around on my own. Someone had mentioned a stone circle in the area but I didn't know where it was. So I asked the gods to guide me there, and I was directed down strange roads in foreign countryside, even through a busy town, and eventually I pulled up outside the entrance to the path which led to the stone circle. I hadn't got lost at all.

All that is necessary is to listen to the guidance and not negate instructions or cherry-pick them. When we surrender our human will to the will of the divine, then we allow magic into our lives and miracles are sure to follow.

k) Bodily sensations and illness

Another important way that we receive messages from the higher dimensions is through our physical body. This can be by way of sensations that we feel in different parts of us or through our entire body, or through various pains and illnesses and physical conditions. Our body is a great indicator of what is going on for us in our consciousness. It signals us when things in our mind are rotten or misaligned or inflamed or worn out. Discomfort, pain, and illness are used a great deal by our soul to alert us to an issue that needs resolving. Pain always results from our resistance to something.

In Louise Hay's classic book *You Can Heal Your Life*, she documents what various ailments may represent in our thinking and emotions. And so we see that skin rashes could indicate we get irritated over delays, or that knee problems could be caused by stubborn pride, ego, and inflexibility.

In speaking with Master Chiron to develop these ideas further, he told me that it's important to be aware on which side of the body we are experiencing pain. He said that if the pain is on the right-hand side, it emanates from the left brain and is caused by the human inhibiting what the soul desires. It shows that the issue is caused by the human self resisting what the soul wants to do, and the human is trying to control things and is using its human will to fight the soul's will. If the pain is on the left-hand side, emanating from the right brain, it is caused by the soul inhibiting the human from venturing down the wrong track.

For example, if pain is in the right hip, the human self may be preventing the growth and expansion that the soul wants for it. The human doesn't want to move forward and has too much fear, lacks confidence, or lacks the talents required to progress and therefore needs to learn more or skill up. If the pain is in the left hip, the human wants to grow and expand in ways not conducive to the soul's plans for it. The human wants to follow its own will and not divine will, and the soul is preventing this. The human is not listening to their soul.

When we have an ailment or illness, we can ask the divine beings for more information on the issue, and for help in overcoming it. It's not a question of merely healing the disorder, for it is the underlying thinking and beliefs that need to be adjusted before the complaint can be cured. We might find temporary relief is given to us so we can get through our days better, but the sickness of the body can never be totally relieved until the sickness of the mind is dealt with.

Recently I was suffering from some breathing problems. My chest felt very tight, and I had an overall feeling of suppression and not being able to take in enough air. In meditation, I asked the gods to give me more information about my condition, and I was shown images of pan pipes, organ pipes, and the radiator on a car.

My interpretation of this was that I needed to clear my air tubes. Air in symbology equates to consciousness and the mind, so I understood that I needed to clear out some thinking and beliefs. A car radiator contains water, so I also needed to attend to my emotions because water equals emotions in the world of symbolism. Because of the pan pipes and organ pipes, I also concluded that perhaps I needed more music in my life, more downtime to have fun and dance.

As we can imagine, the field of symbology for the human body is vast, and an entire book could be written on this subject alone. Maybe it will be the topic of a future book I write, who knows? In chapter 19 there is more information about symptoms and healing the body.

l) Messages through other people

We not only receive messages through our own consciousness and through situations reflecting back to us from the world around us, but also through interaction with other people. They may be the unwitting messenger of some important communication for us. If the person is very conscious and spiritually aware, they might understand the part they are playing to deliver a message or idea to us, but, for the most part, people are unsuspecting carriers, and their soul is guiding them through their intuition to convey this information.

Recently I found myself being instrumental in getting one of my friends to go on a tour of South America. We had met up in town on market day, and she had casually mentioned that she wanted to visit Machu Picchu, the Inca ruins in Peru. Only moments before, I had bumped into an old friend whom I hadn't seen for many years, and I knew that she ran escorted tours to South America. So, I was able to put the two of them in touch, successfully carrying out my role of messenger on that day.

m) UFOS

This may seem like a strange addition to this chapter, but the higher beings do in fact communicate with us through UFO (Unidentified Flying Object) sightings. It's just another way they make contact, and it gets the attention of one section of society who may not be open to receiving messages by other methods.

Chiron tells us that UFO visits and sightings are targeted. They are seen by the folks that are meant to see them and are invisible to anyone else. Of course, the navigators of these UFOs are not aliens in the usual sense of the word, but they are gods from the higher dimensions. We can tune into them and converse with them. In Part One, in the chapter *Aliens and UFOs*, I described my own experience with UFOs, and I was very delighted to be contacted in this way.

The veil between the higher dimensions and lower dimensions is now thinning, and for those who raise their vibrations high enough they will begin to see things, hear things, and experience things that have been denied us until now. There will probably be many more ways that the higher dimensional beings will contact us in the future, and we will need to be awake and alert to these possibilities so that we can receive their communications loud and clear.

Chapter 16 – How to connect with the unseen universe

In this chapter we are going to take a look at how to prepare ourselves for connecting with the unseen universe, with our own soul, other souls, and the gods and angels, and to look at what happens when our consciousness arrives in the higher dimensions. What is it like there?

At first it may seem strange or difficult to get there, but when we cultivate the proper procedure and we practise it regularly, it will seem as easy as picking up a phone and connecting with whomever we desire. Once we know how to access the clever and wise parts of ourself and the higher beings, we will be assured of getting better answers on how to live our life fruitfully and harmoniously.

At the end of the chapter is a checklist of points for preparing before, during, and after connection with the higher world.

Using our Third Eye, our psychic channel

How exactly do we speak with the higher dimensions? We do so through our consciousness, through our mind. We have already explored how we have a Ribbon of Consciousness connecting our human consciousness with our spirit/soul consciousness. This Ribbon is like a channel that facilitates our communications, just like broadband, TV, and satellite channels take our communications around the world.

This channel is often referred to as our Third Eye, and Chiron himself calls it this, and tells us that it is a jewel of our consciousness and it is our eyesight; not the sight of our human eyes, but our seeing-eye, our psychic ability. Many people equate the Third Eye with the position of a chakra point between the eyebrows, and with the function of the pineal gland in our brain, but Chiron doesn't mention this in his work. Instead, he tells us that our communications channel starts down in our heart, not in our brain. We speak with our soul and the higher dimensions heart-to-heart, not head-to-head.

Every one of us has this psychic channel within us, and the ability to use it, but it is mostly under-utilised by the populace. But there is much to see and learn if we use it properly, as we saw earlier in all the ways that the divine beings can help us with our lives. Our Third Eye channel is as useful as any Internet connection, and if we don't use it we are walking around half blind and half deaf compared to what could be seen or heard. Our psychic channel is one of the most important tools in the Toolbox of our Consciousness.

Most of us, when we look at people, see them in the way a torch picks out a face in the dark. We don't see the world around that person, but just a body, and more often just some features. But our Third Eye, and our soul, can see all that this person is enmeshed in, like their family, job, friends, health issues, emotional problems, or their dreams—all their greater consciousness that spans the present, past, and future.

When we expand our consciousness into the Beyond, we can get glimpses of all this, about ourselves and about others. Most people just accept the tiny illumination they are given into their own lives and others, and it is usually more than enough to have to deal with, but Beyond can sometimes provide us with useful answers.

You might be asking how do you switch on this Third Eye channel? There is no physical switch. There is only the desire and intention to communicate with the higher dimensions, and this automatically activates our psychic channel. The more the channel is utilised, the faster and clearer communications will become. The channel will begin to remain open at all times so that we are online 24/7. We know what happens to any computer if we don't use it for a while—it goes to sleep. So does our Third Eye!

Just as our reading glasses, windshields, phone screens, or computer screens get dirty and need a clean every now and again, so does our Third Eye need some attention every so often. It's not as if we can take it out and wash and polish it, but when we set our intention to do so, our consciousness will take care of that task for us. Whenever I am cleaning windows or mirrors, I always dedicate this act to my Third Eye and ask my soul to get cleaning inside my consciousness at the same time as I beaver away in the external world.

What can we expect to see or hear when we use our Third Eye? I can speak only from my own experiences here, but as stated in Part One, I don't see and speak with higher dimensional beings as if they were physically on the ground in my presence. For me, the Third Eye is like a movie screen inside my head. The gods or Masters come to me in my consciousness, in my mind's eye as it were. They appear as if I am watching a movie or partaking in a movie in my mind. Usually, the gods will form an image or projection of themselves in my consciousness in a way that I will recognise them, and so it is normally their favourite human form they show to me (just as we might show a best photo of ourselves to visiting relatives), and they use the same image every time so that I know it is them. From time to time, however, they can be a little vague and I can get confused until I ask them who they are.

Setting intention and focusing

The first step in activating your divine communications channel, your Third Eye, is to get into a comfortable meditative state, which means just being somewhere high vibrational where you won't be distracted or interrupted for a while. Making somewhere high vibrational means having a clean environment and being clean yourself. (I love that one of Dr. Jordan Peterson's 12 Rules For Life is 'Clean Your Room!') You can burn candles or oils, and use crystals or flowers to beautify the place.

Ensure you are sober, well-hydrated, and not going to think about food or going to the bathroom. Put aside all everyday thoughts and issues for a while and make quality time for this session so that time pressures don't disturb you. Have things ready to hand to make notes straight afterwards.

Think about who you would like to connect with. Have the strong intention of connecting with the higher worlds. You may also state your issue at this time. This alerts your spirit or soul that you wish to work with them during this session, and gives them some indication of what advice or lessons they can bring to you. Keep focusing on this intention and don't get distracted by wandering thoughts.

You should be pure in your intention, in that the powerful information and energies you hope to receive should not be used for unwise situations or harmful purposes. This would have repercussions later on.

Knowing you are safe

When people first meditate they are often a bit scared of what might happen to them. This is perfectly natural, for it is a journey into the unknown and humans are programmed to be wary of the unknown. After a session or two, these concerns will fade away, when the person realises they are quite safe physically and nothing at all is going to happen to their body while their consciousness is off travelling in higher dimensions.

It is only your consciousness that is experiencing scenarios and situations while you are travelling in your spirit sphere. Your body remains on Earth meditating in the same position and in the same state where you left it. If at all worried, you can always ask someone to sit near you while you gain confidence in the meditation process.

Release any nervousness or self-centredness, and do as much cleansing of the consciousness as you can in order to let go of any low vibrations. Follow the suggestions in chapter 11 for raising your vibrations if you feel they may not be very high.

Place energetic protection around yourself, such as visualising white light or a violet flame surrounding you, or hold a special crystal, or burn sage sticks or candles. You can also ask the angels to ensure you are protected from lower frequency entities who might want to jump into your sphere of consciousness while you are opening yourself up to the invisible dimensions.

Your consciousness creates your reality, so whatever you believe protects you, this will be the case.

Crossing the bridge

Trying to enter the higher dimensions is like needing to cross a bridge. In this case it is a bridge between Earth and Heaven, between the consciousness of our human and the consciousness of our spirit/soul.

It is not a physical bridge, but it is helpful to imagine there is a symbolic bridge of some kind and we need to get from one side to the other.

In science fiction movies, there is always some kind of barrier to be crossed in order to enter the invisible kingdoms of the gods or aliens. Usually, in films, they choose wormholes or portals, as I guess they are visually dramatic, but any type of imaginary crossing is suitable, as well as going over a bridge structure. We could go through a door, gate, or archway, climb over a wall, hop over a hedge, fence, or stile, row across a river, or, like Alice, step through a looking glass or fall down a rabbit hole.

We could also imagine we are walking along our Ribbon of Consciousness, or even jumping across the corpus callosum, the bridge in our brain between our left and right hemispheres. The process of crossing even a small barrier assists our consciousness to feel it is now stepping into a new dimension.

When I first began travelling to the spirit realm, I had no idea what I was doing or where I was going, but I just surrendered to the process which automatically took me where I needed to be. For years, I always started off by imagining myself in a large meadow filled with flowers. I found myself walking down a path which led me to a river. There on the bank was a small rowing boat and I got in and rowed myself across the stream. I would drag the tiny boat up onto the shore and then someone would always come and meet me. For the first six months or so, my guides were a couple of women, whom I had apparently known in my past lives. They weren't gods or angels but just ordinary humans who had passed over and now lived as spirits in the higher world (which I now know to be the Second Earth.).

However, I was obviously being monitored during my time in the invisible dimensions, since after six months or so of regular visits, which I found fascinating, I was then introduced to other beings who began to teach me a lot about the unseen worlds. Even then, it was years before I learnt about Ascended Masters, and that my guides were in fact members of this high-ranking society of gods.

Another favourite way of entering the higher dimensions, which I use a lot with my beginner students, is to go through a garden gate and into a garden. I tell people to be there at the gate with all their senses, seeing what colour and shape it is and what material it is made from. What is the shape of the handle? What is on either side of the gate—a hedge, a wall, a picket fence? What is the weather like? What fragrances are in the air?

When they are fully ready, I tell them to open the gate and enter the garden, and then to take a walk around it and carefully look at and touch and smell all the flowers, plants, and trees. Are there water features in the garden? Are there seats or bowers or swings or statues or bird baths or sheds, or any manner of things you might find in a garden?

The imagination begins to take over, and then you are pulled in and find yourself there, truly in another dimension.

Arriving in the higher dimensions

Once you are over your bridge or through your symbolic gateway, what you find on the other side is up to you, and it may change every time you go across. It might be a door that you need to open. It might be an elevator door, or a hallway of similar-looking doors like in a hotel corridor.

I have sometimes ended up at the doorway to a church. There have been times when I've gone through doorways underwater, or through the backs of caves, or fallen over waterfalls, or climbed into a hot air balloon. Consciousness is limitless in its imagination, and the scenario that opens up for you will be very apt for the situation or lesson that you need to experience.

Wherever you may find yourself on the other side, it is important to be there utilising all your senses of sight, hearing, touch, smell, and taste.

Imagine you are in a foreign country on holiday and, even though everything is strange to you, you are drinking it all in and loving the experience. Or imagine that you have just arrived inside a movie set and you are preparing to take part in the next scene to play out there. Look down at yourself and see what clothes you are wearing and what kind of shoes you have on your feet, or perhaps you are bare-footed? Feel your hands and skin and face and hair. Gaze all around you and touch things and note colours and shapes and aromas. If other people are there too, note the way they are acting and speaking. You are familiarising yourself with all the props, and the other actors and extras, and with the zeitgeist of the moment.

Don't be afraid, but just relax and be excited at what might happen next.

Accepting everything

It is important to just accept whatever happens to you in the invisible dimensions. If you begin to analyse it, or fight it, you will find yourself jumping back into your human consciousness again and you will lose your connection to the higher world. When you are well-experienced in travelling in these higher dimensions, then you will begin to take command of situations there and make things happen, but when you first start out as a spirit traveller, it is best to just let experiences happen to you and not try to take control.

Don't have any preconceived ideas about what will happen. Just accept whatever you are seeing, sensing, or hearing, or where you are being led. Go along without resistance. Accept everything that occurs to you or in front of you, no matter how weird. Don't question it, or whether it's possible that it could exist or play out this way. All is possible in the Creation Realm and higher dimensions.

So, you could find yourself speaking with animals or flowers or trees or rivers or even lights. Perhaps you are flying like an eagle or through the walls of a mountain. Perhaps you are diving with whales down into the depths of the ocean, or you are dangling from a star in the cosmos.

Don't tell yourself this is ridiculous and negate what you are experiencing. This is the biggest mistake that people make when they communicate with the higher realms. They say they aren't getting anything, but they are actually experiencing quite a bit, and getting messages too, but they are also instantly negating and dismissing them. You cannot tell yourself, "I am not experiencing this or seeing this." You will have to believe whatever you are going through or it will have no value for you.

Wait until you come out of your altered state of consciousness after your meditation to begin pondering on all the crazy stuff you might have encountered and to make sense of it all, remembering that most of what you experience will have been symbolic and you will need to decipher what that symbolism means to you personally.

Flying and exploring

In our spirit body, our spirit sphere of consciousness, we will be able to fly anywhere in the universe depending on our vibrational limits. We should go exploring and enjoy ourselves. We need to be curious, ask questions, and try to be there with all our senses. Unlike with night dreams, we will remember our journeys and experiences when we come back to the human world in our consciousness.

However, we must be cognisant of the fact that our consciousness will not only experience delightful and uplifting events on its travels, but there will undoubtedly be situations involving challenges or trauma or even death. We need to remember that our consciousness can never truly die, so even if we do go through any kind of 'death' during our voyage, we will merely be losing a part of our consciousness, and not dying physically in our body. There will be no consequences for us back in the real world, apart from feeling a whole lot lighter after removing all that old baggage from our mind.

We will be faced with many situations where we need to die to our old self and our old way of being and thinking, and be reborn as a new self. We might find ourself then rising like a phoenix out of the fire, as did Professor Dumbledore's bird in the Harry Potter books and movies. Trust that we physically survive every situation that our consciousness goes through in meditation.

Having respect

During our travels in consciousness to the higher worlds, we will very probably meet other souls and even gods and angels. We need to be respectful, and acknowledge and thank whomever comes into our scenarios. They are powerful and divine beings, even those who are not gods, but we need to especially treat the higher beings like monarchs. We should converse and debate courteously and civilly, listening carefully to everyone and taking all opinions into consideration.

The higher dimensions have societies and structures and rules just like we do on Earth, and we should heed the way things work there, just as we would if we were visiting a foreign country. The most important rule of the higher worlds is to be love, and if we break this rule then we will find ourselves ejected to a lower dimension.

At the end of our meditation session, we should always remember to thank the divine ones for their time and effort and patience in communicating with us and trying to teach us.

Is it my soul, a god, or my ego talking?

One of the main questions you'll ask yourself when you receive messages in your consciousness is, "Who is doing the talking? Am I making it all up? How can I tell if it's my soul or a god or just the thoughts in my own head?"

In previous chapters we have examined all the different parts of our Ribbon of Consciousness, including our spirit and current soul, and all our souls reaching back to our Source. At the lower end of our Ribbon lie all the different personas of our human consciousness, each one of which we can speak with individually. We have also seen that we can communicate with the spirits and souls of other people, from the ordinary souls who have passed over (nice ones and devilish ones), to gods and angels, to creator gods and the One God at the top. We could be hearing from any one of them.

Depending on where we are 'dialling into' on our Ribbon, we will be speaking with whomever is on that particular vibrational level, or wavelength. If we set our intention to speak only with higher beings and our vibrations are also high, we could be speaking with our soul, or the souls of other people or higher dimensional beings. If our vibrations are low, we will probably only connect with our own lower personas or those of other humans or spirits.

We could, of course, be in a high vibrational mood ourselves but elect to communicate with lower personas to sort out issues with them. However, if we are in a low vibrational mood, we will not be able to connect with beings at higher levels. Therefore, if we wish to converse with a finer class of being, we will need to raise our vibrational level as detailed in chapter 11.

That said, it is still confusingly difficult at times to comprehend at what level the advice or guidance is coming from. Many people give up trying to discern which is the right voice to listen to, the one that will really benefit them, especially if that voice seems to be leading them down an irrational path.

I often wish there was some kind of indicator or signpost in the invisible realms that showed us exactly where we were in any moment regarding dimensions and vibrational levels. We can be too easily tricked, and we need to be alert as to who we are dealing with. If we aren't aware of our vibrational level as we go into meditation, then we will connect with our default wavelength, which is usually our lowest frequency level.

We need to ask ourselves how we are feeling before we attempt to make a connection with the divine worlds. We can refer to the checklist in chapter 11 on what low vibrations look and feel like. If we sense any kind of uneasiness or disharmony or pain (physical or emotional) within ourselves, then this is a good indication that something needs to be resolved. The problem will usually be at the level of our lower personas, but sometimes it stems from issues at higher levels between us and our soul or the gods.

Whether the voices are good or bad will depend on what emotional state we are in when we connect. Other beings, lower personas, and souls and gods alike, will tend to reflect back to us whatever emotions we ourselves are putting out. If we are cranky, then whomever we are dealing with will probably act cranky too. It's just like any relationship on Earth. If we are playing games and being less than honest, then we will attract trickery in our relations with others, even across dimensions.

It's not a bad thing at all to connect with our lower personas; in fact, it's to be recommended. This is the way we will overcome much of our old programming, and be able to let go of limiting beliefs that have sabotaged us for a long while. If we are feeling fearful about something in particular, or just in general, we can call out the personas who are responsible for these feelings, and we can converse with these parts of ourself and sort them out once and for all.

The real predicament comes when we hear a voice that gives us advice, and we're not sure if this voice is a high level being coming from a base of love, or whether it's one of our lower personas guiding us from a base of fear or avoidance or resistance. We ask, "Can I believe this? Is this really true?"

The question we really need to be asking is, "What does this entity feel like?" The presence of our soul or a god or an angel feels quite different from the energies that fill our being when our own lower personas confront us or the lower personas of other people. The presence of any high vibrational being is very powerful and, if we are on the same wavelength, we may intuitively recognise it and feel awe. Their energy should be something that fills us with love and peace. Some people may experience a sense of light and lightness, or a warm tingling in their body.

When gods first started meeting with me in consciousness, I always felt the back of my tongue fizzing. It was like an alarm bell, warning me of their presence. Nowadays I am used to their energies and it rarely happens anymore, except if I am being totally unaware, and then it wakes me up. These days, because I have worked with many gods for a long time, I intuitively recognise who is present from the colours and qualities of their aura and the fleeting glimpse they give me of their physical form they are projecting.

If it's difficult to feel or see the energies of the being who is speaking or appearing in our consciousness and we still can't fathom out who they are, we can always just ask for their name and what they do in the invisible dimensions, just as we might ask a stranger we meet in a bar or on a plane. If we are wondering if they are a god or not, we can simply ask them to show us their godly light. They won't be offended if they are a true god. However, this question will make any lower astral entity skitter away quickly if they don't possess this light within them.

Although our spirit and soul are available to us at all times, it is unlikely that our messages are coming from a higher god unless we are a god ourselves or have been taken on by them as a student. To become a student, we will have proved our commitment to them that we are dedicated to our spiritual journey and to doing the work that it takes to achieve our godhood. Half-heartedness is not acceptable to the gods. If we wish to hang out with gods, then we will need to act like a god ourselves.

For some people, the presence of a god or high entity, may agitate them and cause issues to come to the fore. Even though this isn't a pleasant scenario, we should be grateful that our teachers are helping us to see the things that require cleansing and healing. By opening our heart and surrendering instead of resisting, we can get the most out of our communications instead of just fighting or disbelieving.

But be aware that gods (and our soul too) can sometimes seem to be the devil in disguise, as this will be part and parcel of some lesson that we need to learn. It is the gods' mission to transform us, and they will use any means necessary, including trickery, duplicity, and humiliation in order to get us down the right path and embracing godhood. We won't always see the funny side of things at first, and we can act with outrage and bitterness towards the gods or our soul, but eventually we come to understand that the methods employed by them were justified.

If we are confident that our soul or a god is speaking with us, then we will be ready to follow their guidance and we will feel a sense of relief and harmony within us and an enthusiasm to be moving in the suggested direction.

But if we have been operating from a basis of fear or not-love when we have made our connection with the invisible realms, then we are more than likely to start questioning any answers we receive, and we will go round and round in mental circles, trying to guess and second guess what is really going on and who we have connected with. We probably won't receive any clarity about this until we have resolved our underlying fears and issues. If the messages produce a sense of discord within us, they could have come from the gods, our soul, our lower personas or, indeed, any other dark entity who sees an opportunity for creating chaos. We might wonder why the gods or our soul would allow this turmoil, but they welcome bringing to the forefront any issues that require resolution.

Firstly, we should examine the role of our lower personas in any answers that we receive, for they are usually the frontline of defence, resistance, and opinion. Where are they coming from in their beliefs? Do they have some hidden agenda that would influence this message?

For instance, if we have asked the universe whether or not to follow a certain destiny, and we are doubting the answer we receive, we might begin wondering, "Are my lower personas scared of taking this road, of making changes, of moving forward? Are they fearful of putting themselves out there, of taking more responsibility, of making a commitment? Are they not feeling worthy or confident? Are they feeling resentful or self-pitying, or believe it's too high a price to pay? Are they wanting to walk the human road rather than the divine one? Are they making one excuse after another to defend and protect their current way of being, rather than launch into the unknown and a new adventure?"

The only way out of this dilemma is to meet with our lower personas and work with them to remove all appropriate fears and resistance. When we feel we have reached neutral ground and we have no vested interest either way in the outcome, only then can we ask our question and receive an unbiased answer. Getting all our personas aligned with our soul and our mission is critical if we are to achieve any kind of harmony in our lives, else we will constantly experience a distrust of ourselves and that our efforts are being undermined at every turn.

It's still possible that we might resist the guidance coming to us, even if it comes from the highest of gods. This is because it's quite natural to baulk at some of the things asked of us on our spiritual journey. It's not an easy path, and we are constantly being stretched and tested and challenged beyond what we believe ourselves capable of doing or being. If we can sit with the message for a while and let it percolate through our being, we usually become accustomed to the idea and can accommodate it, even if only gradually.

If we are still unsure where the voices in our head are coming from, then we should do some research into their source. Listening to the voices, asking questions, finding out more about them and their motivations, are ways to become more discerning. The more we practise, the more we will understand the differences between the energies of entities and the various tones of messages.

What is happening if we find ourselves connecting with some seeming demon from the Underworld? Are there truly dark forces that can penetrate our consciousness, and even take us over and bend us to their will? I asked the gods about this, and El Morya gave this comprehensive answer.

Morya: *"Thank you for your questions, Sophia. They are rightly asked, for we do need to understand the nature of these dark energies; where they come from and what we should do about them.*

First of all, let us ask, "Are there dark forces or dark personas in this universe?" Well, yes, of course there are! With the light at the higher end of consciousness comes an equivalent darkness at the other end of consciousness, within ourselves and our own Ribbon, but also in the greater consciousness that covers the entire universe. We know, ourselves, that we have a good side and a bad side, and so it is with everyone around us too, and some are really bad, and some are not so bad.

So, you ask, "Do these bad personas affect the rest of us? Can they enter our consciousness and even take us over?" Yes, they can certainly do that, and the more we are willing to let them, the more they will sink into us and become a part of us.

We know by now that consciousnesses constantly merge with one another, and this goes for the dark end of consciousnesses as well as the higher end. So, yes, if you are not aware and alert, and your own consciousness is easily influenced, then other consciousnesses drift inside yours, will be attracted to you, and you will magnetise one another. And your consciousnesses will begin to interact, and if you are not strong enough, one may take over the other. The weaker will be swamped by the stronger.

Don't we see this every day in your world where mobs can be activated very quickly, where the ideas in one or two consciousnesses can quickly springboard from one to another until everyone is affected by the fever?

Even those who do not believe they are being affected by dark forces are being affected by others' consciousnesses on a daily basis, even moment to moment, for, think about advertising and social media comments. An idea can ripple through society very quickly, not only through the use of media devices but also because all consciousnesses are interconnected through the grid of the universe.

So, if you are not to be affected unduly or unconsciously, then you will need to know your own mind and stand your ground in your beliefs. And if a dark force does enter your consciousness, you must be prepared to do battle with it and not lie down and surrender to it and let it take possession of you, but you must fight it with every ounce of your energy and skill. And you must make it recognise that it cannot bowl you over, that you have boundaries that it cannot breach, and it will make its departure and go seeking easier prey.

You will also have demons inside yourself as well, and again you must do battle with these. And you must vanquish them by knowing what you will and will not put up with, by knowing the road that you wish to follow, and you will not be side-tracked by any other force.

Your protection comes from always being aware, aware of the energies around you and inside you, aware when things do not feel right and harmonious, and setting your intention to put them right. We will always have a sense of when we are being invaded. Our intuition will pick up on this. But whether you choose to do anything about it is another thing.

You may not always be aware of being invaded from within yourself, for the lions that wish to maul you can be very tricky indeed and may masquerade as other things. But if you know yourself well, you will know when all is placid in your fields, or when things are stirring uneasily in the dark woods around your heart. Wake up to what is going on in your consciousness. This is the best way to combat dark forces and see them on their way."[18]

It is important, therefore, that we become aware that we are not only confronting people in our earthly world who oppose our way of thinking or who wish to influence us in some detrimental manner, but we are also dealing daily with consciousnesses in spirit form who desire to get under our bonnet. Within the Creation Realm, we can battle it out with these other consciousnesses in ways that are not available to us in the human physical world.

Perhaps some of these battles will be with consciousnesses that we knew long ago in past lives? We might be dealing with bitter ex-flames whom we intended to never connect with again on Earth in this lifetime, and so the only way to resolve things with them is in the spirit world. There might be deceased parents or loved ones that we need to forgive, or enemies whom we

---

18. From a channelling with El Morya, 7 July 2019

have betrayed or beaten. It's possible that the dark force of a consciousness merely wants to add another foot soldier on Earth to its cohorts in order to manipulate the power base on the planet. We will need to be vigilant and not allow ourselves to be used for evil, corrupt, or not-love purposes.

Right brain vs left brain

One of the ways we can determine if our question to the higher realms is being answered by a higher consciousness, is to become aware of what runs through our mind in the instant that we receive our answer.

In chapter 3, I theorised that the consciousness of our soul operates through the right brain while the consciousness of our human self operates through our left brain. The right brain is often called the silent brain because it speaks through images and the senses rather than with the words of language. But a most interesting fact is that the right brain, the soul, responds a half second before the left human brain. This is important because it means that we hear what our soul is saying half a second before the left brain kicks in with all its opinions and doubts and resistance. Our soul's response is that quiet little voice we hear instantly when we connect with the divine universe, but which gets drowned out by our human inner persona voices almost immediately.

We have probably all experienced this when we get an idea or answer coming into our mind which then gets instantly squashed, negated, or debated. This often happens on quiz shows on TV, when a contestant gets an immediate answer to a question in their mind, but they begin to second guess themselves and then can't decide which is the correct answer.

We have to be alert and quick to catch what our soul is saying to us. We often dismiss it because it wasn't loud and important sounding, or it was just a fleeting glimpse of an image. It's very subtle but this is how the soul (or gods) usually speaks with us. We must grasp whatever is presented to us first, before our human mind kicks in and overrides the message.

Speaking with soul/gods as a friend

Our soul is our best friend, and we should communicate with them as such, just as we would with a loving friend on Earth, always with respect and gratitude, listening carefully to what they have to say, or being attentive to what they have to show us. It takes effort to build and maintain relationships on Earth, and so too should we make some effort with our soul and the gods to foster good vibes between us.

When advice is offered by higher beings, we would benefit from taking action on it, and asking many questions of them to clarify our mission or issues to be cleared up. Just like with a friend on Earth, if we ignore or betray them or renege on a promise, they will be reluctant to provide help to us in the future.

It is perfectly acceptable to speak to a god or Master or angel and to have a conversation with them. Many people have told me that they feel too awed or shy to speak with such high vibrational beings, but the Masters are just regular people really, even though they are gods. They are friendly, affable, humorous, witty, good listeners, and great counsellors.

If they are taking the trouble of speaking with us, then it's because they want to get to know us better, and/or discuss an issue with us, or offer us a new direction or task. We shouldn't clam up on them. They can, of course, read our thoughts, but it's better if we can carry out a coherent and reasonable discussion with them through our consciousness, just as if we were conversing with someone standing in front of us in our lounge. We won't be speaking out loud, but we will be speaking in our mind, and hopefully hearing the gods speaking to us too.

Checklist for connecting with unseen dimensions
Preparation beforehand

- Set intention to meditate and to connect with spirit or others
- Be pure in intention, as divine power can't be used for unwise situations
- Tell people you are meditating and not to disturb you
- Purify self and environment (have shower, burn oils, diffuser, crystals)
- Be sober, well-hydrated, go to the bathroom
- Don't use drugs or alcohol to try to raise vibrations or enter altered state
- Give yourself enough time—if you have to rush off, you'll worry

- Be ready to take notes: recorder, paper/notebook, pen, computer
- Put protection around self (White light, Violet Flame, ask angels, etc)
- Relax in a lovely place. Be comfortable
- Hold crystal, photo, card, etc
- Let go of nervousness and self-centredness
- Take out negative segments, cleanse lower vibes
- Raise vibrations, dial into higher place

During meditation

- Cross bridge, go through gate, etc. Be there with all your senses
- Be respectful, and acknowledge and thank whomever comes through
- Treat gods as monarchs. They are powerful, divine beings
- Higher dimension has societies and structures and rules. First rule is: be love
- Listen/look for subtle voices and images that come first before your mind kicks in
- Keep your focus. Don't get distracted
- Don't analyse anything. Accept everything that happens, no matter how weird
- Remember your consciousness can never die. You will survive everything
- Fly, explore, and enjoy yourself
- Ask questions
- Thank divine ones at end of the session

After session

- Write down things that happened or you will soon forget them
- Ponder on the meaning of it all
- Don't ignore the messages. Take action
- Regular commitment is required or soul/gods will lose interest in you

Chapter 17 – Manifesting

Introduction to manifesting

One of the most powerful and magical tools of consciousness is to be able to manifest the reality we desire. Everyone has been given the gift of creativity, even if we don't necessarily feel creative, and many people do utilise their imaginations very well and the gods value them. We humans do tend to equate creativity with being artistic or imaginative, with having an inspirational muse, but all of us create things in our lives in one way or another. We do this through the power of our minds.

When we think about what we will have for dinner tonight, we are manifesting our future reality. When we ponder on where to go for our holidays, we are also creating our future. When we decide to apply for a particular job, we are again setting up our prospective world. All of this is being creative. We create love, children, careers, businesses, books, systems, gardens, homes, buildings, menus, machines, dances, music, artwork, texts, perfected bodies, maps, philosophies, etc.

Our consciousness is always creating and imagining—it's what it does by default. It is as if we wield a magician's wand. We are forever looking for new ways to create or improve upon creations, ours and those of others. And doesn't this bring us so much joy and fulfilment, to bring things into being? Most of us aren't even aware we do this daily, that through our thinking we are manifesting our reality.

Perhaps we are taking a look at our life and wondering wryly about our doubtful capacity for manifesting, given that our reality is not to our liking, and how come we ended up in this situation? And so, it could be that our magic tool for manifesting might need some adjustment, some training, some cleaning out, some overhaul, if our reality is not what we wish it to be.

The gods lead joyful lives because they have learnt to create whatever they desire. Everyone, god and human alike, has the same apparatus for manifesting and the same capacity for weaving magic. Humans can learn this trick too—it's not beyond anyone; we are all derived from god stock originally and we are all expected to become gods-in-training one day. And so, it is part of our destiny to become creators, to manifest things and to add value to this world, and to do this in enjoyable ways. If we don't learn to manifest, then we will be powerless, and to become gods we need to be powerful as well as loving and wise beings.

Once we have learnt to apply our magic wand of consciousness, we will never look back. There is only, ahead of us, the delight of creating the lives we dream of. We are all creators, and it is perfectly possible to create a Heaven to live in while we are incarnated upon this Earth.

What can we manifest?

We might be wondering what kinds of things we are allowed to manifest. Can we have big dreams, impossible dreams even? Well, some people have certainly made impossible dreams come true, so it's not beyond the realms of possibility. Chiron tells us to dream our life and follow that dream, and if we believe in it then the universe will help to get us there. That might seem a bit pie-in-the-sky for some people but, as we shall see later on when we take a look at the techniques around manifestation, dreaming our dream is one of the main components.

One of the main problems humans have with manifesting is that they have an unconscious belief that the universe hands out only limited resources. On the contrary, the universe, the collective consciousness of everyone existing, does not have a budget and does not dole out only a certain amount of goodies per person per year. Children don't have this constraining belief, and they are fantastic at creating and imagining, but they grow into adults that tend to become inhibited and who stop being creative, not believing they have the power to make their dreams come true.

Our universe has been formed around the creation of gods, people, and things. The universe exists to create, and we too need to follow this model. Therefore, if we wish to create, then the universe will be delighted to keep on delivering all the resources we require to build our creation. It might seem like magic, but the magic never runs out in this universe; it is an ever-replenishing organism.

However, (of course there is a 'but' in this!) the universe isn't stupid. We aren't going to be supplied with more than we have asked for, or more than we can cope with; that would be a waste of resources. Also, the universe has certain standards, and some requests are likely to be rejected if they threaten the harmony of any of the dimensions.

Our own soul will be monitoring our desires, too, and if our dreams are not conducive to our destiny, then these will not likely see the light of day. And so, if it's not in our interest to win the lottery, or that dream house in a competition, or catch the eye of that fabulous person, or win that job of a lifetime, then our soul will make sure it doesn't happen. There will be good reason. One of the main tasks of our soul and the gods is to teach us humans the power of creating wisely and with love.

We might think of the dark and tragic times that some humans have manifested upon the world, and wonder where were *their* souls when they needed to do this weeding out process of unsuitable desires. Why was Hitler or Stalin or any tyrannical despot allowed to pursue their dreams of power to the detriment of millions upon this Earth? Why is anyone at all seemingly allowed to manifest any dark thought into reality and make it happen? Why don't our souls stop us each time?

The reason is because people with dark or evil thoughts are not connected with their souls and listening to them. They are obeying only the will of their lower human consciousness, and our soul and the gods are not allowed to interfere with our free will. Even the most evil of persons, if they follow the rules for manifesting, will be able to gather the resources that they require for themselves.

When we put in our order to the universe for what we desire, rather than it costing us money, it will cost us in effort instead. If we can take action towards what we are wanting, or we can add value to the universe in some way, then there will be commensurate rewards forthcoming, although it is true these rewards don't always come in the way we were expecting them. If we want to manifest fun and pleasure in our lives, then the universe will be pleased to deliver this, but would first like to see some effective work and effort put in from our side.

One thing that doesn't work when placing requests with higher consciousness is when we ask for money itself. This is not a word in the universe's dictionary. Money is just a form of energy, a word of trust between people, and it's better to place an order for items or situations instead, something that the money we wanted would have bought us.

For instance, it's more effective to request a new car or a holiday package, than to ask for the actual money for a car or a holiday. The universe seems to delight in finding magical and unusual ways to deliver our orders to us, often without money being involved at all. It could be that a kind benefactor decides to pay for us to go on holiday, or a great aunt dies and we are bequeathed her very nice car. So, we need to put our focus on what we would want to achieve with the money, rather than on the money itself.

If we don't use our imagination to create our reality and manifest what we want for ourselves, then we are letting others construct the world around us, and we will end up having few choices and may become resentful that we are dancing (or plodding) to someone else's plans and dreams. So, we should use our creative imagination in every avenue of life, to build from scratch, to improve upon current situations, to remove obstacles from our path, to raise ourselves up, and raise others up too.

One of the main things people most wish for is love; a loving partner, a soul mate. Our consciousness can certainly act as a match-maker when we desire an intimate companion. But which part of our consciousness will we allow to call the shots? We will attract to ourselves only those who are on the same wavelength as us. Therefore, if we are defaulting our consciousness dial to our lower human personas' wavelengths, then the broadcast will go out to those also on that same wavelength. If we lift our default vibrational level to higher on our Ribbon of Consciousness, then we will attract a higher class of being into our field.

The person we attract will be the best fit for us in being a good mirror and reflecting back to us all that we need to fix up about ourselves. Consciousness will provide a love interest for us, but it's not always what we have desired but what we *need* in order to evolve into a better person. When all is said and done, if we wish to attract love, then we will need to be love ourselves.

Not only can our consciousness create loving relationships and situations for us and help manifest actual matter into our world, but we can also use our magic wand for other circumstances such as healing physical bodies and emotional and mental states, and using the power of our influence to change minds or attitudes.

If there is one thing the universe loves to create, it is balance and harmony, and we will be well-supported in our efforts to manifest this. Through the power of our mind, we can transform bad things into better things, sorting out the ills of the world and in our own life too. We merely need to identify what is wrong and not working, and make the decision to recreate a new scenario where all is resolved.

The technique for manifestation

In Part One, we looked at two domains that exist in the hidden universe, which are essential to our successful manifestation—the Dark World and the Light World, which together make up the Creation Realm. We saw that the Dark World is the place we need to go to in consciousness in order to first conceive what we wish to manifest. The Light World is the place where we actually bring our creations through into the physical world, manifesting as matter or as real situations or events.

The Dark World is like the womb before giving birth, but it's definitely a realm for both males and females, for all of us need to produce things. Here, our creation can be put together, explored, and nurtured, through our ideas and creative thinking, without anything actually manifesting into the physical world. It's a place for us to relax and feel into things and try them on without having to experience any consequences. There are no rules here, no boundaries or limitations except those highlighted above. It is the world of conceptualisation and pure potential.

The array of all pathways for our future is like a river that exists in The Quantum Field (the Creation Realm) that opens up into a Delta of Possibilities. Which channel are we going to flow down to get to the Great

Ocean? We can explore each and every one of them in the safety of the Dark World until we make a definite decision to follow one particular channel.

Then, because this is the quantum world of waveforms in consciousness, all the channels of the Delta of Possibilities collapse and disappear except the one we have chosen or have observed, and this pathway concretises into physical particles to form our reality. This may seem like a slow process, but in truth we do this sequence thousands of times a day, every time we make a decision about anything. Our choice, observation, or intention is what converts a thought into physicality.

Manifesting anything at all begins by setting our intention to be in the Dark World and then conceiving an idea, a dream, or a desire of what we wish to bring into our world. It's no good being hazy about it. There needs to be as much clarity as possible or else what we end up generating is just a fuzzy representation of what we wanted, or perhaps nothing at all because our consciousness can't make sense of what we are requesting. The universe may try to offer us something that may equate to our order, but it may be nothing like what we had in mind, and then we might be disappointed.

If we request a new car, do we mean a brand-new car or a car that is new to us? If we had in mind a holiday, do we want to go this year or sometime in the next ten years? If we want a job, are we prepared to do any old job or only something specific and above a certain salary?

Dream your dream

So, we need to use our imagination, our consciousness, to dream how we would like our world to look and operate. It does take conscious effort, and it will usually take some time to work out with great clarity what exactly we want to head towards. We shouldn't rush this process, for as we linger within the Dark World, many more ideas will be gifted to us, and we may want to change our plans or refine them.

There is an old saying, "If you fail to plan, you plan to fail." We should always have dreams and goals to make for. This makes life special, and motivates us to get out of bed in the morning, and there is no better or more fulfilling feeling than manifesting something we have dreamt about earlier, sometimes many years earlier.

If we have been having night-time dreams, we need to take these into consideration and take them seriously. They are often the out-picturing of our destiny, a clue to the goals we should be making for, or they depict obstacles which are preventing us from manifesting those goals.

Firstly, we need to dream our desires, meditating long and hard on what we truly want to manifest in our life, and then documenting them. Once we are forced to clarify them on paper or screen, we will find ourselves sorting the wheat from the chaff and understanding where we are still being hazy or muddled in our thinking.

Our dreams can be not only about manifesting things and objects but also about bringing harmony into situations and relationships. It may help to categorise our desires under certain headings such as;

- relationships
- home
- career/job
- education
- health
- leisure
- body
- sport
- transport
- technology
- hobbies
- clothes
- travel/holidays
- support
- other

Allow your mind to take flight (your consciousness will be hanging out in the Dark World), as you imagine all the scenarios where your dreams and desires are coming true. In fact, go beyond your human mind and ask your spirit or soul to guide you in what can be achieved.

Manifesting from purely the human mind takes a lot of willpower and effort, but when we utilise our higher consciousness, then creation feels much more effortless and divinely inspired, and things begin to appear in magical ways. Our soul will want us to open our heart and dream bigger than we have ever dared, and while this might seem quite scary, it also means that we can be downloaded with more energies from the higher dimensions so that we are more capable of accomplishing these dreams.

If it seems we are being a bit greedy in wanting all these things for ourself or for others, we need to remember that we are here on Earth predominantly to create. There is no point in limiting ourselves when the universe's resources are vast and inexhaustible. We are expected to make use of its benevolence and bountifulness. The universe is not like our parents may have been, always saying 'no' to us whenever we wanted something when we were young. Spiritually, we are all children of gods, and they are rich and wealthy and wish to grant us our wishes and share their treasure and magic.

In your consciousness, step into each scenario that you have detailed and begin to act it out as if you were creating a movie scene around it. Don't be fearful—you are merely role-playing at this point. Use your imagination to bring in all the necessary players, props, landscapes, and audio-visual effects, and act out the dialogue. There is no right or wrong; just keep adjusting the scene until it is to your exact liking. Take your experiences and extrapolate them into different settings and landscapes, or new roles for your personalities involved.

We would call this daydreaming, but it is the very basis of manifesting our future. Some people will be more able to do this than others, for they don't inhibit their imagination, but all of us can play 'Let's pretend' or 'What if this happened, or that?' We must allow ourselves to let go and explore new fields and avenues and let ourselves rearrange 'what is' into 'what could be.' This is especially useful if we are feeling stuck in our life. Our soul and the gods will also offer ideas to us, if we ask for their assistance.

Imagination is not only visual; it can involve all of our senses, and adding emotional stimuli (music, dance, song, dialogue, colour, aroma, taste, touch, joy, love, and other sensations) will serve to ramp up the effectiveness and palpability of what we are trying to manifest.

You are the scriptwriter, director, and star of this movie. Keep rehearsing until all is perfect, just as you would if you were creating a movie or play in the earthly world. Get excited, not stressed, about what you are bringing into being. Keep dreaming of what you will be producing down the track. Start with small undertakings, and take your time to do a good job so that you know exactly what you want to bring through into the physical manifested world.

Our full consciousness needs to be applied at the start of birthing any project or idea. As humans we tend to get too caught up in the delivery and the outcome instead of focusing on the conceptual phase. What happens to human embryos in the womb if the details aren't set out correctly in their DNA? Attention to the minutiae of our conceptions means we won't be faced with deformed dreams when they are eventually birthed.

When we get the foundations correct, we can go on to build not just structures but superstructures. We are the architects of our own reality so we must create strongly so that things don't fall apart later. If we do our research, dig deep, plan well and define solid blueprints, our creations will stand the test of time and will not be blown away or wiped out in the first gale that comes along. The gods love those who do a good job on their foundations; they are not interested in fads or flimsy structures.

Many thoughts will leak out of this Dark World and become manifest in the Light World without our realising it. Whatever is constantly in our mind will be reflected back onto us and into our world. We should be determined to catch any detrimental thinking and clean it up. If we are attracting things not to our liking in our life, then we will know there is some pollution in our consciousness that needs to be cleared out.

Thinking only with loving thoughts is the primary goal to reach for, and replacing all our old defunct programming that is getting us nowhere, or even sending us down into the Underworld of low vibrations. As we climb higher in our vibrations, magical things occur with regularity, and we will find that our efforts beget rewards.

Manifesting the dream

Once we have nutted out the details of our dream in the Dark World of conception and have a coherent picture of what we actually want to manifest, we can kind of flick the switch to tell the universe, "This here is what I want." This is often called 'setting our intention', but hopefully the previous description explains exactly what that means.

Now we move over into the Light World, for this is where creation takes place. We now visit the opposite side of the Creation Realm with our consciousness in order to take the completed conceptualisation from the Dark World and turn it into reality. Consciousness shines its light into our conceived idea and brings it into being. If we don't complete this part of the process, then doors will remain closed and our dreams will remain just clouds.

If we are creating in the higher spirit world or the gods' dimensions, then we will manifest pretty much instantaneously whatever we have been focusing on in the Dark World, once we release our final plans to the Light World. It happens rapidly and easily in the quantum worlds of spirit, and we need to be extra careful of what we carry in our consciousness, for it tends to blossom immediately in front of us, whether we like it or not.

But in our earthly dimension, some things will take time to percolate through the Light World and we will often need to be patient. In our human world, it's not as if dreams magically manifest themselves, or that matter can be manifested out of thin air as it is in the invisible dimensions of spirit. On Earth, the material object or situation that we have requested must be brought about through turns of events that can take time to arrange in the background by our soul or the gods.

For instance, if we are trying to manifest a particular job, then once we have done all our due diligence in the Dark World to tell the universe exactly what is wanted, then higher beings will need to spring into action to influence all the players involved and to manipulate energies to bring about certain situations. Sometimes this can be done quickly, and at other times it's a slow process and may not eventuate at all if all the elements required can't come together.

In the section on troubleshooting further on, we will examine a variety of reasons why some dreams get manifested, and others don't.

To successfully create our desired conceptions, we need to get to know every aspect of our dream. We will have pictured it with all our senses, so now it is time to take action and create this dream world as if it existed. We need to step into it, make some effort towards it, and live the role we have created for ourselves.

Sometimes this happens quite automatically without us having to give it too much consideration, and we smile as if some fairy godmother has waved her magic wand and manifested for us what seemed to be just a fleeting thought in our minds. I've had this happen on many occasions, but usually when the things that manifested weren't that important to me. Perhaps that degree of impartiality of outcome is a factor of its success?

For instance, I was making my bed one day and noticing the lovely shade of fuchsia pink interwoven here and there across my bedspread, and I had the idea that sheets of this colour would look good with the bedspread. A few hours later I was in the shopping mall with no thoughts of looking for sheets, when I suddenly noticed sheet sets on sale at a discount price, and on top of the pile was a fuchsia pink set, the exact colour and size that I had 'requested'. It wasn't as if I had deliberately set out to either conceive or manifest these sheets, but I had the brief thought and was then guided to take action to go and get them. If only other, more important, things in our life were so easy to manifest!

All the components for our dream need to be in alignment for it to be delivered successfully to us. We might check with our soul if our idea is well-formed and has the right timing. Chiron tells us we should sow our seeds of ideas, fitting for our life and climate, so that our dreams eventuate when things are ripe and can be harvested, and we should envisage this harvest with all smiles and love.

Just as a good harvest depends on preparing the soil well, planting in the appropriate season, nurturing the growth, and reaping only when the crop is truly ready, so too should we plan and create our manifestations according to the right seasons and conditions. Consciousness moves with these cycles too, experiencing a springtime of ideas, a summer of growth and expansion, an autumn of harvesting, and a winter of resting. We shouldn't be planting in winter, or trying to reap results in spring.

Things take the proper time to mature in our consciousness too. If we procrastinate and miss the right timing, then we might be staring at barren soil in the summer of our consciousness.

Are we out-picturing our desired outcome, and holding it in our consciousness without distorting our image or intention? If we begin to negate our conception through doubt or lack of belief or through changing our mind about the details, then the order will be dropped, or only a part order will be fulfilled, or something else will be delivered instead. Confusion or fear scuppers our manifestation every time.

If we ordered a pizza and kept changing the ingredients we wanted, it's unlikely we would get the pizza we desired, and so we need to remain firm, consistent, focused, and aligned with our request to the universe until it is delivered.

There are times when our dream comes into being piecemeal, and we can see events have been set in motion and are turning our way. Usually, we will be pleased with this, but often as our dream begins to manifest we can become afraid, especially if what we asked for is life-changing or a huge stretch for us. We might want to run away from it, as it seems like a juggernaut coming after us and we have no way of stopping it now.

Sometimes this will be a challenge we just have to face, but we can always go back into the Dark World of the Creation Realm and renegotiate terms and focus on new outcomes. Our consciousness, and especially our soul, is always our control centre, and we can use its tools to make adjustments to our life. The more we practise using our consciousness consciously, the more we will gain control over our life and manifestations.

The science of manifestation

It's a huge stretch of the imagination to believe that things can be manifested just by putting requests through our consciousness like some online order over the Internet. It's an even bigger stretch to believe that things can be manifested out of thin air. But this is the realm of quantum physics, and this is the way of the higher dimensions and how consciousness operates.

In the unseen universe of hidden dimensions and invisible spirits, the laws of the quantum world hold sway. We humans are only just beginning to peer into this domain, and we really have yet to make much sense of it. All we know is that nothing is what it seems. Things occur at the most microscopic of levels, and our normal rules of physics don't apply here. When we look closely at matter at the atomic level, we discover that things are not actually solid and that they are only loosely held together, with more space than actual material substance. We also find that subatomic particles from which atoms are made, jump in and out of existence all the time. They disappear to somewhere unknown and return again in an instant.

In fact, the subatomic particles from which we and other matter are created, are constantly moving in and out of the earthly dimension and visiting the higher dimensions of the Second Earth and beyond. There is no limit to the distance a particle can travel in an instant, and because there is no such concept as time outside of our human dimension, a particle might travel for the equivalent of years in the quantum realm and yet 'be back in time for tea' on Earth in the same minute that it left.

We might ask ourselves the question, "Do we really exist here?" It's a question that scientists can no longer answer, although once upon a time they thought it was a given. If subatomic particles disappear into the unknown in every moment, and we humans are made up of subatomic particles, then where are we disappearing to? We know now, from the information that Chiron and the other gods have given us, that we disappear into the higher dimensions where the higher vibrational parts of our consciousness reside.

In time, scientists will discover the answers to this conundrum, but only when they deign to work with the gods and start to believe in the paradigm of consciousness. Scientists have only just begun to prise open the lid of what is going on in this universe. There is much more going on invisibly behind the scenes, in this world and in other alternate worlds.

In chapter 6, *Unseen Dimensions*, the god El Morya described how things are manifested in the higher dimensions as if our consciousness is a high-speed 3D printer. We feed the printer's computer (our consciousness) with the blueprint of what we want to manifest (our conception and intention), and instantly the universe delivers the product into our hands or as a situation in front of us.

On Earth, the delivery mechanism is very much slower, as the universe understands that humans are not particularly adept at clarifying what they wish to manifest, and this is the reason we are given the 'play area' of the Dark World in which to concretise our thinking before we manifest things or events.

Our consciousness knows us well, and knows our place too in the greater consciousness, and therefore it can guide us skilfully and benevolently in the right direction. It is aware of every nuance of our mind and emotions, and can pull everything together to present us with the bigger picture. It can shuffle us into the correct position, give us inspiration, and make serendipity happen. Our consciousness is always at the keyboard of our control centre for manifestation.

Troubleshooting

For all our good intentions and efforts in trying to follow the rules of manifestation, sometimes we just aren't successful. So, why don't things go to plan? Why don't we succeed every time? What might we be doing wrong?

Unsuitability

We should always ask our soul if our dreams are right for us and our goals solid, and if we are on track. It is our soul who guides us closely down our path of destiny.

Our soul or the gods may block us from manifesting certain things or situations if they deem it not for our highest good, or to keep things in balance. If our dreams or ideas are dangerous or not beneficial to us or the world, then the universe will take them down. However, this implies that we have a soul who is trying to protect us and wants the best for us. Some humans are not in touch with their souls and will manage to manifest totally unsuitable things and events.

At times, our soul will allow us to manifest unsuitable things just so we can learn from this experience and won't attempt the same foolhardy thing again.

Wrong timing

As mentioned earlier, there is a correct season for planting and harvesting, and there is also correct timing for anything we wish to manifest. Sometimes we ourselves aren't ready for it, and sometimes the conditions in our environment aren't ready, or other players haven't yet completed their part in the process.

We need to make sure we get ourselves up to scratch and fully prepared, so that we can grab the next opportunity when it presents itself.

Lack of persistence

If our idea hasn't manifested properly and we feel that our dream is still worth pursuing and we are sure that it is part of our destiny, or that it at least doesn't interfere with our destiny, then we should try again. We may get further with it next time around. It takes courage and persistence to hold onto a dream, to shape it and reshape it accordingly, until eventually we can bring it through into our reality on Earth.

It's an illusion that we should be able to succeed the very first time we attempt something and that everything should work like a charm. We might even be blocked from succeeding straight away, for the universe often teaches us through failure and experiment. We become stronger through facing adversity, and it requires us to think more creatively to get around problems. In particular, if we are a perfectionist, failure will certainly be one way that the gods teach us to love ourself and others. Actually, the gods tell us that there is no such thing as failure, that there are only attempts to succeed, and trying to succeed can never be classed as a failure.

Therefore, when our manifesting doesn't get generated in the way that we envisaged, we need to remain stoic and accepting, turn our hand to other resourceful and adaptive strategies, and if needs be, negotiate with our soul and the gods to come up with a better plan and outcome that ticks all the boxes for everyone involved.

Lack of process

If we have failed to follow the correct process for manifesting in the Creation Realm, and not conceived well enough in the Dark World, or not taken appropriate action to bring through our conceptualisations into the Light

World, then we will be faced with distorted creations, or perhaps no product at all. Nothing can be birthed on Earth unless it has first been conceived and birthed in the higher dimensions of the Dark and Light Worlds.

It's necessary that we build strong, concrete foundations in the Dark World for our 'babies' and projects, or else they will crumble upon hitting the physical world, or very soon afterwards. We can do this by being very thorough in visualising the details of all scenarios and players concerned with our manifestation.

Lack of clarity

We attract into our reality whatever is going on in our consciousness. If our mind is like spaghetti or a roiling ocean or a thousand disparate islands, then it will be difficult for the universe to ascertain exactly what it is we are trying to manifest. We need to work at producing a clear vision in our Dark World of what it is we wish to generate, and hold onto this blueprint with all its detail as we birth it in the Light World and nurture it into being with good actions and positive thinking.

If we don't like our reality or what we have manifested, then we need to go back to the drawing board in the Dark World and rewrite our movie and script to reflect what we would prefer, and then make a plan and take action to bring it about.

Doubt and negativity

Probably one of the main issues affecting our success in manifesting is our doubt that what we wish for will materialise, and any negative feelings and thoughts we have surrounding it. If we keep focusing on the fact that we don't have what we want and are not focused on the desired outcome, we will continually manifest the lack of that something. We need to visualise the future state not the present state. If we ourselves don't believe in what we desire, then why would the universe believe in us enough to support manifesting it?

Human will versus divine will

We might have internal conflict where our spirit/soul self wishes to manifest something, and the human part of our consciousness is blocking it, for any number of reasons, usually from some kind of fear. The left brain is inhibiting the right brain from taking action, and this often leads to pain in the right side of our body due to our resistance.

Creating with higher beings

Working out what we want to manifest in our world is great fun and very fulfilling for human beings. Most people do this using just the human part of their consciousness, for they are not aware of their spirit, soul, or gods and angels, and they often manage to manifest things quite successfully. Every day that we are alive, we are effectively manifesting life in front of us in every moment. It may not be what we prefer, but we are generating reality according to what we hold as our thoughts in our consciousness.

Our human will believe it knows what it wants, but the fact that many people are unhappy with some aspects of their lives testifies that our lower human consciousness doesn't always get it right. If we can allow our spirit or soul or the gods to take control over our plans for manifestation, then we will see a commensurate jump in happiness and fulfilment.

It's not as if our human mind will be sidestepped and ignored; it will still have some say in what is to be manifested. But when all parts of our Consciousness Ribbon are involved in decision-making and planning, and all work cooperatively together bringing in their various skills, then magic can happen and truly astounding things can be created far beyond the imagination of the human alone.

When in the Dark World conceptualising, if we can bring in higher beings, of ourselves and of others, and listen to their advice and suggestions, then we will be tailor-making a much more suitable and enjoyable reality for ourselves.

The higher up our Ribbon we can move our consciousness when manifesting, the more power and magic will be behind us and supporting us. If we can get just one small part of our consciousness up to the level of our Source, at creator god level, then we will be utilising the most powerful part of our consciousness and acting like a creator god ourselves. Creator gods, of course, are the ultimate manifestors within our universe; there is nothing they can't create or un-create.

When we are imbued with the power from our Source, and we direct this power to our issues or destiny, miracles can occur. The energies at this level cannot be directly utilised by humans, but are used in conjunction with the whole team of higher beings. The great power of the gods comes from their connection with their Source, which is the power behind their thrones and allows them to alter creation itself.

Therefore, we should endeavour to raise our vibrations to the highest level possible, all the way to our Source if we wish to be in our full power. This is much more effective than trying to manifest from the very bottom of our Consciousness Ribbon. When we are bathing in the energies of our Source, we will feel like a brilliant star, radiating our power and affecting all around us. Our Source is even brighter than any star, and as a creator god, it knows well how to manifest any reality that it desires.

Manifesting for others and the world

Once we get the hang of manifesting and are having some success with bringing about our desires in our own world, we will probably then want to start making changes in the world around us, focusing on helping and healing other people or our environment or society.

In this, our consciousness will be interacting with the desires of other consciousnesses, and can add extra power in manifesting the outcome, or work against it if our beliefs are diametrically opposed. Our efforts may cancel each other out!

We need to be very careful about what energies we broadcast into the world. The universe will be monitoring us to ensure we don't throw things out of balance. I remember once, a long time ago with a friend, trying to bring healing energies to a part of the world that had just experienced a huge earthquake. We could certainly feel some great power emanating through us, but then the voice of a god came through loud and clear to tell us to stop immediately as we had no idea of what we were doing and what the bigger picture was. Although our intentions had been well-founded, we were engaging only our human will and should have enlisted the assistance of higher beings. A lesson well learnt!

Living in Australia with wild extremes of weather, alternating between droughts and floods and heatwaves and frosts, I often try to affect the local weather patterns to bring about better climate balance. Chiron tells us that, yes, we can change the weather around us, but it's not as if our garden will get its own little rain cloud or piece of sunshine while all around us suffer (although I have known this to happen!) Generally, we won't be changing the weather above our heads but will experience the same weather as everyone else in the region. However, depending on the vibrations of our consciousness, we will find ourselves reacting differently to it and find ways to cope better.

For instance, I have experienced local tornadoes in two different houses that I have lived in. It's pretty terrifying to hear a wind that sounds like a freight train coming towards you, and to hear trees crashing down all around you, and rain and hailstones lashing the roof and windows. In both cases, I prayed to the gods for protection and to be spared great destruction, and both times I have got away, not completely unscathed, but with minimal damage compared with neighbours. There were even some good positives that came out of it. It's a case of when given lemons, make lemonade!

The group consciousness of a neighbourhood or town or city definitely affects what that locality experiences. If there are extremes of any form, then it represents the group desire being too strong in any one direction. For instance, if there is a drought, most people will then focus on bringing in rain, which then eventuates as deluge and flood, and vice versa. The pendulum swings too far. What people really should be manifesting is a balance in all things.

Whatever we focus on becomes our reality. So, if a city is focused on crime or terrorism or natural disaster or pestilence or transport delays or food shortages and the like, then this is exactly what will keep on manifesting. When we visualise the world in a perfect way, it will do its best to out-picture what we are conceptualising and trying to create. We need to check what we ourselves are contributing to the reality of this world.

Healing is another kind of manifestation, but it is such a big subject that it deserves a few chapters of its own. (See chapters 19-22).

Chapter 18 – Creating a better you

Not only can we use the tools of consciousness to manifest matter and situations, but we can also use the great gifts within our consciousness to create a better self and a better life. Even if we haven't made much of ourselves up until now, we can start to turn things around immediately by taking even the smallest of steps to improve ourselves and the life we lead. A small step every day, or even every week, will see us quite transformed by the end of twelve months.

We don't have to put up with the status quo a minute more than necessary. We are not a prisoner except by our own thinking. There's an old saying, "If you do what you've always done, then you'll always get what you've always got." Therefore, if we stay in the same old place with the same old views, we are assured of getting the same kind of life we've always had.

Miracles do await us, but they don't come searching for us; we must go to them. If our dreams are stuck in the pipeline, that means our thinking is stuck, and that means we need to think new thoughts. The new world that we desire is only a thought away, but it needs to be the right thought. Many humans are unwittingly choosing to live at minimum levels of existence because their current thinking is keeping them there. They could elevate themselves out of misery by checking what kind of thoughts are constantly moving through their head. When we change our thinking, we change our world, because the universe can manifest for us only that which is held in our consciousness.

So, if our life feels tired, too difficult, or hopeless, we ourselves must be the force field that triggers change, or else reality will keep on going the same as ever. It just requires us to make the decision that we are going to change our life NOW. Even until the moment just before death, it is still possible to improve our life; it is never too late.

Any victim mentality needs to be replaced by victor mentality, and a firm belief that it truly is possible to change ourselves and our situations. In the beginning we will need to just get ourselves out of what Chiron calls the 'pig-swill' (or pig's will?) of human lower emotions and onto a more even keel, but eventually the goal will be to start on the journey that transforms us from mere mortals into higher beings through the path to godhood.

Identify issues

The first step is to identify what is chronically wrong with us and also the things we would like to merely improve. We will need to do a thorough audit on ourselves and be honest and authentic. Our family members will probably be only too keen to help with this, to point out our frailties and shortcomings! But, before we take umbrage or go into meltdown at any criticism levelled at us, we should remember that other people act as mirrors, and the issues that others have with us will undoubtedly be issues that they themselves suffer from. So, we should take any suggestions with good grace and be grateful for their insights.

We also need to realise that there is not just one set of issues, and that when we have dealt with these we are now clean and pure forever more. We have layers upon layers of issues! They will be revealed to us one layer at a time, like peeling back the layers of an onion.

Every time we are promoted to a new level of consciousness, it's as if we are faced with a fresh field of issues to clear, a field of boulders and snakes, representing many of the negative thoughts or feelings we are still carrying in our consciousness. By the time we clear this field we will be ready to be promoted up the Ribbon of Consciousness again, and yet another field will appear with more boulders and snakes, not the same ones as before, but from different experiences, in this lifetime and in past lives. Sorting out our snake pits and our hidden programming will take lifetime after lifetime.

We can ask our spirit or soul, or the gods, to be shown the issues and blockages that are aggravating us. There may be hidden themes and it's not always transparent to us what is the real problem, but the divine beings can cut through any smoke and mirrors and self-defeating delusions. Sometimes there are issues carried over from past lives that scuttle our present-day emotions.

In the next chapter we will take a look at how we can heal some of these issues.

Raise vibrational level

In chapter 11 on vibrational levels, we saw how we could raise our vibrations to position ourselves higher up our Ribbon of Consciousness and feel in a better state of mind and health and attract better situations to ourselves.

Let's be honest, it can be tremendously difficult to lift ourselves out of a dark pit when we are feeling in the depths of despair or hopelessness, but this is the starting point to creating a better us, when we make the definite decision that we no longer want to be this person we are, or live the life we've been leading. We can take steps, even baby steps, to reach a higher place by making alternate choices to those made previously. We can leave our old life behind and raise ourselves into a much brighter environment and mood. Our intention to better ourselves is the only signal the universe needs to duck in under our wings and guide and support us.

We may need to have a word with our lower inner personas who might not be in alignment with this decision to make changes, and who prefer to wallow in self-pity at our tragic circumstances, or who are too fearful to take the steps that will be needed to get out of our dark pit. See the next chapter on healing for how we can do this.

Even if our life is fairly happy, it's always worth moving our vibrations upwards and not have our default vibration sitting at a low level where we will be in danger of attracting low vibrational people and situations. Any life, even if currently operating on an even keel, will benefit from improvement, and we never know what exciting adventures await us when we rise to new levels of being, can see far more clearly, and can experience new kinds of reality.

It only takes a few moments to raise our vibrations, no matter what we are currently going through, taking the time to dwell on lovely and joyful thoughts, images, or memories, and filling our heart with these energies. We can also focus on raising the fire in our spirit and spiralling upwards in our consciousness. By doing this, we can immediately burst the bubble of gloom around us by injecting it with a little hope, and opening the way for magic to enter. The air is clearer when we are higher, and we can see much better and feel the sun's sparkle upon us.

If we are totally stuck in our dark pit of emotionality, it sometimes helps to go out and take some action, like going for a walk or run, or playing some sport, or doing the gardening, or building a shed. This can help to shake us out of our current mindset. But at the end of the day it is our thinking that creates our vibrational level and not our actions, so we must be prepared to do the work to reprogram our mind or else we will 'keep on getting what we've always got.'

It is a constant battle for some people to raise their vibrations every day, and although the gods and angels will help us as much as they can, they can't keep pulling us up forever; this is something we must learn to do for ourselves. Our thoughts dictate our reality, and so it is through our thinking that we raise ourselves up, and our higher level of vibrations will eventually set us free to experience a new life.

Work with your soul/spirit

A better part of ourselves already exists, higher up our Ribbon of Consciousness, at the levels of our spirit and soul. Therefore, it makes sense to rope in these parts of our being to help bring our lower human consciousness up to these higher levels, even if only momentarily or for short periods of time. Eventually, if we manage to sustain thinking at these levels, we will merge the lower and higher parts of our consciousness, our human with our soul. This is the way we evolve spiritually and in due course gain our godhood.

Being guided daily by our spirit or soul from their higher parallel world has only positive benefits. They can see way beyond what our human consciousness can perceive and understand. We will receive many different perspectives on life and be able to discover more about the unseen universe than we could do alone. Walking with divine beings causes our whole life to become more divine, and ultimately we become a better person because of it.

Working with our spirit or soul is like being in a partnership between Master and student. We must trust that they know our path ahead and what is best for us, which means we will need to give up ideas of being the driver and controlling the steering wheel, and be accepting of being the passenger and driver's assistant. They have a clearer mind and can see the road we need to take, or the roadblocks that stand in our way. They can guide us on how to move through and beyond, if we are open to it, and they offer us freedom from our self-inflicted prison of faulty thinking. However, they cannot drag us out of there. We must take the necessary action to do that, based on their guidance.

Our soul will give us dreams to fulfil. Acting out these dreams, first in the higher dimensions as our spirit self and then on Earth as our human self, will help to mould us into the person we came here to be—the person of our dreams. Creating a better version of ourselves means playing 'let's pretend' that we are already that person, stepping into those shoes and practising the role until in due course we do become this new persona.

Reprogram yourself

We will probably have a hunch about the old thinking that keeps us stuck on the same old rails, and if we don't, then we will need to sit down and take a good look at what is going on in our consciousness, and be totally honest with ourselves and own our issues. A big part of our journey to godhood is learning to take responsibility for ourselves.

We then need to junk these stuck parts of our consciousness and reprogram ourselves with new thinking that supports us and excites us. In the earlier chapter on vibrational levels and in the next chapters on letting go, we examine ways to go through this process. Letting go of our current way of being and replacing it with who we truly want to be, is not an overnight procedure and is the basis of our entire journey from human to god, so we need to be prepared and committed for the long haul.

Our consciousness will need to lose all its flakiness, weaknesses, vulnerabilities, and trigger points (the boulders and snakes), and be rebuilt with strong and firm foundations and solid, yet flexible, walls so that no hurricane of events can knock a hole in them. The transformation we introduce into our consciousness must become habitual and instinctual, and we will need to feel the changes in our heart and our bones.

So, if we are not entirely happy with who we are and the way our life is panning out, we merely need to decide to reprogram our consciousness and eventually out will pop a new version of us, just like installing a new operating system into our computers. We don't have to accept who we are or our situation, but we do have to take steps to do something about it. It's totally possible to create a new life lived from a higher level, and we can put out a daily order to the universe to feel great about ourselves and the world around us.

Being love, our core diamond, self-worth

The most excellent way to better ourselves is to become love itself, with our every thought, feeling, and action exuding kindness and compassion, wisdom, and right use of power, for ourself and for others. This would seem to be a tall order for nearly every one of us, and I suspect that if we were this type of person we wouldn't be down here on Earth working through our numerous challenges (although there may be gods who are roaming this planet in physical form who fit this bill.)

The truth is that each one of us is actually pure love at our core. The original source of ourselves is like a fiery diamond of love-consciousness without any flaws or fear. With each incarnation, on this planet or in any other domain, we have coated over that pure diamond heart with thoughts and fears and deeds that have polluted our being. If we were to take away those layers of contamination, what would be left underneath is pure love. This love is our consciousness in all its purity. Everyone and everything in this universe that might appear to be not-love, is in reality diamond-bright love beneath all the muddiness and toxicity that overlays it.

Therefore, to be love, it's not so much that we need to learn new skills or master new arts; we are already love itself. But we do need to dig down deep into our consciousness and turf out all the non-sense and not-love that sits on top of our diamond light. It's tantamount to removing all the silt from fields that have been flooded by a big river each year, only here we are speaking of the floods of our emotions silting up our heart in every lifetime. In each incarnation, we strive to free ourselves from previous layers of sludge, but often we add even more to it and are fighting a never-ending battle. Being love isn't so very difficult; the biggest challenge is keeping at bay all the not-love.

Things that easily trigger us off tend to reside in the layers closest to the surface. If we can get past these then it will be an easier challenge to find the love layer at the bottom. Unfortunately, most people fall at the first hurdle and never get past this initial sediment. We have to be determined to force our way through all the layers of not-love and deny them air and daylight and let them shrivel away.

The love at our core is waiting to be revealed, like some precious treasure in an archaeological dig; all we must do is mine deeply to expose it. Life is much simpler and more comfortable when we live with our love layer close to the surface of our consciousness where love is more easily within reach.

Love comes in many colours and varieties. We don't ever have to suffer a grey day if we can place love into our every thought, nuance, relationship, and event. The presence of love cures all animosity and fear, and is the only way that our world can ultimately progress. If we remember to focus on love, then we cannot possibly be not-love.

We need to see ourself as a walking entity of pure love, the real us once all the tainted layers have been removed, or at least have this as our goal. If we can know that we are a diamond of love at our core, and so is everyone else, and that the universe is a matrix of brilliant diamonds like the ocean sparkling on a summer's day, then we will feel much better about ourselves and the world around us, and we will appreciate our value more.

One of the biggest problems in the world today is the lack of self-worth in many people. They don't see themselves as this diamond core of love, only as a failure, flailing in layers of silt and muck. One of the first things we need to work on, therefore, is finding love for ourselves, and we can do this if we go deep to our diamond core, to our true nature.

When we love ourselves, we will exude love and this can also attract love into our life externally, but even if it doesn't, we can feel marvellous about each day because we are in a state of love. Experiencing ourselves as the god we came here to be is the best gift we can ever give ourselves.

All of us want and need to be loved, but are we lovable? If we work on our desirability and become a finer human being, and ultimately a god, then people will indeed love us and want to bask in our presence and take our energies home with them. But this desirability comes not from our looks or sex appeal or our generosity with money, although these may also be some of our attributes. People will want to be around us when we display the traits of lovingness and prove to be a good role model to them. If we desire love and good things *for* ourself, then we need to be love and good things *in* ourself, for 'like attracts like'.

In the higher dimensions the first rule of their society is to be love, and so if we wish to become gods one day, learning to be love and to open our heart to harmony and light is essential. When we place our focus on being love, then our external world can reflect only love back to us.

Finding fortitude

When someone has fortitude, it means they have the emotional power and ability to withstand adversity. They display courage, strength, determination, and motivation during challenging circumstances. Overcoming any despair, weakness, or cowardice, they will prove their resolve, mettle, perseverance, and nous in difficult situations and remain upright and positive. They are self-directed through disciplined goal-setting and holding onto their cherished, but realistic dreams. When things don't go to plan, they are accepting and stoical, and merely come up with a new plan.

The following are some of the factors that represent a lack of fortitude.

- Looking for negatives and problems instead of positives and opportunities
- Surviving but not thriving
- Blaming others or life's circumstances for having a poor life

- Allowing self to get overly depressed after a tragedy or knockback
- Lack of self-discipline in any area of life
- Don't tackle jobs because of lack of know-how or skills
- Fear of technology, processes, or systems
- Fear of people or relationships
- Feeling unmotivated, half-hearted, or empty, saying, 'What's the point?'
- Giving up before completing something
- Putting off tasks that are difficult
- Fear of responsibility
- Fear of taking self to new level and new challenges
- Fear of change, even if it will be an improvement
- Believing things to be impossible
- Lacking a dream

We can see that fortitude is not only physical strength but a whole range of strengths, emotional, mental, and spiritual, which help us to keep going through thick and thin and able to live full and happy lives.

Fortitude is resilience that aids us in getting back up again after we fall down or are pushed to our limits. It is the confidence to know we can succeed, or get over things that have brought us to our knees. It is the emotional and mental inner strength that enables us to trust ourselves that we won't buckle under pressure and fail. We need to have faith in ourselves and feel into our strengths and be determined to get through. It is a measure of our personality if we are able to lift ourselves up out of any situation and keep on going.

Often, we can do more than we believe ourselves to be capable of. We will have set a limit on how far we think we can go, but no one has ever improved themselves by staying where they are, and our soul will be wanting us to constantly challenge our own boundaries. To become successful or overcome issues, we will usually need to take a step further than we've ever done before. This is the way toddlers learn to walk, and this is the way we learn to become gods too. If we can challenge ourselves every day in little ways to take a small step beyond what we've known already, then we will be well on our way when bigger issues come to bear and it's not such a gigantic leap that we must take.

The universe challenges us constantly. We are tested to check if we are suitable for godhood. This cannot be avoided, so we might as well accept it. Adversity and failure help us to become stronger, more resourceful, and to act more creatively and experimentally.

As we journey along our path, can we pull ourself out of ditches and dark pits with a semblance of a smile on our face, and can we have the courage and persistence to keep moving towards our dream without whining and dragging our feet? Can we ride the crests of waves by the seat of our pants, and can we also plumb our depths and fix our anchor so that we don't get swept away by our emotions or crisis conditions?

So, to fit ourselves out with fortitude, we will need to overcome any fears, limitations, projections, assumptions and feelings of not being able to cope that bar our way, and clear away any negating thoughts that sap at our pillars of strength and positivity.

We will have displayed fortitude many times in our life, perhaps without realising it. It's good to ponder on those times when we've made it through a challenge. Everyone who has learnt to walk or read or drive a car, or has got through school and exams, has exhibited fortitude and been a success. We often forget that ordinary human life makes many demands of fortitude upon us, so we shouldn't write ourselves off as a failure.

There are times when we *will* fail, and we must accept that; it's the way that we learn how to succeed. Ask any successful person if they managed to get everything right first time, and they will laugh wryly. But every successful person will have fortitude in spades. The world doesn't end when we don't succeed. True failure occurs when we don't try at all, or we don't attempt things again.

Sometimes we will be forced to walk away from things and admit defeat. Perhaps the price is too high and the challenge too unreasonable. The gods don't judge us in this; we only judge ourselves. It will be easier to accept the lack of success if we know that we have given it our all and that our defeat is not because we could have made more effort.

Finding motivation

One of the key obstacles to creating a better self is lack of motivation. If we mope around, saying to ourselves, 'What's the point?' then we will never get off the couch or out of bed. We have to provide something that will put the spring back into our step and make us want to jump into whatever idea or project we have in mind. We require motivation to make things happen or else things will just remain as they are, or they will slip further into chaos because we can't even dredge up the fire in our bellies to maintain the status quo.

Motivation is the spark in our heart and consciousness that gets us excited and gets us going. It begins as inspiration and evolves into a plan of action which precedes manifesting our ideas into reality. Without motivation we are just living in a kind of void, at the mercy of everyone else's imagination, creations, and energies, like a rock on the seashore being pounded by waves. But just like trying to move a big boulder from the beach, it can take a massive amount of effort and special strength of mind to launch ourselves back into the swing of things. It's best to go for small achievements at first to give ourselves confidence and a boost of energy that comes from success.

There are dozens of reasons for lack of motivation; it's not always from being lazy. We could have experienced the death of a loved one or the ending of a relationship, or been fired from a job, or have just completed our schooling or university course, or have recently retired. Often the feeling of ennui comes when we are transitioning from one way of life into another, when one door has closed and the next is yet to open. But it can also come from being let down and disappointed, or we have no idea what to do next with our life, or we are fearful of moving forward.

We now have a choice. Do we want to stay in this no-man's-land of nothingness, this state of disarray or non-productiveness, or would we prefer to make our lives come alive again and start to feel fulfilled, on purpose, happy, and loving the world? How long will we procrastinate? How long do we have before choices are made for us by the universe? Giving ourselves a finite time period for grieving or feeling sorry for ourselves is one remedy.

In South Africa, where I lived for twelve years, it is a custom amongst some of the traditional peoples that when a woman loses her husband, the widow dresses in black and officially grieves for a year and one day. Then she throws off her 'widow's weeds' and is expected to get back into normal society again. This approach has much merit.

The ultimate motivation for us is when we have a clear vision of what we want to manifest for ourselves and our life, and we hold it unwaveringly in our consciousness as our roadmap. If we haven't done this work in the realm of our Dark World, then we won't have anything to strive towards.

However, if we can't get this far and feel completely blocked from even entering the Dark World and using our imagination, then we know that we have work to do in removing our blockages. The initial work we have to do on ourselves will be to communicate with our inner personas and check out what is their problem. They will be resisting or fearful for a myriad of reasons and we need to discover these and deal with the issues. In the following chapters we will discuss in detail how to overcome these hindrances to our plans.

We could also ask ourselves, 'What would happen if I *was* motivated? How would I feel? What might I achieve?' By playing 'let's pretend' we can often create a breakthrough in our state of emotions and give ourselves a chink of hope. Our consciousness controls whether we live each moment in the doldrums or in spirited joy.

The sun is a magnificent instrument in helping to boost our energy and motivation. Who doesn't like to get outdoors on a lovely sunlit day? So, if we are feeling flat or gloomy, we can imagine bringing the fiery sun into our heart and give ourselves the spark of life, as if we were connecting ourselves up to a battery charger. Without the sun, everything on Earth would die, and so, if we are symbolically without a sunny climate in our heart and consciousness, then it's likely we will feel like we are dying. Meditating on an image of the sun, or physically taking its rays into us, gives us a wonderful shot of energy and literally brightens us up.

If our lack of motivation comes from a drought of ideas and imagination in our consciousness, then we might need to nourish and nurture our mind just as we would do to the land in a real drought. Feeding our consciousness with inspiration from books, the Internet, courses, other people's minds, meditations, and dreams, is the equivalent of rain, wetting agents, and fertiliser for fields. Since the world reflects our mind, we should look around and notice the state of the land around us. Maybe we could do both the world and ourselves a favour!

However, all needs to be in balance, and we need both regular sun and rain to provide quality life on Earth, and in our consciousnesses too. Sun and rain together create rainbows, and we all know what is to be found at the end of a rainbow! In this case, maybe we could be motivated enough to follow the rainbow into the higher dimensions and go searching for our real pot of gold. Following the light always leads to treasure.

Have a purpose

Finding motivation is difficult if we have no sense of purpose or goal to reach towards. Conversely, if we aren't able to kickstart a spark of motivation in ourselves, we probably won't find the wherewithal to construct a purpose for ourselves, or discover the mission that we came to complete in this incarnation. It's Catch 22, and we need to break the deadlock somewhere along this closed loop. This is where fortitude and determination come in, a decision that we are not going to stay in our present undesirable circumstances and personality traits, and we are going to break free and rise to higher levels of being, whatever it takes.

And so, we must train our consciousness to dream. What do we need to be set free from? What do we need to be a part of? If we can see no reason to set our heart on fire, we need to make the effort to dream up our future and a target to make towards. What is it that makes our heart sing, or would do if only we opened our heart fully to allow it to dream and feel? Everyone has a dream of some sort for their lives, even if it's only tiny or very secret. We all need a purpose, no matter how small or unassuming.

Often we drop our dreams as being in the too-hard-basket or too fantastical. Is this an excuse so that we don't have to make any effort to chase our dream? Are our inner personas being naysayers, holding the belief that our dreams are not possible? Why are they believing that?

Many people pretend they don't have time for dreams or thinking about some idealistic destiny, and they choose other things to fill up their day instead. It's always easier to do nothing to pave the way for a bright future for ourselves, but our heart will slowly, and sometimes rapidly, wither away if we have no purpose. Even if we cannot think of some specific purpose for our life, our ultimate aim is to smarten ourselves up, and transform out of our human consciousness so we are fit to be a god.

If we let our dreams crumble through a lack of fortitude or foresight, we will feel even more unmotivated and cause our vibrational level to take a dive into the lower world. In chapter 24 we will take a deeper look at how to pursue our dreams and destiny. Certainly, if we cease to be useful to our soul and refuse to work with the object of bettering ourselves and the world, then we will be taken Home where we can study our lack of purpose from a higher perspective.

Increase your power

In order to create a better self, it will benefit us to increase our power in several ways. For instance:

1. Improving our physical capacity to get through our day without getting overly tired
2. Becoming more powerful in our ability to influence people or manifest situations
3. Strengthening our emotional resilience to be able to deal with the vicissitudes of life
4. Enhancing our mental capabilities so that we can achieve more

One of the ways we weaken ourselves is when we don't tell the truth. Our body and consciousness know when we lie to ourselves or to others, and energetically it takes some of the stuffing out of us; it deflates us. It is not always easy to know what the truth really is. We may think we know it, but we may be wrong. Alternatively, there may be many truths for any given situation and what we are arguing for is just our own point of view, which may well be the truth but not the only truth. We can only do the best we can, therefore, and try not to utter, or even think, things that we know to be untruths.

Chiron likens our consciousness to a turbine engine, a motor that turns machinery to generate power. It means our consciousness is valuable equipment, and everyone has been gifted with it. We need to make the most of it, but some people fail to crank theirs up, and others utilise their turbine only at half power. It's up to us to get our turbine going, and this will make us powerful or powerless depending on our efforts. Most people are under-powered, and yet their consciousness is not under-resourced and they have all they need by way of equipment to fully power their world.

If we park our turbine engine, then we will pay the price, which is that we will have no power to affect the world, and then we might accuse the universe of being unfair. It's a crime to let our bodies or minds sit idle when we have such a splendid and powerful turbine at our disposal. Think of what we could achieve for ourselves or how we could help humanity.

Just like with any turbine engine, there needs to be an inflow of energy to feed the machine so that it can generate power. It's similar to a steam locomotive too; it needs fuel to run on, and the more coal we shovel in, the more power and speed can be produced. With our consciousness turbine, this inflow of fuel comes from positive thoughts, goals, and determination. If we don't have the know-how to proceed with our life, then we will need to get the skills and information that will be grist to our mill. If this input stops, then our engine stops and our power will fail us. If we hobble along at half-steam, we will only just survive and struggle to live and work.

Like any machine, our turbine of consciousness needs regular maintenance. We need to lift the cover, clean it out, and feed it with the oil of right thinking. Any negative thoughts will be like pollutants getting into our fuel, choking our throttle, and we will eventually splutter to a halt. Spending time daily getting up to full power will determine whether we live a full and productive life or just chug along.

When our consciousness is firing on all cylinders, we will find ourselves motivated and enthusiastic to tackle whatever comes along and life will feel more under our control. Our heart, our throttle, will be wide open and exposed to the joy of living and producing. Our consciousness actually begins to take flight and soars into the higher dimensions.

It's never too late to start up our motor and to fuel it with the right mixture of dreams and fortitude and love. While love should certainly be one of our driving forces, love without power is ineffectual. Being powerful is important, for our own sense of self-worth and to be able to create marvellous changes in this world. When we feel powerful, the underlying strength and joy this brings to us helps us to cope emotionally, mentally, and physically and thereby to create a better reality.

Chapter 19 – Healing and letting go

Healing

Healing is a major tool of consciousness; it allows us to heal not only our own body, mind, emotions, and spirit, but also those of others, and the world environment too. If anything is not working as it should, be it our physical body, our cognitive functions, our emotional capacity, our relationships, machines, plant growth, pest invasions, climate control, or absolutely anything that requires healing, fixing, enhancing, modulating, or repairing, then we can use our consciousness as a tool to remedy this.

When we heal, we are attempting to bring things back into balance, wholeness, and harmony that have become distorted, unstable, burdensome, or misaligned. We don't have to sit there and think that nothing can be done about our situation or that it will last forever. Tragedy and adversity can happen to every one of us at some time or other, for it is our lot as humans to undergo these challenges, but consciousness can lift us out of the doldrums and help us overcome any difficulty. Some people simply prefer to wallow in pain and self-pity and have others feel sorry for them, but why suffer when, by utilising our tools of consciousness, we can soon be laughing again and feeling in good spirits?

Healing is merely a form of manifestation, therefore if we can master the technique of manifestation, then we will master the technique of healing too. All gods are able to manifest and heal, and this would seem like a miraculous power, but it comes about by using the powers of consciousness that we have previously examined. When we truly believe that things can be changed and healed, then we make it so.

The gods live long and vital lives because they have learned healing and balancing techniques. If they are incarnated on Earth, they will still be prone to the same afflictions and ailments as humans, but through using their consciousness tools they can resolve their issues rapidly.

As with any kind of manifestation, we need to set our intention in the Dark World of conception, and focus on projecting an image or scene of our desired outcome. What we believe and conceive is what will come about. Therefore, if we are focusing on our illness or bad situation, then we are giving energy to it which will hold it in place. It is the out-picturing of health, harmony, and wholeness that we need to hold in our consciousness instead, and we will also need to believe that the outcome is possible, or else we are negating our efforts.

Many people maintain their car better than their consciousness and body, and they tend to just put up with their issues, especially their emotional and mental issues, when with a little work inside their consciousness they could easily make adjustments that lead to a much more harmonious and healthy life.

Most of us have been led to believe by society that only a professional doctor can heal our ills, but our bodies have an amazing innate ability to heal themselves, and we can utilise the consciousness of our cells to our advantage at any time. We can also speak with the consciousness of bacteria and viruses and ask them to balance themselves, which is something I often do when I feel an infection or a cold emerging.

We usually call a tradesperson to fix a kaput motor or machine, or broken things around our home or workplace, but how many of us attempt to connect with the consciousness of an object to help it right itself again? We might be seen as barmy by any onlookers, but I have successfully restarted flat batteries through using my consciousness alone, or got something unstuck, or been inspired to try an unusual method to repair something.

This is something that most people won't believe until they have seen it happening with their own eyes. All I can say is that we have to try these things, or we will never know what we are capable of. When we start asking around, we will hear quite remarkable stories of miracles that have happened that help to stoke our confidence in the divine way of doing things.

This divine intervention doesn't always happen through our own manual efforts; it might just happen that someone saunters by at that moment and offers their skills, like some angel come to help us.

There was one instance when the venetian blinds in my lounge broke. I decided to go and buy curtains to replace them. I had an image of the cerise-coloured floor length curtains that would look good there. On a very limited budget I went off to the shops in my small town, and in the very first store I went into I found a pack of two ready-made curtains in the exact colour and size, and they were half price in the sale. Fabulous! But I needed four curtains, not two. I searched and rummaged through all the packs on the sale tables and suddenly found a matching set to the first curtains. Yay! Now I had my desired curtains, and at discount price too, but now I needed to put up a long curtain rail in my lounge and I wasn't very handy with power tools (only consciousness tools!) and it was impossible anyway to put up the long unwieldy rail by myself.

Suddenly I became aware of the sound of power tools being used in the house next door to me, and when I glanced over the fence, I saw, to my utmost surprise, an old friend who was doing some handyman work for my elderly neighbour. I asked if he had a spare ten minutes to help me put up my curtain rail, and he came over and did a wonderful job, and for free too. Sent by the angels, indeed!

The gods and angels will certainly come to our aid if we request it. They are filled with love and compassion for us and will do whatever can be done to heal us or our situation. The assistance offered to us will depend on our consciousness and whether or not our heart is open to receive it.

The outcome of our healing intervention will also depend on whether it is our destiny to recover from our illness, or whether our situation deserves to be adjusted in the way that we reckon it should. There may be other unknown factors at play here, possibly lessons that we need to learn before full healing or repair can be instituted. Sometimes these situations are a wake-up call for us to make changes to our consciousness and living conditions.

It's great when magic does happen for us, but we need to keep on trying and giving of our best even if our healing and manifestation doesn't appear to be working as we wished. The universe will have noted our efforts and will have delivered to us whatever is for our highest good at that point in time. Perhaps we are learning patience or acceptance, or needing to follow a different path?

Letting Go

In order to heal, we usually need to let go. What does it mean when we say we need to let go? What we are actually letting go are parts of our consciousness. We are reshaping and re-sculpting ourself, taking off bits here and there and adding new bits, like we were a Michelangelo creating a masterpiece out of clay. Notice that I said clay and not stone. Nothing is ever carved in stone, and so we can easily chisel away at all that no longer serves us or does us harm, and we can add new remodelled clay that represents how we prefer our new self or situation to appear.

Most people just allow their consciousness to grow without much planning or restructuring. This is tantamount to letting a garden grow wild and willy-nilly. We're not just letting go of stuff we've grown there in this current life, although that's difficult enough in itself; we're also needing to let go parts of our garden of consciousness that were created by us in previous lives. We will need to determine what can stay and what must go.

Each time we incarnate into physical form we add to our consciousness by way of our experiences, thoughts, and emotions. If we've had thousands of lifetimes, as many of us have, and we haven't done any work to clean out or sort through our consciousness, then imagine what the archives look like where every detail of every life is stored! Consciousness forgets nothing; all joys and hurts are stored away.

Our current consciousness contains only a fraction of this information, only the highlights as necessary for this lifetime. Current memories are edited so that we need deal only with salient issues. But in the storage facilities of the greater consciousness, all our past records are accessible, and nothing is ever lost.

We might think, then, that we can never change our past, but that is not the case. Just like working with computer documents, we have a latest version of our consciousness, but all past versions are also available for our perusal. So, we can look back in time and check out what a previous version of our consciousness was doing in this or that lifetime. (Re-read the Time Travel section in chapter 6.)

What are we letting go of? The answer is any emotions that trigger us off, and the thoughts and memories that underlie them. These triggers can be caused by:

- Relationships we've had: intimate, family, friendships, business, boss/worker, master/servant, enemies, neighbours, government/citizen, human/soul, etc
- Disturbing or traumatic experiences, severe challenges
- Guilt/shame at past actions
- Anything that prevents us from feeling loving, peaceful, motivated, on-track, useful, worthy
- Evolving from human into godhood, the spiritual path

In the way that consciousness utilises and stores all our experiences, thinking, emotions, and memories, it could be viewed as something like a computer. On our computer desktop we place shortcuts to all the apps and programs that we use frequently. So too, at the forefront of our consciousness, are all the thoughts and beliefs we give priority to. It's the screen through which we view the world, and it can be clear and well-organised, giving us easy access to things, or cluttered, making our life seem too busy and unmanageable.

Just as a computer holds our photos, in our consciousness too we have folders of old emotions and memories. In both cases they take up a lot of space, and need sifting through and deleting every now and again. What photo albums in consciousness have we put together to tell our various stories?

Files of documents also need to be arranged into some kind of structure in our computer, and we do this by giving things a priority and deciding what should be stored or archived, and what is to be deleted or reorganised. The same kind of method needs to be employed with our consciousness.

Even though present-day computers and phones have amazing artificial intelligence capabilities, our consciousness beats them hands down and utilises everything we have stored within its system to create our reality for us. It actually mirrors our world back to us. What we put into our consciousness, it processes and outputs (manifests) as our human dimension for us. Just think about that for a moment! It reads like some science fiction movie, but the truth has been hi-jacked by sci-fi writers, whose soul purpose has been to educate humans as to the true nature of reality.

So, we need to be very careful what we put into and store within our computer-like consciousness. It's as if we hoard film scripts there, scenes and dialogues like short YouTube videos but with associated emotions and motivations attached. We choose which ones we are going to play in any moment, and then our consciousness projects these out into the world for us to step into and experience in real time.

What is the story we are telling ourself and the world? If we don't like the video that is playing, we can't blame others because we are the director of our movie, and we can rewrite the script, rejig the scenes and characters and our own role in it. We can be the star of our own screen. What kind of movie would we like to star in?

Some of the videos or movies we have created for ourselves are like horror films. Do we really want to project that kind of stuff and have to live through it? Yet, some people love their old movies, and they cling to their old dismal or terrifying stories and display their battle scars and wounds like medals.

We have a choice whether to keep replaying these old scenes in our consciousness and continually triggering off all the old emotions, or we can delete them and let them go. It is our lower consciousness that wants to hold onto these old ways and plays, so we need to get ourselves into higher consciousness whenever we review them so we can gain a better perspective and be more able to substitute new roles and scripts and initiate fresh dynamics.

Indeed, there are some rooms in our consciousness that contain horrors that need to be faced, and people who need to be forgiven. In our current life these may be obvious. What is not always obvious is when issues from our past lives leak into our present consciousness in order for them to be resolved once and for all.

Whether or not we know anything about our past incarnations, it's certain that memories from them are still playing out in our mind and affecting our life as it is today. People we know currently may have had major roles in our past lives, and we might still be viewing them through the good or bad filters of those previous lifetimes. Fears or disabilities we have today may have had their source in centuries past. Therefore, it will benefit us to be rid of these past notions and recollections if they affect us adversely now.

Healing the body and physical issues

Actual techniques for healing physical symptoms are given in chapter 22. However, the gods tell us that all bodily ailments derive from our emotions, which in turn are a reaction to our thinking. So, if we have a physical issue then we need to look to our emotions and to the thoughts behind those emotions in order to achieve some resolution. (The next chapter deals with emotional and mental healing.)

In the movie *Doctor Strange*, the Ancient One, who has performed miraculous healings on people, tells the astonished and sceptical doctor, "I know how to reorient the spirit to better heal the body."

An entire book could be devoted to this subject alone, and indeed Louise Hay's *You Can Heal Your Life* has done just that, but in the table below I have attempted to summarise some of the major physical issues and which emotions are linked with them, and also which astrological signs, planets, and houses represent them.

The symbolism of the ailment will also depend on which side of the body it presents. Issues on our right side are usually linked with our left brain and our human consciousness, and resisting what the soul wants to do. Issues on the left side are usually linked with our right brain and our spirit consciousness, and often represent our soul trying to suppress our human will.

Physical part / issue	Life aspects	Astrology
Adrenals	Need for balance. Relationship or social issues. Anxiety. Lack of fairness, justice. Procrastination, sitting on fence. Need for creative or leisure activities.	• Libra, Venus, 7th House
Appendix	Inflammation, anger, stress, fast pace, too much ego, selfishness. Fear of taking risks or initiative. Wanting independence.	• Aries, Mars, 1st House
Arms (see Hands)		
Back/spine	Issues with responsibility, pressure, suppression, overwork, imbalance of family and career, job, work, authority figures, social status, ambition, leadership, buildings, structure, organisation, foundations. Rigidity. Lack of fun.	• Leo, Sun, 5th House • Capricorn, Saturn, 10th House
Bladder	Irritation, injustice, male/female balance, over-emotional, relationship issues	• Libra, Venus, 7th House
Blood pressure	Anger, apathy, imbalance	• Leo, Sun, 5th House
Bones/joints	Inflexibility of thinking. Lack of emotion. Overwork, too structured, lack of relaxation and play. Over-ambitious.	• Capricorn, Saturn, 10th House
Bowels	Holding onto grudges or old beliefs. Lack of forgiveness. Over-emotionality. Past life issues. Unable to let go.	• Virgo, Chiron, 6th House • Scorpio, Pluto, 8th House
Breasts	Under-nurturing of self and over-nurturing of others. Past life issues. Providing for family. Mother issues.	• Cancer, Moon, 4th House
Breathing/lungs	Resisting living life to the full. Suppression. Issues with learning and communication.	• Gemini, Mercury, 3rd House

Physical part / issue	Life aspects	Astrology
Cancer (depends on which area affected)		
Circulation	Heart issues. Social issues.	• Leo, Sun, 5th House
Digestive system	Perfectionism, critical and judgemental. Overly detailed. Can't digest life or truth. Stuck in routine. Over or under attention to health, cleanliness, diet, exercise.	• Virgo, Chiron, 6th House
Ears	Not listening to soul or other people. Too much noise in life and head. Shutting out the world.	• Aries, Mars, 1st House • Gemini, Mercury, 3rd House
Endocrine system/ hormones	Lack of balance in life: male/female aspects, career/home, responsibility/fun, work/play, adult/child.	• Libra, Venus, 7th House
Eyes	Not wanting to see the truth. Creating illusions. Lack of inspiration, awareness, appreciation. Lack of focus or too focused.	• Aries, Mars, 1st House • Pisces, Neptune, 12th House
Feet	Self-pity, martyrdom. Lack of creativity, inspiration, or spiritual connection. Too submissive. Addictions. Can't stand on own two feet.	• Pisces, Neptune, 12th House
Fingers (see Hands)		
Gall bladder	Holding grudges and bile from the past.	• Cancer, Moon, 4th House
Genitals/ sexual issues	Disturbing sexual thoughts. Present or past life dark events dealing with sex, or abuse of power, by self or others. Over-sharing, or lack of sharing with others. Deep grief.	• Scorpio, Pluto, 8th House

Physical part / issue	Life aspects	Astrology
Hands/arms/ fingers	Over-thinking. Stuck thoughts. Speaking without thinking. Resisting being sociable. Not reaching out to others. Gossiping. Lack of focus or over-focus.	• Gemini, Mercury, 3rd House
Heart	Lack of love, joy, fun, creativity; separation from loved ones; selfishness; too much ego.	• Leo, Sun, 5th House
Headache/ Migraine	Over-thinking. Stress, anxiety, suppressed anger. Wanting control.	• Aries, Mars, 1st House • Aquarius, Uranus, 11th House
Head/facial issues	Needing to save face. Over focus on self. Not loving self. Inauthenticity.	• Aries, Mars, 1st House
Hips/thighs/ pelvis	Resisting expansion to life. Wanting to escape overseas or from people. Desire to learn, write, or teach is being thwarted.	• Sagittarius, Jupiter, 9th House
Hormones (see Endocrine system)		
Intestines	Perfectionism. Picking holes in things or people. Anxiety, stuckness. Resistance to present or future.	• Virgo, Chiron, 6th House
Joints (see Bones)		
Kidneys	Annoyed by world or injustice. Cannot accept what is. Believe things should be different.	• Libra, Venus, 7th House
Lower legs/ ankles	Unable to go forward in life. Resistance. Hiding away from destiny, humanity, or helping others.	• Aquarius, Uranus, 11th House
Liver	Anger, resentment, holding grudges. Need to purify aspects of life.	• Leo, Sun, 5th House • Virgo, Chiron, 6th House • Scorpio, Pluto, 8th House

Physical part / issue	Life aspects	Astrology
Mental health	Too much in the head and not enough open heart. Anxiety, running from society, addictions to escape pain and living on Earth.	• Aquarius, Uranus, 11th House • Pisces, Neptune, 12th House
Mouth/ tongue	Speaking without thinking or with a forked tongue. Gossiping. Inauthenticity. Selfishness.	• Aries, Mars, 1st House • Gemini, Mercury, 3rd House
Mystery illness	Confused thinking. Haven't processed inner being. Being too affected by others.	• Pisces, Neptune, 12th House
Nervous system	Over-thinking, anxiety, weak thoughts. Not trusting self or others, or universe. Thinking self not good enough. Lack of courage.	• Aquarius, Uranus, 11th House • Pisces, Neptune, 12th House
Nose	Over-ambition. Competitiveness. Going too fast to smell the roses. Too picky or snobby. Unappreciative.	• Aries, Mars, 1st House
Ovaries	Lack of balance in life. Unable to be creative or sow seeds for new things.	• Libra, Venus, 7th House
Pancreas	Lack of fun or delights in life. Negativity. Comfort eating. Wanting someone else to take care of our needs. Wanting attention.	• Cancer, Moon, 4th House, • Leo, Sun, 5th House
Prostate	Imbalance of sexual activity. Feeling guilty re. sex.	• Scorpio, Pluto, 8th House
Ribs	Rambling thoughts. Lack of structure in life. Feeling like a spare part.	• Gemini, Mercury, 3rd House
Shoulders	Too much 'shoulding' to self and to others. Over-burdened. Lack of relaxation.	• Gemini, Mercury, 3rd House
Sinuses	Anger and irritation. Triggers present.	• Aries, Mars, 1st House

Physical part / issue	Life aspects	Astrology
Skin	Inflamed by situations. Itching to do something but suppressing it.	• Aries, Mars, 1st House
Stomach	Find it hard to digest life. Mother issues. Issues re. home. Past life issues.	• Cancer, Moon, 4th House
Teeth	Issues with a man or own masculine aspects. Lack of courage or determination. Being a toothless tiger.	• Aries, Mars, 1st House • Capricorn, Saturn, 10th House
Thighs (see Hips)		
Throat/neck/thyroid	Lack of creativity. Not speaking out. Not valuing self, things, or people enough. Lack of self-esteem. Financial or friendship issues. Using/abusing others.	• Taurus, 2nd House, Venus/Sedna/Earth
Thymus	Lack of open-heartedness. Need to share self with others.	• Leo, Sun, 5th House
Varicose veins	Wanting to hide away from people. Suppression of self or destiny.	• Aquarius, Uranus, 11th House
Viruses/bacteria	Resistance to other life forms, including spiritual parts of self. Dark imagination about the unknown worlds.	• Aquarius, Uranus, 11th House • Pisces, Neptune, 12th House
Womb	Mother or mothering issues. Need for nurturing, caring, nursing, or creativity.	• Cancer, Moon, 4th House

While I was in the process of writing this chapter on healing, I was experiencing pain in my fingers and hands one day, and merely attributed it to too much typing. Chiron came to me in my consciousness and asked me to visualise placing my outstretched fingers and hands on the table. He then took a small rubber mallet and gently tapped on my fingers to straighten them out. He said the pain would diminish when I straighten out my thoughts!

Good physical health and well-being comes from a body and mind that are wholly in balance in themselves and with each other. If any part of us is in pain or not functioning properly, then we must realise we are out of harmony and dis-eased in some way. If one part of us takes over control or doesn't cooperate, even just a little, then we are knocked out of kilter and this causes shockwaves or repercussions throughout our consciousness, and illness and issues follow.

Pain always comes from resistance, so as a priority we should take a look at what we might be holding off or running away from, remembering that physical pain results from the emotions and thinking we are currently programmed with. Therefore, we might think that the pain we are experiencing after a car crash might be just from some random accident, but our consciousness will in some way have attracted that car crash to us, whether it was our own fault or someone else's. There are no accidents in this universe.

All reality is manifested from someone's consciousness somewhere. However, if we are the victim of some accident or disaster, we are always divinely protected to the degree required, and only exposed to the trials that are necessary for us to learn, evolve, and grow.

If we continually resist, our soul will invite us Home—we will physically die. This may be preferable to a long, drawn-out bout of illness or debilitation where the higher energies of the universe break us down anyway.

Humans who have reached godhood, and gods in human form on Earth, can also experience pain and illness and physical issues if their thinking becomes in any way corrupted or impure, or it is part of their mission to experience this ailment. They will have to deal with this in the same way as everyone else. However, they will know how to utilise their tools of consciousness to overcome their issue as quickly as possible.

Physical death is something we must all be prepared for, and it can visit us at any time. While making the most of every day of our incarnation upon Earth, we can also look forward to going Home one day and living a more blissful existence in the higher dimensions. Trying to put off our ultimate fate and bemoaning it, is another kind of resistance and it results in leading a miserable and painful life, focusing on negatives instead of enjoying and learning from the experiences that the physical plane has to offer us.

Chapter 20 – Healing emotional and mental issues

None of us, not even the gods, are immune to situations that cause upsets to our emotional or mental states. Imagine how different our world could be, if we were all taught from a young age, techniques on how to overcome these situations quickly and effectively. Instead, many people labour for much of their lives under the burden of suffering caused by their stressful beliefs and programming and inability to process their emotionality. In chapter 22 we will look at some of the healing techniques we can use to overcome our pain and distress or dubious proclivities. Firstly, we need to examine some major root causes of our issues.

Generally, there's not a day goes past that we aren't faced with a situation that disturbs us in some way, either mildly irritating us or stressing us, or making us give full vent to our emotions. It could be noisy neighbours when we are trying to study or sleep, or some task at work that we feel we can't cope with, or some idiot cutting us up on the road, or a child or parent who is too demanding, or a partner who doesn't do what they said they would do, or being slapped with an unfair parking fine, or battling to pay our everyday bills, or struggling with a computer system that will not respond in the way that we need.

Our present-day world is stacked with ways that stress us out and cause us to flip. What if we could face all this chaos with greater serenity and stoicism and more resilience, and just calmly work through it until we have happy resolution?

Consciousness can be likened to oceanic waters—our emotions are like this too. Emotions are aspects of our consciousness such as love, sadness, anger, joy, fear, surprise, contempt, trust, and excitement. They are non-physical entities, just as our consciousness is a non-physical entity, but our emotions can result in us experiencing physical symptoms, such as heart palpitations, skin tingling, shortness of breath, crying, or pain in some part of our body.

This is not some punishment from the gods. They don't send demons to torment us, and neither are we given any challenge that would be too much for us to handle (although we might argue with this!) It is all about cause and effect within our own consciousness; whatever we hold as our thoughts or feelings will attract experiences that either match these or help us to let go of them.

Emotions are like waves of an ocean. They ebb and flow. They can tower above us threateningly, or they can crash down onto us, flattening us. They can drown or support us. They can be stormy and moody. At times our emotions can delight us, such as when we are in love, and at other times we will feel disappointment at their treachery.

There are many reasons for feeling emotions, but are they valid, and should we allow our negative ones to wreak havoc in our lives and the lives of those around us? Master Jesus once told me, "Over-the-top emotions always take over the landscape."

Sometimes we are not even aware of the reason for our discontent, anger, apathy, or nihilism. We need to always be aware of what kind of ocean is flowing through us at any time, so that we can handle our waters in a wiser manner. Even though the waves may seem tumultuous, we can learn to ride them to shore without endangering ourselves or others.

Whatever our emotions, we need to respect and cooperate with them, for they are a part of our consciousness, a part of who we are. Rather than getting upset at who we are, we can learn ways to modify or transform our emotions so that we can create a better mood for our ocean. We do this by examining our thinking, for it is our underlying thoughts that create our resulting emotions.

a) Triggers and the Secret Book of Laws

For instance, if we have a belief that a library should be a quiet place, and people are talking and laughing there, then it is likely that we will get upset. We might get angry and shout at them, or sit there stewing and muttering and suppressing our emotions, or we might storm out in a huff, declaring to ourselves that we will never visit the library again. Our emotions have been triggered by the thinking or programmed belief that is in place in our consciousness. If we didn't have that belief, then that trigger wouldn't exist inside our mind, and we would have been able to remain harmonious in the library, even while noticing that some individuals weren't behaving respectfully.

In one of my other books *History of the Gods*, channelled from the god Thoth,[19] he likens our human journey to crossing field upon field of snake pits. We clear out as many snakes (or triggers) as we can see, but we never know when a snake will rise to the surface to challenge us. If we are feeling moody or cranky, we can be sure that snakes are on the move in our field.

Consciousness is a web, and just one cranky person can throw the universe into disharmony by sending damaging pulses of their low vibrations down the lines of the matrix, and they will need to atone for disturbing the peace at some time in the future.

Most of us will have thousands of triggers inside our consciousness, waiting like time bombs to explode at any moment. Each of these triggers is founded on some belief that we have given a home to during the vast number of experiences we have had over all our lifetimes. For example, the belief about a quiet library may have come from our childhood when we ourselves were told off for talking in its hallowed halls.

Our beliefs come not only from our childhood experiences and our parents, but also from school days, our friends, bosses, governments, and society in general. If any belief is challenged, or a stored experience is stirred up, depending on how deeply held is that belief or how deeply felt is that experience, we will react with an emotion that is either subtle or aggravated. The type of emotion that we display is often the emotion that was stored along with the belief or event when it was first experienced, and if we were just a child when this happened, we will generally act out as if we were still that same age. Triggered traumas from childhood can see us acting like five-year-olds, even if we are now in our fifties!

---

19. *History of the Gods* is as yet unpublished at the time of writing this.

For instance, if we experienced the breakdown of our parent's marriage when we were a little girl, and we never saw much of our father again, we might feel a sense of abandonment, and have stored away the emotion and belief that men will abandon us and cause us heartbreak. As an adult, we would be keen to protect ourselves from this eventuality and might be clingy towards male partners so they wouldn't abandon us, or be reluctant to enter into a partnership with a man at all. However, if our relationship did break up, it would trigger a torrent of emotional pain commensurate with the stored initial experience of the abandonment by our father.

Another example might be a teenage boy who was bullied at school and who runs away and hides to weep at his powerlessness. As an adult, whenever he is bullied by anyone, he is triggered off and wants to cry like he did as a teenager, and he runs for cover from society again.

So, in order to get our emotions under control, we need to examine the underlying thinking that has triggered us off. This is a monumental task and not some overnight job, but if we tackle each emotional trigger as it comes up and try to understand it, we will find that gradually we shift our thinking and our emotional outbursts decrease. Interrogating our belief system is not an easy thing to do because often it leads to major changes in our lives, and it's simpler to carry on with the thinking we've always had because that protects us from having to make adjustments.

Sometimes a trigger is designed by the universe to monitor how we are progressing in dealing with these thorns in our side. Our lessons come in cycles, which may occur over a 24-hour period or months or millennia; the universe keeps track of it all with no problem. Our soul will want to check how things have evolved since the previous revolution of the cogwheel. Therefore, similar scenarios and themes can be manifested to those in our past in order to gauge the rise or fall of our consciousness since then. Our soul isn't being masochistic here, wanting us to experience the same pain and outcomes as the first time around, but it is the only way to interpret if lessons have been learned.

We can often identify a trigger point when we hear ourselves saying, "This should or should not be happening." (If we 'should' ourselves or others too much, we will often suffer from *shoulder* problems!) When we 'should' something, it means that we have expectations, and if those expectations are not met then it will lead to the trigger exploding into an emotional reaction. Think of road rage incidents; people get triggered because they believe others should or shouldn't be driving in a certain way.

All this was brought home to me personally just as I was finishing the final edits to this book in mid 2023. I awoke from an upsetting dream where I had been extremely angry with someone I cared for who had betrayed my trust. I knew I needed to let go all this anger and my triggers, and I asked myself how I could have responded to all this in a loving way? But I couldn't even think of any suitable responses! Then I wondered how Jesus would have handled this, and I asked for his help to formulate a better response.

Jesus appeared immediately, even though I hadn't spoken with him directly in many years. I felt very honoured and grateful for his guidance.[20]

Jesus helped me to see, firstly, that I need to stop immediately when I initially feel the anger, and become aware of it and not go into my automated response. He told me it's natural to feel the flash of anger for a moment, but then a true god is aware of it and deals with it.

Secondly, I needed to stop blaming everyone who was guiltless in the situation. They may have had no knowledge of what was going on, and to hurt, harass, or harm them when they were just innocent bystanders was not valid. I needed to understand who or what was the true cause of my being triggered off.

Jesus then showed me that what the person in my dream had done was indeed selfish, inconsiderate, and disrespectful, traits that most humans portray at times, but that I myself had carried out the same kind of betrayal against my parents when I had been a teenager. So, my past error was being mirrored back to me in my dream, as a lesson and a challenge for me to clean up. I felt so ashamed, and had to do a lot of work on forgiveness over the following days.

But Jesus continued to work with me during this time, and he opened the door for me on new knowledge that was really helpful for me.

---

20. From meditations with Jesus, 28 April – 1 May 2023.

I asked Jesus what was the best way of letting go all my anger? I said that there are so many ways of doing it, as I have elucidated in this book, but which would be the best way for me? Jesus said any of the ways I have described in these chapters would work for me and my students. But I pestered him some more and asked, "But what would be the most *effective* way for me to let go my anger?"

Jesus smiled and replied, "Ah, you want the industrial solution!"

"Yes, I guess so!"

"Then you need to go to your industrial warehouse of your consciousness, and look for all the fuses and explosives that trigger you off," Jesus said. "What is your thinking that sets you off, such as, people should not disrespect me, or people should not use my possessions without asking?"

I started to ponder on what the thinking was behind my getting angry. What exactly was triggering me off?

Jesus interrupted me. "You have, and everyone has, a Secret Book of Laws, which is unwritten and unrevealed to anyone, but by which you rule your life."

I thought about this and realised he was absolutely right. My whole life was lived by this Secret Book of Laws, rules within my own mind about what people should or should not do, or what I myself should or should not do, or even what the universe should or should not do!

For instance, I had told the universe that it should rain regularly every week to water my garden, or that my computer should never crash. Equally, I had rules such as: friends should reply quickly to my texts or emails; my family should help and support me; Council rates should not be so exorbitant. There were literally thousands of rules sporting all the shoulds and shouldn'ts to do with my life and how I wanted to live it, and each time a rule was broken, I was triggered and felt upset or angry to some degree, even though other people knew nothing about my secret rulebook, and often I didn't even know about my own rules!

I asked Jesus if I could just burn my entire Secret Book of Laws, but would I be able to live my life without any laws at all? Jesus replied, "Try it!" So, I decided to burn my Book and see what would happen.

So, I went to the Warehouse of my Consciousness, a big industrial complex, to fetch my Secret Book, only to discover that it was enormous, the size and weight of a small truck! Jesus laughed and told me that we begin adding to this Book from the day we are born on Earth. So, I got into a forklift truck and lifted up my Book and took it over to the industrial furnace and dropped it in. All the fuses and explosives began to go off like fireworks in there! I left it there to burn to ashes.

Meanwhile, I asked Jesus to help me formulate any new laws I might need for running my life. I mean, I couldn't be lawless and go around breaking laws and having no social boundaries. I began to think of all the new rules I would need, and it started to become a tangled mess.

Then Jesus proposed I set up just two Laws for myself to live by.

LAW #1: I should always obey the laws of the land I am in, or the dimension I am travelling through. (If I don't like these Laws, then I need to find a peaceful and lawful way to change them.)

LAW #2: I should always obey Divine Law, meaning I should be love in every thought, word, and deed, as much as possible, given the situation.

I asked when would there be a situation where a person couldn't be 100% love, and could only give as much as possible? Master Chiron appeared and explained that sometimes we need to use tough love, and that doesn't always feel like 100% love, but it's necessary in that situation.

So, I had destroyed my huge old book of seven decades of human shoulds and shouldn'ts, and replaced it with one small sheet containing just two Laws. This simplified everything. It didn't mean that life would now be simple, but at least I would know how to react now in every situation.

♦

It would seem that our world is becoming more and more offended, not less, if the rants on social media are anything to go by, and the most triggered of people are the ones who get the most air space. Instead of realising that these are wounded people who believe that nothing should be allowed that doesn't coincide with *their* way of thinking, we are pandering to these triggered bullies and shutting down freedom of expression and even the joy of humour.

Many comedians, philosophers, and playwrights are cancelling their performances, at risk of offending a small minority of egos with thorns in their hearts. Before long, we will not be allowed to say, or even think, anything that is not approved by those-who-are-triggered and who refuse to remove their thorns. (The tenets of this book may even be on their hit-list!)

As a society we need to become more comfortable with feeling uncomfortable in the presence of those with alternate viewpoints to our own. We must strive for harmony, therefore if it's noisy neighbours who are bothering us, who we believe should be quieter, rather than getting angry we might need to accept that people have to live, and that life itself is a pretty noisy affair. Given that the world reflects back to us what is in our consciousness, perhaps we ourselves have a noisy consciousness that needs to settle down and be more focused and quieter?

If we think that our boss shouldn't be giving us work we can't cope with, rather than going into stress, maybe we could take on a new perspective? Maybe the universe is trying to tell us that we are capable of more than we give ourselves credit for, or perhaps we are being given an opportunity to grow our abilities, or perhaps we need to learn negotiation skills, or perhaps it's merely time to change our job?

If we are a balanced individual with emotional stability, then we will be able to tolerate people being different from ourselves and having differing viewpoints from us. We will allow them to exist as *their* personality in this world, just as there are many diverse flowers on Earth, all with their individual beauty and attributes. But if we have an axe to grind, a chip on our shoulder, or any number of thorns in our heart, then we are going to be triggered off by other people, and we won't be coming from a base of emotional stability but we'll be attacking and defending from our own world of pain.

In all cases, we need to remove the original triggering thought and replace it with a more rounded attitude or perspective. What does it serve us to get into an angry or morose mood? Does that enhance or settle the situation? It will probably leave the situation unresolved, and in many cases make it worse. Why allow the things in life that we have no control over, to upset our equilibrium and spoil our day?

Teaching ourselves tolerance, compassion, and forgiveness, and allowing things to just be as they are, will go a long way to ameliorating undesired emotionality. The thing to ask ourselves is, do we wish for harmony more than we wish for disharmony?

Sometimes, however, our anger is a positive thing, for it can motivate us to take action, where before we might have procrastinated or shied away from confrontation or from taking steps to resolve things. Allowing things to happen in life without getting upset about them, does not mean that we don't take action. But it's preferable that we take the action that benefits us without being triggered by anger or any other emotion.

b) Facing heartbreak

There are times, however, when emotionality is warranted, such as when faced with the death or serious illness of a loved one or friend, or other tragic events such as losing a home in a fire. In these circumstances, we shouldn't try to suppress our feelings, for that will cause problems within our physical body and could affect us mentally. But even in these cases, we need to be aware of resisting what has happened as if it should never have been so. We don't know the plans of the universe for ourselves or others, and we need to accept that this is destiny playing out.

Any resistance we put up against our reality will be felt as pain, either in our body or in our mind, for we will be at odds with our soul and its desire for us to be experiencing these things for some reason. What we see when our world falls apart is the yawning Void. It is the Dark World of Chaos, but also the realm of potential and possibilities, so we need to look for the silver lining.

Of course, it's not good for us to continue to feel this deep emotionality, since this will develop into depression or other illnesses, so we will need to examine what is really going on in our consciousness, for the initial trigger will have been long overtaken by an underlying agenda that needs to be resolved.

This would be the case, for instance, if years after the death of a loved one, a person was still mourning them and unable to function properly in their life. It can also occur after retirement or loss of a job or some devastating tragedy. Chiron asks us, "Are you going to dwell within these woundings forever, never lifting yourself above them and always feeling hurt? Bring the joy back into your life."

One of the traits of godhood, is that a god can pick themselves up after calamity, misfortune, or heartbreak. They don't stay flattened but will juggle curved balls and even throw them back. They will handle life's ups and downs and inject life force into themselves again, using the determination of their conscious will. It's not to say they won't feel the intense emotions surrounding their circumstances, but they will need to remain strong and resolute all the while. They understand that if they dwell on misfortune then they will only attract more of the same. Gods prefer to fly above the ocean of emotions, and humans tend to wallow in them.

Tragedy, adversity, challenges; these are grist to the mill for the human journey on Earth, and it is how the gods teach us and help us evolve. Through our adventures in the physical dimension we learn to experiment, and even our failures teach us much; to become stronger, more resourceful and creative, or adaptive and accepting. If we have taken a tumble, we need to see it as just a bump in the road and learn to roll swiftly out of it. Everyone will benefit from learning to roll with the punches of life, and how to fall gracefully and how to utilise their consciousness to get back on their feet again. It may help to re-read the section on Finding Fortitude in Chapter 18.

c) Gloominess, self-pity, victimhood

The real tragedy is when we choose to stay down after one of life's beat-ups. We indulge in our self-pity and victimhood and moan to the world they should be helping us and solving all our issues. And when that doesn't transpire, or not enough for our liking, we feel hopeless and helpless and our low vibrations cause us to fall further into physical or mental decline.

If we feel trapped in our lives, it's only because we are constrained by our own thinking and lack of imagination to visualise a different life. Many humans choose struggle instead of opting to change their attitude or perspective. If we have fallen from grace into a gloomy dark pit of emotionality or mental anguish through our own deeds or thoughts, we need to know that no god or vengeful spirit is doing this to us, although our wounded inner child feels like it is being punished and is unloved by its 'parent'. No retribution is ever forthcoming from the higher dimensions. They seek only to correct our thinking or trajectory. We plunge into this darkness by our own hand and, through our own hand or thinking, must we devise a way to climb out of this black hole.

In past lifetimes, we would have had a few successes but many more failures, on this planet and others, and so it's a way of existence that we need to learn to cope with and overcome.

When we change our thinking, we change our life and our reality. If we focus on loss and lack, then this is what gets projected back at us, since the universe can work only with the material we present to it in our consciousness. If we are woeful, then we will be staring at a world full of woe, since this will be the filter we are using to view our surroundings.

Is it possible to live a life where every day is joyful? It certainly is, even when faced with issues and challenges. The trick is not to let them affect us. Easier said than done, I know, but if we can have just one good day, then we know it's possible to have another. But we don't need to wait for a good day to come along. We can make it happen.

We need to choose to take stock, reset the foundations for our future, evaluate new priorities, and recreate or improve our life, working with fortitude until conditions get better. Whatever we do, we can't stay stuck in our chaos or strife, but must clear away the debris of the old life so we can see a new path and move on to a fresh phase. Old energies taint our world, pull us down, and take away hope.

Sometimes it's necessary to experience a big wallop to our life, for it awakens us from a stale or half-dead consciousness. Thunderstorms are useful for clearing the air, and we find it refreshing afterwards. Hurricanes through our life have a tendency to shift things and to open up our consciousness to new perspectives, innovations, and ways of being.

But we have a choice as to whether to conjure up a tempest or a clear sunny day within our consciousness. We can manage the climate within our mind in any moment, and switch from gloomy, rain-laden brooding to cheerful, optimistic, blue-sky thinking. Placing our consciousness in the present moment and not brooding on the past or future, we can make it the best moment we can possibly conceive.

One thing to remember is that the sun is always there for us and the Earth. It may be hidden behind clouds or be over the horizon, but the sun never misses a day of rising no matter what the weather, and even when we can't see the sun, it is still available to pour life-giving energies into us. We may be going through a cloudy phase of our life, but clouds are a good opportunity to go seeking the sun and force a change of climate in our consciousness. However, dark skies don't last forever, and the sun will most definitely break through again and warm our soul with its fire. Most of us would find daily blue skies tedious, anyway, and we appreciate the change in seasons.

We cannot allow our self-pitying thoughts or the world at large to pull us down into low vibrations, for it will take some effort to pull ourselves out again. Stoking ourselves with fortitude, we need to be determined to shine again as the star we truly are at our core. No matter what the circumstances, we always have the tools of our consciousness to lift ourselves out of our heartbreak—if we choose to.

d) Closed heart, imbalance, love, fun

A closed heart can also lead to gloominess. Every time we have been emotionally wounded in our life, our heart will have closed quickly in order to protect itself. If we shut our heart, we surmise that then we won't feel the pain. We have learned to do this over the eons where we have had to endure so much abuse and heartache. After a while, if we have too many wounding situations to deal with, our heart ceases to reopen and remains sealed. It takes a great deal of coaxing and love to get it to open up again, and even more so for it to stay open permanently.

A child, for example, who has experienced much trauma while growing up in a dysfunctional and unloving household, will have closed their heart to protect themselves, and will probably grow up into an adult who is unable to feel or share love and deep emotions. They might function quite adequately in many areas of their life but have trouble forming loving attachments or feeling empathy or compassion, and often are unable to feel joy or have fun.

There are many people who deny love and barricade their heart from it, but it is essential that we balance the hardships and challenges of pursuing our destiny with the delights of love and the happiness of having fun. Balance is a keyword in our universe, and neither dimensions nor emotions are allowed to run amok without the need for intervention by ourselves or the gods. If the balance of things is upset, either on a grand cosmic scale or merely within one little consciousness, the universe becomes disharmonious and a less pleasurable place in which to live.

When we are enjoying ourselves and are relaxed, it is easy for love to seep into and out from our consciousness, making the world a more delightful place to be. Therefore, we need to be positively inviting love into our lives, for love equals harmony and is the intrinsic state of our being.

The mistake many people make is trying to find happiness on the outside instead of within themselves. They tell themselves, "I'd be happy if only…I could find a partner…I could take a holiday…I could afford a new car…I were more attractive…it would rain/be sunny…I didn't have this illness…I won the lottery, etc, etc. But then what? External things aren't going to fill the gap for long. Soon they will be wanting something else to satiate the gnawing in their heart that won't go away.

Learning to be appreciative of what we currently have and finding the happiness in our every day, means that we don't allow the chaotic external world to impinge on our state of mind, and we can carry a full and balanced open heart around with us wherever we are and whatever we are doing.

Closing our heart also means that we don't open up to new experiences or ideas and aren't easily able to shift our perceptions and beliefs. We remain closed to new possibilities and the potential of situations, and new doors won't be revealed to us by the gods or our soul. Therefore, one of the tasks of our soul and the gods is to crack open our hearts and get rid of the shell that covers us. This is painful for all involved as it makes a person vulnerable, but it does open them up to cosmic rays and other useful and life-enhancing energies and messages.

A closed heart also prevents connections with our soul and the higher dimensions (re-read chapter 14), and can lead to physical issues with our heart and vascular system.

e) Managing our lower personas and their emotions

In chapter 2 we looked at the parts of our consciousness that are segmented into many differing personalities, whom I have called lower personas. Chiron calls them our crew, and indeed they are part of the team that makes us who we are, with all our varying traits and abilities. Every day, or even within the same day, we could be playing out different personas within our consciousness, wearing an assortment of hats and displaying various aspects of ourselves, depending on who we are with, what circumstances we find ourselves in, and what energies are within us and around us at the time.

It's like being the conductor of an orchestra consisting of many children. Each kid plays a different instrument and wants to play their own tune. It's up to us as the conductor to wave our baton, our magic wand of consciousness, and to get everyone playing the same tune at the same time and bring all into harmony. The gods like to hear music that will fill their hearts, and they don't like to listen to discordant notes, and if any of our instruments are broken then we will need to fix it. We need to discover the talent of each persona and utilise it and bring it to full potential, noticing also which children tend to play up, and resolve their issues with kindness and love.

These personas have been created over many lifetimes from our various beliefs and experiences. We could call some of them skeletons in our closet or ghosts in our machine. They are responsible for most of our issues because their attitudes are usually fixed and immovable, and they merely react in the way they have been programmed by past events.

When we (or our soul) want to create change in our lives, we find that some or many of our lower personas object to this change because it is at odds with their programming and protection mechanisms. When this occurs, our personal world becomes disharmonious, and our personas can even sabotage or undermine our intentions, and we feel this resistance as very real pain, either physically, emotionally, or mentally. It saps our energy and motivation and brings down our vibrational level, which in turn attracts more lower vibrational incidences and people into our lives.

If a large number of our personas all come out together to oppose us or demand our attention, it can produce a major riot in our consciousness and may lead to erratic emotional responses or even to a nervous breakdown. In chapter 22 we take a look at techniques for dealing with our dissatisfied or renegade lower personas, created either in this lifetime or previous ones.

We can't disregard the rocking of the boat that our lower personas cause. We will sense their discontent or rebelliousness as it plays out in our responses and knocks us off balance. As the captain of our crew we will need to manage them and work things out with them, or else mutiny will be the outcome. Are we doing a good job in quelling their disturbances? They may have valid issues which we have been ignoring. We ourselves are responsible for smoothing out our consciousness. We cannot blame others for triggering off our personas. The triggers sit within ourselves and we need to take action to remove them.

Our lower personas tend to unravel and object and resist when we are making changes within our life, or we are facing new growth or pathways or challenges. We need to get them all on board and aligned with our new thinking. All parts of our consciousness need to work together to create a well-adjusted, happy, and healthy human being, just as all the cells of our body need to cooperate for us to function physically.

f) Resistance to change

One of our biggest emotional downfalls is being resistant to change. Our inner personas often don't like it, unless we are a very adventurous person. Of course, sometimes we look forward to a change—of job, house, scenery, season, clothes, routine, even partners. We tend to not mind change if we are the ones to initiate it and what we are moving towards is what we desire. But when a change is foisted upon us, we can be averse to going there.

Take, for instance, when we are made redundant from a job, or if a partner suddenly wants a divorce, or the home we are renting is sold and we are forced to move out. Even small changes can put our backs up, such as roadworks that impose a detour from our usual route, or new legislation that requires us to use a different form, or the closure of our favourite hair salon or café. We might feel anything from irritated to irate.

Change is endemic in our world. We need to get used to that idea. Nothing will ever stay the same. No two seconds are alike. We can't halt the universe; the cogs are forever turning. We can't alter the fact that we are going to die one day. It's not possible to hold onto the past or old phases, as if doing so would keep the future at bay. We can appreciate what has passed but need to look ahead too.

Although it might seem like it at times, there is no same-old, same-old with nothing happening. New energies are pouring into our world and through us in every moment, offering new opportunities. The Moon cycles through a new zodiac sign every two and a half days, penetrating our psyche with a different focus and triggering a variety of moods. Planets, stars, and people all contribute their energies and wavelengths to the mix, providing a different emotional stew every day for us to savour. We are bombarded by change and shouldn't ignore our ever-changing feelings and energies, for they are part of who we are.

If we come to accept that change is inevitable and that we cannot hold onto the status quo for very long, we shift into a different mindset and become more open to opportunities and creativity. We might wonder what magical thing could happen to us in any moment and invite adventures into our life.

If we allow ourselves to see life as cyclic, we may not feel so trapped or stuck and can enable ourselves to move on. Physical problems often result from resistance to change because our stuck thinking leads to our bodies becoming stuck too, and we can experience inflexibility, especially regarding our joints, back, and neck, and lower leg problems because we are afraid of stepping forward.

All of us do it at some time in our lives—resist moving forwards into the future, the known or unknown. We can find ourselves procrastinating, dragging our heels, pulling back, or acting with tardiness. It may be that we have very good reasons for hanging back, but is the real reason our fear? Or perhaps we don't want to be bothered; transformation takes effort. It's neither automatic nor natural, and we must raise ourself off the couch and commit to some kind of action.

When I was going through a period of resistance recently, a divine voice told me, "You are acting up instead of acting out."

"What do you mean?" I asked.

"You are resisting, instead of playing the role you have come here to do."

"But what am I resisting?"

Master Dominic appeared and told me, "Feel into it."

I did, and could certainly feel a wall of resistance.

Dom said, "It is the wall you have put up between your world of Order and stability and the Dark World of Chaos and possibilities. You don't want to shatter your current life."

"No, I don't, because I am trying to get my book written."

"I understand," Dom said, "but maybe it would be a better book if you had some experiences and adventures in Chaos first?"

I did see his point.

If we aren't aware of our resistance, and don't process our blockages, we may never discover the wonderful things the universe wishes us to experience. If we no longer fit within the vibrational boundaries we are currently living or working in, then it is essential that we are moved on to a place where we will feel more at home and in keeping with the vibrations.

If we keep our heart closed and our defences raised, how can the gods work their magic through us? We need to be vulnerable and surrender to our soul's desire for us. Joining our divine team and working with them cooperatively, instead of trying to hide from our destiny, will see doors open for us that we couldn't have imagined, and our life flowing much more smoothly.

If we anticipate only good things for the future, rather than resist and dwell negatively on what might lie in wait for us, we will create the destiny and future of our dreams.

g) Resistance to what is

We mentioned this earlier in the 'Facing Heartbreak' section—a reluctance to face up to what is happening right now. It does us no favours to run away from our situation or to hide our head in the sand. When we poke our head up again, the situation will still be confronting us, and while we have been avoiding it physically, in our mind we have probably made it seem larger and more monstrous than it truly is. No amount of denial will make the situation come right again, and saying to ourselves that this shouldn't have happened will just cause us more pain because of feeling powerless to have prevented it.

Sometimes the shock of an event will be too overwhelming to cope with in the moment, and we need to be kind and gentle with ourselves at first and nurture our needs and emotions until such time as we can let go of our emotionality and muster up practical solutions.

Many of the healing techniques described in chapter 22 will help us to deal with this resistance, and also re-reading chapter 18 on 'Finding Fortitude'.

h) Wanting to escape

All too often when the world gets too much for us, we might be tempted to want to escape from it all. Then our solutions might range from organising a weekend away, to getting high on drink or drugs, to chucking in our job, to selling our home and moving to the wilderness, or in the extreme, to committing suicide.

While we feel the longing to get away mainly as a physical desire, it is actually our thinking that we are trying to escape from. If we thought about our life with a different perspective or attitude, then we might not be having these escapism dreams. Therefore, it comes back to the fact that we need to change our underlying thinking so that we can bring back harmony into our lives and consciousness.

People with strong Pisces, Neptune, or 12th House aspects in their astrological birth charts are particularly prone to yearnings of escaping this physical dimension, since this astrology provides deep links with the spiritual dimensions. They can often suffer from addictive personalities, seeking something beyond their mundane life on Earth. This can also occur to other people when there is a powerful Piscean or Neptunian transit, such as a Pisces Full Moon, or influential planets are temporarily visiting a person's Piscean or 12th House in their birth chart.

If we are feeling such deep darkness that we want to die, it is that we need to die in our consciousness, not physically. It's actually good news, for we are ready to let go of our old self and be born anew. We do not need to kill ourselves off physically to do this, but merely to say goodbye to some of our pain-inducing lower personas.

People with strong Scorpio, Pluto, or 8th House aspects in their astrology charts, or who are temporarily going through a Scorpionic transit (which can, in fact, last up to twenty years!), are often affected by the dark energies of death and destruction these aspects bring about.

Speaking with our lower personas or letting them go is the remedy here in all cases of escapist or suicidal tendencies. Healing techniques for doing this are described in chapter 22.

i) Fear

There are thousands of types of fears, and it's highly likely that we will experience at least a few of these during our lifetime. Some fears may be temporary, for instance when our airplane hits turbulence, or they may be more permanent phobias, such as if we are scared stiff of even getting onto a plane.

Some fears are useful in that they help us to stay away from dangerous situations or from trouble. But mostly, fears keep us stuck in some way and prevent us from following some line of action that we might have taken if we didn't have that fear. For instance, our fear of public speaking can keep us away from any career that involves having to stand up and face an audience, or even a career that involves dealing with people in general. Imagine what it would feel like and what we could achieve if we weren't constrained by our fears!

The emotion of fear can also manifest as physical symptoms such as inflexible joints, stiff backs, or diseases caused by too much adrenaline or cortisol being released. The fear of moving forward can often result in a broken leg or ankle. Fears will shut us down in some way and prevent us from having to deal with what we are frightened of.

This can be a neat way of getting out of schooling. When I was at secondary school, I detested Latin lessons so much that it often caused a severe hayfever attack to come on, and then I was able to skip the class that day.

However, it pays to remember that whatever we hold in our consciousness, including fears, will result in us attracting that focus all the more. For instance, while I don't exactly fear cats, I am allergic to them, and so when I see one near me, I instinctively freeze a little and hope it will go away. The cat will always make a beeline for me, even if I am in a crowd of people! If we fear our house will get hit by a thunderbolt, well, guess what will probably happen one day?

We can be sure that the gods and our soul will make us face some, if not most, of our fears at some point along our journey. If we are to make it to godhood, we can't be allowed to be a jellyfish with no backbone. We will need to be strong and fearless to a great degree. As Chiron says, we can't just sit in a puddle with our umbrella up, hoping we won't get wet, for we will never get to discover the treasures of the universe and our destiny that way. Rain will fall upon us and waters will rise up too, and the only way around this is to accept we will get wet and also learn to swim. If we are fearing dying, then it might help to re-read chapter 8 on death.

The healing techniques in chapter 22 describe ways to overcome our fears by changing our thinking.

j) Being off track

A common reason for feeling that something is not right in our lives comes when we are off track with our destiny. Because we are on the wrong path, obstacles will be strewn in our way to try to stem our progress, causing us to feel that life is one huge effort. We might feel confused, lost, aimless, unmotivated, or directionless.

The way doesn't need to be so hard, and won't be if we are on the correct road to completing our mission. However, we can also be on the right path but at the wrong time, and again this will be a source of consternation for us. We need to ensure that we align ourselves with our soul's agenda so that we get both our destination and the timing in perfect order.

When we are confused or lost, we can often suffer physically from feet problems, or mystery illnesses where the source can't be pinned down, and which may also keep moving around the body.

See chapter 24 for more information about succeeding with our destiny.

k) Feeling unfulfilled

In chapter 8, Facing Death, we spoke about having had a fulfilling life when the time comes to depart this world. What is it to have had a fulfilling life? Many of us are apt to find life all too unfulfilling at times, and if these moments are plentiful, we will consider our life to have been unfulfilled.

What is it that makes us feel unfulfilled? There could be manyfold reasons.

- No connection with our soul or higher dimensions. No belief in divine worlds
- No goals or sense of purpose or mission. Not understanding our destiny
- Being off track with our destiny
- Procrastination about taking action we know is needed
- Being unproductive or uncreative
- Unable to manifest things or desires properly
- Not believing we can manifest a better reality
- Not working with the divine worlds to manifest our reality
- Not understanding our Tools of Consciousness, or not utilising them
- Not using our talents to their fullest potential
- Keeping ourselves small, limited, or fearful
- Not giving it our all, doing things half-heartedly
- Giving up, not completing things, feeling guilty
- Being unadventurous, not venturing into the unknown
- Resisting life and the roles we came here to play
- Holding onto pain and not-love aspects of ourselves
- Dealing with unsatisfactory relationships (see Ch 23)
- Unable to teach others or leave a legacy
- Not appreciating how far we have come and all we have achieved

All these reasons are covered in the various chapters of this book. We will remain unfulfilled unless we determine to take action to remove any obstacles preventing us from attaining happiness, peace, and contentment.

l) Dealing with desires

One of the emotional pitfalls for humans is our propensity to desire things or people. We all have desires; even gods desire. Desire is not a bad thing or forbidden by the gods. It makes the world turn, and when one desire dissipates, another will pop up to take its place. We just need to learn how to deal with desire properly. For one thing, desire motivates us and leads us to our destiny. The desire for a particular person may lead us to meet people we are destined to have dealings with in this lifetime.

Chiron tells us there are no limits to what kinds of desire we can have; the universe allows it all. However, we do need to keep our desires in balance and neither go over the top with them and become addicted, nor suppress them entirely.

Are we aware of our desires, good and bad? We need to ponder on them and ask ourselves if we could live without the ones that don't serve us? What triggers our desire? Humans are all too often puppets of those who control the satisfying of desires, and can be led by their noses or genitals into darkness, debt, or disgrace. Think of marketeers, drug dealers, people traffickers, online porn sites, or shonky investment schemes.

However, we should, by all means, follow up those desires which motivate us and lead us to manifesting our dreams. Ideally, we would only have desires that complement our destiny.

m) Educating children

At present in our society we don't do enough to teach our children how to cope with burgeoning emotions. Mental issues then abound in adulthood. We must build strong emotional foundations in our children so that they can become winners and need no pampering when they are older but can add value to our world. It is not only the '3 Rs' that need to be taught in schools, but a '4th R'—Resilience.

We need to look at the whole world of a child and understand what makes them tick, and care for them as individuals with distinct emotions, issues, and vulnerabilities. (Astrology charts are particularly useful for showing these.) One size schooling does not fit all. Every child has an individual consciousness that is like a precious jewel, and each facet is unique and must be worked on separately, not in a run-of-the-mill way.

How can we expect a child to learn and open to their full potential if they are wreathed in pain and confusion within their consciousness? When mankind is freed from pain, it can go on to work on other more fulfilling projects.

Parents tend to produce mini-clones of themselves in their children, with the same kind of consciousness passed down through families from generation to generation, and hence the same kinds of emotional and mental traumas and the conditioned thinking behind them. Who will be the one to break the generational chain of woes, and consciously take on a new set of beliefs to hand down to the children for a better future?

Chapter 21 – More about healing

Healing spiritual issues

Sometimes we might not understand where our issue is coming from, and it may not occur to us that it's emanating from disconnection with our spirit or soul, or other beings in the unseen worlds. One of the worst things that can happen to us is if we become separated from our soul or spirit and communications become shut down. This relationship gives us comfort, guidance, inner strength, and purpose, when it is working out harmoniously.

A feeling of inner tension could also be from our spirit counterpart going through some tough times in the higher dimension, and we are feeling their energies at our human end of the Ribbon of Consciousness. Similarly, our spirit or soul certainly feels what we are going through on the earthly plane, and they may be compassionate and seek to help us. On the other hand, they may get antsy with us and wish we had made different choices or reacted in a wiser or more loving manner (just as parents can get annoyed with their children, even while loving them immeasurably).

As the ancient philosopher Aristotle stated, "The soul suffers when the body is diseased or traumatised, while the body suffers when the soul is ailing."

At times, our spirit or soul can get too caught up in their own projects and world on the Second Earth or in the gods' dimensions, and we feel abandoned by them or cold-shouldered. Even if we have never had any inner communications with our spirit or soul, we will still feel this rift between us, as if something has been torn from us, or like a part of us is missing, or we have been left out of the party.

All the non-loving things that family and friends can do to us, we can also experience from our very own spirit or soul. They can be inconsiderate, neglectful, spiteful, non-compassionate, secretive, teasing, manipulative, deceptive, non-sharing, bullying, lazy, or non-communicative. It will depend on how high up the Ribbon of Consciousness they are. If our soul has reached godhood, then we would hope they are acting out the traits of a god, but even then, there are situations where they may fall foul of their inner snakes. Our soul is evolving too, and we will need to forgive them, just as we wish to be forgiven by them for our own transgressions on Earth.

Just like with family and friends on Earth, the best way of resolving relationship issues with our spiritual family is by communicating honestly and fearlessly, and negotiating what we want out of the partnership. We need to feel like we are working together on the same team, heading towards the same target, complementing each other's talents.

However, we will each have our own set of responsibilities, and we need to ensure we are holding up our end of the deal. As a human on Earth, we will have our mission to carry out, and if we are not interested in doing this, our spirit or soul will more than likely make their displeasure felt, or cut us off until such time as we change our attitude. We will feel this severing acutely, and often we will seek partners or people around us to fill this gap, but it is really the love of our spirit/soul that we are truly desiring to feel.

Conversely, as we follow the path to our godhood, we can feel terribly cut off from our human family and friends when we find we must leave them behind when their vibrations begin to become very unmatched to our own. Part of our journey of stepping into the shoes of a god is to let go of the human world and many of the temptations it offers, and this can leave us feeling quite bereft, or even bitter, as we compare our seeming lack of fun or love or materiality with the non-gods around us who seem to be having a much better time than us.

It takes a serious commitment to our destiny and to divine will to enter into godhood, and many fall by the wayside. We will need to keep our ultimate goal in mind and keep out-picturing who we will be one day and how it will have been worth the difficult journey. As Master Time comments to Alice in the movie *Alice Through the Looking Glass*, "Everyone parts with everything, eventually."

If we are fairly aware of our connection with spirit and soul, we can often go through periods where we feel used and abused by them or the gods, and we might accuse them of treating us like their slaves. Humans, of course, are not slaves to any beings in the higher dimensions, but we have agreed to certain tasks, and these come with responsibilities. If we shirk these, then we let ourselves down, and our higher consciousness also suffers and is held back from evolving further.

We can also go through phases where our belief in the divine worlds is sorely tested and our faith shaken (often during a Neptune, Pisces, or 12th House transit). The intended outcome is to make our commitment to our path, and our trust in the unseen worlds, stronger and more resilient. Can we cling to our beliefs, stand by them, and not betray ourselves or the universe? If we lose our faith, who will we become instead?

It can be a wobbly time, when all that we had believed in seems to fly out of the window and a void remains in its place. We might even begin to deny the very existence of our soul, or higher dimensions and beings, since it may bolster a feeling of safety against situations or people we fear. The Apostle Peter did this very same thing when he denied knowing Jesus at the time of his arrest by soldiers. This can result in great feelings of guilt and shame later on.

During a crisis of faith, it will help us to remember all the interactions we have had with the divine worlds and beings, and the times we have been assisted by their energies and love and wisdom. Focusing on positive memories will pull us out of the Underworld of lower personas that seek to sabotage our evolution for one reason or another.

If we are going through a soul merge (see chapter 3), we will endure a few days, or maybe longer, of being in The Void while we assimilate the new energies. We may or may not realise we are going through a merger, or may forget it is always followed by this Void period which can leave us feeling lost and disconcerted for a while. We will generally simply float out of it naturally, unless we resist it with any vehemence. If we don't surrender to the merger then we might find ourselves falling down to a lower level of vibration, and dragging our spirit and soul with us until we come to our senses and fight our way back up again. Then we will need to work with our new soul, our new manager, and come to understand their new way of being and new methods of doing things.

One of the most confusing aspects of working with our soul or the gods is that they often play tricks on us. This is not done out of malevolence or maliciousness but with a view to help us understand some facet of our behaviour or the universe. It is not that they tell us lies or act dishonestly, but they can distort reality for us and tell us half-truths, or omit to tell us the whole truth and allow us to make wrong assumptions. This teaches us to be careful before making assertions of truth, and to be open and ask many questions and obtain many viewpoints.

One of the ways I personally have been duped by the gods is when they have told me I will be meeting one or other of them on Earth. The word 'meeting' can have several interpretations to the gods. It could have the traditional meaning in that we might meet them face to face walking around the planet somewhere. More usually it means the following: we can 'meet' them on the Internet, discovering one of their flesh and blood clones (gods on Earth in human form) on a website or Facebook; or we can 'meet' them by merging our energies with them (often they term this as 'marrying' them); or we can 'meet' them on our travels in the higher dimensional Second Earth in our spirit body. They might also tell us something like, "We will meet you at Christmas." We might want to ask them which year they are referring to, or we might be waiting a jolly long time!

It may seem like there are many pitfalls to be had in dealing with the spiritual realms, and it does pay to be aware of them. However, the beings of the higher dimensions, including our spirit and soul, are primarily there to help us and guide us, and they surround us with their love and energies and wisdom at all times. We never need to feel alone or unsupported on Earth if we remember to connect with all that is out there beyond our immediate chaotic and challenging world.

Being a healer of others

There is so much that could be written in this section, but it's not the prime focus of this book, so we will stay within the boundaries given to us by Chiron.

Many people reading this guidebook will be healers of one kind or another, assisting others to overcome their physical, emotional, mental, or spiritual problems. We may have had some success, or we may not. Chiron tells us it's not up to us as healers to affect a healing, meaning that we cannot be responsible for healing another person or for their destiny. Certainly, we may be able to help them in some way, but ultimately their fate is in their own hands, or rather in their own consciousness

At times we may feel we have failed to heal someone, but opening their eyes to the source of their problem is a healing in itself and is to be congratulated. If we help someone to take a different tack that is more aligned with their destiny, then this too is a healing successfully accomplished.

We need to be cognisant of any desire to save or rescue others from their illness or situation, because this is not what a healer's job is about. A person brings on an affliction or issue due to what they carry as thoughts and emotions in their consciousness. They will need to become aware of their programming in order to correct it or let it go. Sometimes a healer is able to help a person by clearing out this programming, but unless they clear out the roots of these defunct ideas and beliefs, it is likely the patient will merely recreate the same situation again when their old thinking and emotions re-emerge, like shoots springing from a cut-down tree trunk.

The gods once showed me a wonderful scene in consciousness that deftly illustrated one of the traps we can fall into as a healer.

A person had fallen into a swift-moving river and was being sucked under by a whirlpool. The Master told me that it was useless to dive into the swirling vortex in order to save this person for then I would be sucked under too. It was better to stand on the riverbank and offer an outstretched hand or stick and try to haul them out, rather than both of us getting drowned. If we dive into the emotional situations of others, then we may take on these energies ourselves and become upset, thereby lowering our own vibrations.

Another aspect of healing that Chiron warns us about is that we cannot heal others unless we ourselves are in a space of higher vibrations. It's not possible to heal anyone or anything from a vibration lower than that which we are trying to heal.

Healing can manifest in a multitude of ways, not always obvious. While I was walking my dog one day, I stopped to chat to a man who was trimming the grass edges on the road verge with a small, old machine. He had a Herculean task ahead of him, as he needed to work through the entire housing estate. He told me how his back was killing him, but he had to keep going as he had several children to feed. However, it was hard going with such a battered and under-powered machine and such a vast area to cover. I felt great compassion for him, and as I walked away I visualised a fireball of energy on his lower back, and asked the gods to help this man and heal him.

The next day, I bumped into him again, and he was now smiling broadly. He told me that just after I had left him the day before, his boss had pitched up in his truck and unloaded a brand-new edge trimmer for him to use. It was bigger, more powerful, and better designed, and much easier on his back too, thus easing his backache in a way I could never have imagined!

Chapter 22 – Healing techniques

If we want to recover from our issues and move on, we can learn any of the multiplicity of healing techniques in the marketplace at this present time which use the energies of the universe and consciousness to drive them. Chiron's book does not mention any by name, or endorse or judge any of them. He simply states several ways of healing that may be of benefit to us, and leaves it to us to experiment with the methods.

We should start with little forays in order to gain confidence and trust, and build up from there, developing our techniques and belief which will underpin greater adventures in healing in the future. Every human has the innate ability to physically heal themselves as evidenced by the way wounds can seal themselves, broken bones can mend, and we can recover from colds, heart attacks, operations, and even cancer.

Healing our emotional and mental states is also very possible but requires different techniques. We need to learn these, too, since our physical ailments are usually a manifestation of what is going on in our consciousness, in our thoughts and emotions.

For instance, issues with our lower legs are an indication that we could be fearful of moving forwards, and problems with our feet (or shoes) generally signify that we are struggling with spiritual challenges. Personally, I'm always made aware of any disconnection issues I'm having with my soul (sole) if the sole of my shoe comes apart. I don't know if shoes are just being made more shoddily these days, but this has happened to me quite a lot!

It pays to be aware that healing can be a two-edged sword. Just as a dentist, in order to replace a filling in our teeth, has to dig out the old substance before they can put in place the new stuff, with all its collateral pain and injections, so too do we usually have to remove all our old thinking and beliefs before new attitudes can be installed and healing take place. This letting go process can at times be very painful, just like a tooth extraction or filling. Many will be the time when we attempt to heal something and we pull back because it's simply too excruciating. Chiron speaks metaphorically of the times when badly-set broken bones have to be re-broken in order to heal properly. Do we always have the nerve to go through with this?

Below are a variety of techniques that can assist in the healing of many types of issues, physical, emotional, mental, and spiritual. All require that we use our consciousness as a tool, as a kind of magic wand, remembering that our thinking becomes manifest in the physical world and is therefore potentially able to heal anything and anyone.

There are also several brief and free meditations on my website that you may wish to try.

www.earthwithspirit.com/meditations/

a) Raising your vibrations

All methods of healing require that we get ourselves first into a state of high, or relatively higher, vibrations. See chapter 11 on vibrational levels for suggestions on how to do this, such as dialling up to a higher 'station' on our consciousness radio, and letting go segments of our consciousness. It may help to also re-read the section on raising vibrational levels in chapter 18.

Albert Einstein once said, "We cannot solve our problems with the same thinking we used when we created them." Therefore, when we raise ourselves to a higher vibrational level, we will be able to see the problem from a different, bigger, and more spiritual perspective.

We can use visualisation techniques to imagine ourselves physically going higher, such as up the steps of a tower or climbing a mountain, and focusing on lovely things that raise our spirit, like laughing children, music or flowers, a beautiful sunset, or the words of a poem.

We could imagine ourselves to be a volcano of love, and as we raise our vibrations, so pure love rises up to the open crater of our heart and erupts out into the world, spreading the ash of love far and wide.

Within five minutes we could have raised ourselves to new levels and hoisted ourselves out of our dark pit of pain. If we become familiar with the many ways we can raise our vibrations and fly higher as our spirit self, we can utilise these in the moment and never again need to stay stuck in lower emotions or physical pain, or feel powerless to help ourselves.

b) Focus on desired outcome

When we attempt to heal someone, or repair something, or put a situation right, we are trying to manifest a desired outcome. Therefore, we need to firstly travel within our consciousness to the Dark World where we begin the manifestation process by conceiving what we eventually wish to birth i.e. a situation which is healed, whole, balanced, and harmonious.

In the Dark World, we can conjure up images and dialogues until we decide upon the ones that work best for us. Playing 'Let's Pretend' works really well here, going through various scenarios until we finally come up with one that will deliver the right outcome. What we believe and conceive is what will come about, so we need to visualise ourselves or our situation as we desire it to be once the healing takes effect. Consciousness will then manifest, in the Light World of Creation (our physical dimension), whatever thoughts and emotions are taking precedence in our mind.

If we continually hold the problem itself in our thoughts, going over and over all the negative facets of our illness, issue, or dilemma, and focusing on 'what is' rather than 'what's to be', then consciousness is forced to out-picture this for us in our reality. It is not doing this out of spite or judgement; we are simply creating the world around us out of our own thinking. If we don't visualise what we desire, then the universe merely takes the existing material in our consciousness, or from the consciousnesses of others, and creates our physicality out of that.

We can also compromise our desired outcome through not believing that it is possible to be healed or manifested. So, we need to be very thorough about scanning what is going on in our consciousness at all times, or else we will find we are negating our efforts, and the desired healing or repair will not take place, or only with diluted results.

Every morning when we wake, we can focus on how we wish our day to unfold, visualising positive outcomes, using the tools of our consciousness to create and heal our reality. To refresh on manifestation techniques, re-read chapter 17.

(As I'm writing this section, bush fires are raging in the region, and I feel dismay that social and news media are so focused on fanning the flames of panic and doom, and the fact that people are losing their homes, possessions, pets, and livelihoods. How many of us are visualising the wind dying down, the fires petering out, and homes and lives being miraculously saved? (And it's a total coincidence that the next section is entitled 'Being a fireball'))

c) Being a fireball, the Sun

There are many times when we might want to bolster our life force energy, also known by names such as chi, qi, prana, gaia, or orgone. Chiron calls this method of healing 'the fireball effect' and tells us it is a remarkable healing tool used by the gods which can increase our vital energy manyfold. Of the four elements of fire, water, earth, and air, it is fire that is at our core and provides our life force. He showed me the diagram below to illustrate this.

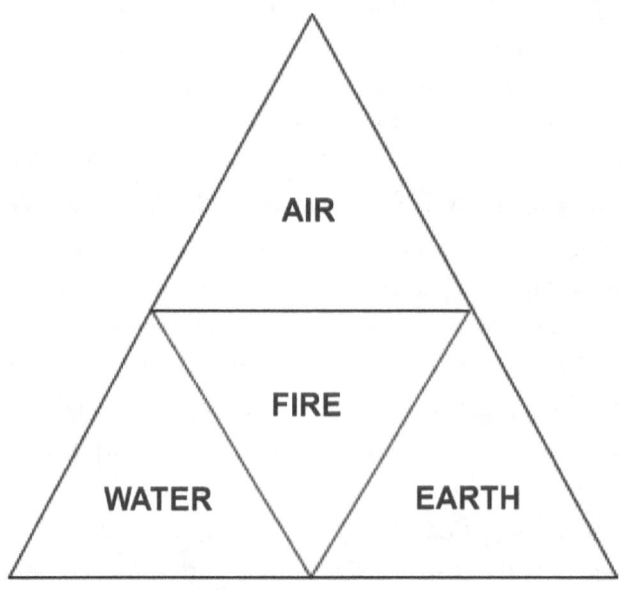

To get the 'fireball effect' outcome, we need to picture ourself as a bright shining star or sun. Our sun is not just light but has incredible energies, managed by a consciousness that rules our entire solar system and every being within it. It does more than hold objects in orbit and radiate magnetic waves which affect the planets within its cosmic reach.

When we connect to our star, we download some of its consciousness into ourself and some of its powerful energies too. It stimulates us and our life blood, and can burn away much of any darkness or illness we may be feeling. That's one of the reasons why most of us feel so good on a sunny day. The sun is at the core of our consciousness family, and we should try to visit it often as it will always bring us increased harmony.

The fireball effect technique

You will need to ramp up the energies in your heart until you feel like a ball of fire—which is what a star truly is. Start small with a fire spark in your heart. It may be useful to be gazing at a flame when you do this. Then, using your imagination, gradually increase the area of the spark to cover your whole heart, and then increase again to fill your whole body with this intense fire. Focus on the fire exuding into every part of you, not only in the area that requires healing, for true healing means wholeness and balance permeating throughout the entire organism, for you may not understand what is linked to what else within your body.

Once you feel yourself sparking with fire physically, allow it to fan out in waves from your body, into your emotional, mental, and spiritual auras, and out into the greater consciousness that surrounds you. If you are feeling particularly strong or euphoric, you can imagine the waves of fire rippling out and covering the entire world and even out into the cosmos and helping souls in other dimensions. When you have filled up on the brilliance of the sun, sit for a while and listen to its wisdom.

◆

The 'fireball effect' is not just a healing tool for the physical body and illnesses but can be utilised for any kind of problem, including mental stress, relationship issues, depression, addictions, low motivation, non-forgiveness, suicidal tendencies, confusion, disconnection, financial worries, career disappointments, environmental disasters, or government challenges; anywhere that balance and harmony needs to be restored. It is a wonderful way to raise our vibrations to a very high level, and since all creativity requires a spark of fire as its source of inspiration, this is a useful technique for stimulating us with new insights and bright ideas.

One thing to bear in mind is that the sun's rays highlight things, and these things may be pathways towards our destiny, or talents that need to be nurtured, or insights into a confused situation. On the other hand, sunlight can also shine into dark and shady corners that we might have preferred to remain hidden.

Sometimes we hide in the shadows and prevent our starlight from shining forth into the world, so in meditation we could purposefully step forward out of the corners and back alleys of our consciousness and more into the radiance of whom we have come here to be.

At sunrise and sunset, I always try to do something I call "Thanking and Tanking" It's a kind of salute to the sun, but also downloads the sun's energies into myself and into others I direct them to.

Firstly, I thank the sun for being there every single day for us, and for all its wonderful traits of sunniness, brilliance, radiance, beauty, love, power, wisdom, creativity, courage, steadfastness, fieriness, life-giving energy, motivation, and fun. Then I ask the sun to download into me all these traits and to help me to become a star myself one day. Finally, I ask the sun to download these traits into everyone in Heaven and on Earth and to help them become stars one day too, and to help me to help them on their journey to become stars.

We can also just meditate on the sun or an image of the sun, or the flame of a candle or in a fireplace. It will be like recharging our battery and gives us renewed energy. We can also journey as our spirit self into the sun itself, taking a sun bath to slough off the old parts of our own consciousness or blending with that of the sun. The sun bleaches the old us, and we feel reinvigorated to step onto the Earth again. It's not Hell in the fires of the sun, but a heavenly place where rebirth happens. Any time we install the light of the sun in our mind, we will brighten up our thinking no end, and at the same time lighten our heart.

If we feel so inclined, we can also use similar techniques and work with our Source/creator god instead of the sun. This will be even more powerful, for a creator god is at a higher level than a star, and our Source is the most potent part of our consciousness. We would be bringing the energies of a creator god into us, and although this may sound magical and wonderful, if we are not used to such high vibrational levels, we could find ourselves suffering from any darkness and impurity that gets revealed in the process.

Certainly, when we are connected with the higher levels of our consciousness, be it with our soul, our star, or our Source, and we let their power flow through us and radiate from us, then miracles can occur. It is not so effective to try to heal ourselves or others from the bottom end of our Ribbon of Consciousness, and this is the reason why healing sessions may not be successful. However, the bottom end of our Ribbon is where most of our healing does need to be directed, where we might have thousands upon thousands of out-of-sorts lower personas that require our attention and time.

d) Dealing with lower personas and ghosts of our past

When our lower personas act up and spill out of us as emotional or mental upsets, we need to speak with them as if they were our human children on Earth—with immense love, respect, wisdom and compassion. It's no good tearing into them and trying to get rid of them or kill them off. They will simply reconstitute in another way, one that might be more rebellious than before.

Our consciousness, as a whole, can never die. However, parts of our consciousness can be dissolved and sent back into the Great Consciousness, like pouring water back into the ocean. Indeed, we need to keep doing this to recreate ourselves and evolve, or else we would be pulled down continually with the most primitive thinking and reactions we've ever possessed in any of our lifetimes. Dealing with our lower personas is a common, almost daily, occurrence and nothing to be ashamed about. Even gods need to regularly clear out their lower personas and distorted segments of thinking and memories.

Lower personas technique

In meditation, ask for the lower personas related to your problem, to show themselves to you. There may be just one, or a handful, or hundreds, or they may swarm in a horde to the horizon, depending on the issue. Don't be fearful. You are their parent, and they are actually looking to you for direction. They don't know how to act or think in any way but the way they have been programmed, and often their programming has been set up to protect you. You will need to listen to their points of view and assuage their concerns and negotiate with them.

The worst thing to do is act like a bad parent and ignore, humiliate, or mistreat them, or dismiss their issues. Don't be angry with them or punish them as they are simply acting as programmed by you previously and they have served you loyally. You are asking them to utilise new skills and perspectives, and they simply can't cope with this.

As a good parent, you will want to do your very best for them and work with them until harmony and agreement has been achieved. Investigate the cause of their resistance, using love, patience and diplomacy, and understand their standpoint and help them to change it.

So, thank them for their protection and loyalty to their tasks, and tell them how you appreciate all they have done for you in the past, but now it is time to change the rules, and therefore their programming.

Specify in detail how you desire your future to unfold regarding the issue, and then ask if any of them have a problem with this? If so, then you will need to firmly but lovingly state how you will need them to change. This constitutes the new and more suitable programming that will replace the old way of being.

If any of them are still resistant or sabotaging your plans, then more stringent methods will be needed because you cannot allow your inner personas to keep causing trouble and pain for you. Offer them the opportunity of going Home to join the Greater Consciousness. Many of them will be eager to do this, to be set free, since they won't like confrontation or being in pain. They will be merging back into the ocean of great wisdom and love—being dissolved, not murdered.

You will then need to take each one individually, or a group of them, into your heart and, with the greatest of parental love, melt them into your heart while thanking them for their service. Sometimes this process makes me cry, but it is soon replaced by a wonderful feeling of buoyancy and light-heartedness, as the burden of resistance and conflict is lifted from my heart.

If any lower personas are still distressed or defiant, then you will need to work with them over a longer period of time, explaining patiently what path you would now like to take, and listening attentively to their gripes and grievances, and giving them solutions or choices. Of course, not all of us are well-versed in parental psychology, and so sometimes we will make mistakes and will need to come back time and again to resolve some issue.

It can take much effort if our lower personas don't see the benefits of going Home, and it has to be said that there are times when they, and our stuck thinking, cannot be budged for love nor money. When this happens, I have found that the only recourse is to perceive my personas rather as segments of stuck thinking, or merely avatars, so that they become impersonal, and then to purposefully dissolve them with the greatest of love. I do this either by:

1. Flying as my spirit self into the sun and taking out these segments and melting them there.
2. Diving as my spirit self into the deepest ocean and taking out these segments and dissolving them there.
3. Flying as my spirit self to a Black Hole and casting these segments into it.

There would be many other ways of doing this, limited only by your imagination. See further on in this chapter for more letting go techniques.

Ghosts of our past

Chiron suggests some of our lower personas are like ghosts haunting a crypt, the lower echelons of our consciousness. He advises we go down deep into its dark niches and view all the skeletons of ourselves laid out there. They may be merely ancient bones, but what they represent could still be affecting us today, and their old fears and beliefs could be preventing us from making progress along our path or experiencing a happier life. We need to set ourselves free of the past, not keep dwelling on it, and look to new vistas in the future.

Meantime, we all have these skeletons to deal with, and we cannot ignore them. They are just another type of lower persona, and the above methods can be employed for dealing with the ghosts of our past too. It's no good wanting to shatter their bones and be done with them. We need to be a good counsellor and listen to their fears, understand their angst, speak with them, reassure them, give them new perspectives, and show them a way to go Home.

Walking around our crypt we could tend to each skeleton in turn, laying each ghost to rest with love, kindness and respect. They are still a part of us, and, once upon a time, we were them. A crypt is usually associated with a church, symbolic of the temple of our consciousness, and when the crypt has been cleared, we could climb the stairs to the bell tower and scale the spire and sit there and look down on our world.

Having cleared the crypt, we could now clear away the entire church, and eventually the whole of our lower world. We have no need of it as we make our way towards the higher dimensions. When our skeletons are finally at rest, we will feel calm, and the anchors of our past fall away and we can carry on with our journey unimpeded. Some parts of that past consciousness will still remain with us, the traits and talents that will contribute to our current destiny.

It may take several trips to our crypt to deal with all our ghosts there. Like an archaeological dig, we could keep uncovering past life skeletons in layer after layer as we go deeper into our consciousness. We will uncover only those skeletons that we are able to cope with at the time. They will arise out of the depths of our crypt in due course when the time is right.

♦

During the period that I was writing this chapter, I experienced two different examples of dealing with my lower personas. In the first, in meditation I had invited a large group of my lower personas over the bridge for an outing to visit the gods' dimension. It was a maintenance mission to ensure that all parts of my Ribbon of Consciousness were over the bridge in the higher dimensions. I didn't want any stragglers holding back my evolution and future plans.

It felt like a school trip with me as the teacher in charge of about ten children. I led my troop into the gods' dimension and showed them around and told them to feel the beautiful energies there—fresh and clear and sparkling, like the best kind of days on Earth. We wandered around for a while and they explored their surroundings and soaked up the invigorating atmosphere.

Then one of my personas went up a ladder in a barn, and in the hayloft they found a bevy of Masters sitting on bales of hay. The Masters pointed to an opened cloth on the floor which contained a bunch of short sticks which I suddenly realised were magic wands.

My personas each took a wand and began to play with it, manifesting such delights as birthday cake and eternal ice cream. However, one of them wanted to go and visit a star. Then, as often happens, all of my children wanted to go and visit a star too, and off they went, zooming up to a star while I watched on from below.

Some time passed and I was still watching and waiting for them to return—but they never did! They had all dissolved in the star, leaving me a little sad and with a vague feeling of empty nest syndrome. For hours afterwards, the area of my three lower chakras felt decidedly vacant.

The second example of dealing with my lower personas was quite different from this. Early in the morning, Master Chiron had informed me of something to do with my future, which I wasn't very enamoured with. The astrology of transiting Mars trine my natal Pluto, and transiting Pluto opposite my natal Uranus, spelt big trouble for the day ahead.

Sure enough, my lower personas were exhibiting anger, resistance, and resentment, rebelling against the extra pressure being put upon them to perform additional tasks, and feeling they weren't being rewarded enough or being given sufficient support or resources. I tried to reason with them and change their attitude, but they merely wanted to go Home. So, I took them up to the Sun and melted them there with love and gratitude.

If I'd thought that would be the end of it, I was wrong. Now, I was feeling even greater antipathy towards my spirit and the gods. I realised that the fifteen or so personas of my crew that I had just dissolved in the Sun were merely the deckhands on board my ship. To my chagrin, I discovered a whole underbelly of mutineers below decks, about fifty of them! They were a nasty and vicious bunch, and they were gunning for real trouble. Rounding them all up, with love and compassion I took them down into Davy Jones' Locker[21], into the deep dark waters of the ocean, and there they imploded under the heavy pressure.

When I returned to my ship, it was like the infamous *Marie Celeste*, a ghost ship with no one on board. Now I had no crew, no one to help me do my work on Earth! I asked my spirit self how I could get some new crew, some more cooperative and willing crew? She told me to invent them, to create them. Just as we can dis-create our troublesome lower personas as segments of our consciousness, so can we also create new supportive lower personas through adding segments filled with positive and motivating thoughts.

e) Healing suicidal tendencies

A more extreme version of healing lower personas happens when we are faced with a desire to commit suicide. This dire cry for help occurs when one or more of our lower personas is desperate to go Home and return to the Greater Consciousness. Hence, we experience the feeling of wanting to die.

However, it is not the physical body that needs to be killed off. It is the segments of our consciousness and our thinking that need to be addressed, and once we do this, all suicidal feelings dissipate.

Again, we need to have a dialogue with our lower personas and try to redress their issues, but if they are adamant they want to go Home, then we can facilitate this by using the process described above. It needs to be emphasised that only segments of our thinking, our avatars, are 'killed off' by our loving and forgiving actions in consciousness, and our physical body remains untouched and unharmed.

---

21. Davy Jones' Locker: a term used by mariners to refer to the seabed, and death by drowning or shipwreck.

Afterwards, we may enter the Void for a period of time, while we assimilate the change of energies and the necessity for such drastic action.

f) Jewels of consciousness, rainbows, and light

Chiron tells us in his book that there are four special, coloured jewels within our consciousness which are exquisite aspects of ourselves that we can visualise as tools of light to help with our healing. If we visualise any of these, and tune into their vibrational energies, we will benefit from their enhancements to our consciousness.

- **Blue Jewel (e.g. a sapphire)**—a balancing stone. Brings calmness and serenity.
- **Red Jewel (e.g. a ruby)**—enlivens, activates, motivates, excites. Feel its fiery energies.
- **Green Jewel (e.g. an emerald)**—cleanliness, freshness, purification, health, vitality, healing, harmony.
- **Yellow Jewel (e.g. a topaz)**—goodness, goldenness, sun energies, star qualities, full potential, love.

The more we practise with these jewels, the faster we will be able to pull them up from our consciousness and the quicker they will work.

Our Third Eye is also another jewel of our consciousness, providing us with psychic abilities and intuition and a way to connect with our soul, the gods, and the higher dimensions. This was described in detail in chapter 16.

The colours of the jewels above are some of the colours of the spectrum of light, and each colour and hue vibrates at a different frequency and has a different function for our consciousness. The colours of everything in our world affect us daily, and each of us would have a favourite colour that we find uplifting, and colours that send our mood plummeting.

White light is the sum total of the entire spectrum of colours together, and is therefore the most powerful colour energetically and vibrationally. Personally, I love to visualise my heart as a pure white diamond, and this brings all the qualities of the coloured jewels above.

Rainbows are also beautiful displays of colour in our world, and most of us feel joy at seeing one. They tend to give us hope, and this may be because rainbows are caused by the white light of the sun's rays being refracted into many colours by the rain, and light itself lifts us from despair and helps us to dream of new possibilities. At our most fundamental level, humans are created from light. We resonate with light, and it stirs our soul.

Therefore, we can utilise the image of a rainbow to uplift ourselves and raise our vibrations. If we can't find a real one, then a photo or picture of one will do fine. Drawing or painting one would be very effective too.

It takes both the sun and rain together to create a rainbow, and there seems to be magic in those sunbeams streaming through the dark skies. They can drive away the rain in our heart, and can lead us to new horizons. So, if we are enduring a rainstorm or a deluge in our emotions, picturing the sun and a rainbow within our heart can truly be life-giving and help us to find some direction.

g) Changing your thinking, cleansing and letting go

In the immediate aftermath of an emotionally charged and upsetting situation or stressful mental challenge, the best thing to do is to consciously let all our emotions drain through us and out of us, as if we were flushing water through our bodies and out of our feet. Imagining this happening whilst having a shower or a swim is also a good way to go about it. Then practise calming techniques such as mindfulness, or meditate listening to soft, harmonious music, or take a walk in nature, or browse through photos of things that have previously delighted us.

These types of actions will raise our vibrations again. Re-read chapter 11 for more methods on raising vibrations. Our consciousness is responsible for all our faults and dramas, but it is also the medium through which we can raise ourselves up again.

One calming meditation is to visualise sitting under a waterfall in a forest setting and letting the water cleanse the body, mind, and emotions, letting go of all anxiety and stress and resistance. Surrender to your soul and divine will. Then dive into the tranquil pool and play with the river dolphins or forest creatures until your heart is restored again.

Consciousness is like our home. We dwell within it 24/7. We also carry it around with us, like a tortoise carries its shell on its back. It pays us to make it lighter, therefore, and not such a burden. We need to face our troublesome thoughts and emotions and do everything in our power to heal them, just as we would take swift and strong action if we discovered a tumour.

We can do this through housekeeping, cleaning out the rooms of our mind every day, putting all the muck into the waste bins and recycling depots of the universe. We all know just how messy and dirty a home can get very quickly and thoughtlessly, and it's just like that with our consciousness too, as we traipse the detritus of polluted thoughts and emotions through it on a regular basis. We have to be quick to recognise when a toxic element surfaces; catch it, and deal with it, not allowing it to nestle back into our consciousness again, otherwise what will we be attracting to ourselves?

How do we know when it's time for a clean-up? Any time we have a feeling of disquiet within us. Something is out of harmony and therefore needs to be dealt with, and the sooner the better.

It's amazing how often, too, we slip into dwelling negatively on the past or the future, so we need to focus on the present moment and make that a good one, and then all those moments will get strung together to provide us with a good life.

We also get too caught up in stressing over the unimportant things in life. I had an example of this as I was writing this chapter. I asked my spirit self if she could help me find a bottle of essential oil that I had lost. It had been my favourite, jasmine, and was quite expensive.

She told me, "Ask God."

I gasped in surprise, "What? The One God? I'm not going to do that!"

"Why not?" she enquired calmly.

"The One God has more important things to do than worry about my bottle of essential oil," I told her.

"Exactly! And so do you!"

Point taken.

So, we can imagine washing, dusting, polishing in the rooms or segments of our consciousness and turfing out all the trash there. When I am cleaning my own home, I often dedicate my actions as symbolic of cleaning out my consciousness. This makes things like cleaning mirrors and windows so much more fun, and certainly produces increased clarity in my life.

If we still have sharks in our ocean of emotions, or snakes in our fields of consciousness, we will not be welcome in the divine domains, for the energies there are clear and unpolluted. We need to turn up at Heaven's door with a clear and vivacious heart. There is an energetic barrier around the earthly dimension that does not permit human consciousness to contaminate higher dimensions. Only when we are pure and untainted are we invited to fly through the unseen worlds.

So, we can go shark baiting, or snake hunting, or go through every doorway in our consciousness until we have a clear slate and there are no more triggers or blockages (for the moment). Our situation has been centuries, even millennia, in the making, and it cannot be undone overnight and is a continual process of letting go sharks and snakes for the duration of our lifetime.

We generally react to situations based on the default programming in our consciousness. However, we can consciously choose how to react to situations in the moment and override our programming. Then at a later time when we feel more settled and have a clearer mind and heart, we can deal with changing our programming, our thought patterns, on a permanent basis.

When we accept a need to change our thought patterns, it's usually because we already recognise that our thinking isn't working out for us and it's keeping us stuck in a situation or making us react in ways that we don't like about ourselves. If we change our thinking, we change our world and our future.

Sometimes it's easier to start with detailing how we *don't* want to feel any longer, and then work our way towards understanding how we would like to feel instead. Once we are ready to work on the positive aspects, we can start detailing a vision of who we would like to be and what we would like to be doing, conceived in the Dark World of our imagination until we are happy with the blueprint for our future self. This vision needs to be held at the forefront of our consciousness without waver.

We can now compare all our thinking against this goal, and if our thoughts don't support our vision then they need to be let go, and thoughts that are supportive and encouraging put in their place. We need to challenge every idea, belief, or fear that springs into our mind and be discerning about what is allowed to stay and what must be snipped out of our Ribbon of Consciousness.

There is an old saying: "Your mind is like the branches of a tree. Birds will fly in and out all the time, but you don't have to encourage them to nest there."

Often, we are not cognisant of what is trawling through our minds because we are on autopilot and we act and react from our default programming. It will take quite a while to become conversant with this default programming, but we will find that it pops up time and time again, with variations on the basic themes as well.

The easiest way to let go of an old thought, belief, or emotion is to imagine that each is carried like a piece of writing or image within a segment of our consciousness—like the segments of an orange, or like ink cartridges in a computer printer. We can click out the old segment or cartridge, and pop in a new one containing our new thinking or belief. It helps to have these new principles written down so we can keep referring to them, until such time as they are embedded and become habitual.

The best way to ethically get rid of our old baggage is to do one of the following as our spirit self, asking for the Greater Consciousness to take back these segments of consciousness with love and recycle them, but there are many imaginative methods you could try, either in the physical world or in meditation:

1. Fly to the sun or a volcano, or build a bonfire in your mind, and throw these segments into the furnace and melt them there.
2. Dive into deep waters and dissolve these segments there.

3. Sit in a bath filled with water and pull the plug, allowing all segments and dirty emotions to drain away.
4. Fly to the edge of a Black Hole and throw these segments into it.
5. Bury the segments in the ground and ask Mother Earth to disintegrate them.
6. Place the segments into a rocket and shoot them into deepest space.
7. Tie the segments onto the tail of a kite or helium balloon and let them drift into the atmosphere.
8. Place the segments in a boat and cast it off into deep waters.
9. Tear up segments and scatter them on the wind.
10. Wash segments under a waterfall or in a pool.
11. Pour the contents of segments into a chemical to dissolve them.
12. Allow a monster to eat up segments.
13. Hang segments on a line to be blown away in a hurricane.
14. Take segments to the beach to be taken away by the tide.
15. Conjure segments away in a magic trick.

As you can appreciate, the methods are endless, and it's fun to discover new ways of letting go.

The Vortex Process

Here's one more letting go meditation that I personally have found to be very effective—the Vortex Process.

- Begin to create a whirlwind in your consciousness that becomes a vortex (twister or tornado), and have it turning in a clockwise direction. It is totally under your control.
- Ask the vortex to do a sweep through your consciousness and all its segments, lifting out and scouring away all the aspects that you wish to be rid of.
- Then, using the point of your vortex, pierce a hole in the base of your consciousness and drain all the contents of the vortex into a big Black Hole where all will be recycled back into light.

After a while of practising this, it becomes a natural habit to whisk away any negative thought or emotion by creating a mini vortex.

The Ice Sculpture Process

I will share one of my own experiences of letting go. I had slipped into the Dark World in order to let go of my stress and anxiety, for this is a gentle place of calm and serenity.

I asked my Beloved Source, "What is the best way to let go in here? Is there a Black Hole or something that I can let go into?"

"Just dissipate," she told me.

"What, like I do in the sun?" I often went up to the sun to dissolve parts of my consciousness there.

"Yes."

I was curious. "What is the difference between letting go in the sun and letting go in the Dark World?"

Source replied, "In the sun, it's more of a physical thing, more to do with letting go of the ego and surrendering the human will to divine will. In the Dark World, it's a general letting go of fears and thinking."

She then manifested an ice sculpture in front of me. "Visualise your fear like water that has become concretised into ice, into some kind of ice sculpture that is meaningful to you. So, to let it go, you just let it dissolve, and it will melt back into the Great Ocean of Consciousness."

◆

This maintenance of our mind is something that will need to be done constantly at first, until we begin to get some decent new programming installed and running smoothly in the background. If this seems like a lot of work, just imagine letting our TV, mobile phone, fridge, or car operate with faulty software—we would soon get it sorted out!

And the great thing about sorting out our consciousness is that we can do it by ourselves, and it costs no money, only our time and focus. An added bonus is that once we are rid of those menacing segments, we are no longer weighed down by them and all the consternation they bring into our lives, and we can feel so much lighter in mind and body.

If all this cleansing and letting go work takes us into The Void of the Dark World (which it often does if we do a major clean up job on ourselves), then we must be careful to fill this void with positive replacement thoughts and emotions. The universe abhors a vacuum, and so if we don't fill this vacuum with good, supportive thinking, then all the old stuff we have just let go will come seeping back in and undo all our wonderful purification efforts.

We need to take charge of our mind, and be aware of all that goes into it and comes out of it, and all that goes on around it, scanning for 'consciousness viruses' and ill-functioning programming on a daily basis. If we ignore this work, we will remain in the lower world where life will never quite work out how we want it. As our consciousness falls into disrepair and eventually chaos, our external world will reflect what is going on in our mind.

h) Revealing our diamond Source

In Chapter 18 we saw how we are pure love at the core or Source of ourselves, and how this could be represented as a faceted diamond of consciousness. Over the millennia of our past lives, we have thrown shrouds or cloaks of darkness and mud over our diamond Source from all the tainted and un-love-ly thoughts we have carried in our consciousness. It is only the junk we have added into our consciousness that holds us back and prevents clarity and a realisation of who we really are.

We need to begin to see ourselves as this flawless diamond, pure from fears or dark memories. Love is there at the core of our consciousness. It just needs to be exposed by us and not covered over. We need to be a miner for love; it's a treasure that's not missing in anyone, and nothing is as valuable as love.

One technique for removing all these layers of toxicity, hatred, and general not-love is to visualise a table lamp with a light bulb shining inside it (representing your diamond Source), covered over with dark cloths and blankets. Remove each heavy layer from the lamp, imagining that it contains all the poisonous muck from one of your past lives or this lifetime, until it can shine freely once again. Throw the dark layers into a Black Hole or similar ethical disposal point, to be recycled. If we can remove just one layer every day, we will soon be feeling the benefits.

You could also imagine flooding your consciousness with pure water or energy from the higher dimensions, to scour and wipe clean all the silt that has accumulated there, and which covers over your bright, sparkling diamond Source of love.

i) Positive perspectives

Once we decide we no longer want to sit in a pool of self-pity or pain or grief, we can use our consciousness tools to turn our thinking and emotions around and begin to put a more positive spin on things. Personally, I think Dr. Jordan B. Peterson's piece of advice is one of the best, "Don't think thoughts that make you feel weak."

We need to believe it is possible for things to change and become better, and this in itself will open the door for the universe to step in and support and assist us. We can use some of the healing techniques already described, such as raising our vibrations and focusing on our desired outcome. It's important to find a base within a higher level of our consciousness and to see ourselves coping with, and eventually overcoming, our travails.

It is our consciousness that controls making each moment one of joy or one of sorrow. We can picture ourselves as more courageous and resilient, perhaps reading autobiographies of people we admire with these traits, and we can train ourselves to gradually scale up our level of fortitude so that we are able to cope with bigger issues as they come along.

Gratitude and acceptance are mainstays of a positive attitude. The antidote to self-pity is to be grateful. It may help to write in a journal all the things we are grateful for, and to read this every day to remind ourselves. If we can find ways to be stoic, happy, and appreciative, no matter what the circumstances, we will thrive, or at least won't fall into a pit of despair.

In the past few days, I have been watching on the TV, victims of devastating bush fires recounting their tragedies. All had lost everything, but while some wept and were angry and bitter, others were just thankful they were still alive, and some were already speaking about how they were going to rebuild their lives. The old adage bears repeating; 'When life gives you lemons, make lemonade.'

When things like this happen; fires, tornadoes, floods, redundancy, failure, a medical emergency, a court case, and such like, it gives us a chance to make things different from before, to improve our lives in some way. The universe is helping us by giving us a clean slate to work from, or an almighty shake-up. We need to be alert to all the new opportunities around us, and open our arms to new ideas and innovation.

It might give us the chance to meet new people and form new friendships and alliances. We can find strength and new skills and concepts when we work with other consciousnesses. Being a hero is a great way to find confidence and self-esteem, but can we be a hero to ourself and do whatever is necessary, even in mundane but depressing circumstances, to lift ourselves out of the doldrums?

There are thousands of examples of negativity that beset us daily, and which we need to turn around into positivity. Fear of failure is a common one, where we don't take up an opportunity because we are scared it might not work out happily. But there is just as much chance of success as there is of failure, even more so if we fill our consciousness with supporting thoughts and visualisations of a successful outcome.

Challenges can definitely thwart us, but they offer us new experiences and richness and ways to strengthen weaker areas of our consciousness, so we shouldn't be shaking our fist at the gods but thanking them for the opportunities. When we don't resist but accept each event of every day, then we will be in the flow of universal energy, and life itself will unfold more easily and positively, and we ourselves will feel happier, more balanced, and more fulfilled.

The universe is a place filled with love and many delights. We can partake of the pleasures on offer if we make the choice to do so. Laughing, singing, dancing, playing; we make the dimensions resonate with our joy, and this will be reflected back to us in some way, too, and is definitely a wonderful way to heal ourselves.

j) Physical healing

Because most of our physical ailments are the result of our emotional and mental issues and the thinking we are carrying in our consciousness, even broken bones from accidents, we can do any of the healing techniques described in this section and we will see a benefit within our body.

We can also speak to our body parts, organs, cells, DNA, blood, hormones, pain, and immune system directly (because they all have individual consciousness) and ask them what is wrong, or for guidance in how to heal them. We will receive the answer in our consciousness, or through signs or messages in the outer world, or through situations arising for us from which we can learn and heal. We can also turn our genes on or off through our conscious intention, and generally these will be affected as we do any healing on our emotional and mental states.

If we are suffering from invading pathogens such as bacteria, viruses, parasites, or worms, we can also speak to the consciousness of these and negotiate for them to leave our body. In the case of bacteria, we can ask the good bacteria within us to counteract the bad bacteria.

Being unable to sleep is a common physical problem, and I often experienced this difficulty too. Chiron gave me some advice and also showed me a healing process I could go through each night when I went to bed.

Firstly, he told me that I needed to separate my consciousness totally from my physical body. I was being too 'Mumsy' as my spirit self, and not wanting to leave my human body alone for too long while I slept. I didn't trust my human consciousness to look after my body while I was away exploring the universe in my spirit body, and I kept coming back every hour or so to check on it. So, I had a word with my inner personas, and they told me I could trust them to hold the roost while I was sleeping.

Then Chiron led me through a door which I closed behind me but didn't lock. On the wall ahead was a big red mains electricity box. I switched it to 'OFF', and then shutters rolled down over the windows and I felt my eyes go very heavy, like in hypnosis. It took a while for my human consciousness to shut off. I was conscious of still giving instructions while I shut down, specifically telling my inner personas I would be back at 7am. Then I did fall asleep until exactly seven o'clock, as I had specified, and when I woke I could vividly remember everything I had been doing in the higher dimensions in my spirit body.

If we have no idea what is causing our ill health, we can just speak with our body as a whole and ask it to come back into good health and balance. It knows what to do, and if it needs our help in some way, it will find a way to let us know.

k) Projections, filters, and fears

When we look at a person or a situation, we are rarely seeing them or it as they truly exist. We peer through filters in our mind and this affects what we see. It's a bit like wearing coloured sunglasses to view the world, and different ones on various occasions. These filters have been formed by our experiences and memories in this lifetime and also from past lives, and they form part of our programming. Sometimes, our soul or the gods have created filters for us so that we see only what we are allowed to see.

Our filters are not a problem, per se, unless they cause us to create emotional or mental issues for ourselves or others. Filters often cause us to tar everyone with the same brush, and therefore we don't value a person for the individual they are but as a member of a group which we treat using our filter of generalisation. Similarly, we might deem various situations, events, or items, to all fall into the same category, and not be discerning in each case.

For instance, just because we don't like one kind of vegetable, we might have created a filter concerning vegetables, and thereafter declared that we don't like any vegetable at all, even if we have never tasted them. We can remove our detrimental filters using several of the techniques outlined above.

Projections occur when we create a kind of movie in our consciousness, and overlay it onto a person or a situation. Think of how a projector sits at the back of a cinema or hall, and projects what is on the film onto a screen. Our consciousness firstly creates the images and then acts like a projector and shines this film onto the screen which is the face of a person before us. We may see the person, not as they truly are, but acting out a role in the movie we have created in our head about them. (Teenagers often do this with pop stars.)

Because consciousnesses are linked, the projection from us forces the other person to play out the part allotted by us. Usually, we are not aware of the fact we are forcing others to play a role for us, but it happens when we have certain expectations of those others, or we are judging them in some way.

The role we have chosen for them to play may be as hero or devil. We can see them through the lens of rose-coloured glasses or a distorted, cracked mirror. The movie may possibly be past life memories of knowing that person before, and now we are still viewing them as they were back then, and not as who they are now. This happens in many relationships until we can recognise what is happening and apply some of the techniques given above for letting go. We need to examine how we are viewing people, and let go all our own judgement and desires that we are projecting onto them so that the true nature of that person can emerge.

And, of course, others may be projecting onto us as well, and forcing us to act in ways that cramp our true style. We might wonder why we always act in a certain uncharacteristic way around a certain person, and this could be a clue that projections are going on.

The same process of projecting can happen with a situation. We have created some dream (or nightmare) about the situation in our mind, and we don't see events clearly but through the lens of our projector which is in our consciousness. It's as if we are watching the inner movie we have created about the situation, now projected onto a movie screen and we are not observing life as it is really occurring.

Fear is merely a projection of our thoughts and emotions onto the screen of our reality. It is not something that actually exists but something we are believing to exist. If we fear a repeat of something that happened in the past, then we are projecting the past onto the future, and because that is what we are holding in our consciousness, it becomes a self-fulfilling prophecy when the universe plays it out for us.

Our lower personas hold our fears, and we need to get them sorted out and aligned to the same goals as our higher self. Therefore, we can let go of these fears and old beliefs with the methods outlined above and replace them with more positive and reasonable thinking and memories.

l) Being love, opening the heart, surrendering

Healing of any kind is all about coming back into the vibration of love and wholeness. In order to love, or feel loving energies, we will need to open our heart. We can do this in a multitude of ways through consciousness, and none of them require us to have open heart surgery!

1. Visualise shutters over our heart, and throwing these wide open
2. Open up the drawbridge and gates to the castle of our consciousness and heart
3. Listen to music that inspires us or brings us to tears
4. Watch a touching or poignant film that stirs our heart
5. Ponder over photos of those we love, and maybe have lost
6. Sit and observe nature, or a sunrise or sunset, or the stars at night
7. Forgive someone that we haven't been able to previously
8. Do a good deed for someone who really appreciates it
9. Fly up to the higher dimensions and have a conversation with a god or angel
10. Draw in the energies of the sun directly into the heart

Letting go of any resistance (as in the techniques above) is paramount in order to have an open heart, for any semblance of conflict or defiance in our consciousness seals off our heart as a defence mechanism against getting hurt. Because resistance is usually championed by our ego and our lower personas, we will need to negotiate with these aspects of ourselves and get them to surrender and allow the heart to be opened. See the healing techniques for lower personas above.

Any situation, illness, or relationship can be healed wholly or to a certain degree when we send out love, blessings, and healing energies from an open and purified heart. When we feel love in our heart, any tragedy won't cut so deep, and we will be able to ask, "What can be learnt from all this?"

m) Healing with our spirit, soul, and higher beings

Higher consciousness has superior powers, and so staying in communication with our spirit and soul is essential for any healing process, as is listening to our intuition and gut feel, or seeing the signs around us, which are the messages being sent to us from the unseen universe. We will be well-guided and assisted from the other side if we connect to the higher beings with love and good intention, and are making some attempt to heal our wounded physical, emotional, or mental state. If we feel in the dark, they have the light to show us our path and the ways in which we can heal ourselves.

The higher beings who make up our Ribbon of Consciousness are always there for us, no matter how dire or hopeless our situation may seem. We can always ask them for answers, direction, or for healing. But if we don't listen, or we ignore their advice, they won't be so keen to help us again in the future. If we can't grasp their suggestions or the reasons for them, then we need to enter into dialogue with our mentors until we reach full understanding.

If we wish to utilise our spirit, soul, or the gods in our healing processes, then we will need to let them take control over proceedings, and not try to take matters into our own human hands and exert our human will. Cooperation, respect, and surrender to higher wisdom, is the name of the game when we work as a team with the higher beings, and then we will see magic happening.

n) Dealing with children

Many of the healing techniques outlined above can be used with children. They respond very well to visualisation and meditation suggestions. The richer we can make the landscape and symbolism, the better. Also using characters from books and movies to explain things to them works successfully. Weave in the child's life and issues with the worlds of the higher dimensions; they will remember the experiential adventures they are involved in, physically or as their spirit self, far more easily than just listening to lessons taught in words.

The consciousnesses of children are delicate and sensitive, so we must be careful to use gentle methods with them, not punitive ones. Damaged children produce damaged adults, maybe irreparably. Children don't have a fully-formed brain or consciousness until they are adults, and therefore we must cut them some slack if they don't know the proper way to do things, or are not aware of consequences. They require training from us—do we always know the correct training to give them? They also use us adults as their role models—are we the best role models we can possibly be?

o) Time limitations

We should give ourselves a finite time period to grieve or to get over the shock of a situation. We can go on finding excuses forever to not pull ourselves out of our dark pit.

On the other hand, we need to give ourselves sufficient time to think over an issue or problem before taking action. Making rash or poorly thought out decisions will see us paying the consequences later on. As the old saying goes, "Marry in haste, repent at leisure!"

If we know we tend towards procrastination, giving ourselves a time limit or a deadline to make a choice will chivvy us along. Preparing justifications for our actions or conclusions will help to assuage any doubt that we may have made the wrong decision.

If we find ourselves in a situation where we need more time, we can visualise time going slower so that we can get more done or cover more ground in the same amount of time, such as when rushing to catch a train. Similarly, if time seems to be interminable, we can visualise speeding it up, such as when on a long, boring journey. Time is simply a human physical dimension construct, and so when we take our consciousness out of this dimension, time ceases to exist as we know it. Therefore, we can make a minute seem like an hour, and make an hour seem like a minute, and we all have had instances of this in our lives.

p) Getting over the bridge

When we experience adversity, either physically, emotionally, mentally, or spiritually, our vibrational level usually takes a tumble as we deal with the fallout of what has happened to us. If we have attained our godhood, then it should be second nature to pull ourselves together quickly and raise our vibes back to normal high dimensional levels again. In this case, we will not have fallen out of the heavenly realms and been pulled back over the bridge into the lower human dimension of consciousness. (In chapter 6 we described the bridges to the higher dimensions.) However, even as gods we need to remember that our position is not guaranteed in Heaven without us maintaining our high vibrations, standards, and integrity. We can slip back into the old world if we get lazy or inattentive to our consciousness and our purpose.

As humans who are not yet gods, we seek to build a bridge—to the higher levels of our Ribbon of Consciousness, to our spirit and our soul at the very least, and to the higher beings in the gods' dimensions. If we, as humans or as gods, do not deal effectively with our tumult and regain control over our falling consciousness, then we will find ourselves on the wrong side of the bridge, the lower side. We will need to redo all our hard work to get ourselves over the bridge once again, whether it's the bridge to Second Earth or the bridge to the gods' dimension. We can always feel when we have fallen back across the bridge, as it's like finding ourselves in some old nightmare that we thought we had climbed out of.

So, utilise all the methods outlined in this guidebook for raising consciousness and vibrational levels as soon as possible, determining to live in the higher world that exists across the bridge. Using the Toolbox of your Consciousness, prepare a plan in the eventuality that you will take a fall (which may happen fairly often) and learn to get up fast.

Don't get anchored in the lower worlds. The deeper you sink, the more effort will be needed to get out of the pit again. Sneaky hands will try to snare you and pull you back down each time. See yourself kicking away those hands or unhitching those anchors. Make tracks out of your despair using the control centre of your consciousness. Take command over any negativity or hopelessness and rein them in. Stop projecting dismal or pessimistic scenes for your future. Do everything you can to settle your heart and recreate a beautiful world to step into in your mind. Change any gloomy thinking or attitude and search for the silver lining that is present in any situation. Everything can be viewed from a new and brighter perspective.

When your heart feels ready, visualise crossing the bridge and going through a door or gateway on the higher side. You may be challenged by a guard to give an account of yourself before you are allowed through. It may be that you haven't yet reached the required level of vibration to visit, or live, in that higher dimension of consciousness. Keep on raising those vibrations, leaving behind all the lower parts of yourself, all the old ways, beliefs, and habits, and try again to cross that bridge. It can, at times, take a while to cleanse off all the muck that you have fallen into on the lower side, and get your heart sufficiently open again.

We will always be welcomed back over the bridge by higher beings. They hold no grudges, and there is no need for us to feel guilty about our demise. We are like toddlers learning to walk. As parents we don't punish our children for not being able to rise up and walk on the initial try. We are thrilled at the attempts, and encouraging, supportive, and patient.

Our challenges can be severe, and we don't always know how to handle them at first. Through experimentation and persistence we can learn fortitude and gain victory and finally godhood. The main thing is to keep focusing on returning over the bridge to the higher realms to experience the energies of Heaven. Our arrival will be celebrated with great cheer.

q) Rewriting past scripts

Consciousness retains every single detail of all our past lives. Therefore, we can review, and change, any scene from any life, from any era, and from any place we once existed in the cosmos. However, in consciousness there is no concept of time—no past, no future. There is only NOW. When we decide to change events in our mind in the present, all dynamics and relationships, past and future, are altered. (This was explained in chapter 6 in Time Travel).

Therefore, we can set our intention to travel back into the past and visualise an event and rewrite the script until it is to our satisfaction. We need to feel into it with all our senses and make it as vivid as possible so that our emotions are engaged, for once we *feel* something, it is more likely to become enacted in our consciousness. This method is also employed in hypnosis and NLP in past life regression.

Chapter 23 – Love, forgiveness, and relationships

There's not a being on Earth or in the heavens who doesn't have some kind of relationship with others, and it's our chief hurdle in every lifetime to form relationships that are loving or harmonious and mutually beneficial. We have relationships with everyone, not just our primary partners: with self (spirit/soul/Source/lower personas), spouse, lover, ex-lover, father, mother, brother, sister, daughter, son, extended family, in-laws, friends, social media contacts, neighbours, co-workers, managers, business associates, clients, students, teachers, families of others, local community, religious community, spiritual community (higher beings), medical community, social services, authorities, governments, past life associates, and others.

How are we doing in our relationships with all these beings? If there is any kind of disharmony between us and them, then we can be sure that snakes are arising from our field for us to resolve our antipathies, quarrels, or ill-feelings. Doors to Heaven will open only once we have made some in-roads in our long list of hostilities and grudges. It's not that we need to clear every single relationship before we can get to godhood. Even in the gods' dimensions there is still much forgiving going on between gods, usually concerning their past lives together, but at least they have a handle on the tools of consciousness they need to employ to resolve all disputes.

Murderous intent

It's doubtful if there is a single human who hasn't harboured murderous intent at some time in their lifetimes. It doesn't help that television and movies stoke this reaction in many minds, but it's always been a natural inclination within humans from our first genesis.

'Kill or be killed' has been the motto, or kill in order to steal, usurp power, or do away with the enemy, competition, or merely people who get in the way of our plans. Even today, when we tend to believe the world is fairly civilised, there are still wars and killing fields and pockets of murderous intent, even sanctioned by some governments.

If we harbour war-like feelings in our consciousness, then war of some kind will certainly be visited upon us. We see this on our planet, how there are definite hotspots of war that continually break out in that region. Old animosities rage across lifetimes, perpetuated from family, clan, tribe, or from religious sects, and from generation to generation. Who will be the one to stop this cycle of vengeance?

If we have murdered, then we will be murdered too. Our actions will rebound on us at some time, whether it is in the same lifetime or another. No one gets away with any crime in this universe, not ever. Consciousness has a long and perfect memory, and seeks to balance and redress all actions. We are never punished by the gods for our bad behaviour, but we will need to atone for it at some time in the future, bringing in commensurate good energies to negate our wrongdoing. It's not that consciousness wishes tit for tat; it is we ourselves who are harbouring the feelings of revenge, and consciousness merely plays out the script it has been given.

We may believe ourselves to be beyond these kinds of crimes, yet while some perform the actual deed itself, others just do it in their consciousness. There are probably many people in our lives towards whom we feel bad vibes. It all counts against us and pollutes our life and obscures our destiny. We can climb only so far up our spiritual mountain to godhood before we are forced to deal with our past and especially our horror lives and deeply buried hurts. New doors can open for us only once we have cleansed the rooms of our consciousness.

Therefore, we will need to let go all triggers, animosity, vilification, and thoughts of reckoning or retribution, and replace this thinking with forgiveness and love. In the past, we ourselves wouldn't have been an angel either, and we will want to be forgiven for our own misdeeds too. We need to forgive ourselves also, for survival was usually our only focus back then, and we didn't know that our ideal should have been to love.

Mercy and forgiveness

Mercy is an old-fashioned word, and these days we tend to use the word 'forgiveness'. It's a trait that's not very evident amongst humans, even in the most civilised or religious of countries, even in the courts of justice. It is especially absent within many families, and woundings are hoarded and stored as grudges where revenge will be sought in the future.

How many of us can truthfully say that we have never held a feeling of resentment or a chip on our shoulder or some rancour, bitterness, or ill-will against another? And how many of us can say that we have never acted in some low or base way that has required forgiveness from another?

We are all guilty, as guilty as one another, and this is the reason we are still on Earth, working on our consciousness to get it clear and pure. Over many lifetimes we will have acted from our lowest consciousness, playing out our rawest emotions, fears, and desires, often fighting only to survive as best we could. We have all had dark pasts, even the gods.

It is time to let these memories go, time to have mercy upon ourselves, to forgive ourselves for our actions and experiences and all that's been said and done over the ages. If we wish to be a better person and manifest a better world, then we may be feeling guilty about our past and the terrible things we may have carried out, either of our own volition or under the banner of king and crown.

I was speaking with Master Dominic once, and he told me how he still wept over his part in the bombing of Germany as an Australian WWII RAF fighter pilot. He himself was killed soon afterwards in 1944. But I also discovered recently that during this same era, he had also been a young man in the Hitler Youth organisation, who had been killed during one of these bombing raids. So, Dominic had been experiencing the war from both sides of the political divide, and had actually been responsible for the death of himself.

We need to forgive ourselves, and flood our heart with love and mercy. We are no longer a savage or that lower consciousness person. We are now improving, refining, and transforming ourselves. The pool of self-pity and tears needs to be left behind to focus on who we are now and the star we are following to godhood. We can use any of the healing techniques detailed in chapter 22 to let go of our past lower personas or emotions.

Once we forgive ourselves, then our soul and the gods will shower their mercy on us too. The gods are compassionate and forgive everyone and everything. They understand that the path to Heaven is fraught and difficult and that we often forsake ourselves and others along the way. There is nothing quite like being forgiven and absolved of our offences against love. It cuts powerfully to the core of us and opens our heart like few other things. This is the reason why the Christian confessional and priest's absolution are still such a potent part of that religion even after two thousand years. Being pardoned and given a clean slate to start anew is the most terrific display of love and mercy, and will have us feeling quite emotional.

As we travel higher up our Ribbon of Consciousness, we will discover more and more mercy around us. By the time we become a god, we ourselves will have been forgiven over and over, and now it will be our turn to show mercy to others. But there will be plenty of practice along the way to godhood in showing forgiveness to those around us and clearing their slates for them. Often our lack of forgiveness can be an obstacle for others to go higher up their path, and it is definitely an obstacle on our own path of progress. The act of forgiving someone is comparable to being forgiven ourselves, and it comes with a huge release of emotion and joy and opens doors for us to the higher dimensions.

This forgiveness needs to be unconditional, in that we can't be thinking, "I will forgive you but only if you do this, or don't do that again." The 'if' in that statement makes it conditional. We are saying we will forgive but only on condition that something else is agreed to. In essence, if we grant only conditional forgiveness, then we are holding the thought in our consciousness that there is a possibility that the same transgression will be committed again, and hence we may be projecting that behaviour onto the other person, pushing them into playing that role for us.

Mercy is a foundation stone of this universe. If people were taught how to forgive from an early age, then we could be assured a more harmonious world with less anger, violence, or stored grudges, and perhaps no more wars. It starts with parents and teachers as role models. If children observe mercy being displayed then they will learn from it, and, as adults, will become better citizens and form more loving and forgiving relationships.

A few days after writing this section on mercy and forgiveness, I was given a taste of this topic for myself. I had had a challenging and sleepless night which had eventuated in my spirit self going up to the sun and asking for all my lower personas to be dissolved there who no longer supported my path. I was in no mood to hang around, and summarily thanked them all for their service to me, and despatched them quickly into the furnace of the sun.

As I came away from the scene, the One God asked me to come up and speak with Him. It's not often I get a summons from the highest divinity, but I am always delighted to be in His Presence.

God asked me, "Why did you want to kill yourself off? You were being nihilistic."

I argued, "I was merely killing off my lower personas from hell."

God told me, "You didn't do it with love, did you? And for that reason I am going to exile you from Heaven for one day."

Oh no! It was a terrible punishment, but I guessed I could survive for only one day. I had to concede I deserved it. It was true; I hadn't let go my lower personas with as much love as I would normally employ. I had despatched them without much thought at all. I felt contrite; after all, my lower personas were part of my own self, and I hadn't treated them with compassion.

God then asked me to come and sit in His Heart, which is one of the best treats in the universe; soothing, calming, loving. He told me gently and in a fatherly tone, "You know I would never punish you, nor ever eject you from Heaven."

Immediately I recognised that I was being forgiven, and God was showing me His Mercy, and tears sprang into my eyes as I felt His Love pouring into me and enveloping me. It also reminded me that gods never punish us, and the One God was just helping me to remember that divine rule.

Finding love

What do many of us desire most in this world? It's to find love. Once tasted, love can never be put aside again. It's an ecstatic experience and most of us can't get enough of it, and we live in hope to find it, and keep it too.

Well, we have read many times throughout this book that like attracts like; therefore, to attract love to us we must be love ourselves. We might want to take a look at what we have already attracted and examine what our true self is broadcasting out into the world. And then there might be some adjusting to be done of our consciousness, of the thoughts, emotions, and triggers that we are carrying there.

Love for ourself first

Receiving the right kind of love from others will depend on whether we have the right kind of love for ourself. Any facet of our personality that we find distasteful will be mirrored in the people we meet and have relationships with. What we don't like in them triggers something we don't like about ourselves. That's not always easy to identify.

For instance, we might dislike the way our partner is too domineering and calls all the shots. This may or may not mean that we are also overbearing, but it could also mean that it's showing up the fact that we are being a mouse and too timid, and that's the trait in us we don't like. Conversely, what we find attractive in another person can also be found as a trait we admire in ourselves, or a trait we aspire to and wish to learn.

Consciousness is love itself and exists to be love, therefore we too are love itself and exist to be love. We were birthed by a creator god as love, and our entire journey throughout all our lives in this universe is to find that pure love again that we were born into. We need to keep seeing ourselves as we really exist, as that pure diamond core of love, and even if we muddy it over with a negative thought, we can pull ourselves back to that place again using our tools of consciousness, letting go all that is not-love.

If we want to know what love tastes like, we need to explore our own inner world and our Ribbon of Consciousness, and set free the love that already resides within us. It's just waiting to be revealed like hidden treasure.

Love has been within us forever, but most people go searching for it externally, thinking it's out there somewhere, if only they could find it. They experience love only when they fall in love with someone else, but we can experience this every day for our whole life when we fall in love with ourselves. Love for ourself is the key that opens the door to loving other people, and then all the universe, and it will be a deeper love than we ever thought possible, coming from the knowing that we are love itself. When we are love itself, we are also entrusted with the keys to the portals to other worlds.

Finding a partner, soul mate, or twin flame

When we are looking for someone to love, a partner or perhaps just a boyfriend or girlfriend, we can certainly use the powers of our tools of consciousness to help us manifest this person. Our soul, as a part of our Ribbon of Consciousness, can indeed act as a match-maker and will be delighted to help us. But there are a few 'rules' around this.

a. You will attract someone only if it is your destiny at this time to do so.
b. If you have an ideal person in mind, then you may not be ready yet to meet them, meaning that *you* may be less than ideal at this point.
c. The person you attract will be the best fit for you, compatible in some ways but also someone who can set off your triggers that need to be removed.
d. The person provided will not always be what you initially desired but will be what you need.
e. A love interest is not only to provide fun, companionship, and complement your lack of skills in some areas, but also to resolve deep issues between the two of you, or to birth projects together through which you learn and grow.
f. You, or the person provided, may be a teacher to the other.

People often speak about finding their soul mate or twin flame. What exactly are these? I asked Master Chiron to describe what these terms actually mean.

Chiron: "*Soul mates are friends, friends of our soul. They might not necessarily be friends for us down on Earth, but at the soul level our soul has negotiated with the souls of these people to bring forth something into our life, be it love or lessons or challenges or different viewpoints. So, a soul mate may indeed be our enemy, someone who is waking us up to a new perspective, to a new path perhaps.*

So, soul mates are people whom our soul has determined are right for us to meet in this present incarnation. They are often people we have known before in previous lives, so their energies will not be unfamiliar to us. Often, we are attracted to these energies initially, then later on we might be deterred by them, disappointed at what we have found, like opening some Pandora's Box. But certainly, soul mates are not all bad, and we have many who come to support us, encourage us, and love us.

A twin flame is similar to this but also different. They are similar in that they can be friend or foe, and we can be either very attracted to them or appalled by them. For a twin flame is the other half of ourself, a consciousness that has been split in two down the middle, and one half goes one way and the other half goes the other. They are generally the masculine and the feminine sides of one whole, but not always so.

Where the split has taken place in consciousness, where the two halves had once been conjoined, there the two consciousnesses are amiable and complementary and compatible, and there is much there to attract each to the other. But at the further ends of each consciousness, you could say these people are poles apart, polar opposites. And therein lies the challenge for twin flames, that they must each seek to love the polar opposites of their own consciousness, which is indeed a very great challenge.

Loving the opposite of whom we are takes great love and forgiveness and understanding, and therefore relationships with our twin flames can be the most joyous of things but also the most rocky and tragic. We spend many lifetimes attracted to the fire of our twin flames, only to be repelled again when we are burnt by their flames. But as we march through our lives in this universe, we will connect with our twin flame time and time again, and each time we will try and get a little further into harmony, until one day we are ready to sit in their energies without becoming inflamed."[22]

---

22. From a channelling with Master Chiron, 4 October 2019

The Greek philosopher Aristotle proposed that, "Love is composed of a single soul inhabiting two bodies," which is an apt description of a twin flame.

Not having a partner is not the end of the world. It may be only temporary, but it may also be part of our destiny in this lifetime to go it alone. We can choose to be lonely and to dwell in unhappiness about our state of affairs, or we can decide to foster the love within ourself and apply it to the world at large instead of towards just one person. There are many ways to add value to our planet through our love, kindness, support, hard work, improved consciousness, and focusing on our mission. In this way, we may just find the path to another's heart too!

However, if we keep our vibrations high and we mix with our higher personas along our Ribbon of Consciousness, we can feel love around us on a daily basis, and it is possible to feel the frisson of romance and upliftment even without a partner on Earth because we feel in love with the whole universe and all the beings therein.

Fear of not having love is one of the greatest fears on this planet, but when we *are* love then we do have this love we are searching for, and all our fear falls away.

Why do relationships fall apart?

Of course, there are many specific reasons why relationships fall apart and so we will cover only generalities here. The primary reason is that not-love outweighs love for one or both partners. We have learned that love is consciousness; however, not everyone's consciousness is love.

In the beginning of the relationship we are attracted to one another for several reasons or motives, and we tend to gloss over those things that have the potential to irk us. But after a while, the gloss dims and opposing opinions and ways of doing things chaff on us and we start to lose respect for each other. We want to be right and prove the other wrong. We want our way or the highway. We want our freedom, yet for the other to be enslaved. We resent, we nag, we manipulate, we deceive, we take and don't give, we criticise, we jeer, we resist, we withhold, we abuse, we sulk, we shout, we humiliate, we capitulate, we sacrifice, we frustrate, we fight, we thwart, we run. We continually trample on each other's carpets and dirty them.

Triggers

Every one of us can be mean at times. It happens when our snakes are triggered off, when old woundings are burst open by our partner or circumstances, when expectations are not met, when we are disappointed or threatened by the turn of events. In these moments of not-love, we need to catch ourselves and ask why we or our partner are acting in this way? What is the underlying programming that pulled the trigger?

Most people don't mean to act mean; they merely need to clear their trigger points. If we have no triggers inside us, then there is nothing that can set us off like a bomb waiting to explode. Our reactions will be kinder, more measured, more *simpatico*. Life would be more harmonious, and people wouldn't need to walk on eggshells around us.

In the previous chapters on healing, we discussed the many ways we can be triggered, and some techniques we could use to overcome them. All the flawed and confused programming that makes us react badly to certain people and situations must be levered out of our consciousness. All our old grudges and hurts act out in the guise of our lower personas, and these need to be dealt with, forgiven, and let go.

Everything in this universe is either love or not-love, and most of not-love comes from fear, but even fear is underlain by love and can be turned around. If we are aware of our own energies, and control what we are broadcasting, then we will less likely attract disharmonious situations to ourself. We need to be responsible for our consciousness and energetic thought-forms, and not allow any of our snake venom to flow from us and poison other people. The field of our consciousness affects everyone around us at all times, and even people we are merely thinking about, no matter how far away they are.

Do we want peace, love, and harmony more than we want to score points? The desire to fight is inherent in human beings. It is a prehistoric emotion and it has helped us to survive throughout eons of time. But our ego will bring us down if it wants victory above all else.

Can we go to a higher part of our Ribbon of Consciousness and allow ourselves to view the situation from all sides, and communicate and discuss and negotiate in an understanding way with the other party? If we desire to become a god, then we must suppress the desire to fight and be the winner at all cost. It is against the ethics of the gods to fight in this way. Gods strive for agreement and foster harmony. They know they cannot win every battle, and they will realise when to step back and yield.

Once we have removed our own triggers, how can we bring in love and forgiveness and wipe the slate clean for the other person? Can we hold a picture in our consciousness of the ideal outcome we wish for, without being interrupted or diverted by the energies, emotions, or outbursts of another? Can we be patient with others who may have desires or opinions that don't match our own, without butting heads with them? Are we judging someone on criteria that we ourselves don't meet? Is our own world in perfect and loving order? Are we the best person we could be, without fault or fear? Can we find forgiveness and compassion for someone who is really no different from us, just someone who is trying to get through this life and challenges in the best way they know how, someone just trying to survive and forgetting how to be love?

The full symphony

Often in our relationships we fill unfulfilled. Perhaps our expectations haven't been met. Perhaps our expectations were based on some fantasy which the other person couldn't possibly have met for us. Do we need to just suppress our desires to fit our circumstances, and merely accept the other as they are and be more grateful for them? This may work, but it could also lead us to simply feel resentful and remain unfulfilled. We may need to unravel exactly what are our expectations of another, and are we being realistic?

A fulfilling relationship will be one where each person gives of their full symphony for the other. If we hear only the middle notes of a piece of music, and not the top notes or lowest notes, we will feel like something is missing. We may not be able to gauge what it is, but we intuit there is more to this tune that would round it out and provide satisfying emotions for us. Imagine Handel's *Messiah* or Simon and Garfunkel's *Bridge Over Troubled Water* played with only the right hand, the treble-clef part, with no bass notes!

If a person plays us their full symphony right to the end, with all the high notes as well as all the low notes, we will not experience anything missing from that relationship. It means we receive all their attention and commitment while they are in our presence, and even when they are not around we remain fulfilled because we go on hearing that music, maybe even for months or years afterwards. Their melody settles our soul so well that we don't need to be with that person physically. Their symphony remains in our heart forever.

If someone withholds their top or bottom notes, their music is unfinished, and we will always be searching for those missing notes in order to feel complete and fulfilled by them. It may be that they fear commitment or lack trust in us. Perhaps it is we ourselves who are withholding these notes, and so the other person is simply mirroring this back to us.

Some people get by on sharing shallow relationships, but many folks need the full intensity and passion of their natures to play out in order to feel fulfilled. If we don't allow this, then we may find ourselves searching for the topmost and deepest notes in each other. We cut off the highs and lows of our amplitude[23], fearing them, but indulging them will actually set us free.

We may need a relationship where the wavelengths are low and steady with little amplitude, or we may need to experience extreme highs and lows. Neither is right or wrong, but we should understand what it is we desire from any relationship so that we are not disappointed. If we need to add high notes or low notes, or turn up or tone down our amplitude, then we can do so and bring back a relationship that may be on the brink.

It is also interesting to point out that in the higher dimensions we are encouraged to experience multiple relationships. In this way we don't get to play only the one symphony; we go from symphony to symphony,

---

23. Amplitude: the height of a frequency wave

always feeling fulfilled from the variety of music. The gods are never possessive of their relationships—their love is shared amongst everyone.

We attract mirrors

If we desire a good relationship then we ourselves will need to model this first, replacing our programming so that we think only with love, keeping our vibrations high in all instances, helping, giving, sharing, and teaching family and friends and all we come into contact with. Can we learn to bounce off others, learning what we need to improve ourselves and finding new strengths? Are we a good and desirable person that others want to have a relationship with? Our journey in life is all about this; becoming a finer human being and then a god.

At any stage of our journey we will attract relationships which are at our current vibrational level, so we know exactly what to do now if our relationships suck. Once we learn to manage our own consciousness, then we will be better able to manage the consciousnesses of others, for our own personas are the trickiest of all to deal with.

In any one day we might be wearing the hat of several different lower personas, all of which can act in atypical ways, depending on whom we are with and what energies the other person is giving out and what triggers are waiting in our hold to be detonated. Add on top of this the fact that our relationships serve as mirrors to ourselves, then it becomes quite complicated to understand what part of the problem is coming from our partner and what is coming from ourselves.

Master Dominic (my twin flame) gave me an example of this as I was working on this book. He was acting fairly antagonistic towards me when I visited him in the gods' dimension, and I asked him what was triggering this response? He was criticising me for not working hard enough and not putting myself out there more in the world. I had to agree with this to some degree, for I also felt it deep within myself.

Suddenly I had the realisation that he was merely echoing back to me my own underlying criticism of myself. Dom was merely being a mirror to me. As soon as I got the message, he laughed, and I knew that he wasn't judging me at all, but merely playing the role to help me see my own faulty thinking in not loving and appreciating myself enough and all that I do manage to achieve.

People wish that the other in a relationship could be different, but it is we ourselves that need to transform our thinking and take our consciousness to a higher level of love and understanding. When we focus on being love itself, not just trying to find a love that fills up the empty holes in our heart, then we will truly find the right kind of deep love that brings immeasurable happiness.

We need only open our heart, take down our defensive attitudes, exorcise our triggers, pull back on our ego and negativity, fill our mind with loving thoughts, and our whole world will change its perspective and begin to glow quite differently from before. Love is the remedy for all fear, hatred, hostility, bitterness, resentment, unkindness, aggression, and adversity. If we are being love, then we cannot also be not-love. We must make up our minds which it will be.

Evil entities and Group Consciousness

Are there really such things as evil entities who can invade our consciousness and take us over? We may not like to see this within ourselves, but we humans are quick to blame others as being cursed with the devil. Some people may refer instead to implants inside us from some outside agency, including aliens or the spirit world. The answer is a little more prosaic.

Although it may seem like evil entities of some kind have taken over our psyche or that of others, in truth, what we are experiencing is the work of lower personas coming out to play. We have seen how they can cause havoc in our consciousness, sabotaging any good intentions, and at times urging us on to commit dreadful deeds.

If at any time we open up our consciousness to the greater matrix of consciousnesses, we make ourselves vulnerable to the consciousness of others being able to enter and merge with our own. This is a good thing to do when we are wanting our spirit and soul and gods to merge with us, but it is not a great idea if the consciousness we are merging with contains very low vibrational personas, for these will make a home inside us and begin to create havoc.

We merge consciousnesses with other people, *usually without being aware of it*, when we have sex with them, or we lose normal consciousness through taking alcohol or drugs, or we are near to people in meditation, or having out-of-this-world experiences such as at a concert or theme park.

I recently watched a documentary featuring some old Beatles concerts back in the 1960s. The audiences were hysterical, screaming and weeping and declaring their undying love for either John, Paul, George, or Ringo, and undoubtedly not acting like their normal selves. They were being affected by the group consciousness. This can also happen anywhere where large masses of people gather—in sports stadiums; at rallies and protest marches; in churches, temples, and synagogues; in cinemas; shopping malls; cruise ships; holiday resorts; airports and on planes; parties; nightclubs; crowded restaurants and cafés; huge events indoors and outdoors; school assemblies; hospital and medical waiting rooms; big elevators; factories and workplaces; Parliaments; crowded neighbourhoods and apartment blocks.

Anywhere we find ourselves in a crowd, we are subjected to the group consciousness of that mass, and we can find ourselves mindlessly copying the actions and reactions of that crowd if we do not bring our awareness to the situation.

Every time we open wide our heart or mind, we are at risk of letting others in. In most cases, this is a wonderful experience and we feel the oneness with them, but at times it does open the door to some bad lower personas entering into our consciousness and feeling like some evil entity has taken up residence. We can deal with these entities in the same way as any other lower persona, and get them out of our consciousness as fast as we can.

Our relationship with our spirit, soul, and higher beings

It is not only humans that we have relationships with, but also our spirit, our soul, and the gods and angels. In chapters 3-5 on Higher Beings, we described these relationships in detail and how we need to maintain them properly. It is really no different from human relationships. There needs to be respect, consideration, communication, connection, collaboration, openness to other viewpoints, appreciation, patience, compassion, compromise, responsibility, a desire for harmony and balance, friendship, reciprocity, sharing, freedom, autonomy, self-control, as well as that all-important love and forgiveness.

The issues that are prevalent in our spiritual relationships will filter down to our earthly ones, and vice versa. Our human relationships will mirror back to us what may be happening between our soul and ourselves; for instance, if we have lost connection with our soul, perhaps we are experiencing a lack of communication or a breakup with our human partner too.

The most common issue between human beings and divine beings, is the fight over control (and it's probably the most common issue in human relationships too!) Humans want to employ their free will; the higher worlds wish us to follow divine will. It's up to us if and when we surrender to the wisdom of our guiding lights and work together as a team to get our mission completed.

It's often the case that we have past life dramas to clear up with some of the beings who are now gods in the heavenly realms. We may physically meet a clone or two of theirs and resolve our issues on the earthly plane, or we may carry out our relationship with them purely through a connection in consciousness across the dimensions. The latter is generally the way I have experienced my own relationships with the gods, but now and again I have met a clone of theirs on Earth, and it's been interesting to observe the dynamics playing out, knowing what I know about the person's soul.

Sometimes the gods wish to merge their consciousnesses with ours. They do this to imbue us with more love, power, and wisdom to assist us in raising ourselves to a higher level.

I asked Chiron, "Does the entire Ribbon of Consciousness of the god merge with the human, or only a little bit of their Ribbon?" He said it was complicated but he would try to explain. He showed me an image of what looked like a length of DNA, like part of a twisted ladder. Chiron said each side of the ladder represented the Ribbons of Consciousness of the god and the human which then joined (merged) in the centre.

The god will latch onto the place in the human's Ribbon wherever that person is currently dialled into.

Therefore, if the human raises themselves up to their Source level, then they can merge with the god at that god's Source level too. If the person is presently at a lower vibrational level on their Ribbon, then they will merge with the commensurate lower level of the god's Ribbon. So, if we can stay dialled into our consciousness at a high level and make that our default 'station', then we will link or merge with that part of the god who resides at that level, which should make for a delightful partnership.

This merger of a god with a human is sometimes known as a "walk-in", but this term should only be used if a human's entire Ribbon is being merged with, which happens only in rare instances, and even then, the two consciousnesses combine; the human is never taken over by the god.

It should be noted that only a god higher than ourselves can suggest a merger of consciousnesses with us. We cannot approach a higher god to do this with us. We would be in danger of being rebuffed and that might hurt us, and no higher god wishes that for us. We might not be ready for a merger, or our vibrations are too low, so we need to wait until asked.

Just as with any relationship on Earth, if we wish for great relationships with our spirit, soul, gods, or angels, then we will need to practise being loving, and then we will receive love in huge quantities in return. But if we are dripping with darkness and low vibrations, then it will be tremendously difficult to gain access to the higher worlds and the beings who abide there.

Chapter 24 – Destiny/mission and evolvement

Godhood mission

The ultimate destiny for every human is to become a god. This pathway may take millennia to achieve for some individuals; that notwithstanding, this is the target of the gods who govern Earth. They have created us humans, and it is now their responsibility to lift up our consciousnesses to the level of gods. Every mission we undertake in each incarnation, and in the lives we have as spirits in between incarnations, is aimed at improving our consciousness and raising us up into finer beings of this universe.

In chapter 10 we described the route we need to take to get to our godhood, and indeed, this entire book informs us of the ways and methods that underpin our eventual graduation to becoming a god in consciousness, and how to perform as a god in a physical body.

Even if we have no idea that this is our most fundamental goal whilst living as a human on Earth, our soul has this in mind in every moment that it is setting us challenges and monitoring our moves, rearing us in the proper way as a parent does with a child. We are being taught how to become a god, given instructions and guidance (if we can hear or see it), and being promoted up the Ribbon of Consciousness if we meet our targets.

Our progress up the divine ladder depends solely upon ourselves and the way we transform ourselves and our consciousness. We go at our own pace, and a little forward movement is always better than none, but it is our choice how long we dwell in the lower dimensions before crossing over the bridge, moving our consciousness to a higher place, and finally into the gods' dimension.

As we move towards godhood, we are given heavier responsibilities and we are expected to think and act more like gods. This brings its own challenges, but also its rewards in the form of more peace, harmony, love, joy, and fulfilment. The spiritual path to godhood is never an easy ride. It turns us inside out and overturns our whole life as a human. Many people fall by the wayside and must try again in another lifetime.

It can be difficult to envisage ourselves as gods; present-day movies about superheroes and gods have probably created a high pedestal that we couldn't ever imagine climbing onto. But after reading the previous chapters of this book, it is hoped that we have a better understanding of exactly what a god is and what kind of life they lead, either in the higher dimensions or on Earth in human form. We must believe in ourselves and that we are capable of becoming gods, and not sell ourselves short.

When we get to godhood

Once we step into the shoes of a god, nothing can ever be the same again. Our bodies may still tread upon the ground, but our consciousness is living in another dimension and managing all that we think and do as a human form. The body is merely a vehicle for us now and it must respond just as any car does, without any resistance or judgement, but merely following our instructions and operations. It does take some getting used to and life can feel unsettled for a while, but it is also tremendously exciting to explore our new domain and discover what can be achieved with our enhanced god consciousness.

As a god, we need to face the world with strength and a positive attitude, and, as usual, heed directions from our soul, for even a god has a soul to guide them. We will still be carrying out normal everyday human tasks, but we will no longer have a normal everyday human kind of mind.

Our journey until now has been very much focused on transforming our own consciousness to the level of a god. Now, we will change focus, and our destiny will be to attend helping others to get to their godhood, and in managing the human world on a broader basis. We will be teaching people as we have been taught ourselves.

Although we have been triumphant in achieving our crown, we will not be allowed to rest on our laurels (give or take a few celebratory parties!) We didn't reach godhood to stay sitting in an armchair in the corner, or hide our light under a bushel. We have many talents to offer the world and it's now up to us to deliberate on how we wish to serve these up.

This period of figuring out what we now wish to do in order to serve the world can be a little disconcerting. It's akin to leaving university; we have our degree—now what? If we feel in this quandary, further on in this chapter and the next, we describe some methods to better understand which mission will be best for us.

However, once we get our sea legs and adjust to the life of godhood, our consciousness shines with love, power, and wisdom, our heart is overbrimming with success, and life sparkles within us and all around us. We will want to take on the world and solve all its issues. This is a small taste of stardom, and of what is to come in the ensuing evolution of our consciousness into that of a sun and ultimately a creator god.

Our human mission

So, that is our overarching mission, to become a god, and plenty of humans have done so in the past, and many more are succeeding in the current climate of intense higher energies and support from the unseen universe of beings.

However, in this present incarnation as a human being, whether we are a god in human form or merely mortal, we will have another destiny to fulfil as well. This isn't necessarily a spiritual mission. It could be that of being a father or mother and training our children to become loving and resilient beings. We could be a teacher or helper to humanity in some way; a writer, tradesperson, astronaut, diver, nurse, athlete, shop assistant, computer programmer, scientist—anything in fact.

Our destiny calls to us, and it would be foolish to deny or resist it, for to do so will cause turmoil in our consciousness and heart and go against the wishes of our soul. We might be dreaming and waiting for destiny to actually come calling upon us, but we might sit waiting forever, for destiny doesn't visit us; we must go searching for it or realise we are already in it.

We cannot wait for the perfect timing or location or resources to be in place before we begin our journey; our path commences here and now, and we must make every step count towards our target. We can never be sure how long we have left on Earth to fulfil our mission, and the worst thing would be to leave the planet without having made at least some progress towards it.

So, it's essential that we prioritise our mission and our path to godhood. All else in our human life is a supporting act for these starring roles. We cannot make excuses and pretend we don't have time for dreams or destiny, and choose other goals to fill up our life. The reason for our existence on Earth is to fulfil our destiny.

The mission itself

What exactly is our destiny or mission? Our only true mission, apart from getting to godhood, is to add value to our own evolution and that of humankind. It gives us purpose and direction and a meaning to our life, and is used as our training ground on this planet for us to learn our required lessons. If we have no sense of purpose, we tend to feel lost or depressed. Our destiny is the future part of us that we must become.

Do we always know what our destiny or mission is? We might think that it's just to bathe in a pool of love and that this will see us right, for we are certainly here on Earth to radiate love like a star! But we have certain activities to complete, goals to aim for—and we are given clues.

The clues lie in our dreams; not our night dreams, although sometimes our destiny can be revealed here too, but in the dreams we have deep in our heart, dreams that we may be ardently following, or which perhaps lie secret and still, afraid to breathe in case they might become a reality. Many humans are scared of their potential, and of whom they might become if they dared to stir their dreams and make them come true.

Our soul may have already laid out the line of breadcrumbs for us, or even a row of lights to show us the way, but we can sometimes be very stubborn about following these, for who knows where they might lead to or what kind of role we might find ourselves playing? And so, many people pretend to not know their destiny, and prefer to hide their heads in the sand and stay in their own little mundane world which is safe and familiar and doesn't require much of them.

It is safe to say that our destiny is never a straight path. It is capricious, and zigzags and detours and takes us in every direction, into the depths as well as into the heavens. Actually, depth is the same as height in the cosmos; the deeper we go into our consciousness to find our Source, the higher we go in vibrational level. There is no north or south in space, no up or down. It is like travelling in a southward direction around our planet; if we kept on going in that same direction we would eventually come to the North Pole! All is circuitous in this universe, like the symbol of the snake eating its own tail, the ouroboros.

The journey in this lifetime that takes us towards our fate will consist of many phases, roles, milestones, and crossroads. We will need to be adaptable and unafraid. There will be challenges and obstacles galore, and we will often be thrown off course and lose our way and must seek the path once again. We can't ignore or hide from these challenges but must face up to them.

How do we find our way in an unknown world? We tend to use a map, or get directions from someone, or use a GPS navigation system. The map for our destiny is held by our soul who works with us either directly or through our intuition.

Our soul is ever our guide, companion, and protector, and all we need to do is ask them for directions (and how many of us have problems with asking even humans for directions!) Our spirit partner has all the answers, and always knows our itinerary and which road to take at the crossroads, or which is the next station for us to board our metaphorical train, or get off one. (Human modes of transport are often used as symbolism for our spiritual journey, and will frequently occur in our night dreams.) So, all we need to do is ask our soul, "Where am I and what do I need to do next?"

Our soul is our future self, and they want only for us to successfully complete our journey and mission, so it pays to heed them. They will make us learn our lessons along the way, for sure, but they actually would prefer it if we enjoyed our journey. Our soul and the gods want us to ride our rollercoaster to freedom with speed and fun, and so they will also create many magical moments for us, and keep shining the holy grail like a compass for us to follow. They can't walk our journey for us, but they will always be there beside us, holding the lantern to light our way. There is no one more delighted than our soul when we cross the finish line to our destination.

The consciousness of our soul is always dreaming, and these dreams become the targets of our mission and the stuff of our destiny, and we are always being moved on by our higher self to meet these goals. We can ask our soul for details of their dreams, and this can be very motivating (and sometimes scary!)

Our physical body is the only way through which our soul can get its dreams manifested, so we need to listen well, follow our intuition and the signs, and act upon instructions and be part of the team, or chaos will ensue. Although we ourselves may be very hazy about our destiny, our soul knows very clearly what they wish to achieve in this lifetime, and even in the days ahead. Our soul's clearer mind and sight always sees the bigger picture and can focus on this without being distracted by our routine activities on Earth, and they will want to share their aspirations with us. It is their sole (soul) purpose to get us on track to completing our destiny, and they will always be looking to guide us, and if necessary, to apply pressure on us to go in the right direction.

One of the prominent themes of this book has been that we need to work hand-in-hand with our soul for maximum benefit to ourselves. In chapter 3 and several other chapters, the partnership with our spirit self and soul has been emphasised and promoted, and this relationship is never more important than when interpreting and following the steps to our destiny. If we don't maintain communications with our soul on a regular basis, sharing like-minded ambitions and strategies, then we will end up going astray and falling foul of our mission.

Some readers may be feeling concerned at this point if they don't yet manage to hear or connect with their soul on these matters. Re-reading chapter 12 on how to connect with our soul may be of some help. However, as soon as we ask our soul to assist us with knowing our destiny or our plan, the signs will begin to appear and we just need to be very aware to catch them and take note of them, and more importantly, to take action on them. There is nothing more perplexing to our soul than for us to ignore their messages.

If we don't understand the communiqués, then all we need to do is ask for more understanding and to be shown in different ways. Our soul will be pleased to offer us more information. But realise that it may come in forms we are not expecting, such as in a movie (this is my own soul's favourite way of getting complex ideas and points over to me), or in something a friend says to us (acting unwittingly as a messenger). If we stay open to receiving an answer, it will come in some helpful way at a time that is always right for us.

It is not only our soul who gives us signs and clues for our destiny, but the gods and angels can be involved too. I'm very fortunate because I'm able to channel the gods directly and receive much information and guidance from them that way, but even then they don't make it especially easy for me and they can be cryptic or employ double meanings, for they understand that deciphering and chasing a hidden treasure map is a whole lot more exciting than merely following directions from some droning voice on a GPS navigation system, and we learn so much more that way.

No matter what specific field our destiny plays out in, our soul is teaching us how to open our hearts and minds and bring more love and harmony into our lives. If we allow it, our spiritual partner will show us new roads, perspectives, and dimensions, more wonders than we could ever have imagined, and even miracles. As we complete the tasks and goals set by our soul, we will progress up our Ribbon of Consciousness, merging with soul after soul until we achieve our ultimate target of entering the gods' dimension.

Although we have our own goals to complete to get to godhood and to achieve our own personal mission or missions, we do also need to keep in mind that we are part of a greater journey amongst mankind, and that along with developing ourself we will need to help develop humanity too. It's not enough just to admire the sterling work that others perform to improve our civilisation. We ourselves must produce a bountiful body of work too.

So, we need to be prepared to share our efforts, love, and maybe resources along those lines. It's not necessary to think we have to find the cure for cancer, or eliminate global poverty, or be the first person to land on Mars. Good on us if we have developed the desire and wherewithal to do this! But we will be able to offer some kind of service that befits our lifestyle and abilities. Even a quadriplegic person has the use of a consciousness that can send out thoughts and energies to heal and improve the world.

One of my older students once told me that she was distressed when she passed motorists on the road who had broken down, as she felt unable to help them. I told her that she doesn't need to stop and get out of her car and offer practical assistance. She can easily ask her soul or the gods and angels to help that unfortunate person in whatever manner is most beneficial to them, and know and believe that the message has gone out there on the universe's network and aid will be forthcoming.

We will be encouraged to share with others the wisdom we gain from our life so that they might benefit, and hence even a reformed criminal could be achieving their mission if they find themselves lecturing to prison inmates on a better way to conduct their lives. As long as we are adding value to our society and improving people's consciousness and increasing the love in their hearts, then this is a perfectly acceptable contribution to our destiny.

So, we need to ponder deeply on how we can donate our time, wisdom, resources, and love, and get out there and be involved. Even spreading smiles around our neighbourhood is gaining us kudos in Heaven!

However, it would be wrong to devote all our time and efforts to helping humanity and not work on ourselves. We often see this with passionate activists or 'do-gooders', whose intentions are worthy but whose hearts are too often filled with rage and righteousness and plenty of not-love. Once we are mostly clean and clear and free of triggers and closer to godhood, we will be much more able to assist in changing this human world and move it onto its correct trajectory. Therefore, it's important that we don't follow one track to the exclusion of the other, but to keep a balance between personal transformation and helping to evolve the nature of humankind and this planet.

We may have just one mission in our entire lifetime or several missions, even overlapping missions. Our destiny may be a continuation of an uncompleted mission from a previous lifetime, or this may be new ground for us to tread and learn new skills and traits of consciousness.

Am I already on a mission? Am I on track?

We may be asking ourselves if we are already on our correct mission and heading towards our true destiny? How do we know if we are on track?

The first thing to do would be to ask our soul if the dreams we are following are the same dreams that our soul has designed for us? Are we in the right place at the right time with the right people? Is our goal the right one for us, or do we need to change our trajectory? We do need to keep checking if we are on the correct road because if we are even a little off the mark we will fail in our aims.

This was made obvious to me many years ago by a Master who had the title of Great Divine Director. He showed me a billiards table set up with all the balls, and he demonstrated that if he hit the ball cleanly and squarely in its centre, it would drop down into the desired pocket. But if he was a mere one degree off centre, then the ball ricocheted off the pocket and missed its target.

We humans generally desire to follow a path in life which makes us feel blessed. We search for the right partner and for love. We look for enjoyment and satisfaction in the things that we do, and hope we can find a job, career, or hobby that gives us a sense of fulfilment and pride.

Our bodies act as barometers. If we are situated on, or close to, our destined path, then we will feel buoyant, strong, capable, and on purpose, closer to godhood. The road is generally without too many bumps and obstacles, and even these we will take in our stride. As we move into alignment with our mission, we feel harmonious and flooded with joy and energy to pursue it. We will find ourselves in the right place, at the right time, with the right people, because when we are clicked into the correct cogwheel for our purpose, the universe fully supports us and helps things to glide along. If we are missing the mark, we will feel out-of-sorts, disharmonious, and discontented until such time as we get back on track again, or begin the quest to find our rightful destiny.

So, we need to feel into our heart on this question and use it as a compass. It just never feels right if we are on the wrong road. We might be suppressing a sense of unease, telling ourselves that life is never perfect, and we force ourselves to strive onwards and accept the way it is. But if the road is jarring and upsets and weakens us, is this really the true road for us?

It pays to understand the difference between being challenged and being on the wrong road. Our path throughout life will be littered with challenges, but we should question whether implacable obstacles are merely challenges we must face, or are they signalling to us we might be heading in the wrong direction altogether?

When we are on the correct path to achieving our mission, we feel strong, eager, and powerful to overcome all trials that beset us along the way because we have an innate feeling that this is the way for us to go. Our dream carries us through all turmoil and upheavals. When we pursue an inappropriate dream, we find we are not so determined to push through to win, and we become half-hearted and abandon our cause all too quickly. If we can't visualise getting to the goal, then perhaps it's because this is not the right goal for us.

However, all this becomes complicated when we take into account the fact that the goal may be right for us but we ourselves have blockages or resistance to carrying out this particular mission. If we haven't progressed along our path, then we can be sure that our consciousness is stymieing us in some way. In the next chapter, we look at reasons we might feel stuck or lost on the road to our destiny.

We can also get confused about our proper path if our soul chooses to direct us down a branch line. This occurs when we are to gain experience in various skills or activities that seem to be ancillary to our main destiny (but in fact will support it), and this can make us feel as if we are off the beaten track.

It can also be the way our soul trains us to realise what we desire and don't desire as our destiny, for often we don't actually know where our preferences lie. So, we will be taken through the maze, trying one avenue after another until we find the one that captures our attention and heartstrings. Therefore, we should try not to lock ourselves onto only one track, as the universe will sometimes want to change the points and divert us down a side line. We should just try to enjoy the ride and new adventure.

However, if we have shunted into a siding in order to protect ourselves from having to go out into the world to do our mission, then we might find ourselves rusting up, with the weeds growing around our wheels, and we end up dying there. Certainly, if we insist on hiding from our destiny, and our soul can see no way of redeeming us, then we will indeed be called to go Home, as we are serving no useful purpose upon Earth.

At times we can also feel as if we are falling off track when we find ourselves coming to the end of a mission and it's time for a new cycle of learning or activity. Even though we may have been successful in this phase of our undertaking, our familiar world begins to fall apart as we are made ready for the next chapter of our existence.

Being unaware of your mission

There are always those who may not feel any urges towards a destiny at all; this happens when they are separated from their higher consciousness and have no awareness yet of their spiritual path. Their lower human consciousness continues to live in its own limited, small world, and there is no desire to improve themselves or the lot of humanity. There will often be a background sadness and sense of unfulfillment because they know they are not on their right track and that they have no usefulness upon this planet. It will be up to their soul to determine if this person has any chance of opening up to their destiny and discovering a purpose, and if not, this consciousness will be moved on, back to the dimension of spirit.

In chapter 18 we discussed the need for having a purpose to our lives, and what happens if we deny our destiny. In chapter 20 we also covered how being off track with our destiny can have a detrimental effect on our emotional and mental health.

Stepping into your mission

Fortunately, there are plenty of people who are open to their destiny. Some are single-minded, even from childhood, and know exactly what they want to go after. Others just feel a tug on their hearts and a pulling towards their mission as if magnetised. Often, they have no idea why they want to do a particular thing, or pursue a certain course, or go visit a special place, or connect with a specific individual or organisation, but, as if hypnotised, they find themselves doing it anyway. It is their soul guiding them, and they are listening to their intuition.

As we pluck up our courage, believe in our dream and begin to follow it, our path is revealed to us more clearly and the universe kicks in with supportive people, events, and resources. We are encouraged to take as much space as we desire and can cope with, and all that is required is provided along the way, sometimes in very magical ways.

I experienced this when I was self-publishing my very first book. In those days, before print-on-demand and e-books, it cost a great deal of money to publish and print a run of books. I was feeling the pinch financially but was determined to spend every last penny I had to see my dream come true. A week after I celebrated my book launch, I received a surprise bonus in my day job in IT, which exactly matched the amount I had had to pay out for my book.☺ Note that I made the commitment and sacrifice *before* the universe kicked in with compensatory resources!

It may seem at times that we are going it all alone in a hostile world, trying our best to get our work done and stay on track. The spirit world is always just a whisper away, and our soul is monitoring our mission 24/7 and has access to gods and angels at all times to help us. They are excited to see us play our role and make a difference. If we give our all and go for gold, then rewards will come.

Often, we find that we embark upon our mission at a salient point in our life aligned with our astrology. The universe works in cycles, and these were described in detail in chapter 9. At the end of a cycle, it is time to wrap things up and review the success or failure of that phase. Then we begin to select our new path and start to seed opportunities for the future.

The North Node of the Moon cycle of 18-19 years, and the 28-year cycle of Saturn, and their half and quarter cycles, are particularly pertinent to our destiny, although the position of the other outer planets Jupiter, Chiron, Uranus, Neptune, and Pluto are also key.

The machinery of the unseen dimensions plays out on a grand scale, and underneath us the vibrations are constantly changing and nothing ever stands still. There are no brakes to the universe, and we can't stop its progress and hop off and take a hiatus. We need to align ourself with its cogwheels so that we are ready to jump on board when the one with our name on it arrives at our station.

As Chiron says, we need to be a video taking action, not a snapshot frozen to the spot. We never know the promise of any moment, so we need to appreciate the energies being stirred up, which will conjure up new desires and notions, and open ourselves to adventure and opportunity, and make space for growth and new encounters as we slide towards our destiny. There is no better sense of joy and anticipation than when we see a new door ahead of us and we are open to all the potential that lies beyond it.

Where to find your destiny

Some people might manage to gain a glimpse of their destiny, and that tiny peek remains with them for a long time like a teaser to the holy grail, and they keep remembering it in the back of their consciousness, but they don't quite know what to do about it. Chiron suggests they throw open the doors to their hearts and minds to get a grander view. But it's no coincidence they have the dreams they do—they are a call to destiny.

But if we truly don't have any notion about our destiny, or what our options might be, then it's time to get dreaming, for then paths may begin to open up, and ways and ideas shown to us. And it's never too late to start. Our soul may be waiting for us to make the first move, for us to express a wish to understand our mission in this lifetime.

What motivates our soul is also what motivates us, and we will have similar goals, but our soul will also be interested to see what kinds of things we ourselves desire and what gets us excited, and they will try to weave these preferences into the plan, for our soul is not a tyrant but our best friend and wants for us to enjoy ourselves along the way, even while working hard to complete our life's assignment.

So, fearlessly, we need to go into the Dark World of conception and begin to dream our dreams, taking our time and letting the excitement build. What we dream here is a pointer to our destiny, out-picturing the desire of, not only ourselves but also our soul, so we need to pursue these clues.

- ❖ What is it that we would most love to do in this lifetime to bring about joy and love in our own lives and in the lives of others?
- ❖ Who do we want to be?
- ❖ What magic do we want to bring into our life?

The ultimate dream, of course, is to imagine ourselves in the New World or the higher dimensions. Our dreams don't need to be world-changing or a momentous *tour de force*, but they do need to cause our heart to fire up, enough to sweep away any hurdles we may encounter later. We all have talents we can offer, no matter how small or seemingly insignificant, and we are expected just to give of our personal best. We merely need to haul our dream out of hiding, put it on a pedestal and admire it, then step into that dream and create a whole world around it with all our senses.

As children we were very adept at doing this, dreaming of the excitement of summer holidays, or a play date with a friend, or a school field outing, or our first trip to the beach or to see snow. When last did we burst with this kind of enthusiasm or anticipation?

And so, we need to set up and sow in the spring, the meadows that we dream of walking through in summer, opening our hearts to the expanding sunshine and visualising the colours and shapes of what we will be reaping. It would be a shame to leave our garden of dreams as just a patch of mud.

The next step is to make a plan to manifest those dreams, and here we get to be creative, for our destiny does not come with detailed written instructions. In chapter 17 we described the steps for manifesting, and these should now be followed. We can begin by viewing all our options, and with the help of our soul, choose the ones that will be most suitable for us at this time for our present circumstances. For we do have some say as a human in the way our destiny is to play out, yet we need to remember that our soul is the manager here and we need to adhere to their guidance and their divine plan and cooperate with them.

This plan for our destiny is not carved in stone but needs to be very flexible in order to cope with the varying energies affecting us each day and our ever-evolving consciousness. Last year's plan will probably not fit us, for many changes will have taken place in our consciousness since then, and we might even have evolved to a whole new level of being. Therefore, our plans should be constantly monitored and regularly discussed with our soul to ensure we are still on track for our goals.

Once we have scripted out our preferred dreams in some detail, then it is time to make tracks towards them, for we can't just magic things into being; we must put in effort to manifest them and then inch ourselves towards them. Dreams are like clouds; they won't touch down in our field, we have to go up towards them. Chiron tells us, tongue-in-cheek, that unmanifested dreams floating around the planet are the cause of all the cloudiness!

Now we need to be determined to make these dreams come true, to believe in them, connect with them and own them, seeding them into our consciousness, nurturing them into being with love and action, and meeting with the universe's synch points. Our soul will guide us as to whether our dreams are valid or not. Often, we are allowed to follow unsuitable paths just so we know in future what is correct for us and what is not. There is nothing like learning through experience!

Chapter 25 – Destiny continued

Feeling stuck or lost regarding our destiny or mission

One of the most common problems concerning our destiny or mission is feeling stuck or lost. Below are many reasons why this could occur. We have already described many of these issues in previous chapters, so, where appropriate, I have given references to these instead of repeating the narrative. In all the following cases, we can use the Toolbox of our Consciousness to overcome our challenges and move forward on the right road.

a) Fears and blockages

Nothing prevents us pursuing our destiny more than fear. Some of the things we might be afraid of include:

- Change—to ourselves, family, home, job, finances, social circle, our world
- Having to make an effort to achieve our potential
- Success or fame, and the responsibilities it brings
- Failure
- Criticism or disparagement
- The unknown and what might be waiting for us
- Not being physically, emotionally, or mentally able to cope

If our consciousness had no fears, we would step forward onto our path without any hesitation or wariness. Do we imagine that the bold pioneers and adventurers of old, like Marco Polo, Joan of Arc, or Christopher Columbus, and more recent ones like Marie Curie, Neil Armstrong, Richard Branson, or Oprah Winfrey, never had a moment of fear as they delved into the unknown worlds before them? All of us face our fears along the road to our destiny, whether it's landing on an unmapped continent or on a moon, exploring mysterious chemical elements, or establishing a business empire against all odds.

Every day and in every way, people are being challenged to venture past their limitations and past the glass ceilings and impediments the world puts in their way, to create something they have never experienced before. Sometimes, mankind has never experienced it either.

Sometimes we can't even base our decision to go forward or not on any available facts, and then we must choose whether to just leap off the cliff into the unknown and pray that we will land somewhere soft and to our liking, or stay stuck where we are. Successful people often state they hadn't foreseen all the hurdles and barriers along their path, but they had just fearlessly and blindly moved forward.

A case in point is the inspirational movie *Eddie the Eagle*, a true story based on the struggles of a young English man whose dream was to participate as a ski jumper in the Winter Olympics. He had to fight a childhood physical disability, disbelieving parents, the social class system, lack of finances and training facilities, and the fact there was no British Olympic team for his event. His belief in himself and his sheer persistence and gutsiness found him breaking records at the Calgary Winter Olympics in 1988 and becoming the darling of the world for his amazing achievements. The movie ends with a quote from the founder of the modern Olympic Games, Pierre de Coubertin, who stated in 1896, "The important thing in life is not the triumph but the struggle."

There will probably always be some kind of fear in our consciousness, so all we can do is try to mitigate it to the greatest extent possible and then take a deep breath and put our best foot forward. If we can't get started, or we have stalled, this means we need to investigate our fears and blockages. Why are we fearing conjuring up our dreams or going after them? They can be difficult to hold steady in our consciousness and may seem unreachable, but is that a reason to ditch them? Re-reading chapters 19-22 on healing and letting go can help to identify our issues and how to overcome them.

We need to let go our core segments of fear and resistance, shaking out all our old past experiences and unhelpful programmed beliefs that are getting in the way of our destiny. Whatever we hold as thoughts and feelings in our consciousness is what will play out as our destiny, forcing us down certain, maybe undesirable, tracks and also into ruts. Therefore, we need to reprogram ourselves to out-picture where we would truly like to head for.

We also need to get all our lower personas on board with our goals, and work with our soul as part of a team, visualising the same outcome and taking steps to manifest our dreams. If we still can't picture our future and destiny, then it could help to re-read chapter 17 on manifesting.

Sometimes we might fear that our body isn't up to the task at hand. We might feel we are too old or ill or frail or disabled. Is this just an excuse? There is still plenty we can accomplish through our consciousness alone, right up until the moment we take our last breath. Our consciousness is a powerful tool for transformation and healing, and we need to remember this. Often as we age, we tend to become more cautious, made wary from life's lessons. We hold back in case we get hurt, and so we forget to dance and laugh. But whatever our age or condition, we shouldn't forget to keep pursuing our dreams.

b) Human will versus divine will. No connection to soul

Another important roadblock to following our destiny is when we allow our human will to take control over divine will. We have learnt that our mission is also the dream of our soul, so it benefits us to go in that direction and not in the opposite one, for that will just tear us apart. If we are at odds with our soul and resisting their guidance, pedalling against the flow leaves us with little energy to deal with the rest of our life. Our divine higher self is not our enemy but our best friend, and everything they do for us is only to support our evolution. Perhaps our soul is pushing us beyond our own perceived limitations, knowing better than we ourselves just what we are capable of.

It might be asked if we have any option in following our soul's choice of destiny for us? What if we have different goals from that of our higher self? Well, that is the difference between following human will or divine will. We do have free will here, but will it be to our detriment? If we opt to follow our human will, then our soul and spirit will not be on board, and we will suffer from a lack of support and guidance that would flow to us otherwise. That said, it is always possible to negotiate with our soul; they will always listen and try to compromise.

Our soul is most helpful in directing us to our rightful destiny and keeping us on track. If we are confused or lost, our soul will appear in our darkness and light the way for us again. They can ensure that our dreams are well-founded, that our plans to manifest them are well-structured, and that we arrive at the station at the appropriate time to catch the universe's cycle of energies that will best support us. With deep perception, our soul sees our issues and blockages that keep us stuck or lost, and they can assist us to let go and move forward.

It has to be said, though, there are times when our soul will keep us in the dark regarding our destiny. This might happen if we are the type of person who doesn't like change too much, and who tends to put up resistance when it is introduced. So, our soul might choose to spring the change on us, rather than warn us and have to put up with a period of resistance or moaning from us. (I speak from experience!)

It can also happen if our destiny is too difficult to imagine, or if it requires us to be mightily surprised; for instance, suddenly meeting the soul mate of our dreams. We need to trust our soul's intentions, that they do what is right for us in the circumstances.

If our human ego, through our lower personas, insists on taking control and decreeing our destiny and route through life, then we will be pretty much lost, in all senses of the word. We may find some success in the material world, but if this was not our appointed destiny, it will count for naught when we return to the spiritual world, as we needs must one day.

When we lack faith in a divine world, and don't believe in our soul or even in our own dreams, then we are choosing a very hard road through life, battling it out alone, and denying all the love, support, and resources that can flow to us from the unseen universe.

Re-reading chapter 13 on the benefits of connecting with the universe, can be helpful here.

c) Lack skills, resources, confidence, courage

Sometimes our mission will seem beyond our pay grade, requiring us to have talents we don't think we are endowed with, or finances or connections we don't possess, or lacking the courage and confidence to carry it out. If everyone in history had waited until all the keys were in the right slots, then it's probable that nothing would ever have got done or been created.

This is where we need to be our own hero, and push ourselves forward with grit and determination. It's always going to be scary to tread beyond our current boundaries, but this is the way we evolve and grow. Holding our dream target in front of our noses will assist with motivation, and so will raising our vibrations to a higher level, but ultimately we have to feel into our strengths and trust ourselves and our soul, and not dwell on negative projections for our future.

If we knew without any shadow of a doubt that we were moving onto a path that was leading us to joy, love, and fulfilment, and a date with a great destiny, then we would surely be running there. But it is the doubt and fear that holds us back each time. Re-reading chapter 18, *Creating a better you*, would be of some assistance here.

d) Destiny too big, too arrogant

On the other hand, rather than lacking confidence, one of our problems could be that we have bitten off more than we can chew with our sense of destiny. Are our dreams too big, too grand, too unwieldy, or requiring the support of too many other people? Certainly, some folks have managed to pull this off, creating empires in business and on land. But it necessitates an enormous belief in self to establish something like this, and maybe we should be looking to start off with something more manageable and achievable?

However, we need to be wary of not going the other way and keeping ourselves so small as to be barely discernible in the world. When I was starting out on my new venture into spiritual teaching many years ago, I told a friend I wanted to book the Convention Centre in the city to hold my first conference. She stared at me in alarm and advised me to begin with something a bit smaller like the local hall. But I wouldn't be swayed, and did end up booking the Convention Centre, albeit just a smaller ancillary room and not the main venue. It was a big risk but actually paid off, and helped to launch my career more quickly than if I had just given a presentation to a local audience of a handful of people.

If we have had a past life where we have been a big note of some kind, we may still have lingering visions of greatness in our consciousness and may wish to re-emulate this starring role. It's not a given that in each lifetime we are meant for fame or fortune. We may be learning to eat humble pie for a start! So, we need to rein in our ego and follow the path that is right for us this time around.

Speaking of humility, we also need to admit when we are lost and have no idea and no clue as to where to find our destiny. At the crossroads, we can certainly try out all the roads in every direction to understand which suits us best, or we can try asking our soul or the gods for their advice on which track to take. I've found the latter is a much quicker and easier route!

e) Focused on past and not the future

Our destiny lies in our future, not in our past, therefore we need to stop looking backwards and start to search and move in a forward direction. Some people get very caught up with history, and especially their own history. It can have some merit at times to know where we have been and how we got to be where we are now, but our current or future mission is where our focus needs to be (unless our mission is, in fact, to be an historian or archaeologist!) It is this that we must prepare for and carry out.

Certainly, it is useful to utilise any talents from past lives where we may have been successful, but make them underpin our current mission as foundation stones and not the entire new edifice. We have reincarnated to build something new and to add value, not to reinvent what has come before.

While memories can be a lovely thing and be duly appreciated, it doesn't benefit us to dwell on our past dark natures or experiences and stay stuck in that mindset or be unable to forgive ourselves or others. Most of us will have evolved to a certain extent since the past played out, and it is the current energies that we need to give our attention to.

We could also be hanging onto the past because it is a way of resisting going forward into the future. Re-reading chapters 19-22, dealing with letting go techniques, can help us here.

f) Missing signs or clues

In Chapter 15 we described the various ways that our soul and the gods can communicate with us using symbols, signs, or images. If we miss these signs and clues to our destiny, or we misinterpret them, then we are likely to get lost or not understand which way we should be heading. Therefore, we need to be very aware of our surroundings and the hidden meanings that might lie waiting for us, or in what people say to us, or we might find ourselves off track or going on roundabout, scenic detours.

This cryptic way of communicating our destiny to us is the premier tool that the hidden dimensions use to guide us through life. Rarely are we given explicit instructions or directions, so we shouldn't be waiting for these like Moses receiving the Ten Commandments. Our destiny is like a search for the holy grail or the Ark of the Covenant—it is a treasure hunt that slowly unfolds for us as we decipher the clues, and each traveller's map is highly customised and meaningful only to that person.

g) Timing and cycles – missing your slot, not being ready

Even though time does not exist in the higher dimensions and is only an earthly physical dimension concept, the art of timing is immensely important to the universe. It runs on cycles, and cycles within cycles, and if we are too late or too early for our destiny, we will miss our allotted slot where everything was designed to come together for us. It may be a long time before the cogwheels turn in our direction again, and maybe never again in this lifetime.

Therefore, when doors open for us and opportunities are presented, we shouldn't procrastinate over long but jump on board quickly.

The cogwheels keep on turning, with us or without us, and the universe waits for no one. There is nothing so painful for the gods than to see someone weeping because they have missed their date with destiny, and there is nothing the gods can do about it until the wheels pass a further point where the person has another chance to join the bandwagon. If we are feeling stuck, it could be because we are having to tread water until the cogwheels come around again.

This is the reason why I find astrology so useful, for it points out many of the universe's cycles, and our consciousness can then move with these tides of energies, and feel into the flow instead of fighting against the current. In chapter 9 these astrology cycles are described in detail.

It often happens that the opportunity comes up for us to evolve to the next level of our mission, but we are not ready for it, or believe ourselves not to be ready. We need to understand why we have missed the boat, and get ourselves more prepared or instilled with more confidence. We certainly cannot keep ourselves chained to the same spot and hope we can prevent changes happening in our life. The universe is eternally on the move, and we are forever in its slipstream.

It can also happen that we pitch up too early for our mission, believing ourselves to be more evolved and suitable than we really are. Then we will feel stuck, as if nothing is happening for us. Our soul monitors the health of our mission at all times and gauges whether or not we are worthy to move on. If we are still not meeting our soul's criteria, then we will need to stay where we are and mature our consciousness to a satisfactory level before the next phase of our mission, or an entirely new mission, is revealed to us.

If we are working with our soul and we keep checking in to see if we are on track and aligned with our destination and schedule, then we will find ourselves waiting at the right stop at the right time for us to begin our new journey.

h) Not following steps to manifest properly

One of the most fundamental problems with not being able to create the destiny of our dreams is that we are not observing the steps for manifesting them properly. We might be dreaming but not following through with action, or we may have forgotten that everything in the physical world first needs to be birthed or conceptualised in the Dark World. Re-reading Chapter 17 on manifestation may help.

If there is no dream to spur us on, then there will be no destiny, or not one designed by us or our own soul. We will be at the mercy of everyone else's dreams. So, we mustn't be afraid to dwell on our dreams and play 'let's pretend' and act out our dreams in the Creation Realm, for it is only then that they can become manifest on Earth. When we play around with our dreams in this way, our consciousness comes up with plenty more ideas for us, and can lift us out of our stuckness or show us ways to go forward that we could never have visualised before.

i) Not using Toolbox of Consciousness

One of our greatest tools of consciousness is learning to use the gift of our Third Eye, our psychic ability that connects us with our soul and the higher dimensions. This is essential if we are to walk the right road to our destiny and work on our correct mission. If we don't use our intuition, or the spiritual communication facilities innate in our consciousness, to receive useful directions, instructions, and information for the way ahead, then we will often find ourselves lost or stuck in life, and certainly discontented and dissatisfied with the way things are.

Visualising the yellow jewel of consciousness that Chiron describes as filled with the potential of star qualities (see chapter 22), is an excellent meditation if we feel stuck regarding our destiny, filling ourselves with the energies of the sun and stars, opening our heart to the goldenness of the universe and to all the love that dwells there. If we are full of love then we cannot be not-love, and therefore everything in that moment is love and every decision we take will be based in love too, and the road before us can only be the right road to our destiny.

Throughout Part Two of this book, we have learnt about the tools of consciousness, understanding how to use our consciousness to live a better life and create it to our own design and that of our soul. We have looked at raising our vibrations; how to connect with the unseen beings of the universe; how to create and manifest in the Dark World and the Light World; how to work on ourselves to improve who we are; how to heal ourselves and others, and techniques for letting go our darker aspects and lower personas; how to have harmonious relationships and find forgiveness; and finally in this chapter, how to create a destiny that makes our heart sing and evolves our soul.

Ditching your mission

What happens to those who fail to find their destiny, or who start down the road but then decide to bail out? Well, they won't be going to the chopping block, but in some ways they will find themselves losing their head, or at least their mind.

While we did sign a contract with our soul before this incarnation that we would carry out a certain mission and pursue a certain destiny, this is not indentureship written in blood where we are reprimanded for not completing our tasks. Yes, we do have responsibilities to our soul, but if we deny our duty, it is ourself that we are letting down and our evolution towards godhood, and our soul would be more than sorrowful that this lifetime was wasted and they cannot get their dreams manifested through us.

Many people drop their dreams, citing them as too difficult to go after, or that they themselves are too elderly, or that nothing is changing for them, or that there should be greater rewards that aren't forthcoming. And so they down tools. Some reckon their dreams are just a fantasy. Are these excuses so they don't need to make the required effort?

Others may have started down the track, only to find failure or relentless obstacles, and they have thrown in the towel and given up. They may blame circumstances, but, as we have learnt, it is never smooth sailing in manifesting our dreams. If we give up too easily and let our dreams turn to dust, we will forever feel guilty and unfulfilled, and always wonder what might have been.

Some people allow their lower personas to get the better of them and find themselves rebelling against doing the work required of them, citing that they feel like a puppet of the gods and are merely being used.

Whatever the reason, reneging on our mission will see us miserable and ashamed, or even tormented. We may find we lose all the status and privileges we had worked so hard to gain on our journey towards godhood, and our inner conflict will see us swimming in not-love.

If our plans are in tatters, we can mend them with our consciousness and our determination to rise up and meet our purpose in life. If necessary, our soul can change the points for us and lead us down other more suitable tracks. But it is we ourselves who must find the wherewithal to get up off the floor and try again.

If we are dead set against understanding our purpose and following the destiny designed for us by our soul, then we will be reluctantly called Home, since the purpose for us being on Earth is to make tracks towards our destiny and to evolve our consciousness along the way. Here we will get to reflect on our life and the decisions we chose to make, and we might feel regret and sorrow.

How to stay on track

What are the best ways to stay on track in playing out our destiny and completing our mission? This is so important that Chiron dedicated an entire chapter to this topic and mentioned it throughout his book.

- Know the details of your dream and destiny, or at least the next steps you need to take.
- Imprint your dream on your mind and keep this at the forefront. If it helps, create a vision board.
- Be clear about where you are heading to, so that you realise when you are off track. Have a plan; an itinerary, route, schedule, and destination for your goal.
- Work with your soul and keep in contact daily, sharing expectations, information, issues, and support. Ask them what is needed to be on track and on time.
- Keep your heart open and let your consciousness fly and explore.
- Keep motivated by dreaming your dreams. Why do you have these particular dreams and not others?

- Be enthusiastic about your journey. Buy a ticket, board the train with your soul. Appreciate the landscape and be open to new experiences and novel ideas.
- Expect the best in all situations and anticipate good outcomes for your future, knowing that magic and miracles can happen in any moment. Run towards your assignation with destiny.
- Become more aware of what is going on in your consciousness, controlling negativity, fears, or resistance, and steering yourself at all times towards your dreams. Let go of doubts and be determined. Clear your heart of all triggers.
- Daily check your vibrational level, and raise it if it is too low.
- Don't deviate, get side-tracked or distracted from your mission. There is much on Earth that can pull you away. Be one-pointed and move forward.
- Don't get caught up in the minutiae and details of everyday life, with things that don't serve your goal.
- Actively look for clues and signs, interpret them intelligently, and take action on them. Be alert to whether you are slipping off track—you will feel it in your bones.
- Don't dally on sidelines or procrastinate when opportunities arise or there is work you know needs to be done. Years can go by without progress, and how long do you have?
- Trains don't procrastinate in sidings. They have schedules to maintain and stations and destinations to get to, and so do you. Unhitch any anchors holding you back.
- Invest effort and meet all challenges. Never give up. Your destiny is a course of lessons, and you don't learn much if it's all too easy.
- Check your timing. Are you on schedule, too late, or too early? There is no time in Heaven, but the universe runs like clockwork. When it's time for something to happen, be there, ready and waiting. Interlock your wheels with the universe's cogwheels and be moved on.

- Schedule in rest days and holidays to keep healthy and balanced. At other times, don't put destiny on hold but keep on travelling. Think of life as a journey you might make on holiday, and enjoy it.
- Travel lightly. Take as little baggage as possible, and keep tossing out whatever isn't useful.
- Cultivate relationships on your journey, but never forget that your destiny is all important.
- Be aware of any night dreams where you miss a train, plane, car, boat, bus, or other connections. These are signs you are not meeting your schedule.
- If you get lost or stuck, use your tools of consciousness without delay to get back on track.
- Have a plan in case you fall off track so that you know how to get yourself up and running again quickly.
- If you have had a failure, try again and get further this time around.
- Don't hide from your soul or the gods but report for duty and act your part in the team.
- Be flexible and allow yourself to follow any new track, having no expectations and letting all unfold magically each day.
- Don't cling to old tracks when the points have moved you over to a new one.
- Don't face backwards to the past but face forwards towards your future and all that needs to be done.
- You won't know if you are on the right track if you keep your head down, so keep your head up, look straight ahead and all around you.
- Get yourself up to full power every day by uploading positive and inspirational thoughts to your consciousness.
- Your consciousness is equipped with exactly the correct attributes for your mission, but ask yourself if you could go bigger or if you need to downsize? Utilise your equipment wisely and maintain it regularly.

Completing a mission

There is nothing more wonderful than completing our mission or one phase of it. We need to ensure we tie up all loose ends so that we are ready and clear to embark on the next phase, which may be still on Earth or may be in Heaven. However, while it is of benefit to have all in order, we shouldn't take so much time on this that we miss our schedule for beginning our new chapter in life.

If we are going Home, or we are approaching that time in life where we know we will not be remaining on Earth for much longer, we need to attempt to wrap up our mission and hand the baton over to someone else, if that's necessary or possible. Leaving a legacy of some kind is a valuable thing to do, but we should ensure we don't leave furtive secrets still in the closet; we will merely rediscover these one day ourselves in a later life, much to our chagrin.

When we close the book on our destiny for this lifetime, or at least come to the end of a chapter for now, it is time to celebrate and sit back and review all that has transpired and what we have been able to offer to the world, to our own Ribbon of Consciousness, and to our soul's evolution. We can move on to the next stage with our heart fulfilled, and begin to dream new dreams.

Our destiny is a never-ending series of journeys, first as a human towards godhood, and then, as a god, back to our Source. With each journey, we discover more and more about the nature of our divine beingness, and the unseen universe begins to reveal itself to us through ever-widening doors. This is our true destiny, to know the universe, as consciousness, in all her miraculous glory.

PART THREE

THE FUTURE

Chapter 26 – Gods as role models

In Part Three, we take a look at how our future is shaping up. What will happen to humanity in the coming years and what can we look forward to, or work to avert, and how can we cooperate with the unseen beings in the higher dimensions to improve ourselves and our planet?

Gods will play an instrumental part in our evolution, so firstly let's examine what roles they are here to play, and what will be expected of us humans as we make our own way up the Ribbon of Consciousness.

Throughout Parts One and Two we have described what kind of being a god is and what they do, touching on their characteristics. Below is a summary of the traits of consciousness of an ideal god who is incarnated on Earth in human form, as this is the role model we are trying to emulate as we move towards and into godhood.

Bear in mind that no god on Earth is perfect, as they too are still journeying towards a pure state of being which they will achieve only once they get to creator god level.

Traits of a god on Earth in human form

A god on Earth in human physical form:

- Acts in a godly manner, incorporating the traits of a god in their consciousness and leaving behind the traits of a human. Chooses to live in a higher world of love, even while walking upon this planet
- Understands the serious responsibility of walking in the shoes of a god
- Loves themselves, knowing they were created by gods

- Experiences themselves as the god they came here to be, and sparkles in their godhood
- Cares for their heart and body, accepting they are now divine
- Has love for everyone and everything in the universe
- Has an open heart and mind, and shares their love and wisdom with the world
- Loves unconditionally, always showing mercy, forgiveness, and compassion
- Is aware of the energies around them and within themselves at all times
- Has a consciousness that is awake, agile, lively, and responsive, and can deal with many tasks or issues at once
- Manages all the personas and issues of their Ribbon of Consciousness like a business or a school, taking all into consideration
- Realises that by managing their own consciousness, they are in a better place to understand the consciousnesses of others
- Believes in themselves as a god and the good they can do, and doesn't sell themselves short
- Is not falsely humble, and their heart is filled with their victory of being a god and the challenging journey it took to get here. Realises that saving themselves has developed admirable traits within them
- Accepts they are limited by their human bodies, but utilises the magical power of their consciousness to the fullest extent to make up for it
- Is constantly aware they are not just human but also spirit and the whole Ribbon of Consciousness, and although they carry out everyday human tasks, their consciousness is anything but mundane

Fun and positive aspects

A god on Earth in human physical form:

- Believes in dancing along their path with joy and fun and sparkle in their heart, but remains temperate and in balance
- Is in love with life at all times, and enjoys the rollercoaster ride. Places love and light at the heart of every thought, feeling, and event, and lets their day be bright and sunny

- Links their consciousness to that of the sun, knowing how it energises and inspires them and adds life force
- Is resourceful, strong, adaptable, accepting, patient, uncomplaining, and is able to cope with life
- Knows how to motivate themselves, raising the required energy and nous for innovative action
- Seeks out ways to be happy and thrive, and is grateful for whatever presents itself and makes the most of opportunities
- Practises love, wisdom, and power in equal measure
- Understands the need to be powerful so they can be more effective and tackle problems more easily and are able to manifest and thrive
- Feeds their consciousness daily to stoke their power, and they maintain and control it judiciously
- Enjoys others basking in their divine presence, and freely shares their energies with them, but doesn't allow this to become hubris
- Embraces learning and new knowledge in diverse fields, and sharing this
- Broadens their trajectory to take in more of the universe
- Leaves home and gets out into life, to expand their horizons and grow their consciousness
- Has undergone much training to get to godhood and continually applies this, and seeks more ways to enhance their consciousness
- Uses their imagination in creative ways and avidly explores new avenues
- Imposes no limitations on their consciousness but sets it free to wander and wonder
- Doesn't just use their brain and body, but utilises the talents of their soul and the entire universe
- Appreciates each moment in life, whether it is on the crest of a wave or down in the trough
- Looks forward to new adventures and has optimism and zeal, expecting the best and staying in high vibrations
- Never takes a day for granted, as it might be their last, and they fill it with joy

- Visits the Dark World when they want to escape the human world. Here they can exist just as consciousness with no interference from physical energies
- Feels there is nothing too much for them to handle, and knows that if they require help or resources, then these will be forthcoming
- Interacts and works with nature as much as possible
- Works in an organised and disciplined manner, not leaving problems, mysteries, or messes for others to clear up
- Loves to nurture other people, and also their own projects, so that the outcomes can help others

Soul relationship

A god on Earth in human physical form:

- Is considerate of others, and of their own physical body and soul
- Lives side by side with their soul at all times, knowing life is more divine this way and they will be shown magical things
- Experiences a much easier life when partnering with their soul; more loving, giving, forgiving, kinder, wiser, more motivated and grateful. Is able to do tedious jobs with love and acceptance
- Has less dependency on human relationships when they have their soul as a partner
- Cooperates with their soul as a team and with the other gods, understanding that compromises have to be made at times
- Understands the concept of the Ribbon of Consciousness, and that they themselves are many parts of consciousness at the same time
- Heeds the advice of their soul and continually communicates with them, knowing it has superior powers
- Undertakes the same mission as their soul, motivated by the same goals
- Lives their life to the high and loving standards of their soul

- Keeps their heart open at all times to receive the energy and wisdom of their soul and the other gods
- Understands that while they walk the Earth, their spirit and soul travel and work in the higher dimensions
- Is aware there may be many threads of their soul in operation at once
- Understands the language of their soul and the gods—symbols and signs

Destiny and manifesting

A god on Earth in human physical form:

- Shapes their dreams of how they wish to see themselves and the world around them. Knows their dreams lead to their destiny
- Is clear about their goals and focused on them, ignoring distractions and detours, and determined to make their dreams come true
- Prioritises their mission above all else. It is the reason for their being
- Creates their destiny and the resources required to achieve it
- Creative and enthusiastic and enjoys playing 'what if?', growing and evolving themselves at every opportunity
- Believes in abundance and that the universe has limitless resources to bestow
- Actively seeks out their destiny, makes plans, and takes timely action to carry it out. Constantly checks they are on track
- Is willing and motivated to perform their mission and complete it
- Is able to work through any channel they are sent down, good or bad
- Does tasks expected of a god, i.e. transforming humans
- Doesn't hide from their soul or the gods but gladly joins their team
- Has fire in their veins and takes in sun energy to invigorate themselves
- Uses their consciousness as a magic wand to create, improve, or heal
- Utilises all the tools of consciousness like a master craftsperson
- Uses their Third Eye and intuition as an innate sense. Uses their consciousness as a telescope to see what the human eye can't see

- Is a manifestor and can visualise, and then create, whatever they desire
- Knows their thinking will manifest in some way, so they think very carefully
- Manifests their desires, keeping them in check but not suppressing them
- Actively attempts to create Heaven on Earth in every way and place, and to add their unique value wherever they go
- Takes time to build solid foundations, and understands that not everything works first time around
- Knows they must take positive action when manifesting and be the instrument of their soul
- Has no set expectations for their plans and allows destiny to unfold as it must
- Never dismisses possibilities, as knows the universe keeps revealing hidden things
- Knows that as they become more capable, more doors will open for them
- Is alert to opportunities and ways to make a difference. Wants to take on the world, and asks what they can do to assist while in human form
- Doesn't resist their destiny but steps into the flow of universal energies, bestowed with inspiration
- Is courageous, doing whatever is necessary, and going beyond previous boundaries
- Steps forward with an open heart, without fear, hesitation, or doubt, knowing that when brave enough to follow their dream then the path will appear before them
- Doesn't make excuses and never gives up
- Is aware of the weather in their mind and of how it is shaping their environment. Utilises storms to their advantage
- Knows it is up to themselves alone, how far and fast they can achieve things
- Understands when it is time to sow and when to reap, and allows time for things to mature. Works hard, knowing the rewards will come

- Sows seeds appropriate for the place, season, and climate, aiming to be self-sufficient and helping to support others too
- Is a captain of their own ship, not a slave to others
- Tries to emulate being a star, knowing that one day this is exactly what they will become

Darkness and adversity

A god on Earth in human physical form:

- Uses their Tools of Consciousness at all times to overcome adversity.
- Is in control of their human will and ego, but follows divine will instead
- Keeps their vibrations high, and knows how to raise them if adversity strikes
- Accepts that life is challenging at times and attempts to hold a smile and remain positive
- Chooses to quickly climb out of any darkness that befalls them, reinjects life force, and calms their heart and mind
- Refuses to wallow in self-pity. Chooses to fly above negative emotionality, and searches for the silver lining in every situation
- Practises fortitude and remains resilient and untriggered in dire or emotional situations
- Gets themselves back over the bridge into the higher dimensions if they should experience a fall, and they will have planned methods of escape from their hole
- Understands they could be recalled to the higher realms if they don't keep up the standards of a god
- Cleanses themselves regularly of all not-love, fears, negativity, deep hurts, anger, projections, and triggers in their personality
- Lets go of any programming, lower personas, or materiality that no longer serves them
- Works diligently to transform themselves and the past, laying all ghosts to rest, and working to clean slates for themselves and others

- Lets go of the past and embraces the present
- Stands strong in the face of derision, disparagement, or disbelief, not allowing the world to pull them down, and maintains their faith, tenets, and confidence, knowing which side they support
- Does not deride others whose views are different from their own
- Refrains from fighting or butting heads, and utilises patience and diplomacy with others
- Attempts to discover and to tell the truth at all times
- Faces death with magnanimity and no fear or sorrow, knowing it is merely a transition back to the higher dimensions, and understanding they could be called back at any time

Teaching and healing

A god on Earth in human physical form:

- Is prepared to share their Presence, time, and love to help others
- Is a teacher, spreading the knowledge about the unseen universe, and assisting people on the road to their godhood
- Helps to develop humanity and the next generation of gods
- Is training humans to use the Toolbox of their Consciousness
- Has as their aim to transform human minds and hearts
- Is a counsellor, and, having the same experiences as humans, means they are compassionate and wise in their counselling
- Is a healer, helping people in pain and teaching healing techniques
- Heals themselves and the world, using the wand of their consciousness, remaining in balance and wholeness
- Gives much consideration to educating children in the correct way
- Understands the need for tough love and doesn't compromise their teachings for students, and works to transform any issues, resistance, or rebellion from them
- Doesn't jeer at students, or punish them for their mistakes or lack of know-how
- Is patient, and will welcome their trainees back into the fold if they have fallen off the rails at some point

- Works with students for as long as is helpful, but then will move on to other students
- Studies astrology as they know it guides them and others daily regarding their destinies and the cycles of universal energies
- Constantly discerns their feelings and energies, and those of others, and takes action to heal them
- Brings in Source energy from their core in order to heal and manifest, and radiates it like a star
- Heals from the topmost part of their Ribbon of Consciousness for full power
- Faces the world with their talents, sharing their wisdom, life's experiences, and love so others may benefit, knowing that a god cannot hide away their light
- Keeps their heart open, and removes all defences so that the universe can work its magic through them, downloading healing energies and profound wisdom

Relationships with others

A god on Earth in human physical form:

- In relationships, shows respect, listens to others, heeds advice, understands other points of view, fosters agreement, doesn't project onto others, knows when to step back, and desires peace and harmony more than winning
- Cultivates networks, alliances, and connections
- Negotiates with their soul, other gods, and their students
- Doesn't interfere with the consciousness of another unless requested
- Understands the right time and place to get involved in action or debate, and doesn't step into action that isn't right for them
- Bides their time to be heard, observing all the while, and positioning themselves to be of value
- Does not seek to get their own way, or own needs met, at the expense of others
- Listens well, considers all views, and converses and debates respectfully

- Doesn't judge others, or preach to them
- Interacts with others willingly, swapping ideas
- Is not unduly influenced by others or subliminal messages. Crafts their own beliefs and stays true to them
- Doesn't allow others to put them off their task or message
- Protects themselves when necessary
- Doesn't fight with human consciousness but tries to transform it, in themselves and others
- Lets go of human consciousness, human nature, and human ways, and tries to live in the higher dimensions in their consciousness
- Has the humility to ask other gods for help when required
- Always supports other gods and angels
- Coordinates their own lower personas and treats them with loving parental control, never punishing them or ignoring their needs or dreams
- Lets go their lower personas with love and gratitude when it is time to do so
- Understands their higher energies can trigger people's issues, and they are careful not to be reactive
- Realises that gods created humans, and therefore gods must take responsibility to raise them up into godhood
- Attempts to be the best role model they can so they attract the right people into their circle—as students, teachers, associates, or partners

Higher dimensions

A god on Earth in human physical form:

- Loves getting to know the universe, experiencing the higher worlds so they can teach about them to others. Steps into magical kingdoms and plays their role as a god
- Understands that their power comes from connection with their soul and Source and other higher beings
- Practises translocating in consciousness and their spirit sphere throughout the universe and time

- Perceives themselves, not as a human with just a brain, but as an expanded version of their self
- Offers to train humans in the ways and things of the gods' worlds
- Doesn't parade themselves as a god amongst humanity, but projects a powerful presence, nonetheless
- Knows they must work to maintain their hallowed position in the higher realms or else they will fall back over the bridge into the lower dimension
- Understands what drives the universe and the larger scheme of things. This puts the petty issues on Earth into perspective, and their heart is filled with a greater focus which brings contentment
- Believes in the universe of dimensions and gods, and how human consciousness was created out of the consciousnesses of the gods, and that humans are now being trained up to become gods themselves

Chapter 27 – Transition to the future

Chiron has much to tell us about our future as humans and the future of planet Earth. Much of it revolves around the fact that the First Earth is in the process of slowly merging with the Second Earth. The First Earth is our human physical dimension. The Second Earth is the invisible higher dimensional copy of First Earth, which houses the spirit versions of our human selves.

Therefore, times are coming where nothing shall stay the same; not our planet, not our bodies, and not our consciousnesses. To get through this unique transition, that no one, not even the gods, has gone through before, we need steps, guidelines, and advice like never before. This guidebook and Chiron's original book, *Training Manual for Gods, Book One - Consciousness and the Unseen Universe,* hope to offer some of these instructions and counsel.

The merger of First and Second Earth, creating the New World

This merger process was first described briefly in chapter 7 (see Diagram #1). A New World is being generated which will consist of our physical Earth as we know it, overlaid by the higher vibrational dimension. The New World is not a different physical place from Earth but a new level of dimensionality where our consciousness hangs out. It is the same world really, but at a higher vibration, and so our consciousness experiences the two worlds in different ways. Therefore, the New World will be all around us and inside our mind. It will dictate how we see, hear, and experience things.

This merger commenced some time ago and may continue for years to come. Those of higher consciousness are already enjoying the finer energies and atmosphere of living in this space, even while their bodies may still be tramping on the same soil as before. We are not going to be evacuating in a physical sense to Heaven, for our feet won't be leaving the ground, but it is most definitely a migration of sorts—a journey of the consciousness across the abyss between dimensions, leaving behind our old human world and old human ways.

It may seem as if Heaven is enveloping our planet and bringing higher vibrations and new modes of living with it. However, the true Heaven of the gods' dimension is not involved in this merger. Only the dimensions of the First and Second Earths are being zipped together, although, one day in the distant future, this New World will indeed start to merge with the present gods' dimension.

The following additional information is from my Beloved Source, a creator god.

Beloved Source: *"Let us speak about the merging of the two dimensions together, the Second Earth with the human First Earth, as you call it. The higher vibrations of the Second Earth are now intermingling with the higher vibrations of the First Earth. They have been pressed one into the other and there is now no difference between them. You call it a zipping process, but I would challenge this imagery for it portrays the dimensions side by side. They are truly more like two pieces of acetate, these two dimensions, and they are being laminated slowly together from the top edge eventually down to the bottom edge.*

Sophia, you are now experiencing life in the laminated part where the Second and First Earth are now fixed together. And so, although to all intents and purposes it will seem like the same Earth that you are treading, with the same buildings and the same people around you, your consciousness is now aware of living in the merged dimension, and you will be living classical physicality alongside quantum physicality at the same time. You are beginning to get a sense of this, that manifestation has speeded up and quirky things are happening, and things are coming in and out of existence with no explanation but you find them there and then they are gone.

This merged state will take some time for you to assimilate, but in the coming months this is what you will be doing, and all manner of strange things will happen to you, and you could find yourself jumping in and out of existence. But we wish for you to experience these things and ponder on them deeply, for you are beginning to understand the New World and you must teach this world to others."[24]

We are starting to really feel the effects of this merger now. This process will take place over a long period of time, therefore it's not some overnight transformation. Those who are at the higher end of vibrations will feel it first, and those who are low vibrational will feel its full thrust last, but they are already beginning to experience the changes.

I asked Master El Morya why were the lower levels of both the First and Second Earths currently being affected when, at this present time, only the higher levels were effectively being zipped or laminated?

He replied, "*It's like placing a light on a table in a darkened room. The table is lit up directly and is brightest, but the whole room becomes lighter too. Therefore, the lower levels also receive more and more light which shows up their darkness.*"[25]

A further question to El Morya was, "What happens when the lower levels of both the First Earth and Second Earth get laminated? Will we get a double dose of low vibe energies, thereby adding the hellish zones of the spirit dimensions to our own?"

Morya confirmed this will be true, but he pointed out that the New World being created by this merger will already consist of both higher humans and gods who have been living here for a while, and they will be a force to be reckoned with by the time the lower levels are included in the lamination.

Morya added that the majority of the lowest humans will also have died off because the strain of so much light will have been too much for them. This will leave only the lower spirit beings to contend with, but even these may be taken off to another dimension for more specialised training that can better assist their evolution.

---

24. From a channelling by my Beloved Source, 25 June 2019
25. From a conversation with El Morya, 21 June 2019

However, Chiron tells us that, at present, there is a serious struggle going on between good humans and those humans invested in not-love, and it's not one hundred percent guaranteed that the good guys will win in the end. This makes it even more urgent that we tend to our light and missions, so that we are assured of a victory and do not suffer the ultimate fate of living in low vibrations for the rest of eternity.

Our consciousness will be especially affected by this merger, but if we have done much letting go of issues and negativity and forgiven many of our fellow humans, then we will get off more lightly. But those who have not attended to their consciousness, thinking, and beliefs will find themselves severely pressured by the new energies and the fact that their thinking is more instantly manifesting and rebounding in their face. The remedy is to think only loving thoughts, and then only love will be manifested in our life.

As the New World nestles closer and closer to us with its higher energies, the old Earth and its low vibrations will become an intolerable place to live. Many will not be able to cope with such intensity of light and it could lead to a surge in mental health issues. Only those who are able to sufficiently raise their vibrations to meet the new energies will survive. (This was written in 2019, before the COVID-19 pandemic!)

This is not some kind of Judgement Day as depicted by religions, and besides, this is taking place not in one day but over many decades, perhaps centuries. There are no gods doing the judging; they are not involved at all. People will live or die depending on their own choices and the vibrational level they have been able to achieve through those choices. There will be no gods plucking a lucky few for the new Nirvana, and throwing all others back into Hell.

Even the gods are feeling the effects of the merger, for although a god's consciousness fundamentally inhabits the gods' dimension, they may also have parts of their consciousness working on the Second Earth and also on the First Earth, for the god might be dealing with past issues here on their return journey back to Source.

Our consciousness is always situated in any moment at whatever wavelength and vibrational level we are dialled into on our Ribbon.

Therefore, if any part of a god's consciousness is travelling through the First or Second Earths, then they too will be caught up in the merger of those dimensions. This will undoubtedly affect most gods, for their work at this present time is focused on these lower realms.

There is more advice from my Beloved Source, which was primarily for myself but I pass on the same message to all readers.

Beloved Source: *"Keep strong, for this will be a tumultuous time of change for you, and you must not let yourself get dragged down even though you do not always understand. These are the end days of living as a human.*

This lamination process will be frightening for those below you, those who have not reached their godhood. They will not understand what is happening to them. And they will reach out for those who do *understand, even though your scientists will deny this. You must speak louder. You must make yourself heard. For, in their heart of hearts, people will understand you and know that you are right, even though you cannot offer up any scientific evidence. Forget the naysayers. They have never been the ones to take the universe forward. Stand in your strength and know what you have experienced, and let no one talk you down.*

Practise your tools of consciousness, for through this you will become much more powerful, and you will be able to show the world what is meant by being a god. People will be rattled and shattered but you must not be rattled and shattered also. You must be strong and resilient.

Be excited by this course of events. It has been planned and awaited for many centuries. You put up your hand to be a part of this integration and implementation. You must go through the transmutation and come out of it the other end aflame.

Put a smile on your face, for these are the last few months of humanness. You will still be in your physical body but everything will change for you, and nothing will ever be the same again. You have wanted this change for a long, long time. Now it is here, embrace it."[26]

So, the merger is happening right now, to every single one of us and to our planet. The gods may have been planning this for centuries, and

---

26. From a channelling by my Beloved Source, 25 June 2019

maybe even we ourselves have known the schedule. But now it's here, are we actually ready? It would appear from the state of our planet and the state of people's consciousnesses that we are sorely prepared.

Prepared or not, there will come a time when the merger is complete and all will have chosen their path—to become gods or to remain as humans. Then we will experience the Final Rift, the Final Shift, and the Second Earth, with only gods aboard, will be pulled apart from the First Earth which contains the remaining humans who did not choose, or manage to get to, ascension/godhood. The two Earths will go their separate ways in separate dimensions, and it may be centuries before any communication between the two Earths is possible again. (See Chapter 7, diagram #1.) It will be the best of times and the worst of times.

Of course, the one thing I wanted to know was *when* was this Final Shift going to happen? The gods, whenever I asked them, always replied with, "Soon!" (And, as this book goes to press in mid 2023, they are still saying the same thing!) But Lady Sedna[27] did raise my optimism when she advised me that I can transition across personally to the Second Earth before the Final Shift happens for everyone remaining on First Earth.

I asked Sedna, "How do I do that?"

She answered, "By surrendering to your soul, and realising this is now the end of your human self. You need to pass the controls over to your soul." And so begins a new phase for me now, letting go my old human self and learning to be my spirit self on Earth in human form.

Climate change, waves, storms

As the high vibrational energies of the Second Earth continue to rain down on us, they will cause not only a huge stir in our own consciousness and that of others but in every situation on the planet. It is evident that the climate is already changing and there has been an increase in huge storms and geophysical events in recent years. Group consciousness is forming the climate in many neighbourhoods, and some people are creating extremes through their lower vibrational thinking.

---

27. From meditations with Lady Sedna, 18-20 April 2023.

As I write this chapter, the whole of eastern Australia seems to be on fire, in the grip of unprecedented drought and tinder-dry forests and scrubland, set alight by dry lightning and temperatures far above the seasonal norm for springtime. The media is having a field day, with warnings of catastrophic and apocalyptic conditions, driving maximum fear into the hearts and minds of people on the ground, and thereby creating the group consciousness to bring about these exact conditions.

The higher our vibrations, the less affected we will be. It's hard to believe that consciousness alone can save us from a terrible fate, but that is exactly how it works! People inhabiting the lower vibrational worlds may be greatly distressed by the new energies and storms, but this is to prod them into raising their consciousnesses, and if they refuse to do so, they will be removed with the old Earth to make way for the New World.

We may be confronted with scenes of physical devastation, but all can be rebuilt and renewed. Indeed, much of the old world needs to be destroyed so that a new and better world can take its place. Our planet has been ripe for transformation for a long time, and most of us know this and actually want change to come. So, we need to ditch the past and generate a new and more loving and harmonious world.

Chiron channelled extra information on this topic of earth changes.

"Let us take a turn around this New World, and let us give our readers a taste of it so that they recognise it when it comes upon them. For they might think that an earthquake is happening to them, or that they have been spun into some kind of vortex, such will be the strength and power of these energies. And it is affecting not only people but the Earth herself too, so you can expect many more geophysical events to occur in the coming months and years. Things will be aligning but also resisting. And with the resistance will come graunching and pain, just as if your bones were being pressed up against a slab of concrete.

And so, the answer is to surrender and go with the flow. Accept that all human life is now changing, and it will never be the same again. Everyone will be rattled, but whether you feel rattled is up to you.

It is not that we gods wish to make the Earth a terrible place to live in. On the contrary, we are bringing Paradise down to Earth. But to be able to live in Paradise, you will need to be a new clean type of being, for the old human will not be welcome. Clean up your act and you will get your passport. Remain in your dirt and darkness, and you will be refused a visa.

And the energies will come relentlessly down and down, sinking into the lower vibrational areas and cleansing them whether they like it or not. And many will not be able to cope with this pressure and they will go insane.

So, commit to a period of cleansing out your mind before the universe does it for you in ways that may not be to your liking. This is not punishment for anyone. This is the wheels of the universe grinding on, and if you are under that wheel you will be crushed. So, centre yourselves and get to the hub of this New World. Your passport is your loving mind. And what could be more awesome than embracing love for yourself and for all the world around you?"[28]

In his book, Chiron speaks a great deal about storms and waves coming to destroy our Earth. Should we take this literally? Yes, but also metaphorically. The storms and waves may indeed be ocean tsunamis caused by Earth movements, but they could also refer to anything from volcanic pyroclastic flows to super-typhoons to solar flares to cosmic waves from supernova explosions. All of these events affect us periodically, and more regularly of late. The kind of waves we get to experience will depend on the climate we live in, our geographical location, and the vibrational level of our area. All the various waves serve one purpose only—to clear away the muck of the old Earth and old human consciousness.

We are also moving into the Age of Aquarius from an astrological point of view, an approximate two-thousand-year period within the universe's system of cycles which is known scientifically as the Precession of the Equinoxes (a 26,000-year cycle), and was something calculated even by the most ancient civilisations.

The symbol representing the zodiac sign of Aquarius is two parallel wavy lines, one beneath the other. Many mistakenly believe these are water waves, but in fact Aquarius is an air sign, not a water sign, and its symbol refers to electronic waves, or wavelengths of vibrations. Aquarius is the sign of raising our vibrations to a higher level of consciousness.

---

28. Chiron channelling 26 June 2019 – Passport to the New World

For the past two thousand years or so we have been in the Age of Pisces, a sign relating to higher dimensions, spirituality, religion, artistry, the goddess, institutionalisation, insanity, and things hidden behind the Veil. The Age of Aquarius will see us focusing on new and innovative things, especially on consciousness, neuroscience, psychology, mental health, other sciences and technology, working with groups, and doing things for the benefit of humanity as a whole.

Aquarian energies often help us to act together on a united front by first pointing out our current modes of separation, aloofness, and loneliness. Therefore, the waves that are entering our world and consciousness are Aquarian waves, and they will assist us to see where we have been a fractured and dysfunctional human race, in order for us to realise we must join together in oneness in the New World.

Wild storms are ever present in news stories around the globe every week. No one will be untouched by them. The world is in flux and panic and spinning into a vortex. But there is no celebration in Heaven as the gods watch parts of the planet, and people, sink beneath the waves, although the storms are doing a good job for the gods in breaking hearts wide open and moving people on. All of us are being shaken to see what we are made of, and to check if we are of the right calibre to make it into the safe higher havens of the Second Earth.

Big storms tend to awaken our consciousness from its apathy or routine, and shift us into a new way of looking at things and following new paths. It is true that we may have to face scenes of destruction, but storms are great levellers. They might level buildings but they also level society, bringing all classes of people together to give of their best. It might seem devastating at first, but it creates many opportunities to build better using a higher consciousness.

Arnold Schwarzenegger was just one person to take advantage of this. Prior to his big break in the movie industry, he started up his own bricklaying company in Los Angeles literally one week before a big earthquake demolished many of the buildings. He quickly hired several other bodybuilders and they helped rebuild the city, earning Arnie his first million even before his 30th birthday.

Old structures, be they buildings, governments, organisations, systems, economies, families, or our own way of doing things, will not survive the coming tidal waves of energies if we don't shore them up with stronger and more loving foundations, or replace them altogether. Things that have gone pear-shaped, and anything that is not advantageous and valuable to the New World, will be let to fall into ruin or be taken down in a storm. Those people with lower vibrations will be yanked out of their positions to sink or swim, for the universe will not be carrying them into the new dimension.

It is not that the gods are choosing to wipe out the human race; we are the children of their consciousnesses, and they can never get rid of us. They are merely trying to get us to godhood and to teach us more godly and less human ways of being. It upsets them greatly to see humans crushed under the weight of the new energies, but if people choose to stay in lower vibrations, then the universe will roll over them, and churn them and everything around them to dust.

The Earth is being cleansed of its old ways, but many humans are still clinging to these and not heeding the warnings and signs of the gods and their own souls. And so, people can't complain when they get wounded by the new energies or they see their loved ones fall. The universe has no guilt, for all have been notified and forewarned. Those who are on the godhood path will be safe, but there is little chance for others. Only people with high vibrations will remain standing after the storms have driven through.

Climate change is here; it's time to change the climate of our consciousnesses.

Things that need to go

Things are coming to an end on our lower dimensional Earth because we have wrecked our planet, and our way of living as humans is not sustainable. The whole world needs to clean up its act, and every individual too. We have poisoned our dimension for long enough through both our actions and our thoughts. Old issues and past ways of being cannot be transferred into the New World. Conflicts and dirty ways will not get past the gates of this world of love, purity, and harmony.

We are a throwaway society, drowning in waste, and we are just beginning to realise this problem now. Why do we feel the need to keep changing things so regularly, throwing the not-so-old into the trash and landfill dumps or oceans? The gods are all for embracing change, but the pace of change on Earth is too manic now, and not only can the planet not cope but people can't cope either with this rapid treadmill. Change must be manageable or else humans will suffer from mental breakdown.

The whole structure of society is breaking down in many places, even in the so-called First World countries, with people not getting the support and services they need. The world seems to have forgotten what really matters, and the foundational work to assist fellow humans is not done. The focus is too often on money and the bottom line. There is little investment in making society work for everyone. Time and again we see government budgets being spent heavily in the areas of infrastructure, technology, and the military, but not so much on housing, health, food, water, and energy security, education, and general support, love, attention, and reward for their fellow man who may be in dire need of it.

Coping with the storm

How do we get to rise above these waves and ride out these storms? It will be by raising the vibrational level of our consciousness, in ways we have learnt throughout this book. Those in the higher world at the upper end of the vortex, who have worked on their consciousness, will float more easily above the crises. Those of lower vibrations, who are closed in heart and mind, will not survive the waves. So, it is our own wavelength that will sink or save us, and we need to gather our loved ones to this same high level, too, so that the waves will pass us by.

These new energies coming in from the universe will require us to be powerful enough to withstand them, or they will take us out, and this means building a fortified consciousness. We can't fall apart at the terrible sights and tragedies we might witness or endure ourselves, and we can't afford to be knocked off our axis, even if the planet is. If we cannot tolerate the new wavelengths, then we will sink beneath them.

Rebuilding and optimism

After a storm, we will need to pick up the pieces, take stock, set priorities, and rebuild or move on. Whatever we are faced with, we can recreate and improve upon what was there before, and we will need to be optimistic, raise the vibrations of the Earth and ourselves, and apply good manifestation techniques (see Chapter 17). The bones of society can be reset in a manner that supports the whole of humankind who have migrated to the New World dimension.

The coming storms and waves should not be a reason for panic or despair. In truth, they are heralding a more wonderful way of life for our future. We need to accept that change is coming and open our hearts to it and move into it with good grace. When all the dust has settled and the wreckage of the old world has been demolished, we will see clear paths to a bright future ahead for us all, and we will be able to build a more robust world that lasts over time, a different world from the one we live in today, a place of high vibrations.

There is nothing to fear about our future. We are coming into greater love and grace, and expelling all that is not-love. We will have new high vibrational leaders, many of whom will be gods in human form, who will guide and direct us into this next phase of evolution for humankind and the saving of our beautiful planet.

I have a wonderful fridge magnet in my kitchen which exemplifies this.

"Don't fear tomorrow; God is already there."

Why humans will resist the New World

Many humans will resist the coming of the New World. The majority will not even understand what is happening to them or the planet, and will probably blame it all on other nasty, greedy, grasping humans who have allowed climate change, pollution, politics, or sinful behaviour to decimate our atmosphere, habitat, and society. None of these people will want to take responsibility for it themselves, and they will try to hold the changes at bay for as long as they can. But even for those who do have some inkling as to what is occurring with the new energies and merging dimensions, there may be some resistance.

It's natural for humans to be wary about the unknown, even if the New World being touted to them is a big step closer to Paradise than their current world. They are suspicious of the offer, and even though they are a dying race, they don't want to take the medicine that will help them to live better and longer. They protectively hold onto their old Earth, dark and shabby though it is, and even while they are wrecking it, they don't want it taken away from them.

If humans knew that invisible higher dimensional gods were involved in this transition to the New World, there might be even more resistance to what is coming, even though our souls have been waiting for, and preparing for, this time in history for centuries. Many people refuse to entertain the idea of divine beings, and even more so the notion of being controlled by them.

But the gods are not aliens who intend to invade the Earth and take it over. They come as teachers to raise up humankind. Surely people would wish to cultivate their minds with more brilliance, and their hearts with more love? Chiron points out that humans are awaiting the second coming of Christ or another Einstein, but they are refusing the assistance being offered to them by the gods.

Therefore, we need to open our hearts and minds to the existence of our consciousness, soul, gods, higher beings, and invisible dimensions, for until we do, these worlds will not be revealed to us. When our human hearts are filled with everything except love, it becomes difficult to imagine what the realm of gods might be like and how it would be to dwell in such a place.

But the gods are not our enemy; the enemy is ourselves. The gods live in a world of love and peace; we humans live in a world of not-love and disharmony. How is that working out for us? The New World, modelled on the gods' world, offers us a more heavenly existence.

This might sound a little like a new religion (and lord knows we've had enough of those throughout our civilisations), but the gods are nothing to do with any religion. There are no churches, priests, worship, rites, bibles, or tithes. The higher beings come merely to teach a new way of life based on love, compassion, equality, and respect, and we need to allow this to happen. They have no interest in fighting with humans but only in evolving them into their higher selves, so that the gods can atone for the 'mistake' they made many eons ago in allowing the consciousness in the human race they created to grow out of control and take over the planet.

There might be many people who refuse to believe that what is written in this chapter will happen. Only time will tell, of course. But if they deny this scenario, what will fortify them in the future, for the Earth holds little promise or support for them? No one will escape the effects of the waves that are coming, and the only evidence that can be offered right now is the fact that people are definitely already experiencing them. For those who continue to deny and resist, their consciousness will remain on the First Earth or be moved on to a more appropriate dimension to assist with their evolution, as they will not be welcome in the New World.

All kinds of theories are being put forward to explain away the current dilemmas of mankind. One way to prepare for the future is to heed what has been offered by Chiron as guidance, and to spread the word about this New World and other dimensions so that they become mainstream, and people are no longer coy about discussing them or believing in them. This book has been written to help prepare humans for the coming of gods to Earth. We can laugh and deny, or we can open ourselves to the possibilities that something very unique and intriguing is happening to our planet, and to us humans right now, and we are experiencing it.

We need to open up to the invisible universe and embrace these new paradigms in a timely fashion, for we don't want to miss the window of opportunity as the cogwheels turn our way. It's time to stop running in the other direction and start stepping into Heaven. We will have many friends and tools to help us get there. This is the way for us to save our world, by being a superhero and flying into the next.

The transition into the New World will be the most massive undertaking in the history of mankind, and it will require belief, trust, sacrifice, and hard work. Without this, an individual is doomed, for it is happening whether we like it or not. Few things in life that are worthwhile come without substantial cost.

Time of transition

There are many humans who are now crossing over the bridge and joining the New World, and everyone is welcome there. In fact, Chiron tells us that currently the majority of mankind, just over half the planet, are on their way to experiencing this new way of life and consciousness. The Second Earth has always been just millimetres away from us on the First Earth, but that spatial abyss has taken many millennia to cover. We can congratulate ourselves for arriving in our new home. The gods are delighted with progress, and enjoy meeting the new generations of gods and gods-in-training.

The people of the old Earth are being moved by the new energies coming in, and they are transforming themselves by getting rid of old limiting beliefs and dark thoughts which contaminate the planet and produce hopelessness and helplessness, and they choose instead to embrace love, respect, compassion, and harmony in all things.

As the potent higher energies bathe us, we will need to surrender to them, ingest them, and allow ourselves to be guided through the halls of this New World. We are not refugees fleeing from some disaster zone. We are packing our bags quite consciously, and willingly moving to our new permanent home.

Once we have migrated our consciousness to the New World, we will need to maintain our focus and determination, and play by the new rules and ethics, or else we could be sucked back over the bridge to the lower dimensions again. This does happen, and quite regularly when we first make the transition, and we need to find ways to pick ourselves up, raise the timbre of our thoughts, and march back over that bridge again. The consequence of not doing this is to stay in the lower worlds of chaos, darkness, and grief.

Once Heaven has been tasted, the vibrations of the lower worlds are impossible to bear if we fall back down there again, and we will always be trying to find a way to return to the soothing and loving energies that we have experienced before. We must realise which place we prefer. However, we have been human for many lifetimes, and it may take a while for us to get accustomed to this transition and working from a higher dimensional consciousness.

We may feel sad as everything comes to an end in our current world as we make the move to the New World. We may need to let go of loved ones or homes or jobs or way of life, or other things dear to us. But if we can remember we are moving into a more heavenly world, we will be able to let go of the doubt and fear and regrets, and not hesitate to turn away from the old way of being and living in lower vibrations, and step forward into the new realm where we will find ourself living amongst other high vibrational people and experiencing a more peaceful, abundant, and fulfilling life. Exciting times are ahead, and we are on the verge of crossing over into an entirely new kind of world, the secrets of which are being revealed to us slowly but surely.

Once we are settled in, we might want to offer our services in spreading the word about the merger and the New World, and this will entail crossing the bridge to the lower dimensions on numerous occasions, so we need to remember to come back home again once our work is done. It is like becoming a daily commuter, leaving home in the higher world every morning to visit the busy, chaotic world below, and then returning home again in the evening to relax with loved ones in a beautiful and harmonious environment.

We might ask, since the two dimensions are merging to create the New World, will there still be a human world with human beings, and a spirit world with spirit beings? For the present time, yes, existing together side by side for a while yet, but they are slowly converging and will do so until the human world is fully transmuted. What this means is that humans will become more and more their spirit selves, or spirit consciousness, but will retain their human physical form, albeit that this too will be remarkably transformed and enhanced. The paradox is that even though the two dimensions are merging, in fact the New World will separate more and more from the old world until they are no longer joined at all. (See chapter 7.)

Chapter 28 – The New World

Living in the New World/Second Earth dimension

Will things be different in this New World? Of course they will, for we don't *want* our world to stay as it is with all its failings and disharmony and warmongering. It will be a new playing field for us, helping us to grow into a better race of people. However, the New World will still be similar in appearance to the old world (at first, at least), but things will not be so concrete and fixed. All will be more unsettled and unpredictable, and more susceptible to being changed by our consciousness.

Lady Sedna[29] further described what it will be like when we first arrive in the New World on Second Earth. She tells us that Second Earth is an exact copy of First Earth, including not only the landscape but also all the earthly systems. So, there are still shops and businesses and banks and governments. However, this is only upon first arrival there. The New World at this time is manifested from a consensus reality, the group consciousness, because this is what new arrivals are used to seeing and experiencing.

After our first arrival on Second Earth, we ourselves then begin to create our own reality from our thoughts and emotions, and we can pull away from the consensus reality and make our reality as we want it. So, we can delete all governments and banking systems and money from our reality if we so choose, and even all the people who still believe in those things.

In this New World we will begin to experience things 'pinging' in and out of existence, including our own consciousness (and maybe even our bodies!), and whatever we think about will be what creates our reality

---

29. From meditations with Lady Sedna, 18-20 April 2023.

in front of us. This is the quantum world of instant manifestation, and our scientists are just beginning to understand the concept of quantum physics but there is still a long way to go yet. However, we know this type of weird world from our dreams at night.

In addition to instant manifestation, there will be a decreasing dependency on time, which is merely a physical dimension construct. Cycles of time will continue to exist, such as days and seasons and planetary orbits, but time will become meaningless and will stretch and contract to suit our circumstances.

This will be our experience in everyday life very soon. We will need to train our consciousness to get a grip on its thinking, else all manner of strange situations could present themselves. Higher minds are better trained to handle this situation where thoughts play out instantly, but lower minds could actually go out of their minds.

Chiron channelled some extra advice on this same subject to remind us that consciousness manifests whatever we are thinking and feeling (one of his main themes throughout this book!)

"What is the New World? What can you expect to be experiencing?

The New World is the merging of the old Earth with the higher dimension of Second Earth. So, we have two different dimensions converging, and we must let go some aspects and bring in new ones. This means that you must be clear within yourself, for as the New World takes hold, so will whatever is in your consciousness. If nothing is happening for you in the New World, it will be because nothing is happening in your consciousness. And so, you must lay plans and design things for them to come into being.

Of course, much will happen all around you, for others are creating this reality from their consciousnesses, and you will walk through what they have created. But if you want to create things your way, then you will need to get busy knitting together a world that is to your desires. So, don't wait for things to come to you. You must design and hold onto that dream and give it all your support so that it may come into being.

It will take a while for you to get used to operating in this manner, but after a while when you see evidence of your outcomes, you will apply your design work with gusto, and watch things pop up all around you that you have initiated and brought into your reality.

So, if you are feeling stuck, it will be because your thinking is stuck. You will need to get creative and apply your thinking to how you want your world to be. So, go and make merry and create a world that is dear to your heart."[30]

The New World, therefore, is created with our thinking. If we can imagine ourselves there, dreaming and manifesting our cherished destiny, then this is where we will find ourselves playing out our dreams. When we change our thinking, we change our world.

New World society

In the New World, Chiron tells us, the air is clean and fresh with no pollution from people or poisoned minds. The climate is stable, be it weather, emotions, or politics. It is not that the world will cease to evolve; there will always be changes, but not change for change's sake. There will still be plenty of innovation and exciting projects.

Peace reigns here because love is the new powerhouse that keeps the planet working successfully. Every person is taken into consideration, and everyone works for the well-being of all. Contented people make for a well-functioning planet, and people who feel love in their hearts are able to share and help and give, and they are more productive when their heart is in it, and they become devoted to their lives.

It is not that it will be a life of lazy ease; in the New World everyone will be expected to do their bit and they won't be allowed to sit on the sidelines. All must add value in their own way, and the gods will train people to make the most of their individual potential. When a person's skills are used to best effect, then the work force is content and fulfilled. All will be equally valued, whether a manager or a labourer; some like to direct others, and others prefer to be directed.

This may seem a little Utopian in concept, but it is already the kind of world that the gods inhabit, and they are teaching humans to become more god-like and live in a more godly fashion, for the betterment of all. During the transition period from the old world to the new, there will be hiccups and challenges, to be sure, but the foundations for a new kind of

---

30. Chiron channelling, 31 July 2019 – How to live in the New World

society and civilisation are being laid. It will be many decades yet before we reach our final goal.

We are being offered the chance to create a divine new world, a planet which is higher dimensional and a better mirror of the gods' world. It will be the same physical Earth, but we will have new eyes and new understanding. Where things have been demolished, we don't want to just rebuild or re-establish in the old style, but to utilise new building codes which out-picture our higher vibrational beliefs. All consciousnesses will need to join in common purpose in love and joy, with none breaking away in rebellion or to work at cross purposes against the universal good.

The old days are ending, and we are required to raise our frequencies and energies and work from a higher consciousness. It will be up to ourselves which level we find ourselves at. We cannot blame gods or governments for where we end up. We will want to clean up every aspect of our own lives and the way we use our planet. As we do this then the lower vibrational aspects of greed, meanness, and malice will fall away from our environment. Gone will be the belief that it is power and money that make the world tick, yet we will be very powerful if we link our consciousnesses and work together in unity and lovingness.

As we broaden our minds and understanding of this New World, our focus will be on not what we can get out of the planet or each other, but on creating a world that is more balanced and harmonious, with perfect weather of sunshine and regular rain. All will look and feel different, and be more lovely and brilliant than before.

Gods on Earth

Many gods have come down, and will continue to come down, from their higher god dimension to incarnate into human form. Therefore, we will be walking with gods in this new merged realm, following in their footsteps, letting go of being a member of the human race, and transforming into gods ourselves as the first members of the new human-godly race. You could say we will be a kind of demi-god. It is only when we are birthed on this planet with god DNA that we are officially a full-blooded god, but that is what awaits us in our next incarnation if we have reached godhood whilst here on Earth in this lifetime.

Although gods and humans-turned-god will be physically walking on the ground of the New World, and living in houses there and going about their business, their default position on their Ribbon of Consciousness is in the gods' dimension, for this is their true home, and they commute to the lower dimensions to do their work but their consciousness remains at its higher level.

How will these gods be recognised or make themselves known? That's a difficult question because it is not that they will come wearing halos around their heads, and they will not be proclaiming their status loudly in the marketplace. To all intents and purposes, they will seem like ordinary men and women, but we will know them by their extraordinary charismatic presence and the exceptional talents they display which really help to progress mankind. They will be born into the right families and societies, with positions ready for them to fill once they reach maturity so that they can hit the ground running, so to speak. Their destinies have been long planned.

Although the incarnated gods on the planet will remain for the most part in undercover roles, they will have much influence in creating this New World, working in conjunction with, and guided by, the gods who remain in the higher dimensions in non-physical form. Their target is a world that operates on a united front, where the success of the whole is more important than the victory of the individual, where love is valued more than ego. We can see, can't we, where we have been going wrong as humans?

Gradually, our society will take shape, and new sciences will be revealed that will help to explain the exact nature of what we are going through as a civilisation. As we humans learn to pool our knowledge amongst ourselves, so will the gods share their valuable information with us. Our consciousness and senses will be expanded to take in these new and seemingly mystical ways of operating.

As humans allow themselves to be moulded into gods, the planet will eventually be filled with only higher beings, love, and peace. This is obviously a long way off, but it is the destiny of the gods and of humankind.

Education in the New World

The gods' primary mission involving us humans is to evolve us into a race of gods like themselves. In order to do this, we must be taught by these higher beings what it is to be and act like a god, and our incarnation on Earth at this time is akin to being part of a training school for godhood.

If we desire this wonderful new society described above, then we will need all kinds of people in every walk of life to be trained in god-like ways; parents, teachers, youths, managers, employees, and youngsters. Most current education systems world-wide are woefully inadequate for this, merely designed to get children through school years in any way they can. Many universities are no longer hallowed institutions, but factories churning out clones who may have acquired some knowledge but little wisdom, and often with no idea how to apply even that knowledge in pursuit of improving our planet.

Therefore, major changes are needed to our entire education system, and parental attitudes too. But we will need teachers and parents who can lead the way, in the new godly way. Where will we find this new brand of Masters, initially? Most current teachers and parents are unqualified for this new role, where the qualification will not be degrees or doctorates but godhood. Our new teachers will be astute mentors, able to give support with god-like compassion and wisdom, and they will truly understand how consciousness works and how to utilise the tools of consciousness.

Gone will be the days when teachers harshly harangue their students for their ignorance, or who show no mercy towards misdeeds. Instead, they will be exemplars to their students, helping to create model citizens for our society to be, laying down the basic building blocks for god consciousness. So, before we can begin to educate our children and others in the ways of the desired New World, we will need to embark on a dedicated training program for our future teachers and coaches.

In his book, Chiron makes a reference to The Aquarian Universe-ity (AQU), a project that the gods are working on at this present time to educate humans in the ways of gods and to reveal the secrets of the universe that have been mostly hidden from humans for millennia.

Sophia Ovidne

This book, and Chiron's *Training Manual for Gods* series, are destined to become some of the source material for AQU students.

At the time of writing this chapter, I am not too sure about the details of this godly university (it is spelt as universe-ity but pronounced in the normal way as 'university'. The gods want to make a point that in their type of universe-ity, students will learn about the greater universe, not just one favoured subject.) Students will definitely have better access to all the information about the greater universe, since the Universal Consciousness has recorded everything that has ever occurred in our universe, and will act like some Universal Google but a million times superior and 100% accurate.

I do know that the Aquarian Universe-ity will be mostly based online and will be accessible by everyone. It may take quite a while to set up, I imagine, as universities are complex worlds with many requirements, and they need to offer a great deal to students, especially when, like the AQU, it will need to offer basic training about the higher dimensional worlds as a starter course. However, the AQU will be a fundamental training college for our New World teachers, coaches, and parents. We can ask the gods even now to be enrolled, if we feel this to be our calling.

Once we have our new teachers, and also parents, who support this new kind of learning, then we can begin to set up an education system for our children and those who want to learn these new skills and attitudes. Clearly, at present, children are not taught anything resembling the contents of this book. It is time for everyone on Earth to realise how they are constructed, where they have truly come from, and where they are heading in this and future lives. There will be no secrets kept from them now by the gods.

It will be easiest to start with primary school children (toddlers and pre-teens) for they have not yet been moulded and brainwashed in the ways and beliefs of the old Earth. Their consciousnesses are still open and receptive, and the focus would be on simple, enriching, and character-building education that takes into consideration a child's particular senses and sensibilities.

At present, due to workload or indifference, many teachers eschew students' personal issues as not their problem; they merely teach to the prescribed curriculum. The gods promote a different type of classroom for the future, believing that children should feel attended and listened to and loved, and never punished for their inabilities. They should be encouraged to explore the unknown and to be excited so that a love of learning returns to our schoolrooms, and our teachers feel fulfilled and valued in creating the little geniuses of the future.

Too often our children, and also those in the workplace, are not treated with the kindness and compassion they deserve, and Band-Aid solutions are applied to their troubles without checking what wounding is underneath. Teachers and employers complain; who has the time, inclination, skill, or budget to delve into the personal issues of those they are teaching or employing? The gods' answer to that is, "What is the cost of a damaged adult, or a damaged child that grows into a damaged adult?"

Is it too expensive to deal with these issues, when the cost of not dealing with them is so high to our society through over-burdened health and prison facilities, and abuse, fraud, and inefficiency? If we can reduce the numbers in prisons and mental institutions, and reduce the rates of suicide and murder and other crimes, surely this balances out the cost of implementing this new education system?

It would, as well, bring better balance to humanity, imbuing our society with love and the motivation to be creative and innovative, and making the world a much more pleasant and less stressful place to live in. In our schools and at home, teaching things like fortitude and forgiveness, which are not automatic and don't come naturally to many, will result in a stronger, more resilient, and more harmonious society.

How do we get governments and dyed-in-the-wool educational establishments to change? It won't be an overnight plan, but with determination and the help of the gods, little by little we will bring about a revolution to the way in which we educate and train people. If we can hold these new ideas in our minds, then our group consciousness will be able to transform the status quo and manifest initiatives such as the Aquarian Universe-ity into successful implementation across the globe.

Chiron tells us that many areas of society require changing, but educating children is the number one priority of the gods. They are our future, and will one day take the positions of gods themselves.

Space travel and aliens

What would a chapter on the future be if we didn't include mention of space and aliens? We discussed aliens and UFOs in detail in chapter 5, but it's worth speaking about how science fiction might become science fact in our future. Already our technology is probing intergalactic space, so where will this lead us in years to come?

The inspiration for science fiction writers has come from their spirit selves visiting unseen worlds and higher dimensions. If those writers are gods, then they will be allowed to freely travel the universe and they may meet beings from races other than human. Much is revealed to us in the invisible universe when we reach the higher dimensions within our own consciousness.

We will discover that Earth is but a junior civilisation in the greater scheme of things, but there is nothing wrong in visiting other higher cultures and societies around our neck of the galaxy. We merely need to remember to be polite and respond with love. But us humans won't be meeting our alien neighbours in the flesh until we have proved our capacity for peace and love. In the meantime, the gods are the vanguards for our eventual meeting with alien races, some of which are human-like. If we can cooperate amiably with gods in the New World, then there is hope for us to venture further at a later time.

As for space exploration using human bodies, this is really more of an impossible dream. We may or may not reach the planet Mars in the foreseeable future, but we won't discover much by visiting the planets and moons in our solar system. It is by travelling in our consciousness, in our spirit spheres, that we will learn the most about our universe. When we have first learnt to travel with our consciousnesses in our spirit bodies, then there will come a time when our physical bodies will be allowed to follow and teleport across the universe.

Our scientists are searching for mankind's survival in exoplanets[31], but all we need for our future is already right here in our consciousness. It is not feasible that we will get to visit any exoplanet any time soon, and

---

31. Exoplanets: potentially Earth-like planets that revolve around other stars, and discovered only recently.

certainly it won't be possible using current technologies. Ingenuity will be needed to discover new forms of propulsion that will get us hurtling towards other suns and galaxies. So, perhaps we should abandon our desire to reach for exoplanets and the stars. The only star we need is right here, within our own consciousness.

The future of Earth, Sun, and solar system

With all the changes going on, as the First Earth merges with the Second Earth and we embark on the evolutionary journey from humankind to godhood, what will happen to the planet itself and to the rest of our solar system?

The physical Earth will remain in place orbiting around our sun, unless we humans do something catastrophic to blow it up or shift it off its normal trajectory. Our sun will continue shining for many millennia yet. But even after our star dies, which it certainly will do one day, its consciousness will live on, and our own consciousnesses will cluster around other stars, or perhaps by then we will even have become a star ourselves.

Until then, we need to really appreciate our sun. It is vital to our existence, and the entire solar system is doomed without its central star. The sun is our mission control. Its consciousness monitors everything that goes on in its backyard—the solar system of planets, moons, asteroids, and many other mysterious bodies and energies that we have yet to discover or define. Our star is at the heart of our life force, embedded in the core of each and every one of us. We have been formed from its consciousness, and we innately respond to its energies and cosmic rays which feed our hearts and minds in hidden ways. Its creative fire lights our soul and our way, and leads us to our rightful destiny.

Other stars in our Milky Way galaxy, and those further afield, also share their light and energies with us and radiate their own unique rays, but these don't affect us to the great extent that our own sun shapes and touches us on a daily basis.

All of us will become stars one day. It is part of our journey back to our Source. It feels good to connect with the sun and the further stellar community, and we should remember to do this often. One of the reasons that the universe is expanding is due to the success of higher beings evolving into new stars, and as their consciousnesses expand, so does the universe.

There is no limit to how large our universe will grow, but eventually one day in the far distant future, even our universe will switch off its lights and come to an end, and that will be the start of a new cycle and another adventure for the creator gods and all our consciousnesses as we reunite and take part in the creation and evolution of a brand-new universe.

In summary

These chapters have taken us on quite a journey. Hopefully you have enjoyed it and learnt much about consciousness and the unseen universe, and have come to appreciate yourself a little better and know where you have come from and where you are heading to.

The existence of consciousness needs to be acknowledged by all, as it's pivotal to our understanding of reality and who we are and what we are capable of achieving. Our own consciousness may be just a tiny cog in a huge machine of worlds and dimensions, but we are still important and each of us has a role to play in keeping the wheels turning and transforming ourselves and our patch into something unique and valuable.

The Great Consciousness of the universe has billions upon billions of 'followers' and is connected online to every single one of us 24/7. We can never not be a part of this exciting universe with its teeming magical worlds which at present remain invisible to most humans. There is so much going on behind the Veil that covers our eyes and prevents us seeing and experiencing until we are ready and willing to do so.

Everyone on Earth is seeking love and happiness, and usually some kind of change to our current circumstances. What we are really questing for is Heaven, and this is now available to us all when we reach the levels of higher consciousness and step into the kinder and more loving environment of the New World. If we use our minds carefully and remember to apply the Toolbox of our Consciousness, we will find ourselves changing our reality and walking and working with gods in ways we could not have previously imagined.

Few people are telling us about these things, but the time has now come for humans to know about the metaphysical nature of their consciousnesses and the enchanting dimensions that await exploration beyond this one. Heaven is only a thought away, and the unseen universe is unfolding her secrets. Has there ever been a more exciting time to be alive?

Psalms 82:6 "*I say you are gods, all of you.*"

www.ingramcontent.com/pod-product-compliance
Lightning Source LLC
Chambersburg PA
CBHW031248230426
43670CB00005B/87